DATE DUE

HOW TO BE A TRANSFORMED PERSON

HOW TO BE
A
TRANSFORMED
PERSON

E. STANLEY JONES

ABINGDON-COKESBURY PRESS

New York • *Nashville*

HOW TO BE A TRANSFORMED PERSON

Quotations on the following pages are copyright:

Pages 3 and 6, from *Guilt and Redemption* by Lewis J. Sherrill. Used by permission of John Knox Press and the author.

Page 17, "Sometimes" from *The Shadow of the Perfect Rose*, Collected Poems of Thomas S. Jones, Jr., with a memoir and notes by John L. Foley. Copyright 1937 by John L. Foley. Used by permission of Rinehart & Co., Inc., publishers.

Page 61, from *The Everlasting Mercy* by John Masefield. Copyright 1911. Used by permission of the Macmillan Co.

Pages 92 and 116, from *The Best of Studdert Kennedy*. Used by permission of Hodder & Stoughton, Ltd.

Pages 142, 144, 145, 161, from *In Search of Maturity* by Fritz Kunkel. Used by permission of Charles Scribner's Sons, publishers.

Page 188, "Overtones" from *Collected Poems of William Alexander Percy*. Copyright 1920, 1943 by LeRoy Pratt Percy. Used by permission of Alfred A. Knopf, Inc.

Page 228, from "Build Soil" from *A Further Range* by Robert Frost. Copyright 1936 by Robert Frost. Used by permission of Henry Holt & Co., Inc.

Page 281, from "What Lips My Lips Have Kissed." Copyright 1920, 1948 by Edna St. Vincent Millay. Used by permission of Brandt & Brandt.

New Testament quotations designated "R.S.V." are from *The Revised Standard Version of the New Testament*. Copyright 1946 by the International Council of Religious Education. Scripture quotations designated "Moffatt" are from *The Bible: A New Translation* by James Moffatt. Copyright 1922, 1935, 1950 by Harper & Bros. Used by permission.

SET UP, PRINTED, AND BOUND BY THE
PARTHENON PRESS, AT NASHVILLE,
TENNESSEE, UNITED STATES OF AMERICA

ACKNOWLEDGMENTS

MY FIRST ACKNOWLEDGMENT OF GRATITUDE MUST BE TO THE Ashram groups in India and the United States, where studies in "How to Be a Transformed Person" were presented. Out of the give and take of these groups this book was born. Many thoughts and suggestions from many people have gone into its making. But in the end, of course, I'm responsible for the book.

Personal and grateful acknowledgment is given to four people in various parts of the world who helped to copy and prepare the manuscript: to my daughter, Mrs. James K. Mathews, of Montclair, New Jersey; to Miss Bess McFadden, of Brooklyn, New York; to Miss Grace Wood, refugee missionary from Korea residing in Japan; and to Miss Ruth Christopherson, missionary in Burma, who came to Sat Tal, India, to help get the manuscript in final shape.

INTRODUCTION

THE THESIS OF THIS BOOK IS SIMPLE: EVERYTHING IS BEING TRANS-formed up or down—and this includes men and women especially. It is not a question of whether you would be or would not be transformed —you are being transformed, for better or for worse. The life forces which flow from you and through you are transforming you into a pattern. You stand in the midst of those life forces and you decide the pattern. Even if you apparently do not decide anything, but allow those life forces free rein, yet in not deciding you decide not to decide.

Everything is being transformed into something else and every person into someone else. Of all the commonly accepted statements about man one of the most widely accepted is this: "Human nature never changes." This is completely false. It is the nature of human nature to change. The man who repeats that statement changes himself through that very statement into a more fixed type of person. The statement produces change—for the worse. In mentally shutting the door to change upward he opens the door to change downward.

The science of semantics is based on the fact that human nature is changing every moment. So when you use a word to describe a man, you must define which man—the man a year ago, a month ago, five minutes ago, or the man *now*. You must therefore change your words to describe the changed man. Even if he is apparently not changed, you must heighten your words up and down to describe him accurately. There is nothing changeless about life except change.

The story is told of the statue on top of New York's old Madison Square Garden, the beautiful statue of Diana. A lovely girl posed for the statue and became famous. But she became gay and then dissolute. Years later into a Salvation Army kitchen there stumbled an old battered woman begging for bread and soup. When the Salvation Army officer asked her name and was told, he in surprise said, "Why, you are Diana." A crooked smile twisted across her wretched face as she replied, "I *was* Diana." Every person can say concerning himself, for better or for worse, "I *was* that person. I am not now that person."

INTRODUCTION

A man of forty pulled a picture out of his inside pocket, laid it before me and said with a sigh, "To think I was that." It was a picture of a handsome youth of twenty-one, so handsome and well built that he was an entrant in a world competition for the most perfect specimen of manhood. When he was not chosen, it so hurt his pride and wounded his ego that it started a chain reaction into conflicts and infirmities that left him a wreck at forty. Had he reacted rightly to that blow, he could have become handsome in character as well as in body, but the wrong reaction let in the forces of decay, let in conflict, and conflict let in inferiorities and the result was a wreck.

These two poems by Emerson describe the two Daniel Websters:

> "Webster" (written in 1831)
> Let Webster's lofty face
> Ever on thousands shine,
> A beacon set that Freedom's race
> Might gather omens from that radiant sign.

> "Webster" (written in 1854)
> Why did all manly gifts in Webster fail?
> He wrote on Nature's grandest brow,
> "For Sale."

Emerson W. Harris, commenting on this, says that "Webster's early manhood was spent in a continual blaze of glory, he was given the envious title, Defender of the Constitution. But his last days were spent in sadness. He began his public career as an antislavery man. Later, in hope of gaining the presidency, he sacrificed his convictions and urged a law compelling the return of fugitive slaves. All the good he did, all his brilliant oratory could not blot out the haunting sting of the words of a former friend:

> He wrote on Nature's grandest brow,
> "For sale."

Webster was transformed into the image of his decisions. He let a conflict in, became a conflict, and ended in looking like a conflict. He ended in sadness.

But this inevitable change can transform us into higher patterns—

if we choose it shall. We can decide which forces shall mold us. When Henry F. Lyte wrote: "Change and decay in all around I see," he expressed only a half-truth, for change *and decay* need not necessarily be linked, for change and transformation upward can be linked—if you decide. Only those forces which we allow to affect us do affect us. It is our response that decides. It is possible to allow the forces that reside in Jesus Christ so to operate in you that you can become a transformed person—upward. Nothing the same, except your name. And that name too might have to be changed, as people did in the New Testament, to express the changed character.

I need not emphasize in this Introduction the necessity to be a transformed person. The facts themselves emphasize it. The people around us who are living with a sense of failure and futility, of defeat and disaster, of conflict and division, of fears and resentments, of inferiorities, of self-loathing, of boredom—and deeper, with a sense of guilt—all these, and more, cry out for some basic transformation. It is a *must*—if life is to be tolerable.

This book undertakes to show you *how*. My British publishers asked, "Is this proposed book on the transformed person to be a book on the theory of the transformed person or on the practical steps into the transformed life?" I had to reply, "It is to be both, but with an emphasis on the *how*." I say that the emphasis is on the *how*, for in education, in psychology, and in religion the weakest place is at the word *how*.

In education the discussion method is emphasized. Everything is thrown back to the student, "What do you think about it?" Willard L. Sperry said that if the modern technique had been in vogue, Paul would have answered the Philippian jailer when he asked, "What must I do to be saved?" by saying, "Well, what do you think about it?" The discussion would have ended—in discussion, in a verbalism. Paul put down a ladder into his pit of despair and the man climbed to freedom and transformation. He told him *how*.

In analytical psychology the psychologist is supposed to sit and listen while the patient talks interminably about himself. The talk itself is supposed to be healing, the exposure is supposed to bring composure. Sometimes it does, but only if somewhere along the line the analyst puts down a ladder with steps of how to get out of the pit of tangled mental and spiritual states. I sometimes wonder if the technique of interminably listening to interminable descriptions of

INTRODUCTION

the patient's inner states isn't in itself an escapism—you don't have to give any answers, for the talk itself is the answer. That *may* be used to cover up the fact of having no answer to give. It may be used learnedly to cover up bankruptcy. For all the learning in the world will not lead to transformation unless the imparter of the learning is imparting it out of experience. He must show the way, and not merely tell the way. A person who is himself a problem cannot deal with problems, for two problems never add up to a solution. This business of transformation must be vitalism, not verbalism. Psychology on the whole, with noble exceptions, is weak, almost to bankruptcy, at the place of the *how*.

But much of religion is in the same boat. It is long on the exhortation to be transformed, but short on the *how*. The fact is that if a pastor after his sermon should tell his congregation that they were going to enter into an afterservice to present the *how*, there would be embarrassment on the part of many. They would feel that this was an intrusion, an innovation, for the *how* is not supposed to be an integral part of the process. It is all left at verbalism. And very often the pastor himself doesn't know the *how*. A prominent pastor relates that a discerning friend said to him, "Doctor, you know everything about Christianity except one thing—how to make a man a Christian." The pastor said in comment, "I didn't get angry, for I knew it was true."

This book tries to answer the *how* of being a transformed person, but it also tries to unfold the meaning of transformation. A content has to be put into the transformed life to make it desirable. The possibilities must be so alluring that the heart is set on fire to get it. We must *see* before we will *seek*. But in the seeing we must see that this has total relevance for the total life, individual and collective. We must see a total answer.

This book is written as my other page-a-day books were written. They seem to have met a need. That need is for three things: (*a*) A book which can be used as a devotional—a page a day; (*b*) a book arranged as a basis of study for a study group—hence the grouping into weekly units; (*c*) a book that can be read straight through as any other book, since it is a unit, dealing with one thing—how to be a transformed person.

The prayers at the end of each day's meditation are prayers I imagine a beginner would pray as he takes the first uncertain steps toward transformation. I am praying his prayers. For I begin at the bottom of the ladder and go on up to the more developed types of Christian living. For transformation can continue clear up to the very end of life—and beyond.

E. STANLEY JONES

CONTENTS

CONTENTS

CONTENTS

CONTENTS

HOW TO BE A TRANSFORMED PERSON

AN URGE THAT ENDS IN AN URGE?

You begin today the quest to be a transformed person. You probably begin with the half suspicion that it may be a wild-goose chase, a will-o'-the-wisp that will allure you on and leave you in the end mired in a swamp of despair. You feel that you may be striving for goals which are not there. "Play the game of life according to the rules," said a professor to his students, and one of them replied, "Yes, Professor, but suppose there are no goal posts?" He wasn't sure there was anything to aim at, for he wasn't sure that the universe itself wasn't aimless.

Perhaps you will have to start where you can. Is there something basic from which you can start, no matter how full of doubts you may be? Yes, there is. It is this: "There is one great and universal wish of mankind expressed in all religions, in all art and philosophy, and in all human life: *the wish to pass beyond himself as he now is.*" The fact that you have taken up this book shows that you have within you the inherent desire to pass beyond yourself as you now are. You didn't create it—it is a part of you, it is a "given."

But the question inevitably arises: "Is there anything out there in the universe that will answer this craving to go beyond myself? I admit that there is an urge to be different, to be a transformed person, but is it just an urge with nothing to meet it from the side of reality?" Well, if a child in the womb could reason, it might say: "I have a brain, but is there any intelligence out there in the strange world into which I am going to answer my brain? I am made for food, I hunger, but is there any food in that outside world to meet that hunger? I am made for love, but is there any love to meet me, or do I go into a loveless world?" These questions answer themselves: There is no known hunger where there isn't something also there to meet that hunger. Cry and supply are both inherent in the nature of reality. The fact that you have this urge to be a transformed person shows that all the resources necessary for you to be a transformed person are inherent in the nature of reality. That is something to tie to.

O God, I call Thee God, but so far but a name. I come to Thee for help. All I have to begin with is an urge to be different. But I am grateful for that. Amen.

AFFIRMATION FOR THE DAY: *I have an urge; that urge may become a divine urge.*

A CRAVING FOR RIGHT DIRECTION

We began yesterday with the basic fact that there is an inherent urge to go beyond yourself, to be a different and better person. Does psychology agree? Dr. William H. Sheldon, in *Psychology and the Promethean Will,* says: "Continued observations . . . lead almost inevitably to the conclusion that deeper and more fundamental than sexuality, deeper than the craving for social power, deeper even than the desire for possessions, there is a still more generalized and more universal craving in the human make-up. *It is the craving for knowledge of the right direction—for orientation.* . . . Every system of philosophy, whether called religious or not, is at bottom a human attempt to satisfy the craving to be pointed in the right direction."

We saw yesterday that there is an inherent and basic urge to go beyond yourself as you now are. Here we add another basic urge: "the craving for knowledge of the right direction—for orientation." We not only want to go beyond ourselves, we want to go beyond ourselves in the right direction. We want to be oriented. But oriented to what? Here the psychologist puts up a vast question mark. But religion steps into that vacuum and says, and says it without equivocation: You must be oriented to God. If there is a God, that's important. You cannot be at cross-purposes with Reality and not get hurt.

We now come to a third basic urge. John Elof Boodin, a philosopher, says: "But in us is the longing for unity. We are impelled by a hidden instinct to reunion with the parts of the larger heart of the universe." Here philosophy hesitates to say "God" and talks of "reunion with . . . the larger heart of the universe," which is vague. We cannot have reunion with vacuity. Religion again steps in and says: You desire basically a reunion with God—with God your Father. You are homesick. All sickness is homesickness. Not basically related to God, you are like lungs without air, a heart without love, an aesthetic nature without beauty. You are centrally *starved.* Therefore irritable and unhappy.

O God, I'm starved—starved for Thee. Nothing this side of Thee can satisfy me. So I'm on a search for nothing less than Thee. Amen.

AFFIRMATION FOR THE DAY: *My homesickness for my heavenly Father is going to lead me to Him.*

SCAPEGOATS ON WHICH WE LAY RESPONSIBILITY

We have seen that there are three basic urges within us, part and parcel of our nature and therefore inescapable: an urge to go beyond ourselves; an urge to be oriented—to go in the right direction; and an urge to reunion with "the larger heart of the universe"—with God.

You gladly admit these urges and cling to them as pointing in the direction of hope. But perhaps you are also caught with a fear that there are other facts in the universe that make this hope of being a transformed person seem questionable—even worse, impossible. Aren't other things beside our basic urges deciding our fate: malign powers in the universe, karma of a previous birth, being born under a bad star, the subconscious, heredity, the mechanical necessity of adaptation to environment—doesn't one or the other of these decide?

Now let us look at these before we go on. The Greeks believed that since the gods were all-powerful they were responsible for man's plight—who else could be? Then they saw through such a flimsy evasion of what they knew was their own responsibility. The gods were dismissed—with laughter. In *Guilt and Redemption* Lewis J. Sherrill describes their dismissal: "With such laughter at their farewell, the gods died—those earthborn gods whom the Greeks had made responsible for man's plight. But what laughter it was! . . . This laughter had no sound of joy or clear-eyed humor. It was the raucous noise which men make as they go out into the dark, and who in going can make no sense out of either the light or the dark. In short, when the Greeks made the gods responsible for man's situation, the point they reached was spelled out in one word: *Nonsense,* to the Greeks more dreadful than tragedy."

When man goes wrong, his first impulse is to look around to find some way of evading responsibility, some scapegoat upon which he can lay his sins. But deep down man knows that this won't do. His moral nature revolts and says with the Greeks one word, "Nonsense." Something within us sides with the moral universe against ourselves. We have the feeling that in any struggle with the moral universe we will come out badly.

O God, maybe I'll have to side with Thee against myself if I'm to get out of what I am. Help me to do it. Amen.

AFFIRMATION FOR THE DAY: *If I try to find scapegoats, in the end I know I shall become the goat!*

ARE WE IN THE GRIP OF KISMET?

We saw yesterday that man, beginning to be caught in the net of his own evils, looks around to find some person or fact upon which he can lay responsibility. This is as old as Adam: "The woman whom thou gavest to be with me, she gave me of the tree, and I did eat."

In Western civilization we no longer blame it on the gods. India still does in large measure—smallpox comes from the goddess of smallpox instead of from preventable contagion. But vast portions of East and West still lay responsibility on God for the plight of mankind. God is all-powerful; why didn't He do this, why didn't He prevent that? I watched a man at a large switchboard directing the traffic of a vast railway system stretching for hundreds of miles. The position of every train was shown and he directed them when to move and when to stop. I said to him, "Suppose these trains should decide to be free and move as they please, regardless of your orders. Would that complicate your work?" "Complicate it? It would ruin it. We'd be a mess in an hour." "But," I replied, "God has limited Himself and has allowed an area of freedom in man. God is no longer absolutely free since He made another will. He must step back and let that will operate." That complicates God's game, especially if man keeps blaming the results of his own mistakes and sins on God. But to blame our predicament on God doesn't get us out of it—not one step.

When a Mohammedan gets into trouble, he blames his kismet—his fate. But his kismet is ordained by God, hence he indirectly makes God responsible. But blaming his kismet doesn't save the Mohammedan from living in a land of backwardness and sterility—as every Mohammedan land is—the direct result of laying responsibility on his kismet instead of on his own actions and attitudes. The laws of God don't listen to our attempted evasions. They are color-blind, class-blind, race-blind, religion-blind. We don't break them—we break ourselves on them. Evasions don't evade, excuses don't excuse, dodging doesn't dodge, except into deeper mire.

O Father, Thou art hedging me in, hedging me in to redeem me. For I see I cannot be redeemed except as I accept my responsibility for what I am. Help me. Amen.

AFFIRMATION FOR THE DAY: *I shall become a fool if I try to fool the universe.*

"MY KARMA IS BAD"

We continue to look at the doors into which people duck to evade responsibility. Let us look at another: karma. When a Hindu or a Buddhist gets into difficulties, he turns over his hand and says, "My karma is bad"—the result of the deeds of a previous birth now finding him out. He removes the responsibility from the *now* to the *then* and to a person of whom he has no memory. It saves him from the necessity of finding the causes in his present actions and attitudes. It adds up to an attempt at evasion. And it doesn't save India from a slowing down of every reform, to the degree that the doctrine of karma is held. It is a paralysis on the will to change, for that will is held by the past.

Others blame their difficulties on unlucky stars. As if lumps of matter floating in space could decide the destiny, for good or ill, of a free moral agent! Of all the nonsense palmed off on ancient and modern minds this has more bunk in it to the square inch than anything I know. The Burmese government was launched on an auspicious day, according to the stars, and immediately went from calamity to calamity. The whole government resigned and five minutes later was reconstituted as it was, in order to have a fresh beginning on an auspicious hour. This is on a par with the governmental order to beat all the drums of Burma in temple and home simultaneously so that the devils of strife might be frightened at the noise and leave!

When we leave these crude attempts at evasion of responsibility, we come to some more supposedly learned and scientific attempts. One is that our conscious life is determined by the subconscious, and the individual subconscious in turn is determined by the racial subconscious. We inherit these racial drives, and these drives are in the subconscious and therefore in large measure out of our control. Our actions are determined by forces not of our making and not in our control. This tends to blur or obliterate moral responsibilities.

O Father God, I do not want to hide from responsibility for I may thereby be hiding from salvation. I want not to be excused, but to be saved. Save me. Amen.

AFFIRMATION FOR THE DAY: *Today I shall keep repeating to myself the statement of Andrew Carnegie, "The first condition of success is to assume responsibility."*

5

TRAPPED BY ENVIRONMENT?

Yesterday we ended by looking at another attempt at evasion—the attempt to blame our condition on the subconscious mind. There is a measure of truth in the statement that the subconscious determines a good deal of the conscious. But we are in large measure responsible for the kind of subconscious mind we have. We can determine what drops into it and can determine what forces we allow to operate there. We make the subconscious and then it in turn tends to make us. Each person has the kind of subconscious mind he has built by thought, attitude, and action.

We come to another learned attempt at evasion—the attempt to place everything on response to stimulus. Writes Lewis J. Sherrill in *Guilt and Redemption:* "Man is not obedient to his fate, but is adapting to his environment. Man does not act in response to a god, but in response to a stimulus. . . . It was once the fashion to sing in religion's name that we are worms of the dust. To celebrate that view of man's nature in song now brings only disgusted protest. Our lowly estate is illumined, instead, by drawing 'laws of learning' from the movements of bewildered animals entrapped by the environment. The Greek, who made the gods responsible for man's plight, finally reached Nonsense as his result. Perhaps the placing of responsibility in the environment, and the conception of man as animal-in-cage-adapting-to-environment, yield us the modern equivalent." The environment is being crowned Lord of all. And man has no soul with which to defy this all-determining environment which seeks to crush him—he has only mechanical response to stimulus. Not only is responsibility evaded, but there is no soul to be responsible. Thus man learnedly works himself not only out of responsibility, but also out of a soul. The result is *Nonsense.* Environment does affect us, but not mechanically, for only that part of the environment to which we respond affects us. And we can decide to respond or not to respond. The choice is always ours.

O God, my Father, I see I cannot get out of my inner tangles by laying responsibility here, there, and everywhere—everywhere except on myself. Help me. Amen.

AFFIRMATION FOR THE DAY: *Today I shall give responsive attention to only that part of my environment which I desire to influence me.*

CONFESSION IS THE CATHARSIS

The last way we take of evading moral responsibility is to say that we are doing only what everybody is doing—we lay it on the example of other people.

A man who had been caught in a moral triangle said to me, "I did only what any man in my circumstances would have done." But whether this is true or not, it did not untie the knots into which he had tied himself and his situation by going off with another woman. Two wrongs don't add up to a solution. "Everybody does it" may be true, but then "everybody" who does it is getting more and more frustrated and unhappy.

There is only one way out and that is to lay the blame where it belongs—squarely on ourselves. A young man told his father and mother he was leaving home, "I cannot stand any longer mother's piety and father's strictness." Early before daylight the father heard the son's footsteps on the stairs. He met him and said: "Son, your mother and I haven't slept any tonight. We've been talking it over and we have concluded that there must be something wrong with us to make you want to leave home. I've come to ask your forgiveness." The boy broke down and said: "Dad, it's not in you and mother—it's in me. I'm all wrong. Forgive me." Mutual forgiveness and adjustments made it possible for the boy to live happily in the home.

The confession was the catharsis. When the boy laid the blame squarely where it belonged—on himself—then transformation began. Transformation will begin in any life—in yours—when you stand up and say: "I'm responsible for the kind of person I am. I am what I've wanted to be. Now I've changed my mind. I'm sorry for what I am and have done. I'm going to be different. God help me." Immediately the healing, transforming forces of the universe set in—the work begins. The grace of God begins to operate. In that moment you cease to be a whining evader, laying blame here and laying it there, and you become a person. There the birth of a soul begins. You're taking no longer the role of a puppet, but of a person.

O God, I'm through with being a supposed victim of this and that. I'm now going to be a person—Thy person. Make me over again Amen.

AFFIRMATION FOR THE DAY: *I have been and am what I have decided to be; today I decide to be another person.*

"I'M BEATEN—BY MYSELF"

We saw last week how under one guise or another we seek to evade responsibility for what we are. Before we go on, we must look at one more evasion.

The Marxist propounds what he calls the economic interpretation of history, that history is determined by the economic forces of a given situation. There is some truth in this of course. But interestingly enough, the Marxist says that the economic determines history, and then he turns around and determines to change the economic. In other words, persons change the economic, which is supposed to change persons! In the last analysis: The choice is always ours. We know that, and as a result we feel ourselves morally accountable persons no matter how we twist and plead and try to evade. Something rises up within us as Elijah did in Ahab's garden and says, "Thou art the man."

We must face one more semievasion. I say "semi," for the person who uses it accepts responsibility, but says nothing can be done for he has tied himself up hopelessly. He surrenders himself to his own fate, a fate for which he is responsible. "I've created out of myself two persons, and the worst of these two persons is too strong for the better person, so I'm fated to be that worse person. I'm not the victim of the karma of a previous birth, but of my karma in this birth. I'm beaten—by myself."

Browning expressed this divided condition in these words:

> Sadly mixed natures: self-indulgent, yet
> Self-sacrificing too; how the love soars,
> How the craft, avarice, vanity and spite
> Sink again!

We created that divided self and that self is our destiny. When Milton pictured Satan flying through space and crying, "Which way I fly is hell, myself am hell," he depicted many of us.

O God, I'm responsible, but I'm so responsible I'm sunk. I cannot bear the weight of being "I." Love me—if Thou canst. Amen.

AFFIRMATION FOR THE DAY: *I decide to live no longer with a hell-self, but with a heaven-self.*

"FOR WE ARE TWO—NOT ONE"

We are looking in passing at the type of person who acknowledges the responsibility but feels that he is caught in the nemesis of his own past attitudes and deeds. This is sometimes true. David Seabury, in *Unmasking Our Minds,* tells of a man who lived in Africa for nearly two decades and then contracted a form of malaria which persisted for over twelve years. The condition made him irritable, morose, impatient, and so unsociable that his friends came to consider him a most unpleasant character. But medical assistance, after his return to England, cured the last remnants of the malarial conditions. His body was cured but the disposition was unchanged. The man continued to be impatient, irritable, and melancholy. He thought of himself as a solitary and rather impossible person and acted under the autosuggestion in an almost unspeakable manner. He had completely identified himself with the condition that he had so long endured.

His surrender to himself was his destiny. As long as there were two of him, one struggling with the other, there was hope, but when there was only one—the bad one—then the condition needed a miracle. That that miracle can take place we shall see.

Some feel that being two persons is destiny, an irretrievable destiny. We feel that this divided condition is our destiny.

> Oh, we are forever divided,
> Despite what love has done
> To draw us close together,
> For we are two—not one.

But those words "forever" and "we are two" are questionable. Life can be changed however fixed it may seem to be. The present is not destiny.

O God, my Father, is it true, is it true that what I am is not destiny— that I can be changed? Make it so, make it so. Amen.

AFFIRMATION FOR THE DAY: *I have been two; now I'm becoming one.*

"EXEMPT FROM STRIFE"

We linger a little longer at the place of those who feel they are hopelessly divided. A poet puts vividly this divided soul:

> I like, mislike, lament for what I could not,
> I do, undo, yet still do what I should not,
> And at the self-same instant will be the thing I would not.

This condition is sad but not hopeless, for the struggling person sees that there is a division and hates it. The condition is bad only when there becomes only one—and that one the bad one. When the struggle is given over, then Despair sits on a near-by tree, like a buzzard, ready to pick to pieces the carcass.

The fact that you are struggling, that you have not let go in despair and have not become unified in dull, dead monotony shows that there is not only hope, but the very great possibility of your becoming a transformed person.

One can be unified on two levels—one on the level of low desires with no fluttering protest within. But that unity is the unity of the beast or worm, where no spark disturbs its clod. You cannot be content with such a unity where you are unified with a grave at the center of that unity—the grave of the immortal part of you, your soul. You would rather be a discontented man than a contented worm.

God is disturbing you, like friends walk a man who has taken an overdose of sleeping powders, lest if he lies down, he will never awaken again. So the everlasting Mercy pursues us, sets us at war with our lower selves, disturbs us until we beg to be let alone—to die. Love will not let us die. Our very pangs are His prods—prodding us to be a transformed person. As long as the prod is there—the Person is there.

Gracious Father, Thou who art "Love that wilt not let me go," I'm grateful at least that I feel Thy prods—prodding me to Thee. Amen.

AFFIRMATION FOR THE DAY: *I shall accept my pangs as God's prods.*

IS THERE ANY DIVINE INITIATIVE?

We cannot go farther until we see if there is something to answer our quest. Is there any divine response to man's upward yearning for a transformed life? Is this all a lifting of one's self by his own bootstraps? Is what man hears from heaven but the echo of his own pleading cry?

I have often said to students that in everything from the lowest cell to the highest man there is an urge for a fuller, more abundant life. "Everything," says Tagore, "lifts up strong hands after perfection." The religious urge is found in that life urge. It is that life urge turned qualitative. It is the cry for life turned into the cry for *better* life. And the moment we say "better" we have standards, and the moment we have standards we have religion. As long as men want to live fully and better we will be religious. The forms of religion may come and go but the spirit of religion is deathless from age to age. For it is the cry for life turned qualitative.

But if man cries for life, is there any answer from the side of God? The answer is found in the New Testament: "I am come that they might have life, and that they might have it more abundantly." When the upward cry for life and the downward offer of Life meet, there real religion sets in. When life with a small *l* meets life with a capital *L*, and living relations are set up, then real religion begins. For the lower life lays hold of the resources of the higher Life, and when that happens, then transformation sets in, sometimes of an amazing character.

Is there any divine Initiative? In this process of transformation does God undergo a transformation in order to transform us? If this is so, then at the very center of the nature of the Divine our transformation is guaranteed. Would God become like us that we might become like Him? If so, then man's quest for transformation is not a lonely orphaned quest. There is Another by his side, and that Another by his side guarantees that the resources of the universe are at his disposal in his quest. It means that we quest because He first quested and is still questing. When we meet, we're on the Way.

Gracious Father, I feel I'm not alone. Where I take one step, Thou dost take two. I feel in my bones we shall meet and go on together. Amen.

AFFIRMATION FOR THE DAY: *God and I are approaching each other. We are bound to meet.*

MANY RELIGIONS—ONE GOSPEL

We must now look at the most stupendous thing which this planet has seen: God being transformed into our image that we might be transformed into His. The Incarnation is the miracle of miracles. Grant that central miracle, and all other miracles in the New Testament become credible in the light of this central miracle.

This stupendous fact is described in these words: "Though he was divine by nature, he did not set store upon equality with God, but emptied himself by taking the nature of a servant; born in human guise and appearing in human form, he humbly stooped in his obedience even to die, and to die upon the cross" (Phil. 2:6-8, Moffatt). Here was not man becoming God, but God becoming man, and becoming man at his lowest place—the place of his sin. He was identified with man at the place of man's sin—He was crucified, and died between two thieves as one like them. This meant that He went so low that He could get under the lowest sinner and lift him to undreamed of heights.

Writes Alan W. Watts, in *Behold the Spirit:* "The meaning of the Incarnation, therefore, is simply that we do not have to attain union with God. Man does not have to climb to the infinite and become God, because, out of love, the infinite God descends to the finite and becomes man. . . . Once we realize the futility of our pride, that we can neither ascend to God nor, by reason of pride, prevent his descent to us, the proud core of egoism as simply dissolved."

The Incarnation is the divine invasion of us, an invasion of incorrigible love. You, then, do not have to find God; you simply have to let God find you. Religions are man's search for God, the gospel is God's search for man. There are many religions; there is but one gospel.

This therefore puts our feet on the right way, gives us a sense of right orientation. We do not have to seek laboriously for God, nor try to lift ourselves into transformation by our own disciplined efforts—we simply have to accept a gift and then belong forever to the Giver. Transformation is so close it is breath-taking. If I reach out, I reach too far—it is here! And here for the taking!

O Christ, Thou dost bring all this so near that I am overwhelmed. I cannot but find, for Thou art finding me. I am closer than I thought. Amen.

AFFIRMATION FOR THE DAY: *Not egoistic striving, but realistic receiving.*

"THE WAY BEGINS IN THE HOLE"

We are now about to put our feet upon the Way. That Way runs right down to where I am. Helen Wodehouse says: "We think we must climb to a certain height of goodness before we can reach God. But He says not 'At the end of the end of the way you may find me'; He says 'I am the Way; I am the road under your feet, the road that begins just as low down as you happen to be.' If we are in a hole the Way begins in the hole. The moment we set our face in the same direction as His, we are walking with God."

Jesus then is that personal approach from the unseen God coming so near that He becomes inescapable. He becomes inescapable for I know if I escape from Him, I escape from—salvation! To find God then is the easiest thing in the world. You don't have to find Him— you simply have to consent to be found. No one is farther than one step from God. And that one step is a short step; turn around and say "Yes" and you are at once in the arms of redemptive Love. But that "Yes" must carry with it *you*—you must be behind the "Yes," not a lip-Yes, but a life-Yes. His "Yes" has been said; the Incarnation is God saying, "Yes." When your "Yes" of response meets His "Yes" of invitation, you are simply there—at the place of transformation.

Someone has said that there are two ways of reaching the house next door. One is to travel all the way around the globe; the other is to walk a few feet. There are two ways of finding transformation—one is to walk clear around the globe in a self-concentrated effort to get rid of your faults and blemishes and discipline yourself into being worthy of attaining the Divine. The Hindu method of austerities, pilgrimages, and discipline is an example of the globe-encircling method. The other is to step next door, a few feet away. This is the Christian method of accepting a gift—the gift of grace. Transformation then is not an attainment, but an obtainment. It is a God-centered salvation instead of an ego-centered attempt at salvation. "Egoism is like trying to swim without relying on the water, endeavoring to keep afloat by tugging at your own legs; your whole body becomes tense and you sink like a stone." Transformation is nearer than you are to yourself.

Gracious God and Father, I begin to see. And my soul is all atremble at the thought that I may be at the door even before I begin. Amen.

AFFIRMATION FOR THE DAY: *I accept the gift and gladly belong forever to the Giver.*

"THE WORD IS NIGH THEE"

The Incarnation is the most important fact in the Christian faith. If you by-pass this, you by-pass the center and are forever upon the margin. Get this and you get Life.

A little boy, child of missionaries, was in school in the United States at Christmas time. The principal said to him, "Son, what would you rather have most of all for Christmas?" The boy looked at the picture of his father framed on his desk and remembered acutely the absence of the father in a far-off land, and then quietly said, "I want my father to step out of that frame." The little boy voiced the cry of humanity: We want God our Father to step out of the frame of the universe, out of this impersonal relationship and meet us personally. Jesus is God stepping out of the frame of the universe—God simplified and God personalized, God become intimate and tender and redemptive.

Let this then be burned into our minds so we will give up our self-lacerations in favor of self-surrender. Until we take the way of self-surrender and acceptance of the gift, we are "like birds flying in quest of air, or men with lighted candles searching through the darkness for fire." "The word is nigh thee." You don't have to ascend up to heaven to bring God down by your efforts—He's down by His love. All you have to do is to "let go and let God"—let go of yourself and take His self. But this letting go is the rub. It hurts our pride that we can't earn something to boast about.

In saving ourselves even in the quest for salvation from ourselves we lose ourselves. "Pluck a flower and it dies. Take up water from a stream and it flows no longer. Pull down the blind and the sunbeam is not trapped in the room. Snatch the wind in a bag and you have only stagnant air. This is the root of every trouble: man loves life, but the moment he tries to hold on to it he misses it. And the harder man hangs on to his life, the sooner he dies of worry," says Alan Watts.

Here we are at the very crux of our problem: If you really want to be a transformed person, want it enough to surrender the center—your self—then you are not merely at the Door, you're in!

O Christ, it all seems so amazingly simple. Help me not to complicate it by egocentric tantrums. Help me to be as simple and direct as Thou art. Amen.

AFFIRMATION FOR THE DAY: *I am becoming simple, therefore wise.*

14

LIFE IS NOT WHAT IT OUGHT TO BE

We are led in our quest to the very center: *It is the conviction that life is not what it ought to be.*

God apparently is convinced of that, hence the extraordinary step of becoming man that man may become like God. Is man convinced? Fritz Kunkel, a psychologist, says, "The collaboration of religion and psychology must be based on the unanimous conviction of both parties that man is not as he should be." Is this conviction "unanimous"? To the degree that men have any convictions at all there is the conviction that life has slipped a cog, is out of gear, has lost its harmony, is missing the mark, is in real need of fundamental change.

It is true that Swami Vivekananda speaking in the United States exclaimed, "Ye divinities on earth—call you sinners? It is a sin to call you sinners." But men smiled a wan smile at the rhetoric and knew it was only rhetoric; at least they did to the degree that they looked into their own breasts. We know that there is a cleft in our natures, a cleft we cannot heal. James Smetham wrote each man's confession: "One of the most formidable enemies was a vivid and ill-trained imagination. Against outward and inward evils of this kind there existed a very powerful love of truth and purity. . . . The antagonism of these two forces . . . went nigh to threaten my reason."

Modern man may be indifferent to religion as he knows it and yet, says Alan Watts, "His nervous restlessness, his chronic sense of frustration, his love of sensationalism as an escape, his fitful use of every substitute for religion from state-worship to getting drunk, shows that his soul still desires that release from itself." It is a fundamental release he vaguely longs for. But he also knows that he hasn't within himself the resources to heal himself. He may run to cults of self-realization, of self-healing, of self-cultivation, but in his heart of hearts he knows that what he needs is not self-realization—he realizes that too much now—but self-release. He knows he needs conversion—fundamental and radical.

O God, I see, I see what I need—I need "a man to rise in me that the man I am might cease to be." Help me. I need it. Amen.

AFFIRMATION FOR THE DAY: *No attempt to hold the untenable status quo by excuses; I'm out to be different.*

STUNTED SOULS

We come now to the very central thing the divine invasion offers—a freedom and release from what we are and what we have done. When I landed in India forty-three years ago, the next day I preached my first sermon on India's soil and I took a text which I felt instinctively was the crux of the matter, "Thou shalt call his name Jesus, for he shall save his people from their sins." The first mention of sin in the New Testament is not a fierce invective against it, but a promise of its removal as the central thing the Incarnation would mean. It meant a double saving: *from* their sins, *to* Himself, the Savior. The "to Himself" meant the opening of amazing possibilities in being made over again in to a new pattern—after His image.

This fundamental change here sounded as the keynote of the gospel is variously described in the New Testament: conversion, a new birth, a new creation, partakers of the divine nature, alive to God, being transformed. All language has been laid hold on to describe this most important thing that can happen in human living.

Stanley Hall, the psychologist, says, "Every life is stunted unless it receives this metamorphosis, called conversion, in some form or other. If the church allows this to fossilize, then psychology, when it becomes truly biological, will preach it. Indeed the chief fact of genetic psychology is conversion, a change of momentous scientific importance and interest." "Every life is stunted"—is that true? Yes, there is a fundamentally tied-up condition within until this central release takes place. The Japanese very cleverly stunt great forest trees and make them into potted plants by a simple expedient of tying up the taproot. The tree then lives off its surface roots only, with no taproot going down into the soil and drawing sustenance from the depths. Every person, religious, irreligious, or nonreligious, is an inwardly tied-up person until conversion in some form releases him. And there are no exceptions. Many are tied up with fears, guilts, resentments, inferiorities, and self-preoccupations. They are stunted and runted

O God, my Father, I know I'm a 25 per cent man until Thou dost touch me into 100 per cent and beyond. I need that plus. In Jesus' name. Amen.

AFFIRMATION FOR THE DAY: *A full-sized man in a full-sized job with a full-sized goal—that's the me I want to be.*

16

"THE MAN I MIGHT HAVE BEEN"

Someone has said: "I am the tadpole of an archangel," and this is true, but it may be that the possible archangel may remain in the mud a tadpole and the archangel never emerge. "Born a man and died a grocer," might be the epitaph of many. Wrote Thomas S. Jones, Jr.:

> Across the fields of yesterday
> He sometimes comes to me,
> A little lad just back from play—
> The lad I used to be.
>
> And yet he smiles so wistfully
> Once he has crept within,
> I wonder if he hopes to see
> The man I might have been.

David Seabury, in *Unmasking Our Minds,* tells of "the tall lad who looks like a young Shelley, blasé now, goes about dreaming of the musician he might have been had not a flippant slip of a girl broken his heart, and turned him into a professional cynic. He watches the blue smoke curling from cigarette after cigarette, and takes revenge on the whole fair sex. His life is sophistication and ennui. He hasn't a remote idea why he was born or what he should do—nor has anyone else."

But not only blasé irreligious youth is tied up without conversion— many religious people are too. A bishop once said to me: "I don't see how you do what you do and keep so poised and happy. I am a conflict. I live as though God were not. I am upset, especially since I've retired." He needed conversion exactly as a man in the gutter needs it. Jesus sat one night with a religious leader of the Jewish people, sensed his deepest need, looked him straight in the eye, and said, "Nicodemus, you must be born again." Here was a terribly startling thing: a morally good and religious man needed a new birth. Why? Because he was essentially self-centered, and when you are self-centered you are not God-centered. He came to Jesus by night, afraid of what would happen to him if it were known that he was interested in this Prophet.

O God, I see that we all stand before Thee with one simple need— the need of a new birth, a new beginning. Give it to me now. Amen.

AFFIRMATION FOR THE DAY: *If I am to be born only once, it would have been better had I not been born at all.*

THE PRESSURE OF THE KINGDOM OF GOD

We pause to see the meaning of the new birth which Jesus said everybody needed: "Except a man be born again, he cannot see the kingdom of God" (John 3:3). We divide people into races, classes, sexes, nationalities, rich and poor, educated and ignorant. Jesus divided men, all men, into only two classes—the once-born and the twice-born, the unconverted and the converted. No other distinctions mattered. If you are converted, you're in the Kingdom and if you're not, you're not in the Kingdom. And there were no exceptions— "Except a man," any man, *you.*

Jesus seldom used the word "except," but when He did, He usually used it about one fact: "Except ye be converted"; "Except a man be born again"; "Except ye repent." That piercing word "except" cuts like a surgeon's knife, cutting away all make-believe, all veneer, all seeming.

In one of my books years ago I called attention to the fact that there are five kingdoms, each representing a stage of life. At the lowest is the mineral kingdom, above that the plant or vegetable kingdom, above that the animal kingdom, above that the kingdom of man, and above that the Kingdom of God. Each kingdom might suppose there is nothing higher than it—the mineral kingdom might say there is nothing higher than the mineral, but the plant kingdom knows of a fuller, more abundant life. The plant kingdom might say that life stops with it, but the animal kingdom is sure of a higher form of life. The animal kingdom might say it is the acme—nothing beyond. But man knows of a completer life. When we come to the kingdom of man, he might claim that man is the apex—this is humanism. But something presses upon us from above, awakening us to aspiration, longing, spiritual hunger. That pressure is the pressure of the Kingdom of God. It is Life pressing on life, the Holy pressing on the unholy—redemptively. That higher Kingdom offers us a birth "from above," and when we accept that birth by surrender and faith, then we enter the fellowship of the twice-born, where we have a new Center of life, new desires, new goals, and a new language.

Gracious God, I would enter the fellowship of the twice-born. I am this side of satisfaction until I do. Take me and make me. Amen.

AFFIRMATION FOR THE DAY: *I am pressed on from above. Today I respond to that pressure rather than the pressures around me.*

BORN FROM BELOW OR FROM ABOVE?

We saw yesterday that man stands between the animal kingdom and the Kingdom of God. He is pulled between the two. For he has one foot in each—he is akin to the animal with his physical desires, and he is akin to God in that he is made "a little less than divine." He can "be born from above," or born from below; can be controlled from above or controlled from below.

The animal kingdom stands for self against the rest; the Kingdom of God stands for the divine Self for the sake of the rest; the animal kingdom is red in tooth and claw; the Kingdom of God is red with the blood of the Son of God in self-sacrifice. The animal kingdom is the survival of the fittest in terms of the sharpest tooth and claw; the Kingdom of God is the revival of the unfit in terms of redemption; the animal kingdom is life organized around the hunger motive, the Kingdom of God is life organized around the love motive; the animal kingdom is a feud, the Kingdom of God is a family. We can be born from below, or we can be born from above—life can be dominated by animal instincts or life can be dominated by God.

We stand at the center of these forces and our decisions turn on the currents—from above or from below. These life forces are directed from a single center—our wills. "The choice is always ours." We decide to be transformed from above or from below.

How can we get from the kingdom of man to the Kingdom of God? Perhaps the clue can be found in the lowest kingdom—how does the mineral kingdom pass into the plant kingdom? Here is foul, polluted mud in a swamp, and above it is a lotus flower. How can the slime be transformed into a lotus flower? It cannot lift itself; there is only one possible way to get up there: the higher kingdom comes down into the lower, and the lower kingdom surrenders itself to the roots of the plant and is lifted up and transformed and transfigured and blooms in the beauty of the lotus flower. It is born from above.

O God, I'm like that mud—I'm polluted, but I cannot purify myself. But I can consent. I do. I'm consenting to redemptive power. Amen.

AFFIRMATION FOR THE DAY: *My response to the Higher Pressure is nothing less than the acceptance of a new birth—from above.*

BORN OF WATER AND OF THE SPIRIT

We saw yesterday that polluted slime cannot rise to the kingdom of the lotus flower except in one way: the roots of the lotus flower must come down into the kingdom below, and if the slime will do two things—let go being slime and will surrender itself to the lotus flower —then it will be lifted up, and be transfigured and transformed into the beauty of the lotus flower. Except the mineral kingdom is born from above, it cannot see the plant kingdom. There is only one way up and that is the way down—the way of a higher invasion downward, the higher transforming itself into the likeness of the lower that the lower may be transformed into the higher.

How can we get from the kingdom of man to the Kingdom of God? There is only one way up and that is the way down—the Kingdom of God, personalized in Jesus, comes down into our polluted world and says, "Let go your old life, be willing to surrender to my life, and I'll transform you into my image." We do "let go and let God," and we are transformed into a new image, infused with a new life. We are born from above.

This new birth John (1:13) says is "not of blood"—it cannot be inherited from the bloodstream of our parents "nor of the will of the flesh"—you cannot get it by the efforts of the will, lifting yourself by the bootstraps; "nor of the will of man"—no man can give it to you, neither pastor nor priest nor pope, "but of God." It is direct from God or not at all.

Jesus said, "Except a man be born of water and of the Spirit, he cannot enter into the kingdom of God." The being "born of water" is the coming by baptism into an outer fellowship—the Christian fellowship; the being "born of the Spirit" is the inner birth. It is possible to be "born of water" and not be "born of the Spirit"—to be outwardly in and not inwardly in. These two things do not necessarily take place together; they might coincide, but not necessarily. A lot of people are horizontally converted, but not vertically converted, their labels changed but not their lives. The new birth means life and label changed.

O God, I cannot tolerate this birth into a physical universe unless it is supplemented by a spiritual birth. I cannot stand being half born. Amen.

AFFIRMATION FOR THE DAY: *God wills total conversion, inward and outward—so do I!*

THE OLD URGES BECOME NEW

We turn to another important passage, where Paul says, "If any man is in Christ, he is a new creature: the old things are passed away; behold, they are become new" (II Cor. 5:17 A.S.V.). The basic drives—self, sex, and the herd—have been cleansed and united and directed toward new ends. Note that they have not been eliminated. By no known process can these instinctive urges be eliminated. Put them out by the door, and they will come back by the window. If they cannot be eliminated, neither can they be repressed without setting up complexes and conflicts. There is one thing, and one thing only, that can be done—they can be cleansed, redirected, and united under a single controlling purpose by the Spirit of God.

Note this passage says: "Old things are passed away; behold, they [the old things] are become new." Self has passed away as the center of one's life and the center of festering interests, and yet, behold, it has become new—it is back again, an old thing and yet forever a new thing. The self now cleansed of its conflicts and its guilts is a self you can live with, and live with it with joy. You can love yourself now for you love something beyond yourself.

Sex as an old dominant corrupting force has passed away, its dominance gone, but it is back again—behold, sex has become new. It is now a creative force functioning within the marriage relationship as procreation and a deeper fellowship, or outside the marriage relationship as creating newborn souls, new hopes, new movements, new life in dead souls and situations. Sex as an end in itself has passed away, but sex as eternal creation is back again, for it has become new.

The herd urge as dominant has passed away. The herd is no longer God—God is God. You come out from under the fear and dominance of the herd, its spell is broken, it has passed away. And yet it has become new. Now you can go into the herd with an emancipated heart. "Delivering thee from the people . . . unto whom now I send thee"—delivered from the herd, now you can be sent to the herd; you can love the herd since you love something more than the herd, God—the herd has passed away, but behold, it has become new.

Father, Thou art taking away with Thy left hand to give back with Thy right hand. Take all I have and give it back cleansed. Amen.

AFFIRMATION FOR THE DAY: *All my old things are new things because directed to new ends!*

THREE STEPS TO TRANSFORMATION

We pause at another reference to this transformation called conversion: "Except ye be converted, and become as little children, ye shall not enter into the kingdom of heaven." In this there are three steps:

1. *A new direction*—"except ye be converted." Converted is "con" —"with," and *vertare*—"to turn," a new direction. Conversion is first of all a new direction, a reversal. But it is a turning *with*—it is not turning around in general. It is a turning around specifically—with Christ. He joins you the moment you turn.

2. *A new spirit*—"and become as little children." A fresh beginning, the spirit of a child possesses you, you are reduced to simplicity from the complexities and complications of evil. "I feel like a newborn babe," said a very sophisticated and able, but now radically changed, person.

3. *A new sphere of living*—"enter into the kingdom of heaven." You pass out of the sphere of the kingdom of self and enter the sphere of the Kingdom of God. You change worlds. There is a difference of heaven and hell between those two worlds. Here in this new sphere of living you and God work out life *together*. You supply willingness and He supplies power. Life is no longer on the unit principle—it is now a co-operative affair—you and God in partnership, with God the senior partner and managing director. The lonely, orphaned striving is gone, and now a sense of being together with One who has all the answers and all the resources for carrying out those answers takes possession of you. You feel you *belong* and belong to Adequacy.

In the first step you are responsible. No man, not even God, can turn around for you. You are endowed with free will and you decide. In the second step God is responsible. You cannot give yourself a new spirit—only God can do that. But you can consent, and that consent looses the power of God upon your inner life. In the third step it is the part of both God and you—you offer willingness and the surrendered you, and He offers power and His presence. Life now takes on power, direction, adequacy. You are a transformed person.

O God, I thank Thee that I am no longer adrift at sea. I know my goal, I know my resources, and I know whose hand is on the helm. Amen.

AFFIRMATION FOR THE DAY: *"In Him who strengthens me, I am able for anything"* (Phil. 4:13, Moffatt).

FROM CONFLICT TO CONCORD

Having looked at the biblical basis for transformation, we now turn to see what psychology says about it.

Here is what one says: "Here is a life divided, consciously wrong, inferior, and unhappy. That life becomes united, consciously right, superior, and happy by its firm hold on religious realities." That pattern is familiar: "A life divided"—the inner life in conflict with itself, mind against emotion, emotion against will. "I'm not a man, I'm a menagerie," said a man of himself. "If that girl is a civil war, then I'm a world war," said a girl who thought she could taste sex experience without regard to God or the moral law. She tried to bend the moral universe to her desires, and succeeded not in bending the moral universe but in breaking herself. A young man said, "I feel like a lot of pieces of person thrown together."

Then, "consciously wrong"—no voice from the sky proclaiming our wrongness, but we have a sense of being morally out of gear, not meshed into anything significant, and worse, of not having cosmic approval.

As a result, "inferior"—no sense of fulfilling life's possibilities and destiny. Made to soar, we crawl in the dust. Made for harmony, we are "like sweet bells jangled out of tune." An inferiority complex eats away confidence and assurance and leaves us a definitely inferior being.

And finally, "unhappy"—of course unhappy, for no one who is divided, consciously wrong, and inferior can be anything else than unhappy.

Then conversion takes place; the soul forces are fused into one under the burning fires of the Spirit; we feel a sense of cosmic approval through divine forgiveness; we feel humbly superior with all the inner inferiorities cleansed away, and then we are happy with an incorrigible happiness, for our happiness now is not based on happenings, but on inner relationships which outer happenings do not disturb. We have come to the most exquisite happiness which this planet knows— the happiness of being right with God and ourselves and life.

My Father God, I cannot thank Thee enough that Thou art throwing open to me the gates of life. I enter and rejoice. In Jesus' name. Amen.

AFFIRMATION FOR THE DAY: *My happiness today shall not be based on happenings, but upon eternal, hence unshakable, relationships.*

THE EMOTIONS ARE PRIMARY

Here is a psychological definition of conversion: "It is the birth of a new dominant affection by which the God-consciousness, hitherto marginal and vague, becomes focal and dynamic."

This writer puts the center of conversion not in the will or in the mind, but in the emotions—"a new dominant affection." He is right, for conversion is not a strained whipping up of the will, determined through thick and thin to be good. That would leave us strained, hence drained. That is not the New Testament pattern. That pattern is not a humanism lifting itself through will power. This attempt at self-lifting is self-defeating, for those who know tell us that "in any battle between the imagination and the will, the imagination is always victorious." Then how is the imagination fastened on the right thing? It is through the emotions. What the heart loves, the imagination sees, and what the imagination sees, the will does. The emotions are primary.

Rufus Jones says: "Matthew Arnold said that conduct is three-quarters of life. But it isn't. Getting your imagination captured is almost the whole of life. The minute the eyes of your heart are enlightened, the minute the imagination gives you the picture of your path, your goal, your aim—it is as good as done." But note that Rufus Jones says that "the minute the eyes of your heart are enlightened"— the eyes of your heart, not the eyes of your mind—it's the heart that sees, through finding a new love. Love clarifies the vision and the rest follows. And love comes through self-surrender. For self-surrender is the very essence of love. Where one or the other withholds the inner self in a marriage, there no love can spring up—it is blocked. So the first step is to transfer the center of your love from self to God by self-surrender. Then there arises "a new dominant affection" and that casts out, by the expulsive power of the new affection, the lower desires. You don't fight them; they drop away like a dead leaf before the rising sap of spring.

My God and Father, I see I cannot create this love. I can only create conditions, by self-surrender, in which this love can grow. So I surrender that self. Amen.

AFFIRMATION FOR THE DAY: *Today my surrendered self shall be the soil in which love can grow.*

ALL LESSER LOVES BEAUTIFIED

Yesterday we were considering conversion as "the birth of a new dominant affection." The lesser affections take their place under this new dominant affection—they are not cast out if they are legitimate, but they are made subordinate. Life organizes itself around love to Christ. That love glorifies and beautifies all lesser loves.

"Christ is not first in my life—my music is," said a young woman obviously in deep conflict. The wrong thing was dominant, and although that wrong thing was music, she had no music within her. All her music had turned to discord. Had Christ been first, then her soul would have sung with a strange, deep joy.

This new dominant affection makes the God-consciousness "focal and dynamic." Just the moving of the God-consciousness from the margin to the center makes the jigsaw puzzle of life turn from nonsense to sense. Everything falls in its place and everything has meaning. The God-consciousness becomes focal; everything in life has its focus there and everything is "found," since it is found in God. Self, at the feet of God, now stands straight before everything else. Sex, subordinate to God, now becomes creative in the total life. The herd, now surrendered to God, becomes no longer a fearsome tyrant, but a kingdom of relationships that might become the Kingdom of God. When God is focal, life is fruitful and full.

And then the God-consciousness becomes "dynamic." God is not a usable power in most lives. How could He be, for with self at the center we would use God for the purposes of the self. So God has to stand untapped for the purposes of life. Only when God comes to the center does He become the center of power. A little fellow was sweating as he carried a large stone across the yard. "Why don't you use all your strength?" asked his father. The little fellow felt hurt and said, "Daddy, I am." And the father replied, "You haven't asked me to help you." There stood his resources in the person of the father, but uncalled on, for the lad was centered in his own. Conversion puts God at the center, and therefore puts an inexhaustible center of power at our disposal. Life is centrally rich, full, and adequate.

Gracious Father, come in from the margin—take the center and take it without a rival. Then I shall be free to live. Amen.

AFFIRMATION FOR THE DAY: *Today I shall use all my strength—in God, my Father.*

25

"IMMEDIATE LUMINOUSNESS"

We continue to look at conversion through the eyes of the psychologists. William James says in *Varieties of Religious Experience*: "The best fruits of religious experience are the best things that history has to show. . . . To call to mind a succession of such examples as I have lately had to wander through . . . is to feel encouraged and uplifted and washed in better moral air." And then he gives these three things as the tests of the validity of this experience: "Immediate luminousness, philosophical reasonableness and moral helpfulness are the only available criteria."

Now note the first characteristic: "immediate luminousness." Pascal describes this change thus: "The year of grace 1654, Monday the twenty-third of November, St. Clement's Day, . . . from about half past ten in the evening until about half-an-hour after midnight—FIRE. God of Abraham. God of Isaac. God of Jacob, not of the philosophers and the learned. Certainty; certainty; feeling; joy; peace."

> Whoso has felt the Spirit of the Highest
> Cannot confound nor doubt Him nor deny:
> Yea with one voice, O world, tho' thou deniest,
> Stand thou on that side, for on this am I.

Alan W. Watts describes this transition from despair to certainty thus: "The soul striving to attain the divine state by its own efforts falls into total despair, and suddenly there falls upon it with a great illuminative shock the realization that the divine state simply IS, here and now, and does not have to be attained . . . wherewith the first turns into the second satori, or sudden awakening."

Or to put it in the words of a converted Lancashire drunkard: "Religion has changed my home, my heart, and you can all see that it has changed my face. I hear some of these London men call themselves Positivists. Bless God, I'm a Positivist. I'm positive God for Christ's sake has pardoned my sins, changed my heart, and made me a new creature."

O God, my Father, I thank Thee that I am not left to grope in darkness; Thou dost come bringing an invincible certainty with Thee. I thank Thee. Amen.

AFFIRMATION FOR THE DAY: *Illuminated, I become luminous and illuminating—today I shall be all three.*

"PHILOSOPHICAL REASONABLENESS"

We continue to look at the three tests of the worth of an experience: "Immediate luminousness, philosophical reasonableness, and moral helpfulness." We must now look at the second: philosophical reasonableness.

The philosophical reasonableness of this experience comes not merely from the sense of verbal consistency of argument, but from a vital consistency of life meaning. Life begins to add up to sense. Frank T. Bullen, in his autobiography *With Christ at Sea,* says: "There was no extravagant joy, no glorious bursting into light and liberty such I have since read about as happening on such occasions; it was just a lesson learned, the satisfaction of finding one's way after long groping in darkness and misery—a way that led to peace. I love that description of conversion as the new birth! No other definition touches the truth of the process at all, so helpless, so utterly knowledgeless, possessing nothing but the consciousness of life just begun, is the new born Christian." Note "the satisfaction of finding one's way after long groping in darkness"—that's it.

There is a sense of being drawn together from a scatterbrained, scatter-affectioned, and scatter-souled condition. A missionary writes after undergoing a spiritual change: "Since I returned I have worked harder than ever—on that which was my greatest problem. It was impossible for me to sit down and stick to the Santali language. I preferred to do other things, with the result that I felt the Santali in my tummy! But now I like sitting with difficult books. I enjoy the studies. And feel well!" A coherent soul made a coherent mind and set him to work to make a coherent world.

Among the people of the Khasi Hills in Assam their poetry has this distinctive characteristic: the first line is utter chaos, a jumble of meaningless phrases so you cannot tell which way the poetry is going to go—it arouses curiosity. The second line is a line of sense, a wise saying giving a sense of direction. That is what conversion does—takes a life which starts out with nonsense and makes it into sense and direction.

O God, I'm grateful that life is no longer at loose ends—it's all been gathered into a pattern. It means something now. I thank Thee. Amen.

AFFIRMATION FOR THE DAY: *If the first lines of my life have been nonsense, the rest of my lines are going to be sense—the sense of God.*

"A MODIFICATION OF CHARACTER"

We come now to the third test of the worth of an experience: moral helpfulness. Said Mark Rutherford in *Catherine Furze:* "I can assure my incredulous literary friends that years ago it was not uncommon for men and women suddenly to awaken to the fact that they had been sinners and to determine that from henceforth they would keep God's commandments by the help of Jesus Christ and the Holy Spirit. What is more extraordinary is that they did keep God's commandments for the rest of their lives."

It was said of Thomas Chalmers that in his early days he preached morals alone and with no moral result. Then he became filled with the love of Christ, and with that power behind him, he engraved the ethical precepts upon the heart of Scotland.

In 1840 Bishop George Selwyn, missionary among the cannibal Maoris of New Zealand, wrote: "I am in the midst of a sinful people, who have been accustomed to sin uncontrolled from youth. If I speak to a native on murder, infanticide, cannibalism, or adultery, he laughs in my face and tells me I may think these acts are bad, but they are very good for a native, and they cannot conceive any harm in them. But on the contrary, when I tell them that these and other sins brought the Son of God, the great Creator of the Universe from His eternal glory to this world, to be incarnate and to be made a curse and to die—then they open their eyes and ears and mouths and wish to hear more and presently they acknowledge themselves sinners and say they will leave off their sins."

This is illuminating—preach morality, and the moral life is largely unchanged; preach the atoning love of God in Christ, and conversion and a total renovation of the total life results, especially a moral renovation.

John Watson classified conversions as moral, spiritual, intellectual, and practical. But the moral runs through all of these other three. As Ramanes says: "In all cases it was not a mere change of belief or opinion. It is a modification of character more or less profound."

O Christ, Thou art a redeemer for Thou dost redeem—dost redeem now from what we have been and are. I'm grateful. Amen.

AFFIRMATION FOR THE DAY: *I am no longer a part of the disease—I'm a part of the cure.*

"MORAL HELPFULNESS"

We ended last week on the last of the three criteria of the worth of a religious experience: Immediate luminousness, philosophical reasonableness, and moral helpfulness.

We must tarry a little longer on this last point—moral helpfulness. Richard W. Church, in *The Gifts of Civilization*, describes this redemptive impact in these words: "It seems to me that the exultation apparent in early Christian literature, beginning with the Apostolic Epistles, at the prospect now at length disclosed within the bour is of sober hope, of a great moral revolution in human life—that the rapturous confidence which pervades these Christian ages, that at last the routine of vice and sin had met its match, that a new and astonishing possibility had come into view, that men, not here and there, but on a large scale, might attain to that hitherto hopeless thing to the multitudes, goodness—is one of the most singular and solemn things in history." Now note: "A new and astonishing possibility had come into view, that men, not here and there, but on a large scale might attain to that hitherto hopeless thing to the multitudes, goodness." But it was not really an attainment—it was an obtainment, a gift of grace. Had it been an attainment, it would have shut out the multitudes but because it was an obtainment, a gift of grace, it opened the door to the multitudes.

And this miracle still takes place today. A few weeks ago this letter came from an Indian teacher: "When I came out of the sitting room after talking and praying with you, I felt that a heavy load was taken from my heart and body. I became so light that the whole night I dreamed, semiconsciously, of flying about in the air. Five years' bondage was broken in five seconds. It is really so amazing." It is. But it is a fact and a recurring fact to the degree it is tried.

Just two days ago a student said to me: "Why, I am so free from condemnation that I am afraid. I expected to be depressed and it is the opposite. I'm surprised at the freedom from guilt and condemnation—I'm free and released." And he looked like it, for his face glowed!

O God, my Father, this is breath-taking. I need to be under the tyranny of nothing. I can be free and free now. I thank Thee. Amen.

AFFIRMATION FOR THE DAY: *I am being redeemed, and today I shall look redeemed, think redeemed, act redeemed, and be redeemed.*

SAVED AND SOBERED

We continue to look at conversion as moral helpfulness. G. B. Cutten says: "Were it desirable, the church could eclipse the patent medicine advertisers with the thousands of testimonials which might be produced by alcoholics cured by religious conversion."

In my early ministry I was preaching on a soapbox in a public square in Harrodsburg, Kentucky, on court day. Just in front of me was a drunk with a long peeled stick. I kept one hand on his shoulder, trying to keep him quiet. At the close he followed along with the others, those who wanted to find a new life at the mission. When I asked him if he wanted to be converted, he replied, "I'm drunk." "I know it," I replied, "but He can save you, drunk or not drunk." "If you say so, it must be so," he said as we knelt in prayer. As I prayed he suddenly opened his eyes, looked around surprised, and said: "Why, He has saved me, and I'm drunk too!" He arose, took out a whisky bottle from his pocket, handed it to me, and said, "You can have that. I'm through with it." I threw it out the window. Then he handed me his stick upon which he had leaned for support and said, "You can have that. I don't need it any longer." And he didn't! He walked down the aisle perfectly sober. God had not only saved him, He had sobered him as well. A clear-cut miracle!

A leading editor recently said to me: "I was an alcoholic. It had me. I was beaten and I knew it. I went to a sanitarium to get scientific help. One day a case was brought in and I said to the doctor, 'That man is in a terrible condition.' And the doctor replied: 'Yes he is. But within a year he'll be well, but in a year you won't be.' It struck me like a blow. That night I went out under the stars, lonely and defeated, and raised my hands toward heaven and repeated what the leper said to Jesus, 'If Thou wilt, Thou canst make me clean.' Immediately the answer came back, 'I will, be thou clean.' From that moment the power of alcohol was broken in my life. I have never touched a drop since. Have never even wanted it."

O God, my Father, this miracle of inner change is taking place in me. My old life is dropping away. I'm becoming a new creature. Amen.

AFFIRMATION FOR THE DAY: *"Be not afraid; . . . here am I alive for evermore, holding the keys that unlock death and Hades"* (Rev. 1:17-18, Moffatt).

"MY HEART STRANGELY WARMED"

We continue to look at the moral helpfulness of conversion. James Gardiner says: "I was effectively cured of all inclination to that sin I was so strongly addicted to, that I thought nothing but shooting me through the head could have cured me of it; and all desire and inclination to it was removed, as entirely as if I had been a sucking child." Someone reports hearing Gardiner say that he was "much addicted to impurity before his acquaintance with religion; but as soon as he was enlightened from above, he felt the power of the Holy Ghost, changing his nature so wonderfully, that his sanctification in this respect seemed more remarkable than in any other."

Carlyle describes his conversion: "You know what my manner of life hath been. Oh, I lived in and loved darkness, and hated light; I was a chief, the chief of sinners. This is true: I hated godliness, yet God had mercy on me. O the richness of his mercy." This he said was his conversion, a new birth when he "authentically took the devil by the nose." That is the reversal: up to conversion the devil leads us by the nose; after conversion we lead the devil by the nose!

John Wesley, whose conversion produced an epoch in the life of Britain, according to Lecky, the historian, tells of his change: "In the evening I went very unwillingly to a society in Aldersgate Street, where one was reading Luther's preface to the Epistle to the Romans. About a quarter before nine, while he was describing the change which God works in the heart through faith in Christ I felt my heart strangely warmed. I felt I did trust in Christ, Christ alone for salvation; and an assurance was given me that He had taken away *my* sins, even *mine,* and saved *me* from the law of sin and death." This strange warming of the heart sent a moral cleansing through the soul of Britain and the world. "You seem to be a very temperate people here," Augustine Birrell once observed to a Cornish miner. "How did it happen?" The miner replied, solemnly raising his cap, "There came a man among us once and his name was John Wesley."

O God, my Father, I open the depths of my being to the moral cleansing of Thy Spirit. Make me clean within. In Jesus' name. Amen.

AFFIRMATION FOR THE DAY: *Perhaps I can be a miniature John Wesley to some group or town through which I shall pass today, and leave it changed.*

31

"THE ONLY JET OF LIGHT"

I once asked leaders of the Khasi Hills people of Assam: "Can you give me cases of transformed lives through Christianity among your people?" They looked bewildered and said, "Why, everybody and everything has been transformed by our becoming Christians." They had been head-hunters! The Hindu governor of Assam said to me: "The only jet of light in the hills is the work of Christian missions. Take that out and all will be darkness. The houses of hill people are notoriously filthy, but the homes of these people are neat and clean."

When Pundita Ramabai went to England as a Hindu to learn methods of social work to apply to India, she saw pure-faced, radiant women rescuing fallen girls in the houses of prostitution in London. "Who are these devoted, happy-faced women?" she asked, and was told that these women themselves had been rescued from lives of prostitution. She replied, "Then this is what my country needs." And she opened her own heart to it, took it back to India, and set up that wonderful women's home at Kedgaon, where she had two thousand women, many of them rescued from prostitution.

A leading Indian congressman, not a Christian, said to an audience at the close of my address in the Punjab: "Our problem is now different. Before, our problem was to gain independence, now it is to retain independence. To retain independence we must have character. There is no doubt that the impact of Christ upon the framework of human life creates miracles of changed character, and as such we welcome it."

I asked a Japanese aviator to tell the story of his conversion before a large audience. He had hated Americans, and through undernourishment and resentments he developed tuberculosis. In the hospital he found he was eating food supplied by Americans. "What makes Americans give food to their former enemies?" he asked himself. "It must be because they are Christians." He got hold of a Bible, made a surrender to Christ, and his resentments dropped away. His tuberculosis healed at once. His child, who contracted tuberculosis from him, began to get well, and is now the picture of health.

O God, I thank Thee that Thy power is available for the best human living, that life can go anywhere—with Thee. I come, I come. Amen.

AFFIRMATION FOR THE DAY: *When men think of the moral helpfulness of conversion, may they think of me.*

"RADIANT AND ON TOP"

We come now to look at lives transformed with less spectacular change. A friend of mine, a mediator between labor and capital at Washington and elsewhere, had a rich nephew who did not go to church. He talked to the nephew about what the church meant to him, got him to promise to go. This rural church was about to close, needed $500. The nephew went around and got twenty-five farmers to give $25 each, and made each one promise to go to church. The church is renewed and alive, and the nephew is happy and quietly on fire. Here was a conversion that began in a deed.

In a Visitation Evangelism Campaign in a West Coastal city two laymen with fear and trembling called on their first prospect, a leading lawyer. They told the lawyer they had come to ask him to join the church. "Is that all you want of me?" asked the lawyer. "A lot of people have asked me through the years to join the church." "Well," said the laymen, "there is this other side of our campaign—surrender to Christ—but frankly we ourselves don't know much about that, so we have begun on the level we know, membership in the church." "Well," said the lawyer, "I'm interested in this other side, this deeper thing. Haven't you a card with something about this on it?" for he had read about it in the newspapers. They produced the self-committal-to-Christ card. He read it carefully, slowly took out his pen and signed it. "Now," he added, "where do you go next? I'd like to go with you." And he did, and he went out every night during the whole campaign and called on people. When people come to see him about a divorce, he gives them a copy of *Abundant Living*, tells them to read it, and after a week if they still want a divorce, they can come back and he will talk it over with them. His conversion was the sensation of the city!

I was speaking over the radio and used the statement of Ananias when Jesus called him to go to the stricken Saul, "Here am I, Lord." As I repeated that phrase a woman, an alcoholic, heard it and quietly repeated it after me, "Here am I, Lord." She told me afterward: "My alcoholism was gone. I've been new ever since." She was radiant and on top.

O God, everything is awaiting my inner consent. I give it. Here am I, Lord. Make out of me what Thou wilt. I follow. Amen.

AFFIRMATION FOR THE DAY: *In every situation when you want a man today, you will hear me saying, "Here am I, Lord."*

"NEVER-BEFORE-KNOWN HUMILITY AND GLADNESS"

We continue the recital of these transformations.

"Oh, Father Latimer," cried one, "I prithee hear me, when I read in the New Testament, Christ Jesus came into the world to save sinners, it is as if the day suddenly broke." It is a daybreak!

Hugh Fawcett describes his change thus: "I became conscious of a subtle change stealing over me. I was invaded by some will in which was infinite love, peace, wisdom, and power. I felt a never-before-known humility and gladness, an inexpressible certainty that within all the discords of life there was divine intention and a final harmony, that the darkness in me was in this timeless moment resolved in light and the error redeemed in the ultimate comprehension."

I once heard a Negro bishop introduce his wife in the most beautiful introduction of a wife I have ever heard: "This is the gracious lady. Thirty years ago I looked into the limpid depths of her eyes and I've never gotten over the spell of it." That is what happens in conversion: we look into the limpid depths of His eyes and we never get over the spell of it.

Here was my friend E. V. Moorman, inwardly shattered by conflict and confusion. He went to a pagan psychiatrist who bled him, soul and mind and purse. He spent $60,000 in consultations. He told the psychiatrist twelve hundred dreams. A pad of paper was kept beside his bed to write them down. Under this pagan probing he grew worse. So one day he sadly left the hotel, giving up the psychiatrist, his last prop gone. As he walked down the hotel steps a voice seemed to say, "Look this way." He felt it was the voice of Christ but couldn't contact Him. I happened to come along, and when he heard the gospel of the Kingdom, he said to himself: "This is it. My quest is over." It was. He became adjusted, radiant, happy, useful. He left a Laymen's Trust for Evangelism to share with others what had meant so much to him. He was responsible for founding the Christian Ashrams in the United States, through which many thousands have been transformed. Transformed, he became transforming.

O Christ, help me to "Look this way"—Thy way. For I know there is life for a look—a straight look at Thee. I take that look. My quest is finished. Amen.

AFFIRMATION FOR THE DAY: *Today I shall look where to look is Life.*

"ARE YOU IN LOVE?"

We finished yesterday on the story of my beloved friend, E. V. Moorman. There is being set up in India, in Sat Tal, a Christian psychiatrical center named after E. V. Moorman and run by Dr. Dagmar Norell, who is trying to start India on a Christian basis in psychiatry, instead of on a pagan basis, as in the United States.

Dr. Norell has a Swedish medical degree, with, in addition, four years of psychiatrical training there and two years in the United States. She had everything to be a successful psychiatrist, thorough training, an outgoing, friendly personality, everything except one thing—a transforming Christian experience. She found that in one of our Ashrams by simple surrender to Christ. This surrender brought life into a living unity and focused everything around the core of Christ. She went back radiant to the pagan hospital where she was working, and her psychiatrical friends, seeing her all lighted up, asked, "Are you in love?" Then she told them what had happened in her conversion and of her accepting the call to go to India. "Why don't you psychoanalyze me and see what has happened?" she said to them. "All right, we will," they replied. They put her through the mill. When they got through, they gave this report: "We can't find any martyr's complex in you. The fact is that we can't find anything pathological about you at all." They saw that she had arrived at one bound at the place they were inching toward by their slow and laborious methods, namely, inner integration. Now she is free to use the best in the methods of psychiatry, for she is not confined to them. She can work up from science and down from Revelation.

After long dealing with people who have been psychoanalyzed and left more disrupted than ever, I have come to the conclusion that psychoanalysis will not work except in a Christian atmosphere and with a Christian technique of ultimate surrender to God. For psychoanalysis, when it is pagan, leaves you centered on yourself and preoccupied with yourself. It doesn't know how to get you beyond yourself. Since it doesn't believe in God and His availability, it leaves you preoccupied with its techniques, with yourself.

O Father, I know I must lose my life to find it again. I must be lifted out of myself to Thee. Then, and then only, am I free. Amen.

AFFIRMATION FOR THE DAY: *Not self-preoccupation, but Christ-preoccupation is my way out.*

PSYCHIATRY WITHOUT GOD, QUESTIONABLE

We left off last week on the note of the inadequacy of pagan psychiatry. It picks you to pieces and doesn't know how to put you together again. It is psychoanalysis, but not psychosynthesis. The self-knowledge is supposed to be healing. It does help to get up buried complexes and that brings relief, but if it doesn't get you beyond yourself to some allegiance beyond yourself, it leaves you a person preoccupied with yourself, and that means a frustrated person—frustrated because self-centered. The Chinese have a saying, "Don't take hold of a tiger's tail to get out of a flood." Another: "It is no good calling a tiger to chase away a dog." The remedy is often worse than the disease.

Some years ago Carney Landis of Columbia University underwent a full psychoanalysis which was paid for by the Rockefeller Foundation. When it was over, Landis, who is principal research psychologist of the New York State Psychiatric Institute, wrote a report in which he said: "'What is normality?' I asked my analyst one day." "I don't know," replied the analyst, "I never deal with normal people." "But suppose a really normal person came to you," Landis asked. "Even though he were normal at the beginning of the analysis the analytical procedure would create a neurosis," the analyst admitted.

It would if it ended in analysis. But here religion steps in and shows the way to synthesis through self-surrender to God. Leave God out and there is nothing to be centered on except the patient's own self or the analyst. Often he is allowed to fall in love with the analyst as a method of freedom from self-preoccupation. A husband wrote to a "worry column" that he had a very happy home. His wife, however, developed a neurosis and went to an analyst, who greatly helped her, she says. But she lost interest in her home, her children, and him. She called up the analyst several times a day to consult him—and to talk to him! This is taking hold of a tiger's tail to get out of a flood!

Anything that leaves you centered in yourself or in something less than God, whether it is religion, psychiatry, or just plain secularism, is leaving you off-center, for you are not God.

O God, if I am centered in Thee, then am I free—from myself, my real problem. In Thee I am on-center, hence free and released and happy. Amen.

AFFIRMATION FOR THE DAY: *Today, no taking hold of tigers' tails to get me out of a flood!*

"THROUGH WHEELING INTO A NEW CENTER"

We saw yesterday that any system of philosophy, religion, or psychology that leaves you centered in yourself is self-disruptive.

Take Henry Overstreet's brilliant and popular book, *The Mature Mind*, in which he says we must give up the categories of "good" and "bad" and take only the categories of useful and nonuseful. He lets go an objective moral universe in which morality is written into the nature of things—a dangerous procedure. He then ends the book by making the goal, not "practice the presence of God," but "practice the enjoyment of maturity." You are to enjoy your own maturity, as the goal of "the mature mind." But if you do that, you won't have maturity, but infantilism, for infantilism is preoccupation with oneself. You are not mature unless you lose yourself. Maturity is a by-product of a mature purpose attached to a mature object, God, and working out a mature plan—the Kingdom of God.

Hiram Corson puts the matter in these words: "Not through knowledge, not through a sharpened intellect, but through repentance, . . through conversion, through wheeling into a new center its spiritual system, the soul attains to saving truth." Note "through wheeling into a new center its spiritual system"—that is the essence of the whole matter. Your self on your own hands is a problem and a pain. Your self in the hands of God is a possibility and a progression.

This makes conversion a possibility now. But if conversion is the end of a long, long process, then of course it is indefinitely postponed. I. A. Hutton says that Browning had an "impassioned confidence that the soul may, in one grand moment leap sheer out of any depth of shame or subtle bondage, and leap to the breast of God."

> Where God unmakes but to remake the soul
> He else made first in vain.

The unmaking here is to get the soul off its idolatrous center, self, to get it on to its proper center, God. The center of conversion is the conversion of the center.

Gracious God and Father, Thou art moving me from myself to Thee. Thou art my home. I'm at home only in Thee. I'm coming home! Amen.

AFFIRMATION FOR THE DAY: *I'm allowing God to unmake me in any area of my life, to remake me there.*

FROM FRUSTRATION TO FRUITFULNESS

We now return to look at some other types of conversion. Here is a girl in her early twenties, laid aside for a year with a rheumatic heart. The prospect of spending a year in bed made her beat her wings against her confining bars in resentment and bitterness. After a week of bitter rebellion someone gave her my book *Christ and Human Suffering*. She saw the possibility not only of bearing frustration and pain, but of using it. It opened a door of possibility to her. She surrendered herself and her illness to God, became a changed person with a changed attitude toward life, had fifty-one wonderful weeks in bed. At the end of the year, having been awakened in mind as well as in soul by her conversion, she determined to go to college, though she was past the usual age. She became the head of a student foundation in a state university, radiant and useful. The simple turning from self-pity and rebellion to self-surrender was the axis upon which the whole of her life turned from frustration to fruitfulness.

That simple change changes the whole of life. Charles Kingsley describes his conversion: "June 12, 1841—My birth-night. I have been for the last hour on the sea-shore, not dreaming, but thinking deeply and strongly, and forming determinations which are to affect my destiny through time and through eternity. Before the sleeping earth and the sleepless sea and stars I have devoted myself to God; a vow never (if He gives me the faith I pray for) to be recalled."

Here was a strong woman needing conversion and finding it: "I was a very resistive person. Therefore I was always creating antagonisms. I have been domineering. I'm letting God take this out of me." He did.

Here was a weak woman needing to get out from under a fear of her mother: "My mother has always been domineering. Has bossed my life. I had a nervous breakdown. I'm still tense." But she let go and let God, and came out from under her fear and tenseness when God became the center, not her mother nor her fear. When conversion makes God dominant, then you come out from under the dominance of fear of people—you're released and free.

O God, I thank Thee that Thy dominance is my freedom. I'm free to be myself since Thou hast myself. I'm grateful, so grateful. Amen

AFFIRMATION FOR THE DAY: *I am my nervous breakdown; Thou art my nervous build-up.*

"CHRISTIANITY FIRST, LAST, AND ALWAYS"

We continue to look at the various types of conversion. Here was a businessman economically down and out and discouraged. He went by a church in Richmond, where I was speaking, and heard a soloist singing a song he loved when he was a good tenor. Drawn by this song, he came in and was converted. He carried on a great Bible class, and became the spark plug in forming a laymen's convention which met annually. Someone said of him: "He was one businessman who put Christianity first, last, and always."

A druggist in Virginia Beach told me this story: "A man came into my store beaten, wanted some drugs to carry him over. His wife was about to leave him, as she was drinking heavily. I gave him a copy of *Abundant Living*. Three months later the man called me and said: 'Our home has been re-established. We have gone back to the church. We are happier than we have ever been. Thanks for giving me *Abundant Living*.'" This druggist added: "The doctors aren't prescribing much of anything now except sedatives and drugs to get people off their hands—they don't know what to do with them."

Srinivasa Shastri, a Hindu, one of the greatest men of India, said in reply to my question whether he shared the skepticism of Poona: "Well, I'm not religious, but I'm not irreligious. My heart is as ashes. I have no spark to kindle this movement called The Servants of India Soicety, of which I am the head. Now religion seems to be real to you. How did it become real?" I told him simply and straightforwardly of my conversion. At the close he thoughtfully said: "I see what I need —I need conversion. I must find conversion for myself, or I must warm up my heart against someone's heart who has been converted." He was a morally upright man and able, and yet he felt the need of conversion. Shastri once remarked to an audience at the close of my address: "We always know where Stanley Jones is coming out. If he begins at the binomial theory, he will come out at the place of conversion." He was right, for life comes out at that place.

Good God, help me not to excuse myself on my morality, for morality or no morality, I need conversion and I need it now. Amen.

AFFIRMATION FOR THE DAY: *Today I shall put Christianity first, last and always.*

VARYING TYPES OF CONVERSION

Here are some more contrasting types of conversion. John Biegeleisen is a professor in Eden Theological Seminary, St. Louis. He was a Russian Jew, and when a colporteur visited his native town in Poland, many of his people bought New Testaments. But the rabbi, incensed at this, gathered up all of them and publicly burned them in the square. As Biegeleisen went past the charred pile, he noticed the black print on a burned page of the New Testament, and the verse read: "Forasmuch as ye know that ye were not redeemed with corruptible things, as silver and gold from your vain . . . tradition from your fathers; but with the precious blood of Christ, as of a lamb without blemish and without spot" (I Pet. 1: 18). It struck straight home. That charred page let him see straight into the heart of God's redemptive purposes. He is today a radiant, contributive personality.

The father of one of the outstanding pastors of India, a Punjabi Moslem religious teacher, walked past the show window of a Book and Tract Society and read this motto: "Come unto me, all ye that labor and are heavy laden, and I will give you rest" (Matt. 11:28). It went straight to his heart, and though it meant an awful wrench to break family ties, he followed the Gleam and became a changed man.

Cyprian, it is said, was brought to God by the reading of the book of Jonah. Savanarola referred to his conversion: "A word did it," but what that word was, none of his closest friends ever knew. It was the sight of a tree, dry and leafless in the winter, that first kindled in Brother Lawrence the high thoughts of God that cut him loose from the world.

A young man told me that he was an agnostic—and empty. He was sitting in a bus when out of a clear sky he felt a deep sense of sin. It aroused him. He found out about a "University of Life" in Calvary Methodist Church in Washington, joined it, was soon converted, and began his studies for the ministry. Apparently the Spirit of God spoke the awakening word directly to his inner conscience. God seems to lay hold on any object, any event, any word, to awaken us.

My Father, Thou art seeking Love and Thou wilt not let me go. Thy love is the Hound of Heaven pursuing us down the years and into the now. Amen.

AFFIRMATION FOR THE DAY: *I am making all words, all events, and all things steppingstones to Him today.*

"FROM A MESS TO A MESSAGE"

We continue to look at various types of conversion. A missionary told me his story. He was one of Doolittle's fliers, the first to bomb Tokyo. They had to land in China and were captured by the Japanese. He was put in solitary confinement for forty-two months. His companion was also in solitary confinement and went mad through sheer loneliness. It frightened the Japanese, so they gave my friend a Bible to read, the only thing he had to read. He devoured it. He came out of there a new man. When the war ended, he determined to get an education and go back to Japan as a missionary to the people who had kept him in solitary confinement. He is happy—and creative.

At the close of a meeting a very fashionably dressed woman came up to me, and as she shook hands, said, "If I had what you have, I wouldn't be in the mess I'm in." I asked her to wait, and as we talked, she laid bare her tragedy: Her home was going to be broken up after Christmas—they would hold together till Christmas so as not to break the children's hearts. We prayed and I asked her to pray when she got home. But she said afterward: "I belonged to the country club cocktail-gambling set and didn't know how to pray. So I wrote God a letter: 'Dear God, life has dealt me a very bad hand and I don't know which card to lead. Please show me which card I am to lead.' And I signed it." God heard that prayer expressed in the only language she knew. The home didn't break up, she held it together by her changed spirit. And now after six years she has two classes on the home. She has been elected the state president of the Christian Woman's Fellowship. Someone said of her, "She is God's good gift to ————," naming the state in which she lives. Her son wrote her on Mother's Day from college and poured out his gratitude "for such a mother." And the mother in a letter added, "To think I came near throwing all of this away." She and her Negro maid have a quiet time together each day. Conversion was the pivot on which she turned from a mess to a message.

O God, how can I ever thank Thee enough for the possibilities thrown open to me through conversion. I'm breathless—with gratitude. In Jesus' name. Amen.

AFFIRMATION FOR THE DAY: *My problems are not problems to God—they're possibilities.*

"FLESHY, FASHIONABLE, AND FUTILE"

Anne Byrd Payson is the pen name of a woman in the upper crust of New York society life. At the close of a dinner where I first met her she took me aside and said: "I'd like to ask your opinion on what has happened to me. I've never had any connection with religion except to take a cocktail with the rector in my country house. So when someone gave me your book to read, *The Christ of the Indian Road,* I took it to bed with me to put me to sleep. But before I knew what was happening, it was morning and I hadn't slept but had read the book. I got up and sat before the fire and let down the barriers of my being, and a warm, living Presence came within my heart. Now I call that hour 'My Shining Hour.' Since then people come to me with their problems, for they think I've found something. Before this, I didn't want to become the head of the Philharmonic Society, for I didn't want to meet so many Jews. Now, since this has happened to me, I'd like to meet those Jews, so I'm taking the job. Now I feel as though I should go to church, and I'm going. What do you think has happened to me?" I replied, "Why, I think you've been converted." "So do I," she said, "and now that I'm converted, how do you act as a Christian? I'm a musician, and we have techniques—what's the technique of being a Christian?" To avoid being embarrassed, for I was rather at a loss for a reply, I suggested that she write about the "technique" she would be compelled to work out as she related this new life to her set in society.

Two years later I received in India a manuscript entitled "Technique." As I began to read it, I saw she had something. It was published under the title of *I Follow the Road,* went into several editions, and was followed by *The Rule of the Road.* Conversion awakened her whole personality. Up to sixty she had created nothing. She said her autobiography up to that point could be summed up in this sentence: "I was fleshy, fashionable, and futile." After sixty she wrote two excellent books and became a living soul—living and life-giving. Futility had turned to fruitfulness. From an animated clod she became a person alive to her finger tips—with God.

Blessed Redeemer, Thou dost redeem me not only from sin and folly but from sourness and futility. I'm grateful, so grateful. Amen.

AFFIRMATION FOR THE DAY: *Not the calendar, but my receptivity determines when I cease to be creative.*

"I'VE GOT IT"

Pride can very often block transformation. Take the case of Margaret Slattery, one of the great women of our age. She taught young people to take religion—they needed it. But for herself, well, she was self-sufficient. She would match her inner courage against outer circumstances. "My head might be bloody, but it will be unbowed under the bludgeonings of chance"—this she kept in her purse as a kind of life motto. It worked for awhile, for she was strong. And then a real sorrow struck her and she found herself a wreck, in a sanitarium. The bottom had dropped out of life.

When she was sufficiently recovered to drag through the days, I met her on board ship going to Europe. She said to me, "Can you help me?" I replied: "You won't take what I have to offer, you're looking for something learned and abstruse and high-brow. But Christ can make you over from the ground up if you'll let Him." In a cathedral she reacted against the service, "It's all too slick and easy; they don't mean those prayers." And Christ said to her, "Yes, these people won't let me do anything for them, neither will you." And she knew she was too proud to let Him help her.

The crisis came in Rotterdam. She arose at five o'clock one morning, dropped on her knees, surrendered her proud, shattered self to God, and He met her there. In the morning as we met on the railway platform she walked over and said: "I'm the happiest woman on earth. I've got it." And she had. She slept eight solid hours that night, the first time she had slept for more than two hours a night for some years. She cabled her doctors a week later: "The miracle has happened. I'm sleeping eight hours a night." When the conflicts were taken out of her soul, the body relaxed and was able to rest. I said to her, "Some of these days it may get dark, but when a train goes through a tunnel and it gets dark, you don't throw away your ticket and jump off. You sit still and trust the engineer." She cabled me after arriving in New York, "Arrived safely, have my ticket!" That experience added twenty wonderful years to her life.

Gracious Father-God, I thank Thee that I can surrender my proud self-sufficiency to Thee. Take it now. And make me over again at the depths. Amen.

AFFIRMATION FOR THE DAY: *Today if it gets dark, I'll trust the Engineer and hold to my ticket.*

FROM SELF-PREOCCUPATION TO GOD-PREOCCUPATION

We are now in a position to give our own definition of conversion: *Conversion is the penitent receptive response to the saving divine initiative in Christ, resulting in a change, gradual or sudden, by which one passes from the kingdom of self to the Kingdom of God and becomes a part of a living fellowship, the church.*

Now note that conversion is a response to divine initiative. We don't have to lift ourselves—we have to respond to God's lifting. The response is in us—all else is in God. That takes our eyes off ourselves and puts them on God—we are released from self-preoccupation and become God-preoccupied. But also note that it is a penitent, receptive response—the turning to God means turning from all that God cannot approve.

The idea that there is nothing to turn from—that sin is only a built-up figment of the morbid imagination—is producing more conflicts in modern minds than any other thing. The moral universe doesn't approve of our futile gestures, waving sin out of existence. It doesn't go. Gaius Glenn Atkins has translated that part of the General Confession into the jargon of modern psychiatry: "We have followed too much the inhibitions and self-expressions of our own complexes. We have not sublimated our libidos, nor considered our neuroses." But that jargon and that attitude does not bring inner release such as comes through repentance and forgiveness.

Someone has said that much modern advice resolves itself into something like this: "Resolve your complexes and sublimate your Id." When the rich young ruler ran up to ask, "What shall I do that I may inherit eternal life?" the correct answer, translated into popular language, might have been: "My dear young friend, you are suffering from a definite anxiety neurosis. Don't let this become an obsession. Don't worry about eternal life. Go home and relax." But that would not have lifted the guilt, or set his heart singing through forgiveness. It just doesn't work. The only open door into release is through repentance, through divine forgiveness.

O God, I know I take roads that run into dead ends unless I take Thy Way. Thy Way is my way—the way for which I'm made. I take it. Amen.

AFFIRMATION FOR THE DAY: *All my roads shall have open ends, for they converge into the Way.*

GUILT, A DIVINE GIFT

Yesterday we were studying the first steps in the definition of conversion—the penitent, receptive response. We saw that it has to be a *penitent* response, no bluffing it through and acting as though nothing had happened.

A trusted man had taken $200,000 but had covered it up with clever bookkeeping. He thought himself safe. But he developed stomach ulcers and migraine headaches, the result of the strain of living a double life. The increasing incidence of nervous diseases is the direct result of passing by repentance and forgiveness and trying to take the way of denial of anything about which to feel guilty.

I believe guilt is one of the divinest gifts of God. Guilt can be pushed into the subconscious and there fester, or guilt can take you by the hand and lead you to God.

Klaus Fuchs confessed to giving atomic bomb secrets to Russia, and though he is still a Communist, and is therefore not supposed to believe in an objective moral universe, nevertheless he said, "I realized that there were certain standards of moral behavior that are in you and which you cannot disregard." These moral standards kick back in nervous disorders, in conflicts, if the way of repentance and forgiveness is not taken.

The attempt to get rid of our guilts by removing moral standards is like the two children of a friend of mine who moved the position of a sundial and then said, "Look, it's such-and-such an hour, the sundial says so." But the sun said otherwise.

An ill lighthouse keeper sent out a bottle, picked up seventy-five miles away, with a message in it: "Come get me, first chance. Sick three weeks, almost died. Can't get out." When they came, they found this note penned before he died—a prayer to God, "Remove from me this burden . . . clean my soul." Anybody who prays that prayer, living or dying, is going to find response from the universe, from God, for the Way stretches straight under the feet of the penitent. He is on it the moment he is penitent.

O Christ, Thou art the Way and that Way stretches clear to the mouth of hell. It begins where I begin—to be penitent. I thank Thee. Amen.

AFFIRMATION FOR THE DAY: *Today: a penitent, receptive response to God's highest for me.*

"JUST TURN THE DOORKNOB"

We continue to look at our definition: "It is the penitent, receptive response." We must look at the receptive side. Receptivity is not mush. A mother was explaining the passive voice to her little girl: "If someone kills me, then they are in the active voice, and when I am killed, that is in the passive voice." "But," said the little girl, "how can you have a voice when you are dead—you can't speak." "Yes, but suppose I am almost dead, not really killed," said the mother. Later the little girl said, "The passive voice is the voice that people have when they are not quite dead." That may be a little girl's idea of the passive voice, but the fact is that you just begin to rise from the dead when you become receptive to God's grace. Faith is receptivity—receptivity to God's invading grace. It is passive activity. Jesus says, "Whatever you pray for and ask, believe you have got it, and you shall have it" (Mark 11:24, Moffatt). Note: "have got it." The word of Jesus is accomplishment, and when I take His word as accomplishment, then it is accomplishment. For behind that word is the character of Jesus, and behind the character of Jesus is the character of the universe—the nature of Reality backs it.

A sign over a door in a Massanetta Springs hotel says: "If the door seems to be locked, just turn the doorknob." Simple? If the door into release seems to be locked, then just turn the doorknob, and turning the doorknob is faith, receptive faith.

Here is a case of active faith: A woman had a neurotic mother, a father who was killed in a drunken brawl, a brother who was an alcoholic and in an institution, and she was on the point of suicide. A pastor gave her a prescription just as a doctor would, "Go home and read a page of *Abundant Living* every day and do what it tells you." She did. Today she is transformed, radiant, and in charge of a young people's society. She had nothing to act on save the pastor's word; she acted on it and it worked. Jesus says, "Thy faith hath made thee whole; go in peace." He would never say, "Go" except to mean, "Go into release."

Dear Lord and Savior, I'm grateful that Thou dost will my release. I will it too. Our wills meet. Mine is released by that meeting. Amen.

AFFIRMATION FOR THE DAY: *Thy Word is Thy prescription for me today.*

GRADUAL OR SUDDEN CONVERSIONS

We look further at our definition: "Resulting in a change, gradual or sudden." Some conversions are gradual and some are sudden. Some unfold like a flower to the sun—the gradual type. Others take a sudden leap to the breast of God. Some children who are brought up in a Christian home "can testify that 'from their childhood' they knew, not the Scriptures, but God Himself; they came to know Him they cannot tell how; they knew Him just as they knew the blue sky and a mother's love; they knew Him before they could understand any name by which in our imperfect human speech we have endeavored to affirm His goodness, His power, or His glory." Probably the number of such persons might be indefinitely increased if we did not imply, in so much that we say to them, that they belong to the devil and have to be brought to Christ, while the truth is that they belong to Christ and have to be kept from the devil.

Jesus said of little children, "To such belongs the kingdom of heaven." They are in the Kingdom of God and get out only by sinning out. If therefore we can keep them in from the beginning, then so much the better. Many wanderings and wounds would be saved. But even where there is an allegiance from the beginning, nevertheless it is well for the child to make an open confession which outwardly fixes that inner allegiance. To confess it before men is to confirm it in oneself.

But most of us need a definite and decisive round-about-face resulting in an unfolding or a sudden conversion. However, even in the decisive type there may be a gradualness, or on the other hand, a suddenness in the gradual type of conversion. They blend into each other. Every child knows about Paul's sudden conversion on the Damascus road, but who can date with any certainty the supreme crisis in the life of Peter? He heard the call "Follow me," and followed, and that following became a flowering. Not the phenomena that surround conversion, but the facts that flow from it are the criteria. "By their fruits ye shall know them." Both types are valid if they are vital.

O God, if I have any lingering doubts left, I lay them at Thy feet now—lay them by a self-surrender now. Thou hast me from this hour—and hast me forever. Amen.

AFFIRMATION OF THE DAY: *I rest, not on phenomena, but in the fact of my conversion.*

"AN INVINCIBLE CERTAINTY"

We talked yesterday about gradual and sudden conversions. Sometimes they are halfway between—half gradual, half sudden. A leading businessman and I had a quiet prayer together after a time of counsel. He writes about it: "You ought to know that when I walked into that little Moravian church yesterday morning, it was with a freedom which I had seldom felt before. In our litany there appears the hymn:

> I praise the God of grace;
> I trust His truth and might;
> He calls me His, I call Him mine,
> My God, my joy, my light.

"The above had a new meaning, each word and each phrase meant more in one instant than they had in all the years of singing them. This morning I go to my business with a sense that it is His business. I shall be under less tension no matter what problems present themselves. I have learned from you that it is not the problems, but our reactions that matter. I am not like the little dog Bang who went to the football field and was confused because he could not discern one dominant voice. I am hearing one dominant Voice now."

On the other hand, there is a very definite type of sudden conversion. William James says: "Were we writing the story of the mind from the purely natural-history point of view, with no religious interest whatever, we should still have to write down man's liability to sudden and complete conversion as one of his most curious peculiarities." "I was," says Lacordiare, "unbelieving in the evening, on the morrow a Christian, certain with an invincible certainty." "In John Duncan," says his biographer, "we behold the most skeptical of men transformed in a moment into the most believing of men." He presents, as Knight puts it, "the picture of a strong man suddenly arrested, struck down in mid-career of linguistic study and speculative daring by the realities of the unseen world; his was one of those swift upheavals of experience which attest the agency of a Higher Power working in the spirit of man." Sudden conversions do occur; they can only be explained vertically.

O loving God, Thou art loving me into love, Thou art believing me into belief. I am responding and Thy redemption is working. Amen.

AFFIRMATION FOR THE DAY: *I am doubting my doubts, believing my beliefs, and affirming my affirmations.*

"I'M IN"

We are looking at conversions, gradual or sudden. Here is one in a dramatic setting. At the close of one of a series of luncheon addresses for the bankers and businessmen of Wall Street, one of these men said: "Where do you go next? I'd like to take you in my car." I saw there was something more to it than a ride. We had scarcely started when he said in the very abrupt manner of businessmen, "How do you get hold of the thing you are talking about?" I asked him whether we could talk about it going through the traffic of the city and he replied, "There is no other place to talk about it." As we went through the roaring traffic I told him the steps: self-surrender, acceptance, obedience. I felt he was inwardly taking them. Then we came to the moment when I felt we should talk with God. "Do you think we could pray going through the traffic of this city?" I asked. "Well, I'd like you to pray, but I'll have to keep my eyes on the traffic," he replied. "All right," I said, "you watch and I'll pray." I'm not sure but what I kept my own eyes open!

But we were borne up into God's help, for God was looking for this hour of self-surrender and acceptance. As I jumped out of the car to go to my appointment he grabbed my hand in both of his and said very simply, "Thank you. I'm in." And he was!

Nobody is ever farther than three steps from the Kingdom of God: (a) Self-surrender, which includes sin-surrender. (b) Acceptance of the gift of God—the gift of salvation. (c) Obedience—obedience to the unfolding will of God. Anybody, anywhere, any time, can take these three steps and he'll be "in." It works with an almost mathematical precision. The infallibility of the Bible is in this: If anyone will take the way of Jesus, he will infallibly find God. This is an infallibility not to be argued about but to be experienced here and now. But really we don't find God; we let God find us. These three steps put us in the way of being found by God. In reality no one is ever more than one step from God—let him turn and he is in the arms of redeeming love. If this sounds too good to be true, remember it is too good not to be true.

My Father, I am so close to being found that I am found in the very fact of grasping this truth. I let it grasp me. I'm in. In Jesus' name. Amen.

AFFIRMATION FOR THE DAY: *I do not hold God—He holds me.*

COILED THE WRONG WAY

We come now to another step: "By which we pass from the kingdom of self to the Kingdom of God."

The center of sin is self-centeredness—all else is marginal. Halford Luccock has defined sin as "disharmony with the moral nature and purpose of God as revealed in Christ." It is a good definition. To be centered in self is the center of the disharmony with the moral nature of God as revealed in Christ. That is an attempt to arrange the universe around the wrong center.

An animal importer was looking for an expert snake winder who could unwind a fifteen-foot python. It was so bad tempered that no one could approach the box in which it was coiled. "It's because the snake was coiled into the box the wrong way. I am trying to find someone who can rewind it the right way." When we are coiled around self as the center, then we are coiled the wrong way. We are ill-tempered, out of sorts with ourselves and people and situations. When the inner life is coiled around God as the center, then we are good-tempered, in harmony with ourselves and people and situations. Conversion is changing us from an unnatural coil around the wrong center to a natural coil around God as the center.

Just as the fingers are rooted in the palm of the hand, so all other sins are rooted in an unsurrendered self. Why do we lie? We think it will be of advantage to the self. Why are we jealous of others? Because the self is thwarted. Why do we become angry? Because the self has been crossed. Why do we commit adultery? Because we think it will be some pleasure to the self. So all dealing with these individual sins is dealing with the fruit and leaving the root—the unsurrendered self.

A man who was known to be the biggest grouch in Trenton called a friend over the long-distance telephone one morning and in an excited voice said: "All Trenton's different—everybody's different this morning since that meeting in the high school last night where we heard ————. Of course, only I may be different, but all Trenton seems different." When he got his grouchy self off this own hands into the hands of God, he and his universe were different.

O Christ, Thou hast come to make me well at the center—at the me. Make me new there and I am new everywhere. Amen.

AFFIRMATION FOR THE DAY: *My universe is going to be different, for I am different.*

GROUCHY BECAUSE SELF-CENTERED

We are looking at the unsurrendered ego as the center of our problems and the center of our unhappiness. A policewoman told me she says to prostitutes and criminals, "You people don't know the meaning of the word 'harmony.'" Why? They started out probably on the assumption that they had a right to their own way, to be free, to express themselves. They made their ownselves the center of their universe. Result? Disharmony. Any other center than God puts life off-center—ec-centric.

Someone has said, "If you are unhappy at home, you should try to find out if your wife hasn't married a grouch." And why are you grouchy? It is because you are self-centered, trying to make the universe bend to yourself, and it won't work. Hence the grouch, which is a sign of frustration.

I know of a prominent man, a religious leader, who got his values so twisted that one day he walked out on his lovely family, said he had a right to his own happiness, and went off to another country with his secretary—in pursuit of happiness. He said he was going to found a new religion, more liberal, more sympathetic, less Puritan. So he tried to build up a new world of happiness around himself as the center. It fell to pieces. The woman saw the falsity of the whole thing, got out of it through repentance, self-surrender, and the finding of a new basis of life. She made good, became honored and respected, married a minister, and is adjusted, happy, and useful. But he was stubborn, tried self-justification, and clung to it in a losing battle. The universe wouldn't back his way of life and he knew it. Years later I sat alongside of his bed in a hospital and he held my hand and sadly said, "I'm an old prodigal who never returned." He could have returned if he had surrendered his frustrated, suffering ego. Instead, he built his house on the sand of egocentricity, and when the winds of ill-health blew, and the rain of adversity fell, and the flood of inner remorse arose, his house of man-soul crashed. "And great was the fall of it."

O God, I know there is no rest this side of Thee. I shall find myself in Thee and in Thee alone. I lose myself in myself. I surrender. Amen.

AFFIRMATION FOR THE DAY: *If my life has been bitter, bitter, now it will be better, better.*

SELF-PUNISHMENT TO SELF-SURRENDER

We continue to look at the crux of the transformation: "By which we pass from the kingdom of self to the kingdom of God."

There is no use trying to repress the self, that only makes it fester. A prominent man in a personal conference told me how he tried to master his ego by penances. As a penance for his sins he would tie his arm to the bedpost, so that he would be so uncomfortable in that position with his arm up that he couldn't sleep. It ended in frustration, for penance is not repentance. Penance is a religious masochism where you inflict punishment on the self. But in repentance and self-surrender the self ceases its own rule and takes God's rule, abdicates the throne and kneels before the throne of God. This man saw this, ceased his self-punishment and passed to self-surrender.

Mrs. Gracie Mannerheim, a former teacher of philosophy in a great university, writes in a letter: "Truly all things are made new. I was doing all the right things for all the wrong reasons. But the wonderful thing about the Kingdom of Heaven is this: the abilities and skills which we develop under the compulsion of a neurosis are not lost. We can shed the neurosis, but develop the skills and abilities we developed for the purposes of showing off the ego. I do think there is a qualitative inner change in the soul which takes place when the subsconcious is surrendered. First, one loses all hostility. Formerly one felt the criticism and then summoned a so-called Christian attitude and controlled one with the other. Now there isn't even a trace of criticism. One simply feels love, sympathy, compassion. One simply understands and loves."

Here was an amazing deliverance from an egocentric life to a God-centric life and it was effortless—no struggling, no trying, just a letting go of the center and the love of God did the rest.

A book on pastoral counseling dealt brilliantly with the solution of minor problems, but nowhere did it deal with this problem of self-surrender, a central fundamental conversion there, hence the book was only marginally Christian with marginal answers.

God, my Father, I know Thou hast Thy finger on the center of my problem, myself. Help me not to dodge or evade or excuse, but to surrender. Amen.

AFFIRMATION FOR THE DAY: *Today, no criticism; only love, sympathy, compassion.*

"NURSES HIS STARVING EGO"

We spoke yesterday of those who try self-punishment to overcome their ego-centricity. Some, instead of surrendering the self when it is frustrated, retreat into illness in order to dominate others through illness.

Alfred Adler puts it this way: "What does every human being want? To be powerful. What cuts him most deeply? Powerlessness, weakness, inferiority, inadequacy. . . . When an individual is unable to compensate for his inferiority, when he is too discouraged, his original desire for power remains, but it is diverted to a useless field of activity which promises nothing more than an easy way of satisfying his personal necessity for recognition. Such an individual forces the members of his environment to give him extra care, sympathy, money, and in turn he rules and tyrannizes over them. Protected in most cases by a sham illness, he thus wins an appearance of superiority with which he nurses his starving Ego." But of course this too is a losing battle—for everybody. An area of unhappiness is created.

George Hartmann, professor of psychology at Columbia University, puts it this way: "Religious conversion is neglected in education. . . . Conversion is not adding 20 points to 100, but a reorganization of the whole 120. Conversion takes place in the whole man." Note that it is "a reorganization of the whole." Before conversion, life is organized around the ego; after conversion, life is organized around God. If that doesn't take place, nothing takes place; but if that takes place, then everything takes place. Pseudo conversion takes place where there are marginal changes around a centrally unchanged self; real conversion changes the center, the self, and carries with it all marginal changes.

To surrender to God is not flattering to the ego, and therefore many would try learnedly to skip around the necessity. If you try to skip it, you will trip over your unsurrendered ego into unhappiness and frustration. The law of self-surrender is the first law of life.

O God, I know I don't break that law; I break myself on that law. Help me today to align myself to Thy law through complete self-surrender. Amen.

AFFIRMATION FOR THE DAY: *Today I shall live by the first law of life.*

"THE SMALL-SCALE INDIVIDUAL"

We pause one more day on the passing from the kingdom of self to the Kingdom of God as the essence of conversion.

"Having no part dark, it will be wholly bright, as when a lamp with its rays gives you light" (Luke 11:36 R.S.V.). "Having no part dark"—that is total conversion. But until the self is surrendered to God, then the center and the margin are both dark. Centered in yourself, you are like an electric-light bulb out of its socket trying by its own efforts to be light. But centered in God, then you are that bulb fastened in the socket, glowing with light and warmth.

When steel is magnetized, the electrons are aligned with each other. Before being magnetized, the electrons are helter-skelter, at cross-purposes, but being magnetized, they are together, working together, hence magnetism has drawing power. Until we surrender our self to God we are inwardly at cross-purposes, life is helter-skelter, canceling itself out; it is ineffective and repels people rather than draws people. But when the self is surrendered to God, then it is aligned to God, which puts us into alignment with ourselves, which in turn makes us inwardly a co-operative order, which makes us magnetic persons. We draw others not to ourselves, but to the thing we stand for. Until that happens we are little souls with little influence.

When someone asked Sir Alfred Zimmern, the famous professor of international relations, "What in your opinion is the greatest obstacle between us and the building of enduring world peace?" the great man slowly replied, "The small-scale individual." The small-scale individual, small because self-centered, is constantly projecting his inner conflicts into outer relationships, and when this takes place in small-scale individuals in authority, then they create chaos on a wide scale. Any small-scale soul creates unpeace around him, for he is not at peace with himself.

Self-surrender enlarges the individual from a small-scale man to a large-scale man. Identified with yourself, you are given to a decreasing and disintegrating entity, but now identified with the Kingdom of God, you take on the significance of this universal entity.

O God, I know I am large-scale only as I give myself to Thee on a large-scale. Take the center—that is my all. I grow big—in Thee. Amen.

AFFIRMATION FOR THE DAY: *Not petty, but big in every situation today.*

"THE ONLY REDEEMING AGENCY"

We now come to the last portion of the definition: "Conversion is the penitent, receptive response to the saving divine initiative in Christ, resulting in a change, gradual or sudden, by which one passes from the kingdom of self to the Kingdom of God and becomes a part of a living fellowship, the church." Note the last portion: "And becomes a part of a living fellowship, the church."

Suppose one tries to take the conversion without the fellowship of the church. Will it work? Across the years I have found that where the fellowship of the church fades out, conversion and its fruits fade out.

In one day two people came to see me, both in spiritual trouble. One was a youth who told me he was staying away from church because he and his girl friend had broken up some months before. He became very unhappy, for he was deteriorating. He came to church that night, surrendered to Christ and became radiantly happy. Another was a pastor's wife who had given up resentments against her husband, but pulled out of the church when she felt he had let her down. She simply stayed away. She deteriorated.

I sat down in a home which was shadowed by tragedy. The father a few nights before had walked out of his lovely home and his lovely family and was found next day with his throat cut, a suicide. There was so little to account for it, for he loved his wife and family and they loved him—an apparently model family. But he brooded over business troubles which really weren't too serious, and in brooding over them he had no faith in God to tide him over. Both the husband and wife had been active in church work, but in moving to a new community, they thought their love for each other and their personal integrity were enough without the church. They inwardly deteriorated, and when the pressure came, he broke. "I've got to return to religion and the church again," she said. But it was late!

A. J. Muste, after leaving the church for Marxian communism, came back to it. "I return to the church," he said, "because these years have taught me that the church of the redeemed is the only redeeming agency."

O Christ, I thank Thee that Thy church is the mother of my spirit. Here I find fellowship, and most of all, here I find Thee. Amen.

AFFIRMATION FOR THE DAY: *I cannot break fellowship any more than I can break a bone and not get hurt.*

"THE SOCIETY OF THE FORGIVEN AND THE FORGIVING"

The church has many critics but no rivals in the work of human redemption. There isn't a spot on earth from the frozen North to the tropical islands of the seas, where they have allowed us to go where we haven't gone with schools, hospitals, orphan asylums, leper asylums, the gospel—everything to lift the soul, the mind, the body of the race. No other institution has done anything like it.

In the days of Abraham Lincoln, Artemus Ward wrote: "If you will show me a place where there ain't no meetinghouses and men don't never pray, I will show you a place where the women are slipshod and dirty, where gates are off the hinges, where old hats are stuffed in broken windows, and where the devil's unknown regions are painted on men's shirt bosoms with tobacco juice." This is no exaggeration, for I have seen just that picture in a different setting. I stood one day watching priests sacrificing goats to Kali, the bloodthirsty goddess. A devotee crept up through the crowd and put his neck between the wooden forks where the goats' necks had been thrust before the head was cut off, and the devotee asked that he be sacrificed to Kali. The priests grabbed the hair of his head and threw him back into the crowd. I left sick at heart, and went to a Christian church where the people from the same race were worshiping and fellowshiping around the cross, where the God they worshiped gave Himself for them. They were cultured, refined, and interested in each other. I said to myself, "I've been hard on the church, but with all its faults, it holds the best of humanity within itself. So I'm for it."

Clovis G. Chappell answers the man who says, "Show me a perfect church and I will join it," by saying: "You will do nothing of the kind. In the first place, such a church would not admit us. In the second place such a church would be a tremendous embarrassment to us. In the third place, such a church would cease at once to be perfect when we joined it." No, the church is made up of Christians-in-the-making. "The church should be the society of the forgiven and the forgiving."

O Father, I thank Thee for this fellowship—this fellowship of those who are emerging out of darkness into light, the sons of the Light. In Jesus' name. Amen.

AFFIRMATION FOR THE DAY: *As a son of Light I shall fellowship with the sons of Light.*

DEFINITIONS OF CONVERSION

We have been looking at a definition of conversion. Before we leave this phase, several more definitions could be given covering other phases:

1. Conversion is the invasion of a man's life by the Spirit of God, who conforms him into the image of Christ.

2. Conversion is the adjustment of one's whole self to God.

3. Conversion is the acceptance of Jesus Christ as Savior and Lord.

4. Conversion is a personal faith in and surrender to Jesus Christ as Savior and Lord, resulting in changed life and relationships.

5. In more modern vernacular: God throws us the ball, we reach out and take the ball and begin running toward the goal.

6. Conversion is a "Halt, right-about-face, quick march."

7. Conversion is conversion from perversion. It is the bringing of the natural powers turned toward unnatural uses back to their natural intention. In conversion you become supernaturally natural.

We now look at the steps into conversion. In reference to John Newton in his *Essay on Evangelical Succession,* Sir J. Stephen says: "There is a natural history of religious conversions. It commences with melancholy, advances through contrition to faith, is then conducted to tranquility, and after a while to rapture, and subsides at length into abiding consolation and peace."

Let us look at these five steps. First, melancholy. Your first contact with this whole thing produces upset and a consequent feeling of melancholy. It is upsetting to feel that here is something that is challenging your whole way of life. You feel the impulse to get angry and fight it or to run away and forget it. It is wounding to the pride of the ego to know that you're wrong, dead wrong, and need to change. Melancholy sets in. This is inevitable. The question is to what side of that melancholy you come out on—on the rebellious, frustrated side, or on the repentant, fruitful side. Melancholy can turn into misery or mastery. You turn the switch one way or the other. It is life's most important moment. Destiny is packed into that moment.

O God, my Father, my heart, heavy with melancholy because of my way of life, comes to Thee to guide that melancholy into transformation. Amen.

AFFIRMATION FOR THE DAY: *I may begin with melancholy, but I am emerging into merriment.*

"PASSED THROUGH MELANCHOLY"

We saw that the first step in transformation is melancholy. Jesus first appears as a troubler. At His appearance "the news of this troubled king Herod and all Jerusalem as well" (Matt. 2:3, Moffatt). The demoniac cried: "Have you come here to torment us?" (Matt. 8:29, R.S.V.) He upsets us to set us up. The molecules of a piece of steel have to be upset on one level to re-form again on a higher level into a higher type of structure.

A prominent woman who had lost her husband ten years before, and who had nursed her grief into self-pity, wanted to run away from our Ashram group—"I am not getting consolation here," she said. She was looking for consolation instead of release. The remedy we were offering was a surrender of her self-pitying self and her grief to God, and that upset her whole pattern of bidding for so-called consolation around a self-pitying self. She stayed through the melancholy stage, passed through contrition to tranquillity, and was released.

A very tied-up woman was disturbed lest people see her talking to me in a hotel lobby—what would they think of her? But she passed through that stage of melancholy when in prayer in a side room, I told her that it takes twice as much power for an airplane to get off the earth as it does to fly. She suddenly opened her eyes, looked around surprised and said rapturously: "Why, I'm off!" After a few hours she handed me her whisky flask and her gold cigarette case, which she said I could sell for missions, and then finally she gave me her bottle of sleeping tablets. "I don't need those any more," she said. She let go all of her crutches. She could stand on her own two feet, a released and ransomed person. Some years later she said to me, "I can look on the person of those days as an entirely different person, belonging to an entirely different world." She had passed through melancholy through contrition to tranquillity.

"I like religion all right, and I'd like to have it, but it's the process of getting it I don't like," said an honest person. He wanted to skip the melancholy and contrition stages and get to tranquillity without them.

Gracious Father, I want release not an easy way. Help me to go through the purgatory of melancholy and contrition to release. Amen.

AFFIRMATION FOR THE DAY: *The old person and the old world belong to yesterday.*

"CONTRITION IS A CATHARSIS"

We noted that the soul passes from melancholy through contrition to faith. The process of smashing down the old to build up the new is a very painful process.

The unmaking is a blow to one's pride and egoism. But God never strikes except the very striking is healing. "So the Eternal strikes Egypt, striking them and healing them" (Isa. 19:22, Moffatt). When He strikes us to the dust, He puts us there only to raise us to the highest heaven.

I shall always remember one thing, the most precious thing among many precious things, when for the first time I had to punish a little granddaughter of four. After I smacked her hand she went downstairs to her mother brokenhearted. We both felt the pain of separation. After a while I heard the patter of little feet upon the stairway, and a little form came nestling close to me as I sat in the armchair, and a penitent voice said, "Granddaddy, I'm sorry." That was all. But it was everything. That contrition broke down the barriers and we were one again, closer than ever before.

Henry Ward Beecher says: "When a man undertakes to repent toward his fellow men, it is repenting straight up a precipice; when he repents toward law, it is repenting into the crocodile's jaws; when he repents toward public sentiment, it is throwing himself into a thicket of brambles and thorns; but when he repents toward God, he repents toward all love and delicacy. God receives the soul as the sea the bather, to return it again, purer and whiter than he took it." And just as the sea asks no questions of how clean or unclean you are, but takes all and sends all back clean, so God asks no questions except one, "Do you want to be clean?"

Contrition is a catharsis. In Thomas Moore's *Paradise* the peri was refused admission to paradise until she brought the most precious thing on earth. She tried in vain with the last drop of a patriot's lifeblood, and the last sigh of a lover's self-sacrifice, and finally was admitted when she bore up to the gate a tear of penitence of an old man. Penitence opens the gates of paradise to anyone.

O God, my Father, in my hands no price I bring except the penitence of my heart. Thou hast me when Thou hast that. Amen.

AFFIRMATION FOR THE DAY: *My penitent tears are my glasses through which I see the forgiving love of God.*

"I GAMBLED THAT THE TRUTH WAS THERE"

We come to the next step in conversion: "Through penitence to faith." William James gave six steps in "the ladder of faith." (*a*) It is a possible view, it is not self-contradictory, it is not absurd. (*b*) It might be true so far as the actual facts are concerned. (*c*) It may be true now for all that anybody knows. (*d*) It is fit to be true, it ought to be true. (*e*) It must be true. (*f*) It shall be true as far as I am concerned, for I shall adopt it as my truth and live by it henceforth.

Now that you are taking the step of faith as your next step, go through those six steps: The Christian way is a possible way, it is not self-contradictory, not absurd; it might be true; it may be true now; it is fit to be true, ought to be true; it must be true; it shall be true as far as I am concerned. For I launch out on it by faith and accept it as my Way. Is this credulity, or is it the way all discoveries, including scientific discoveries, are made? Arthur H. Compton, Nobel prize winner, said to his Sunday-school class, "Every great discovery I ever made I gambled that the truth was there, and then I acted on it in faith until I could prove its existence."

You launch out on Christ as your Savior and Lord and there will come to you a double verification—it will prove itself to you, self-verifying, and you will prove it to yourself as you act on it. That verification may come suddenly, like a rushing wind, or it may come quietly and gradually like the dew on the new-mown hay—you will not know how or when, but it is there.

William James gives this passage descriptive of that state: "There is a state of mind known to religious men, but to no others, in which the will to assert ourselves and hold our own has been replaced by a willingness to close our mouths and be as nothing in the floods and water spouts of God. . . . The time for tension of our soul is over, and that of happy relaxation, for calm deep breathing, of an eternal present with no discordant future to be anxious about, has arrived." In other words, relaxed receptivity—an attitude where you take the gift of God, for it is a "gift."

My God and Father, I pass from contrition to faith. I welcome what I have believed in. I take it. It is mine. I'm grateful. Amen.

AFFIRMATION FOR THE DAY: *Faith is the hand that cleans the window to let the light in.*

"IT FELL IN AND I SAW IT NO MORE"

We come to the next stage in the process of conversion: "Is conducted to tranquillity and after awhile to rapture." That order may happen, but it is often the rapture first and then tranquillity.

Bunyan puts it this way: "So I saw in my dream, that just as Christian came up with the cross, his burden loosed from his shoulders, and fell from his back, and began to tumble, and so continued to do till it came to the mouth of the sepulcher, where it fell in and I saw it no more." Released!

> O glory of the lighted mind.
> How dead I'd been, how dumb, how blind.
> The station brook to my new eyes,
> Was babbling out of Paradise.
> The waters rushing from the rain
> Were singing Christ has risen again.
> I thought all earthly creatures knelt
> From rapture of the joy I felt.

Here is a letter from a woman who at forty-five was a wreck, her home broken up, and she on the rocks. Then conversion and with it a total awakening of her total person. She entered the university at that age, paid her way with a full-time secretarial job, came out at the end of her course for a B.A. *Cum laude.* Got her M.A. with all "A's" in her major field. She writes: "Wasn't Jesus amazing? I don't know why any Christian should discard the miracles. I believe in miracles. He healed me. What could be more miraculous than the forgiveness of sins? Or the taking away of all bitterness, all resentment? And the peace and joy that follow are indescribable. The laughter that comes bubbling up at most unexpected times, in me who thought a few years ago that I would never laugh again. I know the laughter is not what the psychologists call a 'manic' phase, after which will come a depression, but it rises from a well of living water that will never cease. I am grateful beyond words."

A college girl put it this way after her conversion, "I feel as though I've swallowed sunshine." Another girl, recently converted, watching a sunrise, exclaimed, "That's the way I feel inside."

Gracious Father, my heart sings, sometimes in tranquillity and sometimes in rapture, but it sings, it sings. I'm grateful. Amen.

AFFIRMATION FOR THE DAY: *In Christ I'm a sunrise, not a sunset.*

"I FEEL SO CLEAN INSIDE"

We come to the last stage in the steps in conversion: "And subsides at length into abiding consolation and peace."

After rapture and tranquillity there come abiding consolation and peace. But the consolation is not the consolation of someone holding your hand—it is Someone strengthening your arm to give you strength to hold someone else by the hand, it is the consolation of adequacy.

And the peace is not the peace of nondisturbance but the peace of tranquillity amid storm—a peace "in spite of." F. Kiss of the University of Budapest, says: "When my new life became evident, I had to choose between Christ or the anatomical career. I answered clearly: Rather Christ without anatomy than anatomy without Christ. God gave me both. Ten years later I became director of the department in which I found Christ. He is now my power and peace in private life, and He is my wisdom in my research work." Note "He is now my power and peace." The peace comes from a sense of adequacy to meet anything that comes.

Vaughn Shoemaker, political cartoonist of the *Chicago Daily News*, Pulitzer prize winner, says: "I was honest enough with myself back in 1926 to admit I was concerned about my soul. I was simple enough to accept the simple gospel. Jesus Christ became my Savior. I have never been sorry. Having little education or natural ability for any success I have gained as a cartoonist, I must give credit to God. I wouldn't dare start a day without first starting on my knees with God beside my drawing board. I gain wisdom from Him." He could face the demands of the day with peace because he knew he had adequacy through the resources of God.

A very brilliant woman, after surrendering her life to God, went through a night of very severe temptation to yield to the old sex impulses. She resisted and came out on top. The next morning she called up a friend and said, "I feel so clean inside this morning." There was the quivering storm and blinding rain and then a sense of cleanness, therefore a sense of calm peace.

O God, how can I thank Thee enough for the sense of peace through adequacy. Thy reinforcements are my reassurances. I thank Thee. Amen.

AFFIRMATION FOR THE DAY: *The blood of Jesus whispers peace in this dark world of sin.*

"A SUDDEN AND ENDURING CHANGE"

We note the word "abiding" in the last stage: "And subsides at length into an *abiding* consolation and peace."

Is conversion a mere emotional experience which evaporates when the pressure is taken off? Emotions do come and go, but a permanent change in character does take place. George J. Romanes, in feeling his way back to faith after losing it and feeling the barrenness of life without it, put his finger, as a scientist, in his instinct for facts, upon the fact that "Augustine, after thirty years, and other Fathers," he says, "bear testimony to a sudden and enduring change in themselves, called conversion." "Now this experience," he goes on, "has been repeated and testified to by countless millions of civilized men and women in all nations and all degrees of culture." Note "to a sudden and *enduring* change."

This enduring side of conversion is expressed by Edwin D. Starbuck, a psychologist, who after studying a hundred cases came to the conclusion: "The effect of conversion is to bring with it a changed attitude toward life which is fairly constant and permanent, though feelings fluctuate. . . . In other words, persons who have passed through conversion, having once taken a stand for the religious life, tend to feel themselves identified with it, no matter how much their religious enthusiasm declines."

This abiding character of conversion is seen amid many failures and doubts—something permanent remains. A rather rough type of charwoman was converted, and when she lapsed back momentarily in some of her old ways and language she said, "Well, I ain't what I want to be, and I ain't what I'm going to be, but I certainly ain't what I was." That's it! A permanent deposit has been left in character.

When I told the man with whom I was working in a law library in Baltimore that I had been converted the night before, his disgusted reply was, "I'll knock that out of you in two weeks." At the end of the two weeks he was on the defensive and I was on the offensive. He succeeded only in driving it deeper within me.

O Father, I thank Thee I am not precariously holding on to Thee. Thou art holding on to me. I'm in the grip of a love that will not let me go. Amen.

AFFIRMATION FOR THE DAY: *This has the feel of the real and the eternal upon it.*

"BROKEN ARM OR AMPUTATION?"

During the writing of last week's meditations this poignant letter came: "I am making progress on the Way. However, one area still remains troublesome. I have always been extremely anxious and apprehensive. As a small child I lived in terror of my father. I was having horrible night terrors before I ever went to school. My psychiatrist says I have 'catastrophic apprehension.' I feel a terrible inadequacy for living in a world such as ours. It is as though I were in an environment for which I was not made. My psychiatrist evades the issue as much as possible. Pinned down, he will say: 'Of course we can never fully get away from our childhood emotional conditioning. We have to live within our limitations.' I wonder. Should I think of it as I think of a broken arm, that it will heal and I'll have my arm again, or shall I think of it as I regard an amputation—I'll never have an arm again? The issue is: Is my early emotional conditioning, reinforced by forty-eight years of anxious living, *final*? I know of course that by intelligent living and surrender I can modify it, but my question is: Can I hope to be rid of it some day? It would take a terrible load off my mind if I could."

We do not question the statement of the psychiatrist *from his standpoint,* for he is dealing with life without religion, but from the Christian standpoint we flatly challenge the finality of early conditioning. In the Christian Way we subject ourselves to a reconditioning. We expose ourselves to the powerful, sterilizing, remaking love of God. This new conditioning cancels the old conditioning. For the old conditioning is not inherent but imposed, therefore what has been put in can be taken out by our consent and God's redemption. He can and does "restore . . . the years that the locust hath eaten." The arm is not amputated, it is paralyzed; and Jesus says, "Stretch forth your arm." And when we do, it is made whole as the other. If we have had a bad heredity, then a new blood transfusion from the Love of God gives us a new heredity. And if we have had a bad environment, the new environment, the Kingdom of God, reconditions us—decisively.

Gracious Father, I am thankful that in Thee I'm no longer a victim, I'm a victor. I'm not beneath my circumstances; I'm on top of them. Amen.

AFFIRMATION FOR THE DAY: *Today I shall be reconditioned every moment by my higher Environment.*

EARLY CONDITIONING FINAL?

We pause upon the thought with which we closed yesterday—the finality of early conditioning. We said it was not final and could be counteracted and controlled and even canceled. If we have had a bad birth and a bad environment, we have the privilege of a new birth and a new environment. The horizontal influences may have corrupted and confined us; the vertical influence now playing on us can cleanse and convert. We are "engrafted with the divine nature"—a new heredity. We are environed with the Kingdom of God—a new environment. Both are more powerful than the old if accepted and co-operated with. Illustrations leap to mind.

My friend Mr. Santiago was from the carrion eaters of South India, the lowest of the low-people who would carry out the dead carcass of an animal with a song to feast upon it. That sense of inferiority was in every breath he breathed as a boy. But when he exposed himself to Christ and the Kingdom, he became by sheer force of character and ability the head of the South India United Church; though a Christian minister, he was the mayor of his city for twenty years—they would not let him resign. Every one of his six children was a college graduate and in an influential position. His home breathed the air of humble superiority. One American missionary said, "We could afford to lose any five missionaries rather than that man." His new heredity and his new environment canceled the old. It seemed an impossible memory—in any case, only a memory.

A cultured, refined, able man stood up in our Ashram in India and his first words were, "I have been redeemed from the untouchables." Another friend of mine was asked by a landlord in India, "Where do you come from?" He replied in proud humility, "I was your sweeper; now I'm your teacher."

One of the most useful men I know, secretary of the council of churches of a great city and an effective counselor to confused people, was brought up in a saloon, and was converted through a humble Negro Christian, and married the dean of girls of a college. Early conditioning final? Nonsense. Jesus is the Omega, the final Word.

O Christ, Thou art taking the nobodies and making them into the somebodies. I'm a candidate—make me all over again. Amen.

AFFIRMATION FOR THE DAY: *Nothing is final but God—and I'm linked with Him.*

ADOLESCENCE AND CONVERSION

In adolescence there is an awakening, leading sometimes to a revolt against childhood conditioning. The adolescent boy or girl, passing from the stage of dependence to the stage of independence, wants to be a person in his or her own right. Now adolescents sometimes revolt downward into rampart egocentricity and irresponsibility.

But the revolt of adolescence can be a revolt upward. It was so in the case of Jesus. At the age of twelve He revolted against parental dependence, disappeared, and turned up in the temple. When His baffled parents found him they remonstrated, and His reply was, "Did you not know I had to be at my Father's house?" (Moffatt.) He revolted upward into a higher plan and purpose—from the control of His earthly parents to the control of His divine parent, God. It was a constructive revolt.

It is at that moment of revolt that many conversions take place. Edwin Starbuck says that "conversion is a distinctly adolescent phenomenon." Why? Some would say that conversion taking place in adolescence, which is the period of the awakening of sex, is therefore a distinctly sexual manifestation—a manifestation of the libido in religious terms. This of course is "the fallacy of *with* and therefore *on account of.*" Conversion often takes place in adolescence because adolescence is a period of the awakening of the total personality, not merely the awakening of sex. With this total awakening of the personality there is an awakening of the spiritual. A thirteen-year-old girl, convalescing from an illness and cantankerous, suddenly turned to a visiting pastor and said out of a clear sky, "Tell me, why are we here?" Adolescence is the natural period of conversion. Coe illustrates this by saying that when you want the furnace to burn more briskly, you open the draft to the oxygen which is always enveloping the furnace. So the physical changes in adolescence, while they do not produce conversion, nevertheless do open new doors whereby the ever-present divine Spirit may enter mind and spirit. Then the supreme awakening climaxes and co-ordinates the other awakenings.

O Father, I know that amid the other awakenings of life Thou art eager to give this supreme awakening. Help me to throw open the drafts. Amen.

AFFIRMATION FOR THE DAY: *All drafts open to the winds of God today!*

THE FOUR GATES

We have seen that conversion is an adolescent phenomenon; nevertheless it often occurs in childhood and should normally occur there.

Someone has suggested that there are four gates into the city of God: (*a*) The gate of sudden conversion; (*b*) the gate of belonging to God from childhood; (*c*) the gate of being convinced in mind; and (*d*) the gate of a practical change in character. Perhaps the gate of belonging to God from childhood should have been named first, for that is where conversion should normally occur. This is illustrated in Helen Keller, who, shut off from the world of sense by blindness, deafness, and dumbness, got her first inkling of that outside world when a minister was requested to teach her about God. She exclaimed in glad wonder, "I always knew Him, but I didn't know His name."

The glory of the Christian faith is that the gospel is presented not as a creed, but as a Person. The child can understand the Person when he cannot grasp the creed. Someone asked Mrs. Albert Einstein, "Do you understand the theory of relativity?" She replied: "No, I must confess I don't. But I do understand Dr. Einstein." The child may not understand all about Jesus, but he does understand Jesus.

But the consciousness of having sinned out of the Kingdom comes early. A little boy of eight said to me, "Please talk young so I can understand." That same boy talking to a friend said, "I want to be saved, and I don't know how to go about it." This friend explained from a parent's love to a Father's love that to surrender to God's will is to be ready to do God's will, just as one does a parent's will, and then added, "When you do your parents' will, you feel good inside—but when you don't?" The boy replied, "I have a lump in my throat." They prayed and the boy said to God: "I've always felt I belonged to you, but I've been afraid to say so. Now I say so." They arose and the little fellow said joyously, "The lump is gone from my throat." Young and old echo the words of Emerson, "I awoke and *found my feet on a staircase.*" We are going up instead of down.

Jesus, Thou art speaking again, "Suffer the little children to come to me." And they came—joyfully, from every tribe and tongue. And we thank Thee. Amen.

AFFIRMATION FOR THE DAY: *My feet are upon a staircase—I'm on the upward way.*

"GETTING VOCAL FOR GOD"

We saw yesterday that the children belong to Him from birth, but it fixes that fact when they confess it by a public confession. "With the heart man believeth . . . and with the mouth confession is made unto salvation." The expression produces and deepens the impression for it is a law of the mind that that which is not expressed dies.

William James says: "When once the judgment is decided let a man commit himself. Let him do something that will lay on him the necessity of doing more, that will lay on him the necessity of doing all. Let him take a public pledge if the case allows. Let him envelop his decision with all the aids possible." So Christian confession is psychologically sound. Believing faith drives in the nail, but confession clinches the nail on the other side and holds it from being easily pulled out. For a private faith can be privately renounced—and easily. But a public faith is held up by the very fact that it is public.

A man said to Dwight Moody, "Why do I have to join a church, can't I be a Christian alone and in my own heart?" Moody, without a word, pulled a coal from the open grate before which they were sitting, separated it from the rest, and as they sat there watching it, it died. The man got the lesson, "Separated from the warmth of Christian fellowship I too will die."

Faith and surrender light the fire in the heart, but unless outer confession is made, the fire is smothered for want of an open draft. Confession opens the draft and makes the fire burn. Robert G. Le Tourneau, a manufacturer of excavating machines, told me of how he was always a bottled-up Christian till one day he was called on to make an address before a Rotary Club. He turned it into a simple testimony of what Christ was to him. It created a sensation among those business men and it opened a draft in Le Tourneau's life. He never dreamed he could speak in public. Now he is on fire and is speaking everywhere and with great effectiveness. A missionary who went out as a medical missionary to India, so she would not have to speak, said radiantly, "I'm really getting vocal for God."

O Jesus, wisely Thou didst say: "Whosoever . . . shall confess me before men, him will I confess also before my Father." Help me this day to confess Thee. Amen.

AFFIRMATION FOR THE DAY: *My confession will be as open as my convictions are deep.*

A FOURFOLD RECONCILIATION

We have seen how conversion covers all ages and all types. The child can enter, the old can enter.

My first convert, as a lad of seventeen, was my grandmother, eighty-two years of age. I had just been converted and the day after Christmas I was in her room when she said, "I suppose by next Christmas I'll not be here." I asked, "You're ready to go, aren't you?" She burst into tears, "No, I'm not." We knelt and prayed and in the midst of the praying she clapped her hands with joy. She was in—at eighty-two! An Anglican bishop in India stood up in one of my meetings and said, "Life began for me at seventy-two." It did! All his life he had been religious, now he was Christian. It didn't mean that he was changed morally, it did mean that he was lighted up spiritually and set on fire—a dead ecclesiast became a living soul, a living and a life-giving soul.

So conversion has a different meaning for different people: "For one man conversion means the slaying of the beast within him; in another it brings the calm of conviction to an unquiet mind; for a third it is the entrance into a larger liberty and a more abundant life; and yet again it is the gathering into one of the forces of the soul at war within itself." But to all it means a reconciliation with God through forgiveness, therefore a reconciliation with yourself, therefore a reconciliation with your neighbors, and therefore a reconciliation with nature. A fourfold reconciliation with life takes place.

A central characteristic of conversion is that the whole being is awakened and stimulated. A man recently converted stood up in a meeting and said: "Before I was converted I wore out the heels of my shoes walking around the factory—I was run down at the heels. Now that I've been converted I find that I am wearing out the toes of my shoes. Christianity puts me on my toes." It does! Instead of rocking back on your heels, on the defensive and afraid of life, it tilts life forward, gives you a sense of fearless expectancy and adventure, puts you on your toes. Instead of a Nay-saying person you become a Yea-saying person.

O God, my heart bursts with gratitude that Thou hast tilted life forward, hast put me on my toes. Now forward forever. Amen.

AFFIRMATION FOR THE DAY: *I belong to the tomorrows, not to the yesterdays.*

"MY COLD HEART BEGAN TO BURN"

We were meditating yesterday on conversion meaning different things to different people, and yet with a sameness running through them all.

Horace Bushnell was a skeptic, and in a very serious mood one day he sat alone and asked himself, "Is there anything I do believe?" "Yes, there is one thing," he replied to himself, "there is a distinction between right and wrong." Then came the further question, "If there is this distinction, have you ever thrown yourself out on the right?" "No," he replied, "I have not. Then here is something I can do: I can throw myself out on the right. If I have lost God in the wrong, maybe I will discover Him in the right." He knelt and prayed a dim prayer to the dim God to begin a new life, taking the right as his guide. It was a dim prayer but profoundly meant. He was borne up on the hands of that prayer into His very presence. He was flooded with a sense of God. A Being so profoundly felt must be! From that moment Bushnell the skeptic was transformed into Bushnell the mighty believer, one who helped thousands to believe.

Bushnell worked from morality up to God, and Adeline Countess Schimmelmann, a distinguished German lady, worked down from the love of God. She says: "After weeks of darkness and uncertainty, I seemed to hear God saying to me, 'My child, thy salvation does not depend upon thy love to Me, but upon My love to thee, just as thou art.' Then broke in upon my heart a sun of joy in the beams of which I still rejoice, and whose light will shine upon me eternally. Now my cold heart began to burn, not on account of my love to Christ, but because of His love to me."

To others it means a simple change of attitude toward others. A man and his wife were always quarreling, usually because of the radio—she wanted music, he wanted news. He was converted, and when he came home he turned on the music. She looked at him in surprise and said, "But this is the news hour." "Yes, but I thought you would like the music." She looked at him, walked to the radio and turned on the news! From that moment they were friends.

O God, my Father, help me to take a new attitude toward Thee and everybody else. With attitudes converted, I shall be converted. In Jesus' name. Amen.

AFFIRMATION FOR THE DAY: *All my attitudes controlled by love and only love!*

RESULTS OR CONSEQUENCES?

We have been looking at some modern conversions; now we must turn to look at some outstanding conversions in the pages of Holy Writ. Here is one from the Old Testament, a conversion so outstanding that it changed the life of a whole nation. Jacob was notoriously crooked. Jeremiah says, "For a brother will cheat like a Jacob" (Jer. 9:4, Moffatt). And yet he says again, "For he who formed the universe is Jacob's God" (Jer. 10:16, Moffatt). What had happened to make a proverbial cheat into one beloved of God?

In Gen. 31:42 (Moffatt) God is called "the God of Abraham, the Awe of Isaac." Why "the God of Abraham and the Awe of Isaac"? The reason seems to be that in Abraham, God was firsthand, creative, dynamic. Under the touch of God, Abraham went forth, not knowing whither he was going, and founded a great nation. But when it came to Isaac, the next generation, there was a fading-out of the God-consciousness. He was one step removed from reality. He lived on an afterglow of his father's faith. Still he lived in "Awe" of his father's God, but it was secondhand. In the third generation, in Jacob, the moral results of this fading-out of God begin to be seen in moral decay. For when God fades out then the basis for morality fades out with it and moral decay sets in. When God went, then Jacob made himself God. He became a self-centered man, the center of his universe. He began to look for and act on the main chance—for himself. He was Jacob—the supplanter, the heel-grabber. The center of sin is self-centeredness—Jacob became God. And then he began to get the consequences. Some people go through life getting results, others get consequences. If you work with the moral universe, you get results—the moral universe will sustain you, back you, you will have cosmic approval. But others get consequences—they break themselves upon the moral universe, are frustrated. Jacob cheated Esau out of his father's blessing by a clever trick. But here was the pay-off. "Esau hated Jacob" (Gen. 27:41). Jacob got his way—plus the hatred of his brother. He got consequences. He created a situation in which he found it impossible to live. The pay-off was working.

Gracious God and Father, when we revolt against Thee, we revolt against ourselves. Save us from self-hurts. Save us from ourselves. Amen.

AFFIRMATION FOR THE DAY: *In a universe of this kind no one gets away with anything. I would be a fool to try.*

"ONE OF THOSE HALF CONVERSIONS"

We are studying the conversion of Jacob, the man who looked after No. 1—himself. He took advantage of his brother's hunger and bought his birthright for a mess of pottage; then he, with his mother's scheming, got his father's blessing by a clever trick, got it plus his brother's hatred.

And his mother? She got the pay-off in her inner dissatisfaction with herself, a dissatisfaction which showed itself in a dissatisfaction with those around her: "These Hittite women tire me to death. If Jacob married a Hittite woman like these women, some native girl, what good is life to me?" (Gen. 27:46, Moffatt.) Rebekah was bored with women around her because she was bored with herself. She had to live with a bad conscience and a bad conscience is a poor bedfellow. When you are out of patience with people around you, depend upon it, it is most likely a projection of your impatience with yourself. If a person is critical of others, usually it is because he is unconsciously critical of himself. The people who are always complaining of others are simply externalizing their out-of-sortness with themselves. The pay-off of evil is that you have to live with an evil self.

So Rebekah and Jacob again schemed to get Jacob out of the mess he had created by his trickery. They created a set of circumstances in which they couldn't live, so Rebekah recommended—much as the modern doctor does when he doesn't know what to do with a patient —a change of climate! She recommended that Jacob should go to Paddan-aram, to his ancestral place, and get a wife—a legitimate errand with a suppressed escapism underneath. How often we do legitimate things for other than legitimate reasons!

On the way Jacob went through one of those half conversions when he dreamed he saw a ladder between heaven and earth. He awoke and vowed that "the Eternal shall be my God, and this stone which I have erected as a pillar shall be God's dwelling, and I will give thee faithfully a tenth of all that thou givest me" (Gen. 28:21-22, Moffatt). Jacob in his half conversion would give a tenth, but he wouldn't give himself. Jacob the supplanter was intact.

O God, save me from the half conversions which I undergo in lieu of the real thing. I want the real and only the real. In Jesus' name. Amen.

AFFIRMATION FOR THE DAY: *If I am content with a half conversion, I shall have to be content with being a half man.*

"THE CHEATER GOT CHEATED"

We saw that Jacob went through a half conversion, making God
his God and giving a tenth, yet it left the center intact—Jacob the
self-centered was still at the center. It begins to come out again after
the half conversion had suppressed Jacob, the supplanter, for a time.

At Paddan-aram he worked for seven years for Rachel, but on the
wedding night Laban, his father-in-law, cheated him, giving him Leah
his eldest daughter instead of Rachel. The cheater got cheated. When
you build up a false world around you by your own falseness, then
people turn false to you. You sooner or later get into the environment
suitable to your inner attitudes—you build your outer world out of
your inner. The honest man begets honesty around him. The inner
and the outer tend to coalesce.

While Jacob worked for Laban he began to scheme to get his
father-in-law's property. He worked out a plan of which it was said:
"In this way, the weaker lambs fell to Laban, the stronger to Jacob,
who grew extremely rich" (Gen. 30:42-43, Moffatt). He was still
Jacob—the man who used any methods in his own interest. In the
midst of this he was very religious: "However, the God of my fathers
has always been with me. . . . In this way God has taken the stock
from your father and given it to me" (Gen. 31:5, 9). And to himself
he was keeping up an illusion of honesty in the midst of his dis-
honesty, "In this way my honesty will tell" (Gen. 30:33, Moffatt).
Talking to himself in terms of piety and honesty while all the time
the tides of crookedness were flowing down underneath. He was a
compartmentalized soul, switching from one compartment to another
and living there as self-interest demanded.

But he got his way and his ill-gotten wealth at a price: "But he
heard Laban's sons muttering: 'Jacob has got hold of all of our father's
property.' . . . Jacob also saw that Laban's looks were not friendly as
they were before" (Gen. 31:1-2, Moffatt). He got what he wanted
—plus. The plus was the ill-will of those around him—the pay-off.
We reap what we sow—inevitably. There are no exceptions.

O God, I know I can't cheat a moral universe. It will get me in the
end. Forgive me for trying. And help me to stop trying. In Jesus'
name. Amen.

AFFIRMATION FOR THE DAY: *Burn this into my mind: If I try to cheat,
I shall cheat myself first and most.*

"HIS SINS HEDGED HIM IN"

When Jacob took advantage of his father-in-law and got hold of his property by clever tactics, he created the same situation around him in Paddan-aram as he did back home with Esau. Now as he fled from Esau, so he had to flee from his father-in-law. "Jacob outwitted Laban the Aramaean, never letting him know that he fled" (Gen. 31:20, Moffatt). He was always fixing up a false world around him, holding it together by his clever wits. But Reality always bumped into his house of cards and down it went. Laban caught up with him. And when he faced Jacob and asked the reason for the fleeing, Jacob replied, "I fled secretly because I was afraid; I thought you would take your daughters from me by force" (Gen. 31:31, Moffatt).

Jacob got his way—plus inward fear. The pay-off is within. You try to hold a false world together by clever scheming and that false world invades you in the form of fear—the pay-off is within. The pay-off is the person. God doesn't punish so much *for* sin as *by* sin. Your choices become you, and you have to live with yourself and that is inescapable.

But running away from Laban, Jacob found he was running into Esau. He created two hostile situations by his dishonest trickery and now he was caught between them. His sins hedged him in. And there was no place to flee—except into the arms of a forgiving God. But before he tried that, he tried another clever scheme to get out of impending doom. He tried appeasement. For he ran away from the fear of Laban into a bigger fear of Esau. For it was told him: "His brother Esau . . . was already on the way to meet him with four hundred men. Jacob was terrified and anxious" (Gen. 32:6-7, Moffatt). The peril of his angry father-in-law was as nothing compared to the peril of his angry brother coming with four hundred men. So he prayed: "O save me from the power of my brother, from Esau! I am afraid of him attacking me and overpowering me" (Gen. 32:11, Moffatt). He prayed to be saved from the consequences of his sins, not from his sins. He wasn't yet ripe for conversion. He was still pointing to his circumstances instead of to Jacob.

O God, if I'm still trying to point to this, that, and the other, instead of pointing to myself, forgive me. Thy arms are my only way out, I know. Amen.

AFFIRMATION FOR THE DAY: *Let me remember: In most circumstances the question is not "What is wrong?" but "Who is wrong?"*

THE MIDNIGHT WRESTLE

We saw yesterday that Jacob was getting to the place where the final crisis was being precipitated. The consequences of his sins were closing in on him. He was no longer able to dodge those consequences by his own cleverness. His armor was being hewn from him piece by piece. That night he was "terrified and anxious." He sent his wives and children across the ford of the Jabbok. "Jacob was left alone" (Gen. 32:24). He was terribly alone. Everything had dropped away, leaving nothing but himself and his sins. He was alone with the Alone. And he was out of harmony with the Alone. Like an animal trapped in a corner and the hounds closing in, he had no way out.

Except one way—the divine Initiative. "A man struggled with him till the break of day" (Gen. 32:24, Moffatt). Like the Hound of Heaven, the love of God pursued him down the years, awaiting this hour when he would acknowledge that he was beaten, that his strength had turned to weakness, that he was all in. The struggle with the divine Wrestler is a symbol of struggling with yourself and your conscience—the hour of conviction.

The divine Wrestler made as though he would leave him to his consequences: "'Let me go, for the day is breaking.' 'I will not,' said Jacob, 'unless you bless me'" (Gen. 32:16, Moffatt). He had had a blessing from his father, obtained by trickery, and that blessing was returning as a curse upon him in consequences. So now he wanted a blessing that is a blessing and not a curse in disguise. He was through with seeming, with unreality—he would wrestle till he found release from himself and the predicament into which his crooked self had gotten him.

And now the angel asked him the question that was the crux of the whole thing, "What is your name?" To us it seems a simple and innocent question, but in those days the name was the expression of the character—if the character changed, the name changed. So Jacob, with many a struggle, confessed the crucial confession, "Jacob—the supplanter," he sobbed. The depths were uncovered. Jacob was soul-naked before God. The real man was up and out. That was his most honest moment.

O God, help me to tell Thee my name, my real name. Help me to dodge no longer. The game is up. I am I. Save me from myself. Amen.

AFFIRMATION FOR THE DAY: *Complete honesty shall characterize not only the crisis, but the commonplace.*

"WHAT IS YOUR NAME?"

We left off yesterday where the angel asked Jacob the central question, "What is your name?" And Jacob brokenly blurted out, "It's Jacob—I'm the crooked supplanter of others." There he hit rock bottom.

If you have not reached that place, you will have to stop everything and say this one thing to God—your name. Perhaps you will say that your name is "Ego—I do everything for myself." "It's Fear—I am filled with fear." "It's Resentment—I am filled with it." "It's Self-Pity—for I am a self-pitying self." "It's Negative—I'm always saying No, always running away." "It's Pride—I'm steeped in it." "It's Guilt—for I'm conscious of it." "Its Hypocrisy—for I'm not real; I'm trying to be two people." "It's Conflict—for I'm a civil war."

It will be hard to get that name out—you will choke on it. But get it out, no matter the cost, for there is no new name until you say the old name. The saying of the old name is confession—a catharsis.

When Jacob said his name, the angel replied at once: "Then your name shall be Jacob no longer, . . . but Israel (Striver-with-God), for you have striven with God and men, and won" (Gen. 32:28, Moffatt). The moment he said his old name God gave him a new one, a new one to fit the new person. Jacob, the supplanter, the self-centered, became Israel, a prince with God. It was after Israel, the crooked-man-made-straight, that the new nation of Israel was named. Jacob was buried and Israel was alive forevermore.

And your name will be changed from Self-centered to God-centered; from Resentment to Good Will; from Fear to Faith; from Gloom to Gladheart; from Defeated to Victorious; from Barren to Fruitful. "As for the conqueror, . . . I will inscribe on him . . . my own new name" (Rev. 3:12, Moffatt). You'll be a new man with a new name because of a new character. "Can a man be born again when he is old?" Yes! Young, middle-aged, and old alike can be born again. The worst can become the best, the weakest can become the strongest, and the most defeated can become the most victorious. I'm not a trapped animal; I'm a free man—free to go places. Unlimited possibilities are before me.

Father: God, I'm so grateful for this possibility. I take it as my very own—take it by surrender and faith. Am I grateful? I am. Amen.

AFFIRMATION FOR THE DAY: *My character and my name changed, I'm going out to change others.*

THE RECONCILIATION

We saw yesterday that when Jacob confessed his name to the wrestling angel—confessed that he was Jacob, the supplanter—he got a new name, Israel. A new name was given for he was a new man. And the account adds, "The sun rose upon him as he passed Penuel" (Gen. 32:31, Moffatt). When we find this transformation, the sun will rise upon us. The new birth is a sunrise!

And now look at the results. When something happened within Jacob, something began to happen around Jacob. "When Jacob looked up, there was Esau coming with four hundred men!" (Gen. 33:1, Moffatt). His hour of pay-off had come! But a miracle happened. "Esau ran to meet him and embraced him, falling on his neck and kissing him, while they wept together" (Gen. 33:4, Moffatt). When Esau saw the face of Jacob, he saw he was a changed man—it was not the old Jacob. It melted his hostility and they wept in each other's arms. When something happens to us, then something happens to those around us. A changed Jacob made a changed Esau. Many of our problems in our environment are problems within us projected onto our surroundings. When we change, they change. Note: "Then said Esau, 'Let us travel together on our way; I will march in front'" (Gen. 33:12, Moffatt). The man who came with blood in his eyes was now proposing that they travel together and he would be a bodyguard to Jacob! Conversion converts us and our surroundings!

And now note again: "Jacob said to his household and all his people, 'Put away your foreign gods, wash yourself clean, . . . let us move up to Bethel, where I shall make an altar.' . . . Then they handed over to Jacob all their foreign gods, with their amulets of ear-rings; Jacob buried them below the sacred oak at Shechem" (Gen. 35:2-4, Moffatt). A moral and spiritual cleansing began around him—a revival was on! Before this personal change in Jacob, had he suggested this moral cleaning up, they would have laughed at him. They would have said, "Of all things! Jacob, the tricky, what's he up to now?" But when he was sincerely changed they listened to a man like that! Jacob sent a moral and spiritual cleansing tide through the life of a great people.

O God, as Thou didst save the people of Israel through saving this man, so save others through saving me. Change my name and change my influence. Amen.

AFFIRMATION FOR THE DAY: *When I listen to God, men will listen to me!*

"THE NOBODIES BECOME SOMEBODIES"

We have looked at the transformation of Jacob—the most formative conversion of the Old Testament, one that sent a cleansing impulse down through the life of the Jewish nation, saved it to a moral leadership, and made it the vehicle of the coming of the Son of God in redemption.

We now turn to the New Testament, which is a book primarily on conversion. Within these pages is the most astonishing account of transformations in literature. These transformations are of spirit, mind, and body—and of climate. The climate within and between groups turned battling to brotherhood, tensions to tenderness. A new and astonishing power had come into availability—the down-and-outs became the up-and-on-tops, the nobodies became the somebodies. Paul says: "Neither the immoral nor idolators nor adulterers . . . nor sodomites nor thieves . . . nor the drunken nor the abusive nor robbers will inherit the Realm of God. Some of you were once like that; but you washed yourselves clean" (I Cor. 6:9-10, Moffatt). That is redemption!

Wherever the impact of the New Testament is made on life today, the same miracles of changed lives appear. A lieutenant in the Japanese army, now a schoolteacher, told this story: "I kept insisting that the Japanese would win the war. Then came the defeat, and the nation went down. As a Shintoist I felt I should die with the nation, for Shintoism, identified with the nation, would go down when the nation went down. I was about to commit suicide as an expression of my responsibility, but something held me back and I cut off some of my fingers instead. In my despair I went to Tokyo to get a New Testament. When I came across the verse in John 15:16, 'Ye have not chosen me, but I have chosen you, and ordained you, that ye should go and bring forth fruit, and that your fruit should remain,' light dawned upon my heart. My gloom and despair were lifted. I was a changed man." Strange, but the verse he mentioned has been my life verse, given years ago—a verse which I repeat to myself and God as we bow our heads just before I speak to an audience! The New Testament impact is a redemptive impact wherever it touches life—East or West!

O God, how can I ever thank Thee enough that the routine of sin and its consequences has been met and conquered. I accept the possibility in me. Amen.

AFFIRMATION FOR THE DAY: *I am under the law of change: all my goods shall become better, all my betters shall become best.*

HALF CONVERSIONS

Before we look at the real conversions in the New Testament we must look at some half conversions. For many today undergo half conversions and expect full results, and when that doesn't happen, they feel it doesn't work. It works to the degree that you work it. The Chinese have a saying that you don't expect to put out a fire in a load of hay with a cup of water. You get out what you put in. If you give a half, you get a half result. The Spanish have a saying, "Pay the price and take what you want." Full price, full result! Look at the half givers in the New Testament. Many of them get caught in a marginal thing and they miss the center.

The magi who came from the East were converted to phenomena. "When they saw the star, they rejoiced." They were converted to the phenomena surrounding Christ—the star, a dream. They never threw themselves in with the central thing—Christ and His Kingdom. They did not return to be with Him and His movement. As far as we know, no result came from their stargazing, no movement was started by them in Persia to redeem that land. A half conversion.

Many today are converted to phenomena surrounding Christianity, the music, the architecture, the ritual, the eloquence of the preacher, the standing it gives one in a community to be a member of the church, the keeping up of mores from generation to generation—it's the thing to do—and other such phenomena surrounding the Christian movement. But there is no vital saving contact with this saving Person. It's all secondhand and marginal. It lacks luster and vitality. It's an echo instead of a voice. They have not given themselves, so no transformed self emerges. A Negro went to Alcoholics Anonymous, and when asked, "So you want to get rid of drink!" replied, "Not necessarily, I want to get rid of the thing it do." He wanted the results without providing for the cause. He wanted a half conversion with a whole result. But you must give all to get All. Half the church members are converted to phenomena and not to Christ—arrested conversions. There is a sense of halfwayness pervading the churches—a stopping this side of salvation.

O Father, I want to be converted not to things surrounding Christ, but to Christ Himself. For if I don't touch Him, I don't touch Life. Help me. Amen.

AFFIRMATION FOR THE DAY: *The whole cross is easier to carry than the half cross.*

CONVERTED TO THE CONVERTER

Yesterday we saw a type of arrested conversion. Today we look at another type of half conversion—a conversion to the converter.

John the Baptist came to convert men not to himself but to the coming Christ. He insisted that he was only a voice crying in the wilderness, "Prepare ye the way of the Lord"—"of the Lord," not of John the Baptist. And again, "He must increase, but I must decrease." In spite of this original intention, John did what many do today— they start out to lead men to Christ and end by leading men to themselves. People are converted to the converter. John built up a movement around himself. "The disciples of John fast"—"disciples of John." That movement persists to this day. In Iraq there is a survival of that revival under John the Baptist. They have a sacred book called the Ginza, have a trinity made up of the First, Second, and Third, are baptized at least once a year in a white garment, always toward the North, for the gate of heaven is in that direction, are called Sabeans or Disciples of John the Baptist. They never became Christians. I met some of the Disciples of John who are the silversmiths and the boat-builders of that land. They are completely ingrown and sterile, the obvious result of being converted to the converter.

Many today are converted to the converter, and it is so prevalent that it is accepted—"he has a great following"—as if it were a credit that people follow the converter instead of Christ. I remember how my gratitude to the man who led me to Christ made me center dangerously in him instead of Christ. Then came the emancipating word from Christ, "Are you following him or are you following Me?" From the depths I cried, "I'm following Thee." The cord was cut and I was free—free from the converter! Peter said to Jesus, in reference to John, "Lord, and what shall this man do?" And Jesus replied, "What is that to thee? Follow thou me." We must be converted to Christ and stay converted to Christ and not be bound up too much to the converter. The converter may let you down. Christ never does. You have one solid center where you can put your whole weight down—Christ. All other ground is sinking sand.

O Christ, I thank Thee that Thou art Savior—save me from the pseudo saviors. Thou art Life, save me from stopping this side of Life. Amen.

AFFIRMATION FOR THE DAY: *I shall not try to make of any halfway house a home.*

"CHRISTIANS—ALMOST"

We are looking at half conversions. Let us look at two men who were almost Christian, but never made the grade, Nicodemus and Joseph of Arimathea.

Nicodemus, because he was a Pharisee, who belonged to the Jewish authorities, came to Jesus by night lest he be seen having anything to do with this young Radical. He was drawn to Him, but with reservations, hence the cover of night. Jesus, seeing his divided soul, said straight off that he needed a new birth, to become single-minded and not herd-dominated. The herd was his god, but he was drawn to Reality in Jesus. After the interview he sank back into the herd and was submerged into the mass mind. There was a feeble fluttering to be free when once he with Joseph of Arimathea went and asked Pilate for the body of Jesus. "They took the body of Jesus, and bound it in linen cloths with the spices" (John 20:40, R.S.V.).

"Joseph of Arimathea, who was a disciple of Jesus, but secretly, for fear of the Jews" was a case of arrested conversion—the new life smothered by fear of the herd. So he suppressed the urge to follow Jesus. He became herd-centered instead of Christ-centered.

And what they both found was a dead Christ. They never got beyond the corpse and the spices. We never hear of them again. They probably sank back into the herd—with a sigh. They were Christians —almost!

Said a woman in one of our meetings, where people were telling what they wanted and needed, "In a measure I want with all my heart all the fullness of God." "In a measure"—there the subconscious was speaking. She had a dead Christ on her hands.

The fear of the herd is the greatest single thing producing arrested conversions and a dead Christianity. Said a herd-bound soul to a released soul, "Catherine, I admire your convictions, but why don't you have convictions like the rest of us?" In other words, "Why don't you be herd-centered instead of Christ-centered?" If she had, she too would have embalmed a dead Christ; as it was, she was alive with a living Christ. Are you a disciple "secretly for fear"? Surrender the fear or surrender Christ.

O Living Christ, I give Thee not a half allegiance but my whole heart— my all. For I want to follow a living Christ, not a dead one. Amen.

AFFIRMATION FOR THE DAY: *I shall be a dead follower of a dead Christ if I try to live by compromise.*

THURSDAY—Week 12   *Luke 9:59-62*

"A MAN WITH THE BRAKES ON"

We continue to look at half conversions. Here is one: "Another man also said to him, 'I will follow you, Lord. But let me first say good-bye to my people at home'" (Luke 9:61, Moffatt). "I will follow you, Lord, but . . ."—many of us follow with a "but"—a reservation. We give but we don't give up, we follow but with something else "first."

We preach for Christ, but with our ears open to listen to the compliments first. We serve, provided we receive recognition for the service. We give if we are given special credit in the giving. We go as missionaries, but we want to be dominant in a situation.

A Negro minister said, "I'm a man with the brakes on." Many of us are Christians, but Christians with the brakes on. And the brake is usually "but." Some good thing like saying "good-by" keeps us from the best—following Jesus. We are caught by conventions rather than by Christ.

Jesus said, "No one is any use to the Reign of God who puts his hand to the plough and then looks behind him" (Luke 9:62, Moffatt). The man who follows, but with a backward look, cannot fit into the Kingdom of God. For the Kingdom means an utter commitment to an ongoing movement, and has no place or use for half decisions.

It is upon the rock of halfwayness that most conversions go to pieces when they fail. We don't repudiate our faith; we reduce it to conformity with the crowd. The salt loses its savor, its distinctiveness, and for that reason is cast out and trodden under the foot of men. Men despise the people who are half-and-half, and God can't tolerate them either. "So, because you are lukewarm, neither hot nor cold, I am about to spit you out of my mouth" (Rev. 3:16, Moffatt). Lukewarm, tasteless Christians—we spit them out, figuratively speaking; we can't swallow them.

Jesus speaks of him who "relaxes a single one of these commandments"—a relaxed Christianity toned down to the common level. If there is no outer difference between you and the world, depend on it, there is no inner difference.

O Christ, give me the all-out heart. Take away from me the spirit of "Mr. Facing-both-ways." I would face toward Thee with a single allegiance. Amen.

AFFIRMATION FOR THE DAY: *If I live by half allegiances, I shall leave not a mark, but a blur.*

82

"WITH ALL WE ARE AND HAVE"

We look at another half conversion in the New Testament. A couple in the early days saw how much real prestige came to those who laid their all at the apostles' feet. They saw them change the name of Joseph, which means "one more," into Barnabas, or "son of encouragement," when he sold a farm and laid the proceeds before the apostles (Acts 4:36-37).

So Ananias and his wife Sapphira decided they would try to get the prestige without the price. They sold some property and laid only part of the purchase money at the apostles' feet. That was all right; had they not acted as though it was the whole amount. They wanted full credit from a part contribution. Peter said to Ananias, "You have not defrauded men but God" (Acts 5:4, Moffatt). And when he heard this "he fell down and expired."

God didn't directly and personally strike him dead, but the tension set up within him caused a heart attack and this caused his death. The same thing happened to his wife. The moral climate in the early church was so acute that to lie in that climate would set up such a tension as to cause physical death. Today the moral climate in the ordinary church is so relaxed and flabby that to tell a lie in that climate would scarcely cause a flutter in the heartbeat! The fact is, I've known preachers who kept on preaching while living in adultery, and one of them remarked, "I never preached better in my life." A badly sagging moral climate.

These two got nothing out of a half Christianity, nothing but tensions. And today many are getting nothing out of Christianity except tensions. They have just enough religion to set up a conflict and make them miserable. If you introduce Christianity into the life in a halfway manner, it sets up an irritation. But to introduce it fully would set up not an irritation, but an irradiation. That would mean not conflict, but conversion. A half cross is harder to bear than a whole cross. To lay all is to get All. But to lay part is not to get part—it is to get part plus a conflict. When we try to be halfway Christians, then we are not at home in the world nor in Christ. The Hindus have a saying, "Don't put one foot in one boat and the other in another boat."

O Christ, save me from half giving, for that will make me a half person. I want to be a whole person, so I give the whole. Amen.

AFFIRMATION FOR THE DAY: *All I have for all Thou hast.*

"A BETTER CASE OF DEMON POSSESSION"

We come to our last meditation on the half conversions of the New Testament. We come to an instance where a group tried to work the Christian way in a secondhand fashion: "Some strolling Jewish exorcists also undertook to pronounce the name of the Lord Jesus over those who had evil spirits, saying, 'I adjure you by the Jesus whom Paul preaches!'" (Acts 19:13, Moffatt.) "By the Jesus whom Paul preaches"—they were living and working in quotation marks, secondhand life and work.

A great many preachers preach not out of their personal, vital experience, the overflow of their own hearts, but preach in quotation marks, sometimes acknowledged and sometimes not, but it is all one step removed from reality—it is secondhand and therefore second-rate. "I adjure you by the Jesus whom Fosdick preaches," or "by Jesus whom Macartney preaches." It is out of books instead of out of the inner overflow. It lacks conviction, hence conversion. Nothing happens. The evil spirits retorted: "Jesus I know and Paul I know, but you—who are you?" (Acts 19:15, Moffatt.) The evil spirits do not come out through secondhand preaching—they sit tight; or worse, they "overpower" the ones who try to get them out. The man had a better case of demon-possession than they had of God-possession so they were baffled and defeated.

So many live on the faith of someone else—husbands on their wives' faith, children on their parents' faith, preachers on some other preacher's faith or on a seminary professor's or on some author's. It is a muddy pool, or at best a cistern, and not a flowing fountain within. Hence on Monday there is exhaustion, a "Blue Monday" ensues. Why anyone should have a blue, exhausted Monday from preaching the gospel on Sunday is beyond my comprehension. It should exhilarate instead of exhaust. Does this nearby spring flowing from the hillside at the rate of ten gallons a minute take a day off from exhaustion? It is attached to infinite resources, and it is its nature to flow. So we, when we are attached in a firsthand way to the infinite resources of God.

Father, save me from the futility of the secondhand. Help me to have an exhaustless fountain within. Then I shall be no broken cistern, but a well of water springing up to everlasting life. Amen.

AFFIRMATION FOR THE DAY: *I'm out to be, not a secondhander, but a firsthander.*

A VERY REAL CONVERSION

We have been looking at the half conversions in the New Testament; we must now look at some real conversions. If the half converted brought paralysis to themselves and their surroundings, the real converted brought power to themselves and their surroundings. They become the focal point of individual and collective rise. They represent spiritually and morally what Lloyd Morgan describes as "emergent evolution," a radical departure from existent forms and a rapid climb to a new level of life.

Take Zacchaeus, "the head of the taxgatherers, a wealthy man" (Luke 19:1-10, Moffatt). He had the two things that men desire most: position—"the head of the taxgatherers"; and money—"a wealthy man." Someone has said: "O Money, Money, Money—he that hath thee hath health and life. He can rattle his pockets at the devil." And if you add position to money, then you can not only rattle your pockets at the devil—you can rattle them at the herd around you; you are secure, so many think.

But a disturbing thing had happened—a Man was moving in their midst, One who cared for neither wealth nor position; in fact, He was calling on men to renounce both and follow Him. This was disturbing. It bumped with a thud straight against everything men had built up as the ends of life. So Zacchaeus "tried to see what Jesus was like." He thought perhaps he would see a wild-eyed fanatic, for anyone who could sit so lightly to position and wealth must be queer.

Life often comes to a crisis for us out of small happenings: Jesus was entering Jericho and passing through and Zacchaeus thought he'd like to see what he was like—both of them surface incidents fraught with deep significance. Life is like that—a word, an incident, a memory, a face, and a spiritual crisis is upon us. That apparently chance happening brought us face to face with Reality. A personnel director of a large firm thumbed through *Abundant Living* with no intention of reading it, saw the word "cigarette," was intrigued by it, read the book, was converted, and today is on fire.

O Christ, I meet Thee in every chance happening and the commonplace becomes a crisis. Let me look for Thee today. In Thy name. Amen.

AFFIRMATION FOR THE DAY: *Each little incident becomes big with destiny when it leads me to Him.*

SOCIETY DEMANDS CONFORMITY

We are studying the transformation of Zacchaeus. An apparently chance happening—the passing of Jesus through the town and the curiosity of Zacchaeus—precipitated a crisis that changed Zacchaeus forever.

As in many cases a handicap proved an asset—he was short of stature and that made him climb a tree. That climbing of a tree brought him face to face with Jesus—and with destiny. Our handicaps can drive us back into inferiorities and self-pity and self-consciousness, or they can drive us to God and the getting of greater resources for living. Paul had a thorn in the flesh and that drove him to draw on grace more than if he had been normal, and made him say, "I will all the more gladly boast of my weaknesses, . . . for when I am weak, then I am strong" (II Cor. 12:9-10, R.S.V.). His impediments were made into instruments.

Zacchaeus could not see Jesus "on account of the crowd." The herd instinct keeps a lot of people from seeing Jesus, especially young people. They are mortally afraid of getting out of step, of doing and being different. Society demands conformity. If you fall below its standards, it will punish you; if you rise above its standards, it will persecute you—it demands a gray, average morality. So a great many look around before they act. They don't really act; they only react. They are not voices, they are echoes; not persons, but things. The first step away from the crowd is often the first step to God. So Peter said, "Save yourself from this crooked generation" (Acts 2:40, R.S.V.), save yourself from the dominance of a crooked herd. "Everybody does it" is becoming everybody's code. The first step toward salvation is breaking step with a society that is going downhill fast. At that moment you begin to become a person. You are no longer saying "Ditto," you are beginning to say "I choose." But you do not break with the crowd just to be different, you break with it hoping that by your break you can meet with it on a higher level. The lower break is in order to a higher fellowship. Step out of the crowd and you step into the arms of God.

O Father, I would be free to come to Thee. Help me then to throw off the herd dominance and take Thy yoke. Then I shall be free. Amen.

AFFIRMATION FOR THE DAY: *I can be self-centered, or herd-centered, or Christ-centered. I choose to be Christ-centered.*

FROM GREED TO GOD

We are looking at the transformation of a greedy, grasping taxgatherer into a Christian. Zacchaeus "ran forward"—not a very dignified procedure for a wealthy head of the taxgatherers. But the eagerness of his soul got into his feet. It was more undignified to be climbing a tree, but the process of conversion is the process of becoming a child again and tree climbing is a childhood propensity. He was taking the first steps away from the artificialities and complexities of evil to the simplicities of the good.

"For he was to pass that way." Zacchaeus put himself in the way of being found. You do not have to find God, for He is seeking you. You have to put yourself in the way of being found by God. When I have said that to a non-Christian audience in India—"He is seeking us"—I have watched the look of incredulity come into their faces— God seeking man! For with India, men go through incredible austerities—holding the arm up till it withers, sitting on spiked beds, measuring their length on the ground, say fifty miles, to get to the temple to ring the bell to call the attention of the god to them—all this to attain to a darshan, or audience with God. And here in the gospel God seeks us! It is incredible!

If you put yourself on the road of repentance and faith and acceptance of the gift of God and obedience, then you will find Jesus, for now, as then, he is "to pass that way." The moment you put yourself on the way of repentance and faith you are on the Way, for the way of repentance and faith intersects and runs into the Way. I say repentance *and* faith, for many people walk the road of repentance for years and never reach the Way. They live in a state of guilt, wear hair shirts constantly, always lashing themselves over past sins, and never go on and accept the gift of forgiveness and release. They are ever learning and never come into the knowledge of the truth of forgiveness and transformation. They try to present their own blood from their bleeding backs instead of accepting the blood from the wounded side of Christ—a gift of God. They don't get to the Way.

O Christ, Thou art the Way. Help me to take ways that lead inevitably to the Way. For the Way is the only way for me to live. Help me take it. Amen.

AFFIRMATION FOR THE DAY: *I shall wear not my hair shirts, but Thy robe of righteousness.*

"I PUT MY WHOLE WEIGHT DOWN"

We left off yesterday at the place where Zacchaeus put himself in the way of being found—the way that Jesus was to pass. Applied, we said this way is the way of repentance and faith. "And faith." A little girl did something wrong and asked her mother for forgiveness, which was gladly and readily given. But after an interval the little girl came to her mother again and anxiously said, "Mother, are you sure you forgive me?" She was assured that the sin was forgiven and forgotten. Four times the little girl came and each time was reassured. The last time she took it as final. But the first was final! A minister who had worn within his heart the guilt of unfaithfulness, and could never get release from it, heard that story and saw in it a picture of himself and gave up his continual asking for reassurance and took the gift of God. His transformed face expressed his transformed soul—transformed by acceptance.

The account says that "when Jesus came to the place, he looked up and said to him" (Luke 19:5, R.S.V.)—Jesus picked him out of the crowd and spoke to *him.* He was no longer a mere member of a mob, he began to be a person—the most important member of that crowd was paying attention to him, a redemptive attention, but it was attention nevertheless. Conversion is the beginning of being a person. You are no longer a bundle of conflicts, tied in knots—you're a person, a person with whom you can live, and a person who knows where he is going and has power to move on to his goal.

One would have thought that to be an outstanding businessman, perhaps *the* outstanding businessman, of a large city would give one a sense of being able to put one's weight down. But listen to what such a businessman said after he had accepted Christ as his personal savior: "For the first time in my life I really stood on my feet. I put my whole weight down, feeling I was a person and that the universe was back of me." It's an epoch in personality when Jesus looks you in the eye and calls your name. You know you are now a person looking at the Person. You can never despise yourself again for He respects you.

O Christ, when Thou dost look in my eyes, then my eyes are nevermore downcast, looking at the dust. My eyes see Thee, and in seeing Thee I find myself. Amen.

AFFIRMATION FOR THE DAY: *My whole weight is down, my heart relaxed and released.*

NOT "IS" BUT WAS!

We saw yesterday that in the awakening of the personality of Zacchaeus Jesus "looked up and said to him"—to *him*, now no longer a cipher, but a person; he was on speaking terms with the Divine! And more than that, Jesus called him by name, "Zacchaeus, . . . come down." It is one thing to have Someone single you out as a person, but it is another thing for Him to call you by name! How did Jesus know his name? Did Matthew the former taxgatherer whisper to Him in the crowd that the head of the taxgatherers was up a tree? At any rate, the most important person in the country was calling him by name. Something awoke within Zacchaeus. And he must have gasped, for what was Jesus saying? That He "must abide" at his house today! To have Him look at him, to call him by name, and then to say that He must stay with him—well, that was plus on plus. It was overwhelming. So Zacchaeus "came down, and received him joyfully." And we might add, "and received him gladly and fully." For such a complete self-giving to Zacchaeus produced a complete self-giving on the part of Zacchaeus. Like produced like.

But this redemptive mutual self-giving produced a reaction in the crowd: "And when they saw it, they all murmured, saying, 'That he was gone to be a guest with a man that is a sinner'" (Luke 19:7). From their standpoint they were right, for they had been brought up in the tradition that evil was to be corrected by aloofness and a frown, and here Jesus had smashed through their aloofness and frowning and was showering attention and love on a man notoriously unworthy. The distinctions between good and evil, right and wrong, were breaking down. They were dismayed and alarmed. The whole legal and moral system was crumbling.

But they were wrong at one place—the tenses of a verb—"he was gone to be guest with a man that is a sinner"—not "is" but *was!* Zacchaeus may have been a sinner when he went up that tree, but he wasn't one when he came down. For when he dropped from a limb, his feet landed squarely on the Way! With legalism, once "is," always is; but with the gospel the "is" turns to "was." Transformation transforms tenses too.

O Father, I thank Thee that Thou art changing my tenses. All my evils are becoming past and all my good becoming present. I thank Thee. Amen.

AFFIRMATION FOR THE DAY: *I belong no longer to my past, but to Thy present and Thy future.*

RESTITUTION, THE BY-PRODUCT OF RESTORATION

We saw that the crowd got their tenses mixed—Zacchaeus was a sinner, he is not now a sinner. Something stood between him and that past and that something was a Someone. Jesus interjected Himself between the shady past of Zacchaeus and an opening future. He laid one hand of forgiveness upon the past and the other hand upon the latchstring of a new beginning.

But while he knew he was forgiven, he also knew that he must do his part in righting that past as far as possible. "And Zacchaeus stood and said to the Lord, 'Behold, Lord, the half of my goods I give to the poor; and if I have defrauded any one of anything, I restore it fourfold'" (Luke 19:8, R.S.V.). "Zacchaeus stood"—that simple statement is revealing. He felt the rising dignity of a dawning manhood, sure of itself because sure of God and a new sense of adjustment to himself and the universe.

William James puts it thus, "An unseen order, and that our supreme good lies in harmoniously adjusting ourselves thereto." That adjustment to the supreme order puts confidence in us, for we know now we are backed by Reality. We are afraid of nothing.

Zacchaeus was so sure of the new security that had come to him that he didn't hesitate to let the old securities go. They were now irrelevant in the light of what had happened to him. "The half of my goods I give to the poor"—that was no legal bargaining; it was the outburst of a grateful heart. "In the light of what has been freely given to me I freely give to others." Like had begun to produce like—the generosity of Jesus began to produce the generosity of Zacchaeus. This is the new morality: making people good by being good to them. The water of forgiveness and love which Jesus was giving to Zacchaeus was becoming in him a well of generosity springing up into everlasting life. Instead of going the second mile, Zacchaeus was willing to go four miles—"If I have defrauded any one of anything, I restore it fourfold." Restitution was a by-product of restoration, the overflow of a grateful heart.

O Christ, Thou dost break down the barriers of my selfishness by breaking me down. Thou art giving all, and I must give all. Take it. Amen.

AFFIRMATION FOR THE DAY: *My restitutions shall come not from the lash of duty, but from the love of Christ.*

"THEY STOOD ALONE"

We ended yesterday on Zacchaeus' spontaneous restitution. A hotel-keeper called me up and said: "Thank you so much for the mission. A woman just came in with an armful of hotel towels." As her soul was being cleaned, she could not have dirty—dirty because stolen—towels around. After I was converted, I sent money back to pay for stolen pigeons. The white dove of peace had settled in my heart and I could not bear having greasy pigeons around.

Henry Drummond tells of a man who led a woman astray, but was afterward converted and became a prominent preacher. For twenty years he preached through England and Scotland, hoping she might hear him and be saved. At the close of a meeting a woman walked up to him with bent head, weeping. They stood alone. That was the woman for whom he had searched in the restitution of twenty years.

Then came the outer assurance fitting the growing assurance within, "Today salvation has come to this house." The greatest moment in a person's life, barring none, is the moment when he hears the words "Today salvation has come." This is *It*.

And then upon this foundation of solid assurance of salvation Jesus put the superstructure, "Since Zacchaeus here is a son of Abraham" (Luke 19:9, Moffatt). As a taxgatherer he was an outcast from respectable society. And now Jesus restores him to respectability—puts him back into the stream of decency and respectable society. I introduced Starr Daily, a man who spent twenty years in jail and in the underworld, a hardened criminal, to the chamber of commerce of his own city, as "the city's most distinguished citizen." He was. For when he met Christ in solitary confinement, he began to go up and up and up. After he was so completely changed in his cell, some keepers, seeing the change, offered to bring him food from the officers' table. He refused, "It would not be honest." A man whose life was given to crime becomes suddenly and permanently honest.

Tradition says that Zacchaeus used to go periodically and water the tree in which he found his Lord. No wonder!

O Christ, Thou dost restore me to righteousness and to respectability. I can't despise myself, for Thou dost honor me. I thank Thee. Amen.

AFFIRMATION FOR THE DAY: *My superiority that comes from my God-consciousness dissolves my inferiority that comes from my self-consciousness.*

"CONVERSION TAKES PLACE IN THE WHOLE MAN"

We study this week the transformation of the greatest Christian of the centuries—Paul. No other man, save Jesus of Nazareth, has left such an impress upon the ages. What happened to him?

Men have tried to explain him by explaining him away. "He was an epileptic visionary." And yet that "epileptic visionary" has brought more sanity and wholeness to more people than any man that ever lived, save only his Master. Was he off the track when he has pointed more men to the Way than any other man? It would be an effect out of harmony with its cause.

It reminds me of what G. A. Studdert-Kennedy says about Jesus: "You may rail at . . . Him as being inhuman and insane, and then His splendid wholesome sanity . . . will stand up and ask you questions. He was a mad fanatic who played with children. . . . He was a ridiculous visionary with His eyes fixed on Heaven who was always telling men that their first duty was to love one another and do good in this world. He was a megalomaniac madman who was always talking about Himself as King of Heaven, and always thinking about other people, and living the simplest and humblest life of kindly service. He made Himself equal with God, and forgave the men that spit on His face. . . . He was impossible, and infinitely appealing."

This description in lesser degree fits Paul. Could such a pure stream of influence as came from Paul come from any source save from a divine source? He who has converted millions to reality, was his conversion unreal? No, the stamp of authenticity is upon the life and letters of this man. His conversion still converts. His transformation is the most transforming thing in human history.

A priest said to a college girl who had undergone a real conversion, "You are going to hell." "Well," said the girl, "if this is going to hell, I like it." If Paul was insane, then I like his type of insanity! He has produced more sane sanity than any other man. Such a pure stream could not come from a muddled source.

O Christ of the Damascus Road, meet with me and transform me from darkness to light, from hate to love. In Thy name. Amen.

AFFIRMATION FOR THE DAY: *Hallucinations cannot hallow, nor can illusions illuminate.*

EXTERNALIZING OUR CONFLICTS

The beginnings of Paul's conversion are in a man, Stephen, who with the face of an angel prayed for his enemies amid a shower of stones. As they laid their garments at the feet of a young man named Saul something happened—that face, that prayer! Both haunted him night and day. They produced a terrible conflict within him.

He externalized that conflict. Angry with himself, he became angry with others. "Meanwhile Saul still breathed threats of murder against the disciples of the Lord" (Acts 9:1, Moffatt). This is what James A. Hadfield in *Psychology and Morals* calls "projection": "Repressed complexes which we refuse to recognize tend to attach themselves to persons and objects of the outside world. Thus, we condemn in others what we refuse to admit in ourselves. This is the principle of the objectification or projection of our complexes. The principle may be stated thus: *'Our relation to the outside world is determined by our relation to our own complexes.'"* The challenging thing Paul had seen in the face of Stephen produced a conflict within himself, and he projected that conflict on the Christians—he made war on them to compensate for the war within himself. If you are fighting with others, search to see if that fight isn't a conflict within yourself externalized.

But since Paul was a man who believed in being legal in all his actions, "he went to the high priest and asked him for letters to the synagogues at Damascus empowering him to put any man or woman in chains whom he could find belonging to the Way, and bring them to Jerusalem" (Acts 9:2, Moffatt). He would make legal (letters) and religious (from the high priest) his projected conflicts so he could live with himself in the process. So here were three ways conflicting with the Way: the way of legal sanction, the way of religion, the way of personal revenge—all in conflict with the Way. And these ways broke themselves upon the Way. And in the conflict the one who got hurt most was the man who embodied the way of projected anger— Paul. The end of the road for him was stunned blindness.

O Christ, our ways break themselves upon Thee—the Way. We get hurt, and in getting hurt, hurt Thee. For Thou art hurt in all our hurts. Forgive us. Amen.

AFFIRMATION FOR THE DAY: *I cannot be in conflict with the Way without losing my way.*

A PHYSICAL SYMPTOM OF A SPIRITUAL MALADY

This conflict within Paul became more and more intense, and he became more and more fierce in transferring his inner conflict upon his supposed enemies, the Christians. He directed his bitterness upon the Christians for it was the face and prayer of a Christian, Stephen, who began this conflict within him.

"As he neared Damascus in the course of his journey" the crisis came. He had extended his line too far—clear to Damascus. He could be more sure of himself and his position in Jerusalem, surrounded by the symbols and monuments of his ancient faith; but as he got farther from home, he got farther from certainty. The facts closed in on him. He saw he was fighting a losing battle. Then he kicked more fiercely "against the goads." At that moment, his zero hour, Jesus, like the Hound of Heaven pursuing him down the labyrinth of the years, seeing the moment had arrived, flashed on him with a blinding light. Paul lay prone. He who had laid low many was himself laid low. The universe had kicked back.

A voice, "Saul, Saul, why do you persecute me?" And the reply, "Who are you, Lord?" then the answer: "I am Jesus, whom you are persecuting" (Acts 9:4-5, R.S.V.). Saul began to see the stinging, stunning truth; he couldn't see without seeing Jesus in the face of His disciple; he couldn't persecute without persecuting Jesus. He was enveloped by Jesus! The Hound of Heaven had closed in on him and he saw no way out. He was trapped.

This produced such a conflict of values that he was blinded, not primarily by the brilliant light but by the awful inner darkness. Were Jesus and the Christians right, and was he all wrong? He was confused. The moral and spiritual confusion transferred itself to his eyes. He was unable to see spiritually, so he became unable to see physically. Here was a transference of a spiritual fact to a physical fact. He showed a physical symptom as a sign of a spiritual malady. Psychology calls this "conversion," but it is a conversion downward—you become physically ill to compensate for a spiritual illness.

O Christ, I come to Thee, blinded by my follies and groping for the Way. Give me sense not to kick against the goads. Amen.

AFFIRMATION FOR THE DAY: *I see when I walk by Thy light. I am blind if I walk by any other.*

"SHARP DISSENSION IN MY BREAST"

We saw yesterday that Paul was outwardly blinded for he was spiritually blinded. He transferred his spiritual symptom to physical counterpart. I know of a young man who put complete faith in his spiritual teacher, and when that teacher proved less than he thought he was, his eyes became affected. He put on seven different kinds of glasses, but none of them helped him. It was pointed out to him that he was confused in his eyesight because he was confused in his inner spiritual seeing, since the preceptor had failed him. When he lifted his eyes to Christ, and remade his life around Christ instead of the preceptor, his eyesight returned to normalcy.

An arm became paralyzed when a young woman subconsciously wanted to strike her mother because of resentments. When the resentments were faced and given up, the arm became normal again.

"For three days he remained sightless, and he neither ate nor drank" (Acts 9:9, Moffatt). As he was unable spiritually to assimilate this new experience to the old, so physically he was unable to assimilate the light—he could not see, nor could he assimilate food, "he neither ate nor drank." Every spiritual state registers itself in the body. Sooner or later you have a body which is made in the likeness of the soul that inhabits it. If your spirit is ulcerated, then your body is going to be ulcerated. If your soul is rhythmical and harmonious, then the body, all other things being equal, will be rhythmical and harmonious.

Shakespeare says:

> I feel such sharp dissension in my breast,
> Such fierce alarms, both of hope and fear,
> As I am sick with working of my thoughts.

Paul had such sharp dissension in his breast, such fierce alarms, both of hope and fear, that he was sick, very sick with the working of his thoughts. Soul and body he was beaten. He was in "the dark night of the soul," and it was very dark. Everything he had lived for had suddenly become meaningless and empty. His world had gone to pieces.

O God, Thou dost put me low to raise me high. Thou dost smite me to heal me. My dark is just before Thy dawn. Amen.

AFFIRMATION FOR THE DAY: *I make myself sick with my discords; I make myself well by Thy concords.*

"CALLED TO DO THE IMPOSSIBLE"

Yesterday we saw Paul at his lowest ebb. He was on the rocks. Then Grace began the rescue and the restoration. But Grace that seemed so sovereign in the smiting on the road now worked through human agency. The balance had to be restored, lest Paul think it all God and no man. It must be shown to be God and man working redemptively. "Now there was a disciple at Damascus named Ananias. The Lord said to him in a vision, 'Ananias.' And he said, 'Here I am, Lord'" (Acts 9:10, R.S.V.). He put himself at God's disposal in a crisis: "Here I am, Lord." And when he did so, he did the greatest thing in the New Testament, outside of the doings of Jesus. He did one thing and passed off the stage, but that one thing was the most creative thing in human history—he started the greatest Christian of the ages on his astonishing career.

One morning at the Sat Tal Ashram, as we sat on the prayer knoll, the Inner Voice said: "If you'll say one thing in every situation, 'Here I am, Lord,' then I'll take care of the rest. You need worry about nothing." I replied, "I close the bargain." Life was simplified: I had only to do one thing: put myself at God's disposal and He would take care of the rest.

When someone asked Frank Laubach how he accomplished all he did, he replied: "I don't do anything. I just throw open the windows." He let God do things through him. That is the secret: you're not the source, you're the channel.

But when Ananias saw what was involved in putting himself at God's disposal he turned pale, for He was saying, "Rise and go to the street called Straight, and inquire . . . for a man of Tarsus named Saul; for behold, he is praying" (Acts 9:11, R.S.V.). But Ananias objected, saying he couldn't, for he knew the man and what he was after—he had come to murder them. To go to lay hands of healing on a man who had come to lay hands of destruction on him—well, that was asking the impossible! But Christians are called on to do the impossible, with incredible weapons—the weapons of forgiving, healing love. Suppose Ananias had pulled back and refused; history would have been different. Everything depends on our daring obedience.

O Christ, put Thy hand on me today and send me to do the impossible—impossible, except as Thou dost work through me. Amen.

AFFIRMATION FOR THE DAY: *I can do the incredible because of Thy offer of incredible power.*

"THE AUTHENTIC SIGN OF A CHRISTIAN"

We saw yesterday the hesitation of Ananias when called on to go to the persecutor Saul. "But the Lord said to him, 'Go.' . . . So Ananias departed and entered the house" (Acts 9:15, 17, R.S.V.), probably with fear and trembling. But he "trembled bravely." And then he did one of the most Christian things that has ever been done: "And laying his hands on him he said, 'Brother Saul.'"

When the stricken Saul felt those hands so tenderly laid upon his head and those amazing words, "Brother Saul," he must have shaken with sobs: "My God, what kind of people are these? They're calling me 'brother'—I who came to murder them—they're calling me brother.'" The forgiveness of injuries, the loving of enemies, is the chief characteristic of real Christianity. It is the sign of a Christian.

That simple Christian act opened the gates of life to Paul. Until that moment he saw no way out of his dilemma. He was wrong—dead wrong—and had run into a road with a dead end. For three days he was dead-locked. Then Ananias, when he welcomed Paul into the brotherhood of Christians by the use of the words "Brother Saul," let Paul see through human forgiveness the possibility of Divine forgiveness. From this human forgiveness he stepped up into the Divine forgiveness. He saw the heart of God through the heart of a man. And as he accepted that forgiveness, "immediately something like scales fell from his eyes." Here conversion took place.

I do not believe that Paul was converted on the Damascus road. Stunned and blinded, yes, but not converted. Conversion took place only when he saw forgiveness through a forgiving Christian. Ananias fulfilled that word: "God was in Christ, reconciling the world unto himself, . . . and hath committed unto us the word of reconciliation" (II Cor. 5:19)—for the word of reconciliation became flesh in Ananias. A group of Burmese Christians came to India, and one of them called "The Buffalo," because of his strength, was spat upon by an outcaste Telugu after a meeting. "The Buffalo" quietly took out his handkerchief, wiped his face, and said, "Thank you, Brother." He and Ananias were brothers of the same Spirit. And that Spirit marches on triumphantly through the ages.

O Christ, help me this day to forgive all injuries, overcome all evil with good, all hate by love. In Thy name. Amen.

AFFIRMATION FOR THE DAY: *I shall not allow any man to put his weapons of hate into my hands. I shall keep my own weapon of love.*

"SPIRITUAL FECUNDITY"

We saw yesterday that the moment Paul accepted the forgiveness of God as the way out of his moral dilemma, "immediately something like scales fell from his eyes and he regained his sight. Then he rose and was baptized, and took food and was strengthened" (Acts 9:18-19, R.S.V.).

The moment his inner chaos and confusion and guilt were banished through forgiveness, that moment the body began to function normally again, his sight came back and his appetite returned—he "took food and was strengthened." The conflicts in the soul throw conflicts into the body, and when the conflicts are resolved, the body immediately reflects the adjustment and tends to become adjusted. "I have only one objection against Christianity," said a radiant Christian, "and that is that it makes everything digest and makes you fat!" The remedy of course was to eat less! For everything you eat is now digested! Cure a sour disposition and you'll cure a sour stomach. Someone has said, "If a man has ulcers of the stomach, don't ask, 'What's he eating?' but rather, 'What's eating him?'"

I know of a man who was an alcoholic. When Alcoholics Anonymous helped him to a changed life, he put up a house and called it, "The house that A.A. built." But more: his physical life was so changed that his wife had a baby after twenty-four years of married life. He might have called the baby, "The baby that A.A. brought."

But Paul's own life was not only changed, he became life-changing. "When many days had passed, the Jews plotted to kill him, . . . but his disciples took him by night and let him down over the wall, lowering him in a basket" (Acts 9: 23, 25, R.S.V.). Note: "Many days . . . his disciples" —in a matter of "days" after his own conversion he had "disciples"! This is spiritual fecundity! He tasted grace and at once began to share it. He was so evangelical that he became evangelistic. Freely had he received, so freely did he give. Across that uncertain world he went with a message of glowing certainty, and believing hearts caught fire. He was living and life-giving.

O Christ, I thank Thee that a blazing heart sets others afire. Set my heart afire with Thy love so I can kindle others. Amen.

AFFIRMATION FOR THE DAY: *"The first man Adam became a living being; the last Adam became a life-giving spirit"* (I Cor. 15:45, R.S.V.). *I belong to the last Adam.*

"FAITH THROUGH FINGER TIPS"

We look this week at a man who was transformed from doubt to amazing achievement—Thomas. An unfair label has been put on him and we still call a man "a doubting Thomas." We pick out a bad patch in Thomas' life and label the whole of his life from that bad patch. Never did a label less fit a man than the label of "doubting Thomas." In reality he was the believing Thomas and the achieving Thomas, as we shall see.

He must have been a man of independent judgment for he is called "the Twin," and apparently the twin brother did not become a disciple. He must have developed an early independence of judgment that made it possible for him to break with his twin brother and become a follower of Jesus. I know twin sisters, brought up in identical surroundings and subject to identical environmental influences clear through life, and yet one is five years younger than the other, for she faces life with laughter and a smile, while the other is querulous and afraid. The two philosophies of life have made them different in appearance, though they started out as identical twins.

The independence of judgment which it took to make Thomas break with his twin brother and become a follower of Christ made him independent after he became a member of the inner group. He would not be swept off his feet by mass psychology. "When the rest of the disciples told him, 'We have seen the Lord,' he said, 'Unless I see his hands with the mark of the nails, and put my finger where the nails were, and put my hand into his side, I refuse to believe it" (John 20:24-25, Moffatt). He was the forerunner of the modern scientific attitude—faith through finger tips or not at all. He revealed the scientific attitude and climate of today—the spiritual must be seen in and through the material or not at all. It is not an anti-Christian attitude, for the Christian faith is founded on an Incarnation—the Word became flesh. So the flesh now becomes Word, and one can find faith in and through the material.

O Christ, I thank Thee that Thou dost not despise my wanting material corroboration, for Thy field is the material, too. I thank thee. Amen.

AFFIRMATION FOR THE DAY: *Today I shall see Thy blood upon the rose, the glory of Thy eyes even in the stars, Thy Calvary on every hilltop, and an Easter morning in every open cavern.*

"ACCORDING TO THE NATURE OF THINGS"

We saw yesterday that Thomas was the precursor of the whole scientific attitude of today—faith, not apart from the material, but through the material or not at all.

Jesus did not reject this attitude. He invited it: "Look at my hands, put your finger here; and put your hand here into my side; be no more unbelieving but believe" (John 20:29, Moffatt). The Christian faith is solidly at home in the material. It is the only faith that takes the material seriously. It starts by saying that God created the earth and saw it was good. The material is God-created and God-approved. The center of that faith is an Incarnation, where the Word became flesh. "Lo, I come . . . to do thy will." "A body hast thou prepared me." The will of God was to be done in and through the body. The Christian faith then is thoroughly at home in the scientific climate. It is the only faith that is not dissolved by the acids of the scientific attitude. The more science has grown, the more the Christian faith, rightly conceived, has grown. It is no mere chance that Robert A. Millikan, a great physical scientist, could say, "Of all my acquaintances in the scientific world, I know none who are atheists; almost all of them are convinced Christians."

The discovery of the laws of being, underlying nature and human nature, is revealing the fact that these laws are the same laws written in the teaching of Jesus. When Jesus finished the Sermon on the Mount, the people were astonished at His teaching, for He taught them as "one having authority" (literally, "according to the nature of things"). He was teaching something not imposed on life, but exposed from the very heart of life. So His teaching was supernatural naturalism—it was the revealing of supernatural laws embedded in the natural. The Christian faith is therefore not an attempt to escape the natural order, or to work above it or in spite of it —it is an attempt to work in and through the natural and to redeem it and make it the medium of revelation. Faith through finger tips is an integral part of the Christian faith.

O Christ, I thank Thee that Thy Way is the way that is written unto the nature of things. Thou dost hold all things together, including the material, and the material especially. Amen.

AFFIRMATION FOR THE DAY: *The Kingdom of God is written in texts of Scripture and also into the texture of my being.*

"A CHRISTIAN PULSE BEAT"

We meditated yesterday upon the possibility of faith through finger tips. The more this age puts its finger on the pulse of nature, including human nature, the more it is being driven to the conclusion that the pulse beat that is in human nature is a Christian pulse beat. A Christian Heart beats at the center of things.

For instance, the *Reader's Digest* had an article "Science Discovers Love." When Jesus says that the supreme thing in life is to love God and man, human relationships say the same thing. You would expect them to say that the Second Commandment—"Thou shalt love thy neighbor as thyself"—is obviously right; but the first—"Thou shalt love the Lord thy God"—is not so obvious. But it is becoming increasingly obvious, for one of the first things in life is to break the tyranny of self-preoccupation; for a self preoccupied with itself is an unhappy, disrupted self. And there are no exceptions, even if it is a religious preoccupation. Something must lift you out of yourself and make you love something beyond yourself. Only love to God can do that. That is as necessary for human nature as breathing. If you don't love something beyond yourself supremely, you will be suffocated by yourself. Then unless you give love to your neighbor, you can't get along with yourself or your neighbor. Delinquent children come out of broken homes, 95 per cent of them, where they feel unloved and insecure. Babies have to be taken up and fondled and loved or they will be fretful and develop sickness—homesick for love.

The psychologists who love God and people are integrated and happy people; but the psychologists who are fundamentally pagan are on the whole disrupted and queer. They get caught in the meshes of a method and don't get to the message of the Man! There is no new center of attachment—nothing eternal to tie to. In spite of all learning, you have to love God and man or you cannot get along with yourself or anybody else. Science is gaining faith through its finger tips. Life works in one way—God's way, or not at all.

O my Father, I see Thee in the stars and in the stones and in my stomach. Thy laws are written there. I cannot escape them. Amen.

AFFIRMATION FOR THE DAY: *The law of love is as inexorable and as inescapable as the law of gravitation.*

"FAITH HAS COSMIC BACKING"

Thomas wanted a physical corroboration of his faith, and he got it. The physical is just as eloquent with God as the spiritual. And Thomas, getting his faith through the material, went even further in that faith than those who did not demand a physical corroboration, for he cried, "My Lord and my God!"

Up to this time no one had called Jesus "God." They called Him "Messiah," "Son of God," "Son of the living God," but not "God." Here the unbeliever leaped beyond the believers and became the mightiest believer of them all. Is this symbolic of what is happening today? Are those who are being compelled to get their faith through their finger tips, through the touch upon the material facts, going beyond those who merely believe in the spiritual and cry down the material? Are they gaining a larger and more assured faith because corroborated by a wider range of facts?

I can only testify. From the moment I looked into the face of Jesus Christ I've always had a living faith, but that faith has been immensely strengthened and deepened and widened as I began to see that the judgments of life and the judgments of Christ are turning out to be the same. I believed in the texts of Scripture, but my eyes opened in glad astonishment to find those same texts written into the texture of things, written in my nerves, blood, cells, tissues, and in the total organization of life. My faith has cosmic backing. It is not a wedge driven into the nature of things—it's the whole shooting match, it's Life itself.

And when I see the print of the nails not merely in His side, but in my insides, then I do exactly what Thomas did—I bend my knees instinctively and cry, "My Lord and my God!" If He isn't God, who is He? Can anyone less than God open blind eyes, still the waves, raise the dead, forgive sins, and reveal a Kingdom whose laws are the laws of my being and the laws written in the constitution of things? Here either infinite Goodness and Wisdom speaks or infinite blasphemy! I choose the first.

O Christ, the facts drive me to Thy feet. Thou art inescapable. Nor do I want to escape Thee, for to escape from Thee is to escape from—salvation. Amen.

AFFIRMATION FOR THE DAY: *If I try to run away from the laws of God in the Bible, I run into them in myself. I shall obey both—and live!*

"REAL SCIENCE BRINGS FAITH"

We concluded yesterday that the facts are driving us to Christ. Faith through the finger tips is producing a greater conception of and allegiance to this living Christ, who lives everywhere, including the material processes. We are on the verge of a great era of faith, and that era will be brought in by deeper and deeper explorations into the material. "Raise the stone, and thou shalt find me; cleave the wood and there am I." And yes, "Look into the constitution of your being and you will find my laws written there."

I am not afraid of science being too scientific; I'm afraid it won't be scientific enough. Half-baked science brings doubt; real science brings faith.

And this faith of Thomas did not stop at faith—it issued in mighty achievement. For if Thomas believed beyond the rest, he also went beyond the rest. Under this mighty impact that Jesus was God he found himself being driven by a mighty impulse to share this with everybody, everywhere. He went clear to India, founded a great church there, died a martyr, and is buried on St. Thomas' Mount near Madras. This is tradition, but it is well-authenticated tradition. There are copperplate inscriptions dating back to the third century giving the Syrian Christians, or St. Thomas Christians, certain rights accorded only to high-caste Hindus by the maharaja of Travancore—the right to have a red carpet put out for their bishops, to carry umbrellas, and to have two plantain leaves for their plates. There are now a million Syrian Christians on the Malabar Coast—400,000 Jacobites, 400,000 have gone over to Rome, and 200,000 Mar Thomas, or St. Thomas Christians, an evangelical section of the Syrians. They are called Syrians, but are really Indians; for they use the Syriac or Eastern Orthodox ritual and get their bishops ordained by the patriarch of Antioch. About ninety years ago one of the priests underwent a spiritual conversion and began the Mar Thoma Church. This Mar Thoma Church—literally, "Lord Thomas Church"—is the brightest spot in the situation in India. They are evangelical, evangelistic, and may yet evangelize India. They are on fire!

O Christ, I thank Thee that Thy flame in the hearts of men drives them everywhere. Their hearts burst with a divine joy and compassion. We thank Thee. Amen.

AFFIRMATION FOR THE DAY: *When I know that all things corroborate my faith, then I will go far.*

THE BELIEVERS GO PLACES

We were looking at the amazing reach of the influence of Thomas. Almost every year I am in India I go to the great convention of the Mar Thoma Christians, held in Maramon, Travancore, on a river bed which dries up at that time of the year. It attracts fifty thousand people, perhaps the largest Christian audience in the world.

Under the palm-leaf pandal, or tabernacle, are seated twenty thousand women on one side, all dressed in white, and thirty thousand men on the other, all seated on the sand. Bishops in purple robes and miters and priests in white robes with tonsured hair sit upon the platform. Gales of the Spirit go over that great audience and thousands are permanently changed and set on fire. To hear the murmurs of prayer go over the audience is like "the sound of many waters." There is no coming and going—everyone sits in deathlike stillness listening to and wanting nothing other than a pure gospel message.

I have been going to this convention for thirty years, and I cannot remember any attempt at flirtation, though the sexes mingle freely and the women are educated and free. There is one hundred per cent literacy among the people, the highest in India. The relationships among the sexes is the finest in the world—divorce is unknown and unfaithfulness is practically unknown. It just isn't done. The mores make anyone who is unmoral an outcast. Christian morals are built into the social structure. They are much more frugal than their non-Christian neighbors, so that eighty per cent of the land revenue of the state comes from the Christians, though they represent only one third of the population. They are not all saints by any means—they are prone to litigation, it being their football. But they are an amazing product of the man who believed mightily and wrought mightily through that belief. It is the believers that go places. The nonbelievers cancel themselves out with doubt and dilemma. They suffer from "the paralysis of analysis." Thomas had his doubts laid low in one moment of illumination—and then went places, and how! His spirit still lives in India—and in the world.

O God, put into my soul the mighty compulsion of a mighty faith. May it drive me as it drove Thomas. And may there be no limits. Amen.

AFFIRMATION FOR THE DAY: *My faith, at first so tentative, now becomes a driving force—it saves me and sends me.*

THRONGING AND TOUCHING

We have seen that the phrase "doubting Thomas" is a misnomer—he was the "believing and doing Thomas." A little boy stood beside his father as the father sat in his chair and triumphantly said, "Look, Daddy, I'm taller than you are." He was, when his father was sitting down. We thus compare ourselves with Thomas at the moment of his doubt and feel ourselves superior. But look at the man when he was up. Compare yourself when he stands in the regal dignity of a great faith and a great achievement. Then?

Before we leave this week's meditation on faith at the finger tips, we must look at a woman who was transformed through her finger tips. She touched Jesus' garment and was made whole. Jesus, perceiving that power had gone forth from him, turned to the crowd and said, "Who touched me?" Peter replied, "Master, the multitude throng thee and press thee, and sayest thou, 'Who touched me?'" He replied, "Somebody hath touched me." There was a difference—a world of difference—between thronging and touching. Those who merely thronged Him went away essentially unchanged, but one woman touched Him and was instantly healed.

Today the multitudes in the churches and outside throng Jesus—throng Him with their thoughts, their aspirations, their interests, even their affections, but they are not essentially changed by this thronging. Nothing happens except perhaps an indirect and faint moral and spiritual impression for the better. But no drawing of life and power and healing. They have not learned the art of receptivity, of accepting a Gift. They have not learned the art of being a child again, of being able to receive. The Kingdom of Heaven belongs to the childlike—belongs to them, they do not merely belong to it—it belongs to them, all its powers at their disposal. The sophisticated throng; the simple touch. And through that touch of faith healing and power and life stream. The finger tips become the faith tips and the faith tips become the fire tips—letting in the fire of healing love.

O Christ, I've been thronging Thee, and now I touch Thee—touch Thee for everything I need, transformation, life itself. Amen.

AFFIRMATION FOR THE DAY: *When I "touch Thee in the strain and stress," I am whole again.*

GOD'S SEARCH FOR MAN

This week we study the most palpitating recital of transformation ever spoken or penned. The three parables of the lost sheep, the lost coin, and the lost son contain more vital truth concerning redemption than anything that ever fell upon human ears. Had we heard it for the first time, we would have been filled with astonishment bordering on rapture, for what was Jesus saying? *Nothing less than that God is seeking us.* Let that soak in, for if that is true, then no one is ever more than one step away from God. But before we come to that amazing truth let us step back and get the context.

"The taxgatherers and sinners were all approaching him to listen to him, but the Pharisees and the scribes complained, 'He welcomes sinners and eats along with them'" (Luke 15:1-2, Moffatt.) The Pharisees honestly believed that the way to correct sinners was to boycott them, to make them feel the social disapproval of their sins by a scornful aloofness. Jesus believed the opposite. So the religious leaders, feeling that religion was in danger, tried to save religion by discrediting Jesus, "He is like them, therefore He welcomes them and eats with them." It was an attempt to take away His good name. What did Jesus do with this meanest of all attempts? He did what He always did—He transformed the evil into revelation. He took the evil and turned it into a good. He used the incident to reveal the very nature of God as redeeming love. He turned the interruption into interpretation. That is mastery—real mastery, the only mastery. When you can overcome evil with good, then you are a real overcomer.

As they pointed out what they considered His worse side, Jesus turned on an offensive of love and pointed out their best side, "Which of you with a hundred sheep, if he loses one, does not leave the ninety-nine in the open field and go after the lost one till he finds it?" (Luke 15:4, Moffatt.) As He pointed out their own redemptive trait, their hearts softened and they began to see God's best from their best. In one sentence He turned criticism to construction. This is mastery.

O Christ, teach me Thy secret. For I want to know how not merely to bear evil, but how to use it. For knowing Thy secret I live—live masterfully. Amen.

AFFIRMATION FOR THE DAY: *Not what happens to me, but what I do with it after it does happen, determines the result.*

LOST THROUGH HEEDLESSNESS

We are studying the three parables—the lost sheep, the lost coin, and the lost son. Each of these depicts a different method of being lost: The sheep was lost, not through deliberate intention, but through a series of inattentions, of going from one inviting tuft of grass to another—lost through careless inattention. The coin was lost through the carelessness of someone, depicting those who are lost not through their own neglect, but through the neglect and carelessness of others. The son was lost through his own deliberate choice.

These three emphases cover the way people get "lost." Some are lost through their own heedlessness. They, like the sheep, take a series of steps, none of them seemingly important, but each one contributing to the growing distance from the Shepherd. They go with the crowd to the borderland of evil, expecting to stay inwardly aloof while being outwardly near. But the inner defenses begin to crumble, for evil, looked on in the beginning as hideous, becomes bearable, then inviting and desirable: "Everybody does it. You mustn't be a speckled bird, you know." They wake up to the fact that they are "lost." Or a series of neglects takes place—"I'm too busy to have a quiet time just now—I'll have it later." "I'll not go to church this Sunday—I'll go next week." "This duty is pressing, I know—I'll do it tomorrow." Action turns into attitude, attitude turns into habit, habit turns into character. "I didn't intend to lose my religion," said a professor, "I just put it in a drawer for safekeeping and some years later when I came to look for it, it was gone." Lost by a series of tiny steps of neglect. A woman arose spontaneously at the close of an address and said, "I'm lost through neglect and fear." And perhaps neglect causes more lostness than fear. "As thy servant was busy here and there, he was gone" (I Kings 20:40). The descent to hell is so gradual that many do not suspect the road they are following. They think they are "on the level." God fades out through inattention, not through deliberate intention. The lostness, however, is the same.

O God, I know if each little step may take me away, then each little step may bring me back. I take those little steps today. Amen.

AFFIRMATION FOR THE DAY: *The little tufts of grass of worldliness that lure me on may leave me lost. I shall watch them today.*

LOST THROUGH OTHERS

We saw yesterday that the sheep was lost through a series of small steps. The coin was lost through the carelessness of another.

Many are lost not by their own choices, but by the choices, or lack of them, of society. Often the child is "lost" through the parents. We speak of "the prodigal son" but we could just as easily speak of "the prodigal parents." If 95 per cent of delinquencies among young people come out of broken homes, then the child is broken by the breaking of the parents. The older generation wouldn't live with God, now they can't live with themselves, therefore they can't live with each other. The result is delinquent children. "In a broken nest there are no whole eggs," says a Chinese proverb. The securities of the home are broken up and the child, feeling insecure, goes delinquent. "There is nothing wrong with this younger generation except the older," I said one day to a group, and a boy of twelve piped up and said, "Say you said something!" "We don't think our parents are fit to bring us up," said two junior high school girls to their dean. A more severe judgment was never pronounced by one generation upon another. Peter said, "Save yourself from this untoward generation"—a generation that wasn't going "toward" anything, without direction, without goal.

Then there are those who are lost not by family environment, but by social injustices—economic and racial. A German woman doctor wrote, "The acids of injustice have changed the chemistry of my soul." The feeling that the profits of industry are not being more equitably disturbed turns the chemistry of the soul from good will to ill will, from co-operation to sullen obstruction. To have to live in a society where the tint of the skin brands one every moment as inferior, changes the chemistry of the soul from love to hate imperceptibly. The miracle is that the Negro is bitter so little. His religion is the neutralizer of the acids of injustice. The Negro spirituals are pain set to music, the sorrows of a people set to song, the most triumphant religious music of the world. They are deep speaking to deep. Many without that neutralizer are "lost" through the attitudes of society.

O God, save me this day from letting anyone slip through my fingers like a coin on account of my social or spiritual carelessness. Amen.

AFFIRMATION FOR THE DAY: *I shall be on my guard today lest someone slip through my fingers into lostness through my neglect.*

LOST THROUGH DELIBERATE CHOICE

Yesterday we saw that many are damned by environment. A prominent Negro was called on by a team of people doing visitation evangelism and was invited to become a Christian. "No," he slowly replied, "I was ready once as a boy. But when the baptismal service was performed at the river, I, a little Negro boy, was left standing on the bank of the river. The white boys were baptized and I was left out." The acids of that injustice had changed the chemistry of his soul.

And it can work both ways: the acids of prejudice can so change one's judgment of values that the chemistry of the soul is altered from fairness to twisted judgment. "That man is full of race prejudice. He is prejudiced against white people. He thinks they are no better than the Negro." And he was serious, deadly so.

But we must not linger any longer upon those who are lost through social carelessness. We now turn to the third type of lostness: the prodigal son was "lost" through his own deliberate choices. He decided to leave his father. Why? He was under the illusion that his father's will was bondage and his own will was freedom. The central illusion of life is this: we think our way is freedom and God's way is bondage. That is hell's cleverest twist: " 'No,' said the serpent to the woman, you shall not die; God knows that on the day you eat from it your eyes will be opened and you will be like gods' " (Gen. 3:4, 5, Moffatt). "Like gods"—free to do as you like! No bondage, no direction from another! Free! But from that day to this that freedom is the freedom to leave paradise; freedom to hide in fear from God and yourself; freedom to tie yourself up in knots; freedom to be a problem to yourself and others. God's will is our freedom; our will against God's will is our bondage; and there are no exceptions—none. "Four steps to freedom," whispered the treacherous keeper of a French prison to the prisoner, but when he took those four steps out of his cell to apparent freedom, he fell through a hole and was thrown from knife to knife on the way down. Freedom? God's will alone, is freedom. That is the deepest lesson of life. If you don't know that lesson, you don't know how to live.

O God, Thou art my freedom. When I do Thy will, I do my own. I know that. Then help me to choose my freedom in Thee. Amen.

AFFIRMATION FOR THE DAY: *My freedom at its best is to choose God's best.*

ATTAINMENT TO OBTAINMENT

It doesn't matter whether we are lost by unthinking carelessness, or through the carelessness of others, or through our deliberate choices; if we get away from God, we are "lost." It may be a very respectable lostness—all the outer life intact—but the inner life is loosed from its moorings, God; nevertheless we are just as lost as though we were in the gutter. Anybody, anywhere, apart from God is "lost."

Then what happens? Once lost, always lost? Are we caught in the grip of our karma and must we work it out, paying the last penny before we are unlost? That is the teaching of both Hinduism and Buddhism, and millions upon millions surrender hopelessly to this fatalism of evil. But the Christian revelation sounds a strange and amazing reversal—it says that God is like the shepherd who searches till he finds the one lost sheep; like the woman who sweeps the house till she finds the coin; like the father who watches day by day for the prodigal's return. Never, never was such a breath-taking conception of God ever given to the waiting ears of man. No wonder it is called by its only appropriate name: "the good news."

I once heard in India a foreign visitor deliver an eloquent address on man's search for God, and at the close a Scotch missionary said to me: "Have you ever read *The Hound of Heaven?*" I was a young missionary then and had to confess I hadn't. "Then sell your coat and buy it," he added. I read it and saw what he meant: the Christian faith is not man's search for God, but God's search for man. There are many religions; there is but one gospel. Religions are good views; the gospel is good news. One is man's reach upward; the other is God's reach downward. Said a Hindu: "I lifted my hand upward for some handclasp of the Divine and nothing happened, and then one day a hand reached from above and clasped mine—and it was a nail-pierced hand." At that moment he passed from attainment by works to obtainment by grace. Transformation set in. A little missionary girl heard him speak about the cross, and she came home and said to her mother, "You should have been at the service today—a Hindu spoke about the cross, and he spoke as if he meant it." He did.

O God, it is too good to be true. But could anything so good be anything but true? So I accept it with all my heart. Grace, grace, grace. Amen.

AFFIRMATION FOR THE DAY: *If God is seeking me and I am seeking God wholeheartedly, what can keep us from meeting? Nothing!*

"THE ONLY GOODNESS IS A CHOSEN GOODNESS"

How long will God seek? The statement of Jesus points to a continous search: "until he finds." I am not sure that this verse (Luke 15:4) can be stretched into meaning that all will finally be saved. But when this verse is backed by the character of God as revealed in Jesus, then I know that we can say this at least: Everybody will be saved who wants to be saved. Nor can we confine the grace of God to the borders of this life. But that sin can harden one until the desire for redemption is quenched, I have no doubt. You can see that at work on this side of death. Evil causes the personality to go to pieces. The spark can be put out, the personality can disintegrate and perish —perish everlastingly, suffer "eternal destruction," be wiped out, be unfit to survive. But Grace will follow until the end. God will damn no one—if we are damned, we are self-damned. Grace stands by weeping as the last spark goes out.

In the parables of the lost sheep and the lost coin the shepherd and the woman take the initiative, they seek till they find. In the parable of the lost son the father did not go to the far country to seek the boy and force or persuade him to come home. For if he had, the boy would still have been in the far country in thought. The "far country" would still have been within him, even when he got back to his father's house. He must come back of his own accord, for he went away of his own accord. God cannot coerce the personality and take us by the nape of the neck and make us good. For in that case we wouldn't be good. The only goodness is a chosen goodness. "There is nothing good but a good will; there is nothing bad but a bad will." So the father must wait, even though his heart is breaking in the waiting. No "cross" in the story of the prodigal son? Look into that father's face and see there the cross! "Salvation is free," but it is costly to God. The shepherd seeks with swollen feet and torn hands; the woman sweeps the whole house and raises a lot of dust; the father waits and watches and in the waiting and watching silently suffers, every sin of the boy his own. God can give salvation only in a nail-pierced hand.

O Father-God, I know that this cross is on Thy heart until I lift it by taking it from Thy heart through repentance. I take it. Amen.

AFFIRMATION FOR THE DAY: *If God is seeking me until He finds, then I'm going to seek others until I find!*

"YOU PREACH A TROUBLESOME GOSPEL"

We said in our last study that the woman must have raised a lot of dust in sweeping her house. She had to upset things to get that coin back into circulation. For the king's image was stamped upon it even when it lay in the dust under a rug. God would sweep the universe to find the one lost soul, lost in the dust of degradation, for the King's image is stamped upon every human soul. But in doing so, He has to raise some dust.

"Have you come here to torment us before the time?" cried the demons identifying themselves with the man. Jesus raises the dust. He disturbs the *status quo*. He convicts us in order to convert us. He brings on a bitter gloom in order to bring a better gladness.

Sir John H. Harris of London served the African people long and well, and was grateful to an English clergyman named Cripps who had helped him in his work, though he had never seen him. He asked some miners in Africa what they thought of Cripps. Foul language, too foul to repeat, was the reply. "What have you got against him?" Harris urged. Finally one of the miners blurted out: "It's no use telling you anything but the truth. He is too much like Jesus Christ for this country." Jesus and His true followers upset—upset only to set up.

"You preach a troublesome gospel," said a South African white minister to me. "I preach a Kingdom in heaven, and that doesn't upset anything now. You preach the Kingdom on earth, and that upsets everything." It does. But the simple trouble of repentance and change is nothing compared to the vast trouble of a whole nation in fear and turmoil because they will not change their racial attitudes.

Evelyn Underhill says that "the main causes of disharmony in our lives are: inclinations to selfish choices, inordinate enjoyments, claimful affections, self-centered worry, instinctive avoidance of sacrifice and pain," and I may add, an unwillingness to face these things honestly.

We have to raise some dust to get people out of the dust. But all God's smitings are God's healings. He cuts only to cure. Face the dust and get out of it.

Gracious Father, I thank Thee that Thy rod smites me to awaken me, to make me a living soul. Smite on. I kiss the rod that smites me. Amen.

AFFIRMATION FOR THE DAY: *The soul gets on by a series of crises—no crisis, no cure.*

"EXPOSED OUT OF LIFE"

Having completed the general survey of the three parables—the lost sheep, the lost coin, and the lost son—we turn this week to look specifically at the parable of the prodigal son, "the most beautiful story ever told." Through it we step up into the very heart of God.

But before we do that, we must look into the heart of a young man. He prayed a prayer to his father, a kind of life prayer, a central request: "Father, give me." Note the "me." That was the first and the fundamental step down to self-ruin. He made himself the center of his universe. He became God. The moment he became a self-centered man he was "lost." The center of his tragedy was self-centeredness. All else is consequence—this is cause. He was just as much "lost" standing in all his pride of possession and tingling with adventure as he paused on his father's doorstep about to begin his journey, as when he was ragged and hungry feeding swine. The far country and the feeding swine flow from one thing—the fact of his being a self-centered person. He would have been "lost" if he had never gone to the far country, if he had never "wasted his substance with riotous living." Anyone who makes himself the center of his world is "lost," even though he may be cultured, respectable, and affluent. When you shift the basis of life from God to yourself, when you make yourself the center of your loyalty, you're "lost."

This is not a mere religious dogma imposed on life. This is not imposed on life—it is exposed out of life. For psychology would agree that all the ills of personality come out of one thing—self-centered preoccupation. It may be argued that the child is by nature grasping and self-centered, but even if it is, at the same time that child is unhappy, and made unhappy by his self-centeredness. It may be in the child, but it is not natural to him, for he is upset by it.

The son thought his own will freedom and his father's will bondage. If the transition could be made from his father's will to his own will, then an era of freedom would set in. That is the fatal illusion among mortal men: God's will bondage; my will freedom. Life renders a completely opposite verdict.

O God, Thy will is my will made free. Give me the sense to accept that and to act upon it with complete abandon. In Jesus' name. Amen.

AFFIRMATION FOR THE DAY: *God cannot will anything but my highest interest, otherwise He wouldn't be God.*

"THE CENTRAL REVOLT"

We saw yesterday that the moment you pray the prayer, "Father, give me," that moment your feet are upon the path to the far country and ultimate disillusionment. He prayed, "Father, give me" and started down; he prayed, "Father, make me" and started up. Two worlds are in those two prayers.

The boy used the word "father" even when transferring his allegiance from the father to himself. So we, amid our self-centered loyalties, still say "Father" to God thus to hide even from ourselves, the central revolt. But the facts are not fooled. The son in his prayer used the word "father" once and "me" twice. When there is as much emphasis upon "me" as upon the Father, then we are "lost," even amid our religiosity.

I am amazed beyond words that the father acceded to the request and "divided unto them his living." Why didn't he refuse and thus protect the son against himself? This granting of human freedom is a mystery, but was there anything else to be done? For if he had refused, the son would be revolting still, would be in the far country even when still in the father's house. For the far country is a condition before it is a place, just as hell is a condition before it is a place.

God gives us the awful power to ruin ourselves. On what condition? The condition is that God gets into the whole transaction, suffers in Himself the consequences of our wrong choices, makes them His own, and redeems us through that identification. The cross is the acute point of that identification where the continuous fact comes to light in history.

The decision once made, the son "gathered all together" and went into the far country—he would put outer distance between him and his father as the outer expression of the inner distance. The outer and the inner sooner or later become one. Life becomes all of a piece.

There in the far country "he squandered his means in loose living" (Moffatt). Not merely his material substance, but his moral and spiritual and mental and physical substance. He began to deteriorate, to fall to pieces. Sin is waste. For it is an attempt to live life against itself—sheer waste.

O God, I know when I go away from Thee I go away from myself. I waste myself along with my substance. Forgive me. In Jesus' name. Amen.

AFFIRMATION FOR THE DAY: *Freedom of choice means freedom to choose the highest. I do.*

"NO COHESION IN EVIL"

We saw yesterday that the prodigal "squandered his means in loose living," and that that squandering included himself, and especially, as well as his "means." The living was so "loose" it fell to pieces. There is no cohesion in evil. It stands on its own, backed by nothing in the universe, so it falls to pieces. In Jesus "all things cohere"—they hang together, there is cement in Him, for the universe backs, sustains, His way of life. Sorrow, opposition, death bump into the life of evil and that life "goes to pieces."

"After he had spent all a severe famine set in throughout that land, and he began to feel in want" (Moffatt). The outer famine coincided with the inner famine. Another illustration that our worlds become one—the outer sooner or later expresses the inner. "All things betray thee, who betrayest Me."

"So he went and attached himself to a citizen of that land, who sent him to his fields to feed swine" (Moffatt). Here was his vaunted freedom come to the end of the rope and strangling itself with the end: "He . . . attached himself to a citizen." He who would not accept his father's will is now selling himself for bread to the will of another. Outside of God all our freedoms turn into bondages. And what bondages! "Who sent him to his fields to feed swine"—him, a Jew, reduced to feeding swine, an animal taboo to the Jew! He wasted his self-respect as well as his substance.

"And he was fain to fill his belly with the pods the swine were eating: no one gave him anything" (Moffatt). The swine "were eating"—he wasn't; so he was lower than the swine! "And no one gave him anything"—sin doesn't care. His companions, male and female, stayed as long as the money held out, and then walked out on him. When we desert God, men and things will desert us.

One saving thing in the prodigal was that he "attached himself to a citizen of that land," but he never became a citizen himself. He never took out naturalization papers. He kept saying to himself: "I'm here, but I don't belong here. I belong back at my father's house." That was the saving remnant" that was left.

Gracious Father, that core of inner revolt against life in the far country is the one string Thou still hast hold of. That string will open the latch to let Thee in. Amen.

AFFIRMATION FOR THE DAY: *My Father's house is my home, and I cannot be at home anywhere else.*

"IMAGINE YOURSELF AS TRANSFORMED"

We come now to the pivot of the story. "But when he came to his senses," as Moffatt puts it, or as the King James Version has it, "When he came to himself." It is both—anyone in sin is out of his senses and consequently out of himself. Sin is insanity and also inhumanity. The idea that you can have a good time in sin is pure illusion. "It will keep the word of promise to your ear and break it to your hope."

So he began to talk to himself: "I will arise and go to my father, and will say unto him, Father I have sinned against heaven, and before thee, and am no more worthy to be called thy son." He saw that he had sinned in three directions: "against heaven"—the impersonal moral law; "and before thee"—against the personal love of the father; "and am no more worthy"—against himself. When we sin, we sin against the impersonal moral universe, against the personal love of God, and we sin against ourselves. Sin is a hydra-fisted monster that strikes in three directions. And the center of the sinfulness of sin is in sinning against the One who loves us. As Studdert-Kennedy wrote:

> That underworld where lust and lies
> Like vermin crawl and creep
> Across my visions and my prayers
> When sordid passions leap
>
> To slay the very thing I love,
> To crucify my Lord
> And force me spit my sins upon
> The face my soul adored.

The prodigal kept repeating this inner confession to himself, over and over, and soon his feet began to move in the direction of his thought. Ideas are motor. Hold them in the mind long enough and they will pass into action automatically. Thought is destiny. If you want to be redeemed, think of yourself as being redeemed, and you will be redeemed. For your thoughts will begin to take feet and walk you straight to the Father's bosom. Talk repentance to yourself and you'll act repentance to the Father.

O Father, I know Thou art putting thoughts within my mind that these thoughts may lead to Thee. They are born of Thy love. I thank Thee. Amen.

AFFIRMATION FOR THE DAY: *My thoughts ruin me or redeem me; today they shall redeem me.*

116

OUTER ASSURANCES OF FORGIVENESS

And now the drama of redemption shifts from the son to the father: "But when he was still far away, his father saw him and felt pity for him and ran to fall upon his neck and kiss him" (Moffatt). He saw him "when he was still far away," for day by day he had watched that road, early and late, believing that the son would come back. He didn't go after him—there must be no compulsion, he went on his own and he would have to return on his own. But oh, the infinite sympathy—sympathy in its root meaning, "suffering with"!

The father couldn't go into the far country, but he could go a long way down that road when once he was assured that the son was through with the far country. And the old man running down the road with his beard flying and the tears falling down his face like the summer rain is the most touching scene in history. Jesus looks up, in repeating the story, as much as to say "That's God." And it is!

The father let the prodigal repeat his confession, for that confession was catharsis. It had to get up and out. But the father never allowed him to finish it: "Make me as one of thy hired servants"—that was choked off. There must be no unreal talk of being a servant: This is my son—my son still! "Quick," he said, "bring the best robe"—the outer sign befitting a son; "give him a ring for his hand"—the ring as sign of authority; "and sandals for his feet"—only slaves went with bare feet, a son, no!; "and bring the fatted calf"—saved for a special guest on a special occasion. And this was it!

Why these outer signs of the father's forgiveness and restoration? Would his word of forgiveness not be enough? No, the sense of guilt and inferiority and shame had gone so deep that in addition to the word of forgiveness there had to be these outer signs to assure him. So when we come to God in real repentance, we get outer signs of forgiveness—the robe of self-respect, the ring of authority, and the wiping out of the slave relationship. The emotions He gives are not forgiveness, but they are the outer assurances of forgiveness.

Gracious Father, Thou art gracious in saying the word of forgiveness in Thy word and then giving the outer assurance to make us sure. I thank Thee. Amen.

AFFIRMATION FOR THE DAY: *Assurances are the companions who press our hands as we walk along the way, but faith makes the feet walk.*

SINS OF THE FLESH AND DISPOSITION

"So they began to make merry"—so ends the prodigal son's side of the story. And what an ending! It is incredible. He went out to get happiness, got bitter unhappiness and disillusionment instead; he returned home expecting to get a slave's status, and to work out his evil past by wearing sackcloth the balance of his days to atone, and he ran into this! He got the very thing he had wanted—happiness. As a gift!

This is grace. A Jewish rabbi says that Judaism knows nothing of salvation by faith as Christians teach. But it isn't salvation by faith. It is salvation by grace through faith. We are not saved by our faith, but our faith opens the door to let grace come in. "By grace are ye saved through faith." Cheap? Nothing more expensive, for when you accept the gift, you belong forever to the Giver! He's got you—clear down to your toes! Love gives and creates giving in return—forever each other's.

And now the other side of the story—a side which some people think should have been left out because it brings a jarring note in the symphony of joy. But without this side the story would be unrealistic. The elder brother is terribly true to life: he stands for those who sin not in their flesh but in their dispositions. The younger brother sinned low down in his flesh—harlotry and drunkenness; the elder brother sinned high up in his disposition—lack of forgiveness, anger, petulance, pride, self-righteousness, self-centeredness. The sins of the flesh are not respectable sins; the sins of the disposition are.

When the elder brother would not join in the rejoicing, his father came out and reasoned with him, but the elder brother revealed his inner soul as self-centered by using "I" or "me" five times: "Look at all the years I have been serving you! I never neglected any of your orders [very self-righteous], and yet you have never given me so much as a kid [hadn't the father given his living to both, the larger share falling to the elder son?], to let me make merry with my friends" (Moffatt). He was out of tune with his father's spirit. He was a prodigal who never went away—a prodigal in his father's house. He too was "lost."

O dear Father, save me from the respectable sins of the disposition which make me lost even in Thy presence. Cleanse me from respectable sins. Amen.

AFFIRMATION FOR THE DAY: *A self-centered disposition is ugly; a God-centered disposition is beautiful.*

SELF-EXCLUDED

We meditated yesterday on the elder brother—the man who sinning in his disposition, despised the man who sinned in his flesh: "But as soon as this son of yours arrives, after wasting your means with harlots, you kill the fatted calf for him!" (Moffatt) "Your son"—not "my brother."

What was the central difficulty with the older brother, besides being self-centered? The answer is in the father's statement, "My son, you and I are always together; all I have is yours" (Moffatt). "All I have is yours"—yours for the asking, but you didn't know how to ask or receive. For he was on a legalistic, self-righteous basis, a basis which shut him off from everything the father had, except that which had been given legally to him.

The elder brother represents millions of religious people, the vast bulk of them, in fact, who live in their Father's house, attend services, give to good causes, pray and act religious, but they have never learned how to accept the gift of grace—they lack simple childlike receptivity. They stand on their record of self-righteousness instead of kneeling in receptive penitence and faith. So their faces know no joy, for legality never sings and pharisaism is gloomy. The younger brother knew how to take, and hence knew how to give. The elder brother knew neither how to take nor to give—he was tied up in self-righteous criticism.

And when the curtain goes down on this drama, the awful fact remains: The younger brother was on the inside and the elder brother on the outside—"he would not go in"—self-excluded.

And now the gentle but terribly cutting application of the parable. The sting is in its tail: "The publicans and the harlots go into the kingdom of God before you" (Matt. 21:31)—the Pharisees, the elder brother in the parable. The setting of the parable is their criticism of Him, but the end is a revelation of themselves. In deft strokes He reveals the heart of God, the Father, and reveals the heart of man, one penitent and receptive, the other proud and unreceptive. Both of them "lost," but only one of them "found." "He was lost, and is found." The other was lost, but not found.

O God, my Father, this parable shakes me to my depths. It reveals Thy heart—and mine. I bring mine to Thee for forgiveness and restoration. In Jesus' name. Amen.

AFFIRMATION FOR THE DAY: *"All I have is thine"—then I shall inherit my inheritance and possess my possessions.*

119

THE MOST BEAUTIFUL VERSE IN LITERATURE

We looked last week at the most beautiful story ever told; this week we must look at the most beautiful verse in literature. The parable and the direct statement say the same thing—the story of God's search for man. For forty-five years I have looked at that verse wishing I had enough nerve to preach on it. But each time I turned away wistfully feeling that the verse is perfect as it stands. To try to expound it would be to spoil it—like picking to pieces a rose to show its beauty. My readers are already suspecting what verse it is—John 3:16: "For God so loved the world, that he gave his only begotten Son, that whosoever believeth in him should not perish, but have everlasting life."

There is more of the gospel packed into those twenty-five words than in all other literature. It says everything there is to be said, and after saying it, leaves you awed into curiosity at what is left unsaid—only hinted at. After trying to expound it, I shall say, like the queen of Sheba, "The half was not told." Tennyson's lines about the flower in the crannied wall could be applied to this verse:

> If I could understand
> What you are, root and all, and all in all,
> I should know what God and man is.

For this verse unfolds the breath-taking fact of God transforming Himself into our likeness that we might be transformed into His likeness—God coming down into infinite identification that we might go up into infinite identification.

Emerson asked a friend how he liked the sermon he had preached and he replied: "The diction was perfect, the outline adequate, the thoughts sparkling, but no one would be any more in danger of being converted through it than one would be in danger of getting drunk on buttermilk." But this verse is so charged with the new wine of the Kingdom that just to sip it makes you intoxicated—with redemption. To really drink of it is to be transformed in every cell of soul and body.

Gracious Father, I would put my heart up against Thy heart and feel its beat and catch its rhythm. Thy heart is here. Amen.

AFFIRMATION FOR THE DAY: *I am determined to drink deep of God's deepest well—this verse.*

THE INITIATIVE IS WITH GOD

We are studying the most beautiful enfoldment of the most beautiful fact that ever took place—John 3:16. The initiative begins with God —"For God." All other religions begin with man—"For man so eagerly desired God that." The Hindu scriptures are filled with the accounts of men who by their austerities stormed the very citadel of God and disturbed His calm aloofness by their very insistence and persistence. And God would respond only because His calm might not be further disturbed. They had to overcome God's reluctance. But here it is the very opposite—the only problem is to overcome man's reluctance. God takes the initiative—"We love him, because he first loved us."

Quintin Hogg, a businessman, gave himself and his fortune to the outcast boys of London. The boys adored him. Jem Nicholls, one of the wildest characters before Hogg met him, was later asked how he was getting on. He replied: "I have a bit of trouble in keeping straight, but I thank God all is well. You see, I carry a photo of 'Q.H.' always with me, and when I am tempted, I just take it out and his look is a wonderful help, and by the grace of God I am able to overcome all." Jesus is God's photograph. We look at Him and we see God. As Browning says:

'Tis the weakness in strength, that I cry for! My flesh that I seek
In the Godhead! I seek and I find it. O Saul, it shall be
A Face like my face that receives thee; a Man like to me
Thou shalt love and be loved by, for ever: a Hand like this hand
Shall throw open the gates of new life to thee! See the Christ stand!

Jesus is God stepping out of the frame of the universe and coming to me personally and intimately. He is God pressing home upon my heart the pressures of His heart. He is God breaking through—breaking through to my understanding and my heart. He is love seeking its own—its own: me. Jesus is God become understandable and lovable. He is the Personal Approach from the unseen. There is a picture in India of an armless god—Jesus is God's arm stretched out still.

O Jesus, how can I thank Thee for Thy tender intimacy? Thou art God available, at hand—and now. I thank Thee. Amen.

AFFIRMATION FOR THE DAY: If the "initiative" is with God, the "referendum" is with me. I decide to respond wholeheartedly.

LIFE-AFFIRMING AND WORLD-AFFIRMING

We yesterday meditated on Jesus as God drawing near—redemptively near. Wrote William Blake:

> I give you the end of a golden string;
> Only wind it into a ball,
> It will lead you in at Heaven's gate,
> Built in Jerusalem's wall.

Jesus is the end—the human-divine end of a golden string, which if you follow, you will be led into the very heart of God.

"God so loved the world"—that is important, for if the world is the object of God's love, then it is the object of God's redemption. Salvation is not redemption from the world of men and things—the world of men and things are to be redeemed. This sets the love of God at the place where it is most needed—at the heart of the world of men and things. This turns the dynamic of religion into redemption of the world, instead of release from the world. When I see the vast endeavor, involving millions of ardent Hindus struggling to get out of the meshes of the world through their religion, then I see the importance of this concept of God loving the world. Instead of draining off human endeavor from the world's redemption, it turns it toward that redemption. This makes religion life-affirming and world-affirming.

Not that God approves of the world even when He is loving the world. He loves where He cannot approve. The head of a boys' school, noted for its power to transform boys, said to a lad one day, "Johnny, we love you, but we don't like what you do." God loves the world in spite of the world being what it is. A pastor blistered the aching soul of a man who sat in his mother's home, a bleared and bloated sot. The man, knowing he deserved it, sat there with his face in his hands and took the moral lashing. When the pastor finished, the mother got up without a word and walked over and kissed the swollen lips of her son. Afterward the man, telling of the turning point in his life, said that he could stand the lashing but he couldn't stand the kiss—it redeemed him. Jesus is God's kiss upon the blotted lips of a prodigal humanity.

O God, my Father, Thou art astonishing in Thy love—loving the unlovely and the unlovable, loving even me. I thank Thee. Amen.

AFFIRMATION FOR THE DAY: *If God loves the world, I too shall love the world—in God.*

"WHY DIDN'T HE COME HIMSELF?"

We continue our study of the heart of redemption—John 3:16: "God so loved the world, that he gave his only begotten Son."

When I was speaking in India to a group about God loving the world, that He gave His Son to die for us, a village woman spoke up and said: "What kind of a Father was He to send His Son—why didn't He come Himself?" It was a good question—and penetrating. Yes, why didn't He come Himself? "I love Jesus but I hate God, for God wanted to destroy the world and Jesus wouldn't let Him," said a little girl. If Jesus is a third person standing between us and God, she is right. But Jesus is a mediator only in the sense that He mediates God to us. For when we take hold of Him, we take hold of the very self of God. For "God was in Christ, reconciling the world unto himself." I cannot tell where Jesus ends and God begins in my experience. They melt into one. When I deepen the Christ-consciousness, I deepen the God-consciousness. They do not rival or push each other out. They are one.

How deep was that self-giving? He shared our humanity; did He go deeper and share our sins, taking them into His own body on a tree? The account unhesitatingly says so. A girl was told that if she came in late, she would have to eat bread and water. She came in late and was served bread and water while the rest ate their meal. But the father gave her his meal and he ate the bread and water. Could she ever forget or escape it? That was what God was doing at the cross— He took it on Himself. In a school where student government ruled that any boy stealing should be whipped publicly, a hunchback stole a lunch, and when asked to take off his coat to be flogged, he pitifully begged, "Oh, no, not that," for he was ashamed of his crooked spine. A big boy, from whom the lunch had been stolen, arose and asked if there was anything in the rules to prevent his taking the punishment, and when told there was none, he came forward and took it on himself. The hunchback, now a preacher, said he was redeemed through that act, for he saw the cross through it.

O God, Thou art wonderful. Thou dost take my place. The only way I can show my gratitude is to give Thee back my sinful heart. I do. Amen.

AFFIRMATION FOR THE DAY: *Today I shall be a reconciler in every situation—even at cost to myself.*

"HE TURNED BEER INTO FURNITURE"

Yesterday we meditated upon God so loving that He gave His only begotten Son. And the giving was an ultimate giving—He took His place as a sinner and died between sinners. He couldn't go any further.

"The idea of God on a cross reversed all the values of antiquity," said Nietzsche. He was right. But we can't get away from that cross— it holds us. "Today more than ever, whenever things grow dark and God's ways seem difficult to understand, when our own minds are puzzled and confused, people gather at Calvary, stand and look," says George Bernard Shaw. They do. For we know instinctively there is redemption there—if anywhere.

And how wide is that redemption? The gospel writer uses a breath-taking word—"whosoever." That word stretches its arms as wide as the human race and as deep as human need—the sky is the limit. Celsus, an early opponent of Christianity, objected to this attitude, saying that other faiths invited in the respectable, the moral, the upright, but this faith scandalously invites in the riffraff, the immoral, the drunken, the dishonest, and welcomes them! It does! But the riffraff become the respectable, the immoral become the moral, the drunken become the sober, and the dishonest become the honest, and live and die for it!

An old slave woman loved her "Little Boy Blue" given to her by her mistress. But one day it dropped from her fingers and broke. She gathered up the fragments lovingly and said, "I love you, Little Boy Blue, more than ever since you've been broken." That reveals something of the heart of God toward sinners—He loves them especially when they are broken. They need it more.

A skeptic was heckling the Christians. "Do you believe that Jesus turned water into wine?" he asked. "Well, I don't know," said one man, "but this I do know, that in my home He turned beer into furniture." The miracle of changed lives is taking place today to the degree that it is being tried. "Whosoever" works wheresoever and by whomsoever it is really tried.

Gracious God and Father, I thank Thee that thy promise is performance, Thy word is Thy work. I take Thy promise and get the performance. I'm grateful. Amen.

AFFIRMATION FOR THE DAY: *Since God loves me especially when I go wrong, for then I need it most, so I will love others especially when they go wrong, for then they will need it most.*

"I GOT IN TOO"

We were lingering yesterday on the "whosoever." A pastor of a fashionable church was called one night by a little girl appearing at his door and saying, "My mother sent me to ask you to come and get her in." Wondering what she meant, he followed her into a slum section, up a flight of rickety stairs into what was the room of a harlot dying of consumption. He sat alongside of her bed and told her of Jesus, the great teacher, but she shook her head and said sadly, "That's not for the likes of me." Then he tried Jesus as a doer of good, but again she shook her head and repeated the same words. He was at the end of his tether when he reached back into the past and pulled out something he had discarded—he talked to her about Jesus dying on the cross to save sinners. She began to nod her head: "Yes, that's it. That's for the likes of me." Telling of it afterwards he said, "And we got her in," and then added slowly, "And I got in too." The cross met the need of both—"whosoever"!

"That whosoever believeth in him should not perish." The word is not "believeth" but "believeth *in*." Many people believe but they don't believe *in* it enough to surrender their lives to it. For believing *in* passes beyond mental assent and goes into paying the price and taking the Gift! "The devils believe"—and remain devils. But no devil has believed in it enough to surrender his life to it and has accepted the gift of God by faith and has remained a devil. In one of my books I quoted a woman who said of herself, "I'm a street angel and a house devil." Since then she has not only believed but has believed in, and today she is a street angel and a house angel too. And the angel of the courtroom and jails, rescuing others.

"Should not perish"—we see people outside of God perishing here and now, perishing from conflicts, fears, inhibitions, complexes, and guilts. The process of disintegration is taking place before our very eyes. And if the process of disintegration of personality goes on long enough, then they perish eternally, wiped out, unfit to survive. In Christ we are under the process of renewal—eternally.

O Christ, Thou dost arrest the processes of decay. Thou art giving an eternal rejuvenation—soul, mind, and body. I thank Thee, thank Thee. Amen.

AFFIRMATION FOR THE DAY: *I am under the law of eternal rejuvenation. I shall take large advance installments today.*

"IS ETERNAL EXISTENCE DESIRABLE?"

We come to our last phrase of this most wonderful of statements: "But have everlasting life." This "everlasting life" is not merely eternal in the sense of duration, but in sense of quality. It is a quality of life called eternal simply because it cannot be confined to time. It bursts the seams of time as a butterfly bursts its chrysalis. It is so good it just has to be eternal.

A Harvard professor lectured on the question "Is Eternal Existence Desirable?" and came to the conclusion that it is not. I agree if it is just eternal existence, for who could bear mere existence eternally? But if it's eternal *life*—that's different. Life has to be eternal or it is not life—it has the seeds of death in it. George Bernard Shaw once said, "I don't want to have to live with George Bernard Shaw forever." I don't blame some people for not wanting to live with themselves forever. They are poor companions to themselves now! A lot of people hate themselves, and to have to hate yourself forever is no joke. But suppose you have a self with whom you can get along, and even enjoy, for it is a self that is integrated, co-ordinated, harmonized—a self you can respect and love in God—then that's different. With such a self death seems unbelievingly impossible—it knows it is deathless, inherently so. As Emerson says:

> What is excellent,
> As God lives is permanent.

And we can more than accept the statement of George Herbert Palmer about the death of his wife, Alice Freeman: "Though no regrets are proper for the manner of her death, who can contemplate the fact of it and not call the world irrational if, out of deference to a few particles of disordered matter, it excludes so fair a spirit?" Yes, eternal life has to be in duration when it is eternal life in quality. Chesterton said Robert Louis Stevenson "died with a thousand stories in his heart." Of the Christian when he dies, it can be said that "he had a thousand ages in his heart"—had it in the eternal life which he possessed. Eternal life is Christian life in the midst of time.

O Christ, I thank Thee that Thou hast given me eternal life now— now in the midst of decay around me. This shall never decay. I know that. Amen.

AFFIRMATION FOR THE DAY: *Today I shall live as one who has a thousand unrealized possibilities in his heart.*

A CASE OF ARRESTED TRANSFORMATION

We have been stressing the fact that transformation comes through grace by faith—a gift of God. When we learn how to co-operate with God, aligning our lives with His life, our wills with His will, so that we can take the resources of God as our own, then their infinite transformation is not only possible but actual.

We must look at a case of arrested transformation before we proceed. A rich young ruler ran to Jesus, knelt before Him, and asked earnestly: "Teacher, what good deed must I do to gain life eternal?" (Matt. 20: 16-24, Moffatt.) Here he made the almost universal attempt to find eternal life by doing a deed. Eternal life is something we *do*, instead of something we *accept*. If eternal life were something we do, then our salvation is self-salvation, and the finished product is the self-righteous Pharisee praying, "God, I thank thee that I am not as other men." God isn't in the picture except to be informed of the prayer's virtues. But if salvation is by grace through faith, then the finished product is the God-righteous Christian praying, "God, I thank Thee that Thou hast redeemed me, the worst of sinners. I am alive with joy and gratitude."

At first sight salvation by doing seems more virile, more self-dependent, more in the stream of today, and more expensive. This is superficial. Salvation by doing gives the deed and reserves the self. Salvation by self-surrender and faith gives the self plus all its deeds forever. It is an expensive acceptance of a gift, for the moment you take the gift, then you belong to the Giver forever! He has you and all you do!

How did Jesus correct this centrally wrong attitude? He lifted the young man from a deed to a Person, "Why do you ask me about what is good? One alone is good" (Matt. 20:17, Moffatt). He lifted him from a "what" to a "whom"—from a thing to a Person. He was saying to him, "You don't become good by doing a good deed; you become good by coming into receptive contact with a good Person, that Person, God." Here He lifted him from the level of duty to the level of grace. Changed character is caught, not bought or taught. You catch it by contact.

Dear Jesus, lift me from the lashing of duty to the loving of grace. For I know that I cannot be saved except by a Savior—by Thee. Amen.

AFFIRMATION FOR THE DAY: *"By grace are ye saved through faith; . . . it is the gift of God."*

"FROM A 'WHAT' TO A 'WHOM' "

The next few verses in the story of the rich young ruler seem t
contradict what I said about Jesus lifting the young man from a "what
to a "Whom," for He immediately refers him to the Commandments
But this referring him to the Commandments was simply to let hir
see that after he had replied that he had kept them all from youth up
he was still in need. The young man suspected this and asked: "Wha
more is required?" And Jesus showed that what he needed was nc
"what more?" but "what other?" What he needed was not "more," bu
utterly "other." And what was the "other"? It was this: "Go and sel
your property, . . . then come and follow me" (Matt. 20:21, Moffatt)
The "other" was in the last phrase—"follow me." Here again He wa
lifting him from a "good deed" to a good Person—"follow *me*." "Yo
will become good as you get into contact with my goodness."

What was it the young man lacked? The usual answer is—poverty
That is to miss the point completely. For that would be another "goo
deed"—something "more." What he lacked was following Jesus. Th
riches stood in the way, therefore they had to go. But if he had sol
all his property, had given it to the poor, but had not followed Jesus
he would not have been one inch nearer eternal life. Every step h
took on that road would have taken him farther away from the goal
for he was faced in the wrong direction—eternal life by a good deed
He was faced toward himself and his deed instead of toward Go
and His deed.

The rich young ruler had to turn around, about-face from a "what
to a "Whom." He was only one step from salvation—that step
"Yes." But he never took that step—"He went sadly away, for he ha
great possessions." No, his great possessions had him. He had his affec
tions twined about his possessions and couldn't untwine them. Jesu
today is saying: "Go, break that relationship and follow me"; "Go
burn that book and follow me." The end is following Him. If yo
bring your possessions along with you in following Jesus, and yo
and the possessions both belong to Him, then the end is fulfilled—
following Jesus.

O Jesus, I know I become good only by surrendering to Goodness—
to Thee. Take me as I am and make me as Thou art. Amen.

AFFIRMATION FOR THE DAY: *My possessions do not possess me, for
and my possessions are possessed by Christ.*

"DIFFERENCE BETWEEN RENUNCIATION AND REPRESSION"

We have come to the central insistence of this book—the way to self-transformation is the way of self-renunciation. You must lose your self to find your self again—lose it in the will and purpose of Another, God.

But as Joshua Liebman says: "It should be noted that there is a difference between renunciation and repression. A person who represses all his ambitions and wishes and denies any reality to them is on the road to misery. . . . We shall be free of inner conflict and burden only when we have looked renunciation directly in the face and persuaded ourselves that it is essential for the fulfillment of our true and permanent happiness." Self-renunciation is not sitting on a lid —it is the free and full surrender of one's self into the purpose of Another to be possessed, controlled, and guided by Him. But Liebman's objective must be corrected a bit—the objective is not our "happiness"; that would still be self-surrender to one's self, to one's happiness. Happiness is a by-product of surrender to God. Seek it as an end in itself and it will elude you, but seek God first, and all these things, including happiness, will be added.

Bertrand Russell once said that the best that man can do is to hold "an unyielding despair." But he saw a glimpse of the way out: "The gate of the cavern is despair, and its floor is paved with the gravestones of abandoned hopes. There Self must die; there the eagerness, the greed of untamed desire must be slain, for so can the soul be freed from the empire of Fate. But out of the cavern the Gate of Renunciation leads again to the daylight of wisdom, by whose radiance a new insight, a new joy, a new tenderness, shine forth to gladden the pilgrim's heart." Here Russell saw the Gate but never got beyond "unyielding despair," for he never saw the One for whose sake we must renounce self. His transformation remained verbal—"Logic," instead of Life. For if you don't actually do it, then like the rich young ruler, you "go away sadly," but if you do, actually do it, then you go away gladly.

O Christ, possessing Thee, I possess all things, for in Thee all things come back to me, including myself. I am free when I freely give. Amen.

AFFIRMATION FOR THE DAY: *My self-renunciation results in self-realization. I can safely express a God-centered self.*

"FREE AT THE CENTER"

In my reading I came across a quotation which I liked, wrote "Good" alongside of it, and then discovered it was my own!

"No man is free until he is free at the center. When he lets go there then he is free indeed. When the self is renounced, then one stands utterly disillusioned, apart, asking for nothing. He anticipates the buffeting, the slights, the separations, the disappointments of life by their acceptance in one great renunciation. It is life's supreme strategic retreat. You can say to life, 'What can you do to me? I want nothing! You can say to death, 'What can you do to me? I have already died! Then is a man truly free. In the bath of renunciation he has washed his soul clean from a thousand clamoring, conflicting desires. Asking for nothing, if anything comes to him, it is all sheer gain. Then life becomes one constant surprise.

"Everything belongs to the man who wants nothing. Having nothing, he possesses all things in life, including life itself. Nothing will be denied the man who denies himself. Having chosen to be utterly solitary, he comes into possession of the most utterly social fact of the universe, the Kingdom of God. He wants nothing of men and matter. He has God. That is enough. Now he is ready to go back into the world. He is washed clean of desires, now he can form new ones, from a new center and with a new motive. This detachment is necessary to a new attachment. The fullest and most complete life comes out of the most completely empty life."

Would the best in psychology agree? Listen to Anton T. Boisen: "To be at one with that which is supreme in our hierarchy of loyalties, that to which men generally give the name God, is ever essential to mental health; to be isolated or estranged through the consciousness that there is that within which we cannot acknowledge without being condemned means mental disorder and spiritual death." Self-adjustment through self-surrender to God equals mental health.

O Christ, Thou art calling me out of conflict into concord, out of confusion into certainty, out of myself into Thee. I come. Amen.

AFFIRMATION FOR THE DAY: *Washed clean from conflicting desires in the bath of self-renunciation, I go gaily and gladly about my tasks.*

"OUT OF THE SWAMP OF PREOCCUPATION"

We now turn to a phase of our study to which most modern writers turn in the beginning of the discussion on being a transformed person, namely, the transformation of the mind. We have waited, deliberately so, till certain things have been established in our discussion before turning to the renewing of the mind.

Modern discussion puts this first: Change your thinking and you will change your personality. Books, magazines pour out a steady stream of emphasis on salvation by your thinking. It is the modern climate. And yet with all this emphasis, with all these techniques, the number of disrupted people is steadily growing. Even among those who advocate these mental disciplines and techniques one seldom finds one truly integrated, adjusted, and radiant person. In talking to two doctors they said to me of a certain psychiatrist: "She is the only integrated, radiant, and happy person we have ever seen among psychiatrists themselves. The rest, for the most part, are bordering on the things they talk about. They are bordering on the queer." But this psychoanalyst had at the center of her knowledge of the mind and techniques, self-surrender to God. As simply as a child she surrendered herself and her conflicts to God. That brought central integration and lighted up the whole method of psychoanalysis. Without it the whole method seemed an attempt to make life hold together without any central cement. Self-knowledge will not bring self-integration—self-surrender to God will and does, does to the degree that it is tried.

As Fritz Kunkel, a psychiatrist who combines self-analysis with self-surrender, says, "We cannot pull ourselves out of the swamp by our own hair as the famous knight in the fairy tale did." The method of lifting ourselves by our own bootstraps, or our own hair, ends in a straining at a recalcitrant self with pitifully small results. But when we surrender ourselves to God, then we rise out of our swamps of self-despair as if by magic. It is so easy it becomes incredible—incredible but for the fact that we're out, out of the swamp of preoccupation. We're free. Glory be!

O Christ, one touch of Thy healing hand upon us and we are every whit whole. It was so then, it is so now. We thank Thee, thank Thee. Amen.

AFFIRMATION FOR THE DAY: *Not self-knowledge, but God-knowledge lifts me out of what I am to what I want to be.*

"YOUR MIND RENEWED"

Now having established the fact that self-surrender is primary, we can turn to self-cultivation through mental attitudes. For now we have changed the center from ourselves to God, and around this new center we can discipline ourselves by thought processes. But if we try to cultivate an unsurrendered self, then we are sitting on a lid which constantly blows off from the unmastered self within.

This verse expresses the Christian position at this point: "Instead of being moulded to this world, have your mind renewed, and so be transformed in nature, able to make out what the will of God is, namely, what is good and acceptable to him and perfect" (Rom. 12:2, Moffatt). Note: "Have your mind renewed, and so be transformed in nature."

The mind has a powerful influence upon nature—human and material. The experiments in telepathy at Duke University have proved beyond a reasonable doubt that telepathy, or the influence of one mind over another, is a fact, and it doesn't matter whether that mind is in the next room or a hundred miles away. It has also been established that one can influence the rolling of dice by concentrating the mind. Hatfield in his experiments has shown that in testing one's strength by a strength-testing machine where the average would be, say 100, under waking conditions, when the subjects would be put under hypnosis, and were told they were weak, the average strength would be 40. Then they would be told under hypnosis that they were strong, and they would act upon it and it would go up to 140. The difference was in the mind.

A missionary from the Philippines told me that when they were ordered to go into prison camps by the Japanese, they were told they could take all they could carry in suitcases, and no more. His wife weighing 105 pounds, and not strong at all, carried a load of 200 pounds, mostly canned goods, 4½ miles—a load that neither of them could even lift after they arrived. Mannheim says that we normally use only about one eighth of our physical reserves. If the mind can tap these hidden reserves, then we can multiply our present selves.

O God, my Father, teach me how to tap the resources Thou hast stored up within me awaiting my ability to call on them and use them. Amen.

AFFIRMATION FOR THE DAY: *My mind, cleansed of weeds, and watered with Thy Spirit, will be the soil from which creative projects spring.*

"RESHUFFLING OF VALUES"

We continue to meditate upon the use of the mind in transforming our natures. The first step in the Christian plan for this transformation is metanoia, or repentance. Now metanoia means "to change your mind," in other words, "to get a new outlook on life," "to reverse your values."

Someone has imagined a department store where all the price tickets would be changed by some wag so all the expensive things would bear cheap labels, and all the cheap things, expensive labels. The confusion would bankrupt the business. That is the fundamental point of confusion in life—we've got the wrong values placed on things. Repentance means a reshuffling of values—a putting of first things first and wrong things in the garbage can.

S. B. Dunn tells of coming out of a house where he had prayed with a family and was met by a man who fell on his shoulder weeping, "Pray for me, for I'm a lost sinner." He took Dunn into his house a few doors away. Telling about it afterwards, he said: "I had an armful of liquor bottles when I saw and heard you pray in that house. I ran home, dropped the bottles, and came back to meet you. What must I do with that stuff?" They went out into a lot and broke the bottles on a rock. The whole family came into the church and they are now all changed and happy. He underwent a change of mind, which meant a change in value—one moment the bottles seemed precious, the next they seemed poison. That change in mind resulted in a change in nature.

One moment the self seems precious and worthy to be defended, and the next it is loathed as the center of all our disruptions and must be renounced—a change of mind. Resentments are held to and bitterly defended before the tribunal of the value judgments, the next moment they are seen to be disruptive and loathsome—a change of mind. "I was a ninny to do it," said a penitent woman bitterly about her sex relations—a change of mind. The most important moment in life is the moment when you get a new set of values—when you change your mind, repent. For repentance closes one door and opens another—the door to eternal life.

O God, I thank Thee that Thou art showing me the difference between the precious and the vile. I'm choosing, and I'm choosing Thy value. Amen.

AFFIRMATION FOR THE DAY: *All my values become valuable—in God.*

"SWALLOWED AN ELECTRIC-LIGHT BULB"

We continue this week our study of the transformation of our thinking—the renewing of our minds. We saw that the first step is metanoia, repentance or a change of mind.

Jesus said: "The eye is the lamp of the body: so if your Eye is generous, the whole of your body will be illumined, but if your Eye is selfish, the whole of your body will be darkened. And if your very light turns dark, then—what a darkness it is!" (Matt. 6:22-23, Moffatt.) The "Eye" is your outlook on life, the point of view from which you look at things. If your "Eye," or point of view, is selfish—if you look at things from a point of self-reference, "How will that affect me?"—then the whole of your personality will be darkened. Metanoia is a change of mind—you cease to look at things from a standpoint of self-centeredness, for you are now a God-centered person and life is viewed from God's viewpoint. From that new center your new life and the whole of your personality is illumined. You are a lighted-up personality. "You look as though you had swallowed an electric-light bulb," said someone to a young mother whose "Eye" was "generous," whose outlook was God's.

This radiant young mother told me that when her husband proposed to her she replied: "You propose to me before your sister [with whom the husband lived] and I want to see her face. If she approves, I'll take you." It was done. The reply of the sister was, "Well, I always wondered whether John would have sense enough to ask you." The young mother commented: "I got not only a husband; I got a sister as well. I never had one. We love each other tenderly." Her "Eye" was generous and her whole personality and the whole household was full of light. In one year she has grown spiritually, more than anyone I've ever known.

Said a schoolmaster: "I was kind because I wanted people to be kind to me. I was interested in people because I wanted people to be interested in me. I did everything, even my good things, for selfish reasons. But this didn't go with the children of my school. They saw through it. Now I've come to the end of my road. I've surrendered myself."

O Christ, help me to change my basic attitude toward life. May I see life through Thy will not mine. Then—light! Amen.

AFFIRMATION FOR THE DAY: *"The generous eye" will characterize my outlook on life today.*

"WHAT YOU THINK, YOU ARE"

Our basic thinking is important. For the mind and the whole personality are dyed by our thoughts. "As [a man] thinketh in his heart, so is he."

Someone has put it this way, "You may not be what you think you are, but what you think, you are." If you think positive thoughts, you'll be a positive person, but if you think weak, negative thoughts, you'll be a weak, negative person.

Go over your vocabulary and your habitual thinking and cleanse your vocabulary and your thinking from all weak and negative words and thoughts. Replace them with the strong and the positive. If you've been saying "No," begin to say "Yes." A friend, a management engineer, remakes sick businesses and sick personalities. When he takes hold of weak persons, he makes them straight off say "Yes" twenty-five times. They have been saying "No" to themselves—"I can't do this"; "I'm afraid of that"; "This is too big for me"; "I'm not feeling well"; "I'm worried sick"; "I may fail," and so on *ad nauseam*, literally *ad nauseam*. For under this sick thinking the whole person turns sick.

Since life is ongoing and positive and creative, to be in line with life you must say "Yes," not "No," for in saying "No" you step out of the stream of creative life into the stream of negation, the stream of decay, the stream of death.

Listen to this trapped soul, trapped in her own negative, backward-looking attitudes: "Even normally I seem to live in a state of self-condemnation much of the time. You see, I am continually wondering if I have sinned here or sinned there until it has become almost an obsession with me. All in all it makes me a very self-centered person until I don't know which way to turn. I have just returned from a place where I had a wonderful teaching position, yet I have failed again. It was blamed on surface reasons; yet down in my heart I know it is the same old problem, that is the only problem in life for me, namely, my relationship with God." But I wonder if it isn't her relationship with herself. She's saying "No." And just as you cannot live by denying yourself food, so you cannot live spiritually on a "No." It must be a "Yes."

O Christ, teach me to affirm—to affirm thy promises written in the Scriptures, in the universe, and in me. Amen.

AFFIRMATION FOR THE DAY: *I am an affirmative person, affirming great affirmations and denying denials.*

THE DIVINE "YES"

We are emphasizing the necessity of positive thoughts and words, the necessity of saying "Yes." A disciple asked his preceptor, "What is the one ultimate word of truth?" The preceptor replied, "Yes." "I asked what is the one ultimate word of truth?" And the preceptor again replied, "I'm not deaf." The ultimate word of truth is "Yes." But not a hit-and-miss, random "Yes" to anything that comes along—good, bad, and indifferent. That is the mistake of those who insist on being positive, but do not clearly state—positive to what? They say we must say "Yes," but "Yes" to what? The Christian defines his "Yes," and then says it wholeheartedly.

"The divine 'yes' has at last sounded in him, for in him is the 'yes' that affirms all the promises of God" (II Cor. 1:19-20, Moffatt). In Jesus the divine "yes" has at last sounded. Men were not able to say a full-throated and a fullhearted "Yes" to life until they saw it incarnate in Jesus. Up to that time it had to be "Yes" and "No." But when we saw the full meaning of Life in Jesus, then at this place we can say "Yes" with no inhibitions or hesitations. My "Yeses" must be "Yeses" to His "Yes." Here I am not saying "Yes" at random, a "Yes" for the sake of saying "Yes," which ends in mushy sentimentality, but I'm saying "Yes" in Him, for in Him life is good, is creative, is open-ended.

Here you can say "Yes" with the stops out. Think, affirm, say, act the "Yes" of Jesus, and life itself will become a "Yes." For you are affirming something which the universe affirms. You are echoing the creative Word of God—the Word which created the worlds, sustains them, and which redeems into affirmation all who affirm life with Him. In saying His "Yes" you align yourself with the creative purposes of God, and all of them work in you and through you.

This saying "Yes" at random, just to be saying "Yes," is better than saying "No" at random—it lifts you a bit, but only a bit. For it is only an orphaned "Yes," with no universe necessarily behind it. It is bootstrap lifting.

O Jesus, in Thee I can be all out. I can face life with no hesitations or fears or inhibitions. Here I am backed by everything that really is. Amen.

AFFIRMATION FOR THE DAY: *When I affirm Jesus and His Way, then the universe confirms me and my way.*

THE NAY-SAYING ATTITUDE

We continue our meditation on thinking affirmatively. The sacred writer puts the matter thus: "Finally, brothers, keep in mind whatever is true, whatever is worthy, whatever is just, whatever is pure, whatever is attractive, whatever is high-toned, all excellence, all merit. . . . So shall the God of peace be with you" (Phil. 4:8-9, Moffatt). Here he asks to "keep in mind" the true, the worthy, the just, the pure, the attractive, the high-toned, the excellent and the meritorious. No wonder he finishes by saying, "So shall the God of peace be with you."

But if you "keep in mind" the critical, the negative, "So shall the devils of unhappiness and conflict be with you." Listen to this woman telling in one of our Ashrams her needs: "I do not forgive myself— I need to. I forgive others but not myself. I'm a coward and I've been running away. I've not had the guts—I've been backwatering." The unhappiness on her face reflected the backward-looking, the Nay-saying attitude.

Some women of India were filled with stories of tigers and leopards as they traveled for the first time in the hills. They went to bed at night with the thought of tigers and leopards in mind. One woman awakened during the night with a shriek and all the others began shrieking. There were eyes glowing under the bed! The tiger's eyes turned out to be glowworms! The negative type of person is always turning glowworms into tigers.

Canon Hooper of India was staying in a bungalow in a section where there were tigers and leopards. He and his wife went to sleep with the thought of them in mind. During the night he awakened his wife, "Listen to the rustling in the bushes." Tigers! Their hair almost stood on end. Just then Christmas carols burst out, for it was Christmas morning and the Indian Christians had gathered to sing. If you keep in mind fearful negative thoughts, you will turn Christmas carols into tigers and glowworms into leopards. If you think tigers and leopards, you'll see them—see them in everything, even in the good. Go to bed with positive thoughts of good, of God.

O God, forgive us that we die before we die and are sick before we are sick, because we are thinking dead or sick thoughts. Amen.

AFFIRMATION FOR THE DAY: *I will think health, talk health, and be health this day.*

DON'T PROVIDE FOR FAILURE

We continue our meditation on being positive and affirmative in thinking. Don't think defeat; think victory.

But not a phony victory—it must be real. It was said of Napoleon that he used to deliberately deceive himself, making out his battle plans and talking in terms of hundreds of thousands of men here and there when there were only tens of thousands available. When someone remonstrated with him, he replied, "You don't want to take away my comfort do you?" But it was a false comfort and his false comfort ultimately let him down. There must be no false, impossible ideas projected on the universe to bolster courage. To bolster prayer this statement was put out in a call to prayer: "A hundred people in 1939 through love and prayer stopped Hitler even before the war began: and then in November 1, 1942, when the war was on, a greater wave of love and prayer, spread all over the United States, turned the tide to victory." This is closely akin to magic and produces not real prayer, but ultimate paralysis. Our affirmations must be in line with reality or they will let us down however affirmative they may be.

Here is the Christian position: "But put ye on the Lord Jesus Christ, and make not provision for the flesh, to fulfil the lusts thereof" (Rom. 13:14). Don't provide in the thought for failure—make no provision in your thinking for the flesh to get the upper hand. If you think you're going to fall, you will fall. You've already fallen in thought. Expect victory and you'll have victory. Expect defeat and you'll have defeat, for you're already defeated in mind.

But this is not just autosuggestion, good as it is as autosuggestion. There is something deeper, "Put ye on the Lord Jesus Christ, and make not provision for the flesh." In putting on Jesus, affirming His affirmations, we adequately provide for mental re-inforcement against yielding to the flesh. It aligns us with adequate resources—we are affirming reality and not merely autosuggesting what isn't true. We are affirming Affirmation; we are promising the Promises; we are living Life. It is realizing the Real.

O Jesus, I put Thee on—take Thee as my life and now I am free to be free. I make no provision for defeat since Thou hast provided for victory. Amen.

AFFIRMATION FOR THE DAY: *I am victorious in His victory, strong in His strength, and alive in His Life.*

"THEN SHE IS VERY ILL"

We look today at another phase of renewing the mind—affirming health. I do not believe that you affirm out of existence all evil and all sickness by mere affirmation. Some diseases are structural and the changing of the mind about them will not change the facts. But the mind does have a tremendous influence upon the body and its health. "As for me, Daniel, my thoughts greatly alarmed me; I lost my colour, but I kept everything in mind" (Dan. 7:28, Moffatt). "At this I Daniel was for some days ill; after which I rose and went about the king's business. I was appalled at the vision; I could not understand it" (Dan. 8:27, Moffatt). "No strength was left in me, paleness ruined my fresh colour" (Dan. 10:8, Moffatt). "I was shaking; no strength remained in me, I could not breathe" (Dan. 10:17, Moffatt). Here Daniel, a model of physical health, was physically upset by his thinking. You can think yourself into illness and you can think yourself out again.

If you are always talking about your illnesses, you'll have a lot of illnesses to talk about. As someone has put it, "When a woman thinks she is ill when she is not, then she is very ill." If you have a mental image of yourself as ill and depressed, then you'll be made in the likeness of that wanted illness. But if you think health and affirm health, then you are health. I have sometimes played the game with myself as I walk from a train carrying suitcases which are far too heavy to carry, and no porter in sight, of imagining myself raising those suitcases above my head and carrying them along in that triumphant fashion. The actual carrying then seems easier. Autosuggestion? Yes, of course. You're always suggesting something to yourself—victory or defeat, health or sickness. Then why not suggest the constructive instead of the destructive? Your very organs will respond if you talk health to them instead of sickness. They will blush with pride, and the very blushing will send the healthgiving blood coursing through them. But if you think sickness to your organs, they will blush with fear and the bloodless organs will turn sick for want of blood.

O God, Thou hast made me for health. Then may I think Thy thoughts after Thee and think health instead of sickness. In Jesus' name. Amen.

AFFIRMATION FOR THE DAY: *"In Him who strengthens me, I am able for anything"* (Phil. 4:13, Moffatt).

STEPS INTO POSITIVE ATTITUDES

Today we take positive steps out of negative into positive ment.
attitudes.

1. Stand off from your life and look at it objectively and honestl
to see what your "eye" is. From what standpoint do you look at life—
from fear or faith? From defense or offense? From apology or aggre
sion? Decide what kind of person you are.

2. If you find a basically negative attitude, then surrender it
God. Don't spit on your hands and say you'll fight it. That will mak
you tense and strained. Ask God to take it over with your consen
and co-operation.

3. After surrendering it, now accept the positive resources of Goo
Begin to live on God's Yeses. Be God's Yes-man in the sense of sayin
Yes to God's Yeses.

4. Spend enough time in prayer to expose yourself to God's Yese
The quiet time is the acquiring time.

5. Now go over your vocabulary and cleanse away all weak an
negative words. Since they have become grooved in the mind, they wi
tend to hang on after the basic attitude has been reversed.

6. When these negative words come back to the mind, point ther
to the permanent sign, *Verboten*. Don't let them beyond the fron
porch.

7. Cultivate the new vocabulary of strong, positive words. Use ther
on yourself and on your friends. Use them until they become real t
you and habitual.

8. Remember the dangerous ages are forty and above. Remembe
that the wisest can be infected with negativism. "For years Shakespear
seems almost maniacal in his blind hate of life, and his stinging con
tempt, his nausea indeed of men and women. As Raleigh put it, 'H
blasphemed the very foundations of life and sanity.'" Watch cynicism
as you would watch a deadly germ.

9. Look for the positive and strong and you'll begin to see it every
where. For the creative God still creates.

O God, my Father, Thou art bringing me in line with Thy creativ
processes. I surrender to them completely. They are at work in me now
I thank Thee. Amen.

AFFIRMATION FOR THE DAY: *I belong to a creative God with a positiv
plan, the Kingdom of God, and therefore I shall be a positive
creative person.*

"LIFE MAKES SENSE"

We have been thinking about the renewing of the mind. According to the verse, "Have your mind renewed, and so be transformed in nature, able to make out what the will of God is" (Rom. 12:2, Moffatt), the central thing in the transformation of the mind is the ability to make out what the will of God is"—the linking of your mind with the mind of God. When your mind and God's mind come together, then all things in heaven and earth fall into their place. Life makes sense.

Then you find out that the will of God is "good"—"good" intrinsically and "good" for you. The next step is that it is "acceptable"—he accepts it as "good," and when it does, then it finds that it is "perfect." So the steps are these: When we look on the will of God as "good" and accept it as a working way, then it turns out to be "perfect." The mind is at rest.

We might dismiss the matter there were there not not a factor in the mind which we haven't yet looked at—the subconscious portion of the mind. Can the subconscious be transformed?

David Seabury says: "All of our real thinking, and three-quarters of our mental activity, transpires below the depth of our awareness, and only comes to the surface as the time of active use arrives." If this is true, then when we try to straighten out our conscious thinking and leave out the subconscious, then we are dealing with only one quarter of our problem. For that reason thought-control movements, which deal only with the conscious control of conscious thought, so often end in frustrated trying. For the subconscious is untouched. If our faith has no adequate word for the subconscious, then it too will suffer from the same frustrated trying, for the bigger part of the personality is unredeemed. As Kunkel says, "Religion without awareness of conscious and unconscious . . . is not religion, but blind idolatry." The Christian faith takes in the whole of life, and life includes the subconscious, includes it especially.

O God, we have now come to the crux of the matter: Heal me at the place of the subconscious or I'm healed lightly. So heal me there. Amen.

AFFIRMATION FOR THE DAY: *I shall talk faith and victory to my subconscious mind when I am awake, so that my subconscious mind may talk faith and victory to me when I am asleep—or awake!*

THE TRANSFORMATION OF THE SUBCONSCIOUS

I have looked down from a plane flying between Newfoundland an
Ireland and have seen the huge icebergs floating below. Even fron
twenty thousand feet in the air they seemed huge, but we are told tha
only one eighth of the iceberg is above the water, with the seve:
eighths below. G. Stanley Hall says that the subconscious is like th
iceberg—seven eighths of it below the level of consciousness. D
Charles Mayo declared before a medical association in Chicago tha
75 per cent of human action is controlled by the unconscious, and 2
per cent by conscious thought. Whatever the proportion, we are dea
ing with a preponderant and hence powerful force in our make-up
If, as Maeterlinck says, "It is what we do not see that makes the worl
go round," then it is certainly true that it is that which we are no
conscious of that makes our inner world go round for good or ill.

How do we know the subconscious is there? Sigmund Freud, a
quoted by Kunkel, "has pointed out that some of our blunders, . . . an
at least part of our forgetfulness are due to unconscious tendencie
which conflict with our conscious intentions. For example, a woma
who is very anxious to have children always reads the word 'stock,' a
'stork.' That happens against her conscious will, and is caused by th
deeper instinct which controls her reactions more than she knows."

This brings an inherent conflict even after the conscious mind i
converted. This conscious mind has accepted the Christian way whil
the unconscious mind is still under the control of elemental drives—
self, sex, and the herd. Hence many Christian lives are at a standstil
for the unconverted subconscious cancels out the converted conscious
"Many a man's starboard turbines are pushing forward with his por
engines backing up." The result is confusion and conflict and a gettin
nowhere. All of life, conscious and the subconscious, has got to b
brought under a single control, directed toward a single end, with al
the forces harmonized, or else life is frustrated.

My God and Father, Thou hast made me—made my depths too, mad
them for Thyself, so cleanse and remake them for I want to be every whi
whole. Amen.

AFFIRMATION FOR THE DAY: *My subconscious mind, surrendered t*
and controlled by the Holy Spirit, is safe and creative.

SOMETIMES THE DEPTHS ARE REVEALED

We continue to look at the unconscious. We saw that the conflict etween the conscious and the subconscious can give an undertone to fe of unhappiness and frustration. For there is an uneasy sitting on lid. Sometimes the depths are revealed.

Charles T. Holman relates: "In the town where I was born lived a oman and her daughter, who walked in their sleep. One night while ilence enfolded the world, the woman and her daughter, walking yet sleep, met in the mist-veiled garden. And the mother spoke, and she aid: 'At last, at last, my enemy! You by whom my life was destroyed— ho built up your life upon the ruins of mine! Would I could kill ou!' And the daughter spoke and she said: 'O hateful woman, selfish nd old! Who stand between my free self and me! Who would have y life an echo of your own faded life! Would you were dead!' At hat moment the cock crew, and both women awoke. The mother said ently, 'Is that you darling?' And the daughter answered gently, 'Yes, ear!'"

Each during waking hours lived on the polite but suppressed level of he conscious. Both were unhappy and frustrated. These resentments estered underneath. But sometimes it is unconscious fears that work avoc in the subconscious. Seabury quotes the story of Miss Lily andon, who at the age of three was closed up in a closet by a nurse. his produced an unconscious fear of dark, shut-in places. Subways, unnels, narrow, dimly lighted streets at night, somber shadows in the oods filled her with horror. But she was forced to travel. When her rain was to pass through a long tunnel, her teeth would chatter for ours beforehand, her feet would be cold, her face white and set. With ll her will she would restrain screams of wild anguish. And yet her ntellect knows perfectly well that there is no more danger in the unnel than when the train is speeding along the sun-lit tracks. The ears had dropped into her subconscious and there they worked havoc. Many wake up in the morning tired because of the conflict in the ubconscious, working while they slept.

O God, I come to Thee with my deepest need, the need for cleansing he unconscious. Heal me there and then let the world come on. I'm afe. Amen.

FFIRMATION FOR THE DAY: *My subconscious is the storehouse of victories upon which I can call in a crisis.*

"AN INJURY TO THE SUBCONSCIOUS MIND"

In one of my books I told the story of a music teacher friend who when she came to write her name, wrote it laboriously as the writing of an old woman double her age. When she came to playing the piano her thumb worked perfectly; when she came to write, her thumb was nearly paralyzed. Why? It began after she wrote hundreds of letters in longhand to people who had sent letters of condolence to her family upon the loss of a wonderful father. What was happening subconsciously was this: every time she picked up a pen to write she was subconsciously reminded of that bereavement, became inwardly tense and her finger refused to work properly.

Norman Vincent Peale quotes a similar case of a man who had trouble writing his name. When he came to a hotel register he would always get at the end of the line so no one would see his awful scrawl. Why this paralysis? When he was a small boy, his father suffered a muscular accident which destroyed the ability of his fingers to write. The father became horribly self-conscious about it. He told the boy the story so often that it amounted to an injury to his subconscious mind.

The depth psychology, says Kunkel, was never more accurately described than by Jesus, who said, "You are like tombs whitewashed; they look comely on the outside, but inside they are full of dead men's bones and all manner of impurity" (Matt. 23:27, Moffatt). Kunkel adds, "The existence of our unconscious desires and our repressed tendencies could not be described more strikingly."

The question arises that if Jesus described the subconscious so accurately, did He prescribe a remedy which is adequate? Or did He, like the priest and the Levite, look at the half-dead man and pass by on the other side? If so, He is only a half Savior, dealing with the conscious but making no provision for the release from subconscious conflicts. His salvation in that case is arrested conversion and we must pass Him by. But must we? He who was so right in everything else will he be wrong in this?

O Christ, we turn breathlessly to Thee, for we feel Thou hast the answer and that answer will not be an answer, but *the* answer. Amen.

AFFIRMATION FOR THE DAY: *"Who healeth all thy diseases," including hurts to the subconscious mind.*

"THE LAW OF REVERSED EFFORT"

We raised the question yesterday whether Christ had an adequate answer for the subconscious. We must face that question now.

First of all, we note that nowhere in the New Testament is repression of suppressed desires advocated. It is foreign to the gospels. Here modern psychology and the Christian faith are one. They both teach that repression results in a complex. The experience of Paul, under the law, fighting with his suppressed desires (Rom. 7) is pre-Christian and sub-Christian, and something to be superseded by a more excellent way, "The law of the Spirit of life in Christ Jesus hath made me free from the law of sin and death" (Rom. 8:2). Here is freedom from the lower law of sin and death, not the suppression of it. The remedy is not repression, for this brings on what Baudouin calls "the law of reversed effort." An unusually conscious effort brings about an opposite result. If you try too hard to miss a stone on the road while riding a bicycle, you'll probably hit it.

Nor does mere confession of the ordinary transgression get at the root of the matter. Kunkel has a penetrating passage when he says: "Both the sinner and the absolver live in an unconscious agreement never to touch the poisonous roots, because the same explosion, the same revolution would upset the whole outer and inner lives of father confessor and parishioner alike. 'Keep off!! High voltage!!' That is one of the reasons why two thousands years of confessional practice have failed to discover the unconscious. The result of this wrong practice is that scarcely anything can be more boring and more useless psychologically than the usual routine of confession."

If the two proposed remedies, repression and "confession," as routinely practiced, do not touch the problem, then what does? Does conversion, if it stops at the conversion of the conscious mind, give the answer? No, for it sets up another conflict between the new life in the conscious with the old life in the subconscious. The subconscious must be converted or we are not fully saved.

Father, Thou art probing deep. For Thou art seeking to make me not merely better, but well. Take me by the hand and lead me to the promised land of full freedom. Amen.

AFFIRMATION FOR THE DAY: *The God who made the depths can remake them. I turn them over to Him.*

"YOU CAN LOVE YOURSELF"

We have been looking at inadequate or sub-Christian answers to the problem of the unconscious. What is the Christian answer? It was hinted at in the quotation: "The law of the Spirit of life in Christ Jesus hath made me free from the law of sin and death." "The Spirit of life in Christ Jesus" is the equivalent of the Holy Spirit. The Holy Spirit "fathoms everything, even the depths of God" (I Cor. 2:10, Moffatt). And we may add—"and the depths of man." Here is the depth psychology—not merely revealing the "depths," but redeeming the "depths."

For the Holy Spirit, when we surrender to His control all we know —the conscious—and all we don't know—the subconscious—then He does nothing less than move in to take over, cleanse, control, and co-ordinate the whole of the inner life, conscious and subconscious. And more: He fills it with the unutterable sense of His presence, so that the exquisite joy of that presence makes irrelevant and absurd any conflicting lesser joys. It is the expulsive power of a divine affection. Everything is caught up in the love of God and the power of the lesser loves is not broken but fulfilled in a higher love. You can love yourself —in God; you can love sex—in God; you can love the herd—in God. Then you are not sitting on a lid; you've taken off the lid and you're letting nature caper! For nature, conscious and subconscious, is made for Him, and when it finds Him, it finds itself. Then you are free, free to express yourself—in Him.

This is more than sublimation—it is total self-expression. You are expressing yourself in the way and in the sphere for which you are made—God—and now you are truly natural. You are truly natural because possessed by the Supernatural. Everything then becomes a dancing joy—a play spell.

No wonder when the early Christians received the Holy Spirit on-lookers thought them to be drunk. They were—intoxicated with God and with their own consequent freedom. Such a sweeping answer to all their fears, inner conflicts, inhibitions, and guilts was enough to make them appear intoxicated—with joy.

O Holy Spirit, whose area of work is the subconscious mind, take over depths I cannot control, and cleanse where I cannot touch. In Jesus' name. Amen.

AFFIRMATION FOR THE DAY: *With the Holy Spirit at the roots, then all my fruits will be fruits of the Spirit.*

"THE GOOD STORE"

In considering the subconscious the question arises: Why did a good God create the subconscious portion of our minds and leave it out of our control? Isn't that a moral liability, especially as the subconscious is the residing place of the driving instincts or urges? Can the subconscious work beneficently and to our advantage?

Yes. Suppose the conscious mind had to take over the complete load of responsibility for being good and doing good. That would load too much on conscious decision and would make goodness to precarious, depending every moment on good decisions. So God has provided for what Jesus calls "the good store": "The good man brings good out of his good store, and the evil man brings evil out of his store of evil" (Matt. 12:35, Moffatt). Every good deed, every good thought, every good attitude is dropped into the subconscious mind and thus becomes a part of "the good store" which is being built up within. This good store in the subconscious takes over in conscious crises and while we are asleep, and predisposes us to goodness. We thus become good by habit. Habit is working with us and not against us. This makes goodness not a precarious thing depending on the passing good act—it becomes a constitutional thing, a part of our make-up. We become naturally good —it becomes second-nature to us to do the right thing, say the right word, take the right attitude.

The driving urges in the subconscious have had a long association with evil by racial inheritance when we take them over as individuals. Hence a certain bent toward evil. But intrinsically they are not evil. They can be surrendered to the Holy Spirit, cleansed by Him, redirected and brought into co-ordination and unity with the conscious mind, so that conscious mind and subconscious under a single control are directed to one end—the Kingdom of God. Then a man is a truly co-ordinated and integrated person. And not precariously so. The good store holds him to goodness. You make the subconscious, and then the subconscious makes you. We become almost automatically good—automatic because we have chosen through infinite decisions the character of the subconscious.

O God, I thank Thee for the subconscious, Thy beneficent way to make me good even when off-guard. I thank Thee. Amen.

AFFIRMATION FOR THE DAY: *My good store holds me to goodness by disposition and by habit.*

CANCELED OUT BY UNTRANSFORMED EMOTIONS

We come now to meditate upon the transformation of the emotions. We have looked at the transformation of the mind, conscious and subconscious, so we must now take the next step—the transformation of the emotions.

Some people are converted in mind—they accept the Christian faith in their way of life; and they are converted in their wills—they try to live the Christian way, but their emotions are not converted. Their emotions are still filled with fears, griefs, resentments, self-pity, jealousies, inhibitions, egocentricity, conflicts, a lingering sense of guilt. Their emotional life has not been cleansed and co-ordinated and Christianized. Hence they are canceled-out Christians—canceled out by untransformed emotions. The emotions are the driving force of the personality, and if they drive in wrong or contrary directions, then the personality is a battleground instead of a smoothly working whole.

It is difficult to separate thought from emotion, for every thought has an emotional tone almost inseparably connected with it. Besides, we can almost say that we think with our emotions, for the mind gathers reasons to justify the emotions. Just as a magnet gathers iron filings to itself, so an emotionally charged mind gathers reasons or excuses to justify the emotional attitudes. A mind filled with wrong emotional attitudes can't think straight, for the emotions twist the thinking. To think straight you've got to be emotionally straight. If wrong thinking has slain its thousand, then wrong emotions have slain their tens of thousands, for wrong emotions slay right thinking as well.

William James defines an emotion as "the state of mind that manifests itself by a sensible change in the body." So the emotion does not merely influence the body—it produces a sensible change in the body. And the changes take place not merely in some portions of the body—they affect every single cell of the body for good or ill. There is not a single cell of the body clear down to the marrow in the bones which is unaffected for good or ill by an emotion. Emotions, then, are important; yes, all important.

O God, my Father, if I'm to be straightened out, my emotions must be straightened out too—and especially. So I come for emotional transformation. Amen.

AFFIRMATION FOR THE DAY: *The God who has made the emotions has made provision for their redemption and redirection.*

"THE EMOTIONS MADE THE DIFFERENCE"

We are meditating on the transformation of the emotions. First of all, we must remind ourselves that emotions are a good endowment if directed toward right ends. As someone has said, "People never do anything unless they feel." The feelings or emotions are the driving forces of the soul. If properly harnessed, they can drive you to great goals, or if loose and unharnessed, can drive you "nuts." Or a lack of driving emotion can leave you just cold and fishy.

Emotions can affect every cell of the body for good or ill. Here is a man who was carried to a hospital at 9 A.M.—carried because he couldn't walk, faint, heart going at 180 times a minute, vomiting, couldn't control his bowels. He stayed in that shape for three months. Up to 8 A.M. he was perfectly normal, never sick. At 8 A.M. he walked into his wife's bedroom and found his wife had killed their only girl and had committed suicide. Every organ was structurally the same at 8 A.M. and at 9 A.M. But functionally they were entirely different. One moment they functioned into health and well-being, and in another moment they functioned into ill-health and upsetness. The emotions made the difference.

The power of the emotions to affect the organs and their functions is seen in a test given to a woman in Leviticus. If she was suspected of immorality she was taken to a priest and her hair let down. A curse was written on a piece of paper, the paper soaked in water, and the woman drank the water. If she was guilty, she would have pains; but if not guilty, no pains. The emotion of guilt produced the pains. In India the eating dry rice test is given to a number of suspects in a crime. The one whose rice after chewing remained dry, is guilty. The emotion of fear stopped the salivary glands from functioning. Emotions can upset every gland of the body. Therefore emotions are important, very important.

O Father, Thou hast made my emotions; help me not to unmake them so that they become disruptive by my wrong attitudes. Amen.

AFFIRMATION FOR THE DAY: *My emotions, now the servant of the Kingdom, will furnish driving power to bring in the Kingdom.*

"THE GUINEA PIGS WERE SICK AGAIN"

We continue our thinking about the effect of emotions on the body. Michael de Montaigne says: "I knew myself a gentleman, who having treated a great deal of good company at his house, three or four days after bragged in jest (for there was no such thing) that he had made them eat of a baked cat; at which a young gentlewoman, who had been at the feast, took such a horror, that falling into a violent vomiting and a fever, there was no possible means to save her." Her emotions caused functional disturbance in perfectly healthy organs.

A group of people ate soup, liked it and said so. But when told that it was real turtle soup they began to vomit.

A pastor told me that he lost his lunch thinking about a purple cow, suggested by the Purple Cow restaurant. He could eat beef and assimilate it, but the mere thought of a purple cow aroused feelings which upset him.

This is not confined to people. Scientists gave guinea pigs cream with ipecac in it. It made them sick. Then they gave cream without ipecac, and the guinea pigs seeing the cream were sick again.

A pastor told me that every time he was with his wife in the days of their courtship he would be upset and would lose his previous meal. But as soon as they were married the vomiting stopped! Obviously it was the uncertainty about being able to get her for his wife that upset him, but as soon as the matter was settled and the uncertainty dropped away, his digestion was normal.

An aviator got ill in flight during a war. A doctor gave him some pills to take which he said would cure him. They did. Later the doctor told him he could cease taking them. They were nothing but aspirin tablets!

A nurse who had given an ice pack to many patients was required to take it as a part of her training. She became hysterical, and the whole attempt had to be abandoned. She was suffering from claustrophobia, a fear of closed places. In her childhood she had probably been shut into a closet and a fear was lodged in the subconscious. It came out in the crisis.

O Gracious Father, help me to get my ideas and my emotions straight, for I would be straight. I cannot be straight unless they are. Amen.

AFFIRMATION FOR THE DAY: *My emotions may play tricks on me; they can also do the trick for me—drive me to my goal.*

"GRASSHOPPERS WE WERE"

We are looking at the effect of emotions on the body. Doctors tell us 85 per cent of the people who have headaches, with a pain in the back of the neck going down into the cords of the neck, have it because of emotional stress. There is nothing structurally wrong with the nerves, but wrong messages are being sent over these nerves. Many people lay the blame on the nerves—"My nerves are upset." But the nerves are only wires—they transmit what is sent across them, good, bad, or indifferent. It is the person behind those wires who determines what messages are sent. If he is sending fearful, negative, resentful, critical messages across those wires, then of course the results will be upsetting. To blame it on the nerve would be as intelligent as to swear at the telegraph wires when you get an upsetting telegram.

And the serious thing is that we are made in the likeness of the messages we continually send. If we send fearful messages, we become a fearful person; if negative messages, then a negative person. "They made us feel like grasshoppers, and grasshoppers we were to them" (Num. 13:33, Moffatt). If you send grasshopper messages to yourself long enough, then you will be a grasshopper.

John A. Schindler says that half the people who have pains that seem like ulcer pains have no ulcer. He tells of a man in the grocery business who had a pain in the region of the stomach all the time. He was in competition with the chain stores, had a bad-tempered wife, and a son who was always in trouble. Every time he went on a fishing trip and got to a town twenty-five miles north of where he lived the pain would cease and would not return until he got to the spot where he could see the towers of his town, then the pains would begin again. The towers awakened memories, which in turn sent messages of fear of renewed strain and conflict, which in turn produced the pains. And they were not "imaginary pains," they were real pains, just as real as though they were structural in origin. The pains were caused by emotion resulting in functional disturbance.

Father, I thank Thee for my nerves. Help me to send helpful, healing things across them. I accept the responsibility for my nerves. Amen.

AFFIRMATION FOR THE DAY: *I shall send across my wires, my nerves, messages of faith and confidence today.*

"THE PAIN BEGINS"

We pursue our meditation on the effect of emotion on our bodies. A great deal of high blood pressure comes from the emotions and not from the heart or arteries. That this is true was pointed out by a doctor, by the fact that if such a person is put under an anesthetic the blood pressure will come down to normal. The pressure was not in the physical, but in the mental and spiritual. Something, buried deep perhaps, in the subconscious was causing emotional disturbance, which in turn caused high blood pressure.

A doctor in the Mayo Clinic told of a pain he had in the abdominal region that seemed like ulcer. He said: "I know there is nothing there, but in Rochester I'm driven; I've got things to do; and that thing keeps hurting me. When I get into the train and get to Winona the pain stops; when the train gets back into the station again the pain begins." The pressure of work and his inability to do it in a relaxed way tied up his intestines and caused pain—real pain too. Someone has said: "The colon is the mirror of the mind. When the mind gets tight, the colon gets tight."

Many a person gets up tired in the morning—more tired than when he went to bed. Why? The reason is that some wrong emotion is setting up a tension in the subconscious mind and the subconscious mind is working in tension and fear even when the conscious mind is unconscious in sleep. He is running his motor even when his car is parked, so he is using up his gas and wearing out his engine needlessly.

A medical authority says that half the people who seem to have gall bladder trouble don't have it at all. If the pain happens to be in the lower abdomen, it would seem like appendicitis. And then he adds, "It would take a wise doctor not to open that abdomen." Bushels of teeth and buckets full of appendixes have been taken out when the trouble has been caused by emotions and was not structural at all.

Two doctors, D. T. Graham and Stewart Wolf, making a study of hives, found that twenty-nine out of thirty cases had hives because of a particular attitude toward life. The patients felt resentments against the fact that they could neither retaliate nor run away. They felt they were stuck.

O God, give us the sense to see that we are upsetting ourselves and causing pains in our bodies because of our wrong emotions. Amen.

AFFIRMATION FOR THE DAY: *Since my emotions can upset me or set me up, I'm going to make them set me up.*

"YOUR GASTRIC JUICES WILL FIND IT OUT"

We tarry another day to look at the effect of wrong emotions upon the body. If we get this straight, then perhaps we will be straight.

A woman writes: "The next day I asked him if he wanted a divorce. No answer. Now I am flippant. I put on a false front of flippancy. But I don't sleep and my stomach is tied in knots. Please help me. For I love him so much." You cannot tell the subconscious mind a lie and have it believed. For the subconscious mind sees past or through subterfuges like outer flippancy, sees the real condition—an emotional upset, deep down.

In the *British Medical Journal* were these lines:

> Eat all kind Nature can bestow,
> It will amalgamate down below
> If the mind says so!
> But if you once begin to doubt
> Your gastric juices will find it out!

An osteopath, able and prepossessing, told me that he got all tied up and frustrated through emotional upset. Though he had an excellent practice, his patients fell off, for he could radiate no confidence, no health—he transmitted his own sicknesses of mind and soul to his patients. Then through reading *The Way* he got straightened out. He was released from his inner tied-up condition and frustrations. He began to be confident again. His patients came back—more than ever. He is now on top of the world. When his emotions got straightened out, he got straightened out.

But some don't get their feet upon the Way. Here is the son of a very outstanding doctor. He did not want to go to school. He actually became ill in the schoolroom, for he resented going. After high school he wanted to go into the army. His father allowed him. But after two years he had enough and wanted to be released. When news came that his time was extended, he became sick, with a temperature of 105°. Any limiting thing closed in on him and made him sick. He wanted to be free and didn't know how. His emotional conflict made him a conflict and hence his physical illness.

O Father, save me from self-imposed illnesses. For Thou hast made me for Thy health. Thou dost will my wholeness. Help me to will it. Amen.

AFFIRMATION FOR THE DAY: *All my autosuggestions will be suggestions not to illness, but to health.*

STEPS TO TRANSFORMED EMOTIONS

We now come on the last day of this week of our meditation on transformed emotions and ask what the steps are to have the emotions transformed.

1. *Reject from your thinking the pre-Christian and sub-Christian fatalistic statement,* "You cannot straighten out what is twisted" (Eccl. 1:15, Moffatt). You can. What man has made by God's grace and help man can unmake. The twists are no integral part of your nature. God wills their removal. When God and you both will they should be straightened out, they will be.

2. *Don't stand up and fight your emotions.* That will only make you tense and will produce "the law of reversed effort."

You cannot be fruitful by the *will* willing to do so. There must be effortless faith that naturally brings forth fruit.

3. *Don't defend your wrong emotions or deny they are there.* That will only drive them into the subconscious where they will work havoc.

4. *Now surrender them to God.* They are not on your hands now; they are in God's hands. Ask Him to take them over. That means that you are willing to part with them—really willing.

5. *Since God has your emotions, now you can relax.* Let go the fighting, tense attitude. Be receptive of grace to overcome these emotions. Since God has your emotions, they are now being cleansed and are fastened on Him. Since your emotions are now centered in God, you need no longer be afraid of them. Let your transformed emotions now drive you to great goals.

6. *Cultivate now the opposite emotions.* If the wrong emotion has been fear, cultivate faith; if it has been resentments and hate, cultivate love to everybody and everything; if it's been self-hate, now love yourself in God. If negative emotion, put your mental emphasis on the positive. Your emotions are now with you, not against you. You're free!

Gracious God and Father, I thank Thee that Thou hast shown me the Way. And now I walk in it joyfully and freely. I thank Thee. Amen.

AFFIRMATION FOR THE DAY: *My emotions, now broken to harness and working with me, are now my allies.*

"WORRY EATS UP THE HUMAN FLESH"

We have been looking at emotions in general; we now come to look at specific emotions. The first emotion we shall look at is fear.

The first fact about fear that needs to be stressed is that fear can be a very constructive emotion. Fear is a hedge set up around the personality to keep it from harmful things and influences. It keeps the driver from driving too close to a precipice; the surgeon from cutting into the wrong places; the mother from feeding the wrong things to her child; the good man from breaking a moral law lest it spoil his goodness. Without wholesome fear the human race would have destroyed itself physically, morally, and spiritually. So wholesome fear is God's good gift—the gift that helps us to say "No" to some things in order to say "Yes" to others. Fear is God's preventive medicine.

But fear, like almost everything else, can get off the right track. It can jump its God-intended track and then it can be the most destructive of emotions. Harnessed to constructive ends, fear is constructive; but unharnessed and running wild, it can be the most destructive thing ever let loose in the life. It can leave the life in chaos and ruin.

Akin to fear is anxiety. Anxiety is an undertone of chronic fear. It can be even more destructive than fear, for it may not become acute as fear does, but may exist, perhaps in the subconscious, as a state of tension. This tightens up the whole inner life, and thus produces functional disease.

A Persian saying goes, "Worry eats up the human flesh." Kabir, an Indian poet, puts it this way, "Worry, like a funeral pyre, reduces to ashes your intelligence, your substance, and you." Another Indian saying says, "Worry is bigger than a funeral pyre." In the parable of the sower Jesus names three things as the chief causes of unfruitfulness: "The worries of the world and the delight of being rich and all the other passions come in to choke the word" (Mark 4:19, Moffatt). He puts "worries" first. He was right. Worries not only choke the Word, they choke the worrier—literally. The worrier is always the shallow breather.

O Father-God, I want to be at my best—at Thy best—so give me courage to face all fear and anxiety and by grace be released from them. Amen.

AFFIRMATION FOR THE DAY: *Anxiety is self- and God-mistrust. I trust both, so I have no anxiety.*

A VICIOUS CIRCLE

We continue our meditation on fear and release from it. But before we look at the release, we must look at the results.

Here is a letter from a very devoted and useful woman, but cramped at one place in her otherwise adjusted life: "I'm wanting help to be delivered from a fear that keeps me from traveling long distances. Years ago I started having heart attacks caused by a goiter. I was a thousand miles away from home and my loved ones and was unable to travel. It was a horrifying experience to be so ill so far away, and I didn't get much better until I got back to my home and family. Since that time I've been afraid to get too far away, and when I do, the fear makes me so nervous that sleep is almost impossible, and then my heart acts up, which makes me more nervous. You know the vicious circle." Here is a fear associated with long distances because of what happened once far from home. Long distances had nothing to do with this fear except by association. The fear was off-base. After that letter was written I persuaded this woman to travel a long distance to one of our Ashrams. She did. Nothing happened. She is radiant. The fear is gone.

Here is another letter from another woman with a similar fear: "You see, I can't go anywhere alone without feeling panicky, and I want to, oh, so badly. I even hate to go any distance away from my home, and even sitting still in church or a good movie is becoming rather hard to do. I am not afraid of people, I love to entertain and I have a nice home, husband, and son. The doctors say it is a safety complex and eventually I'll get over it, but they don't know how deeply it is impressed in my mind." She was trying to be safe and making herself more and more unsafe in the process of trying to be safe. Another vicious circle.

The worrier meets things three times: before they come, while they are here, and after they are gone—triple duty, hence premature decay.

O Christ, Thou canst break our vicious circles of fear and make us free. Thou hast done it. Thou canst do it. Do it for me. Amen.

AFFIRMATION FOR THE DAY: *God has me and my worries, so I am anxious about neither.*

"THE CAUSE IS UNEASINESS"

We continue our thought on the effect of fears and anxieties on our total life. Dr. Walter C. Alvarez, the stomach specialist of the Mayo Clinic, pronounces this judgment: "I am coming to believe that in a considerable percentage of those many cases of diarrhea, in which we physicians cannot make a diagnosis, the cause is uneasiness or attacks of panicky fear." "Uneasiness" is equivalent to an undertone of worry, and the "panicky fear" is the undertone of worry become acute in fear.

The same authority gives this illustration of the effects of worry and fear: "The current of the digestive tracts can be reversed. One day a nervous woman received a menacing letter from an income tax collector. It so frightened her that instead of going to find out what the trouble was, she took to bed and vomited night and day for a week." Another girl vomited for two weeks after she learned her mother had cancer of the stomach.

Vash Young wrote: "In my first days as a salesman I often became so nauseated as I contemplated my next calls that I lost my food not once, but time after time, and always due to fear."

Here is the case of a woman who told me she had what the doctors called "anticipatory asthma." She anticipated having an attack, and anticipated it with fear, and the fear itself produced the thing she feared, asthma. While well she was dominating, and now she was dominating still—dominating the household through illness. She orders the household—passively! All unconsciously, of course, for she is a very able and loving mother.

Fear—hidden fear—dominates more of our actions than we often care to admit. Fear is the internal climate. We live, move, and have our being in it.

The oldest lie detector in history, a rice cake shaped like a demon, is forced down the throat of a suspect. If he is guilty, he chokes. But fear produced the choking. Fear chokes everything within and around us. The world climate is so full of fear that life commercially, socially, politically, and spiritually is choked.

O Father, give me the inner climate of confidence and faith, for I would be a confident person—able for anything. In Jesus' name. Amen.

AFFIRMATION FOR THE DAY: *I shall breathe the inner air of quiet strength and peaceful calm—my climate is God's complete adequacy.*

"WE ARE AFRAID"

We are studying the effects of fear on the personality and on the body. A very able and apparently poised friend wrote: "I am about to take the plane for the long hop half way around the world and there are butterflies in my stomach." If the effects of fears were only "butterflies in the stomach," then they would not be too serious, but those "butterflies" often lay eggs, and they become worms that gnaw at our inwards and create disease, especially ulcers. Shakespeare puts it:

> The thought whereof
> Doth, like a poisonous mineral, gnaw my inwards.

Dr. Franz Alexander says: "What is disturbing is not primarily a fear of death. It is a much more complex form of anxiety. It is a sense of instability, a fear of unpredictable change, bewilderment as to the future which cannot be planned in any intelligent, orderly fashion." It is an ill-defined fear of life—oncoming life—because we feel inadequate to meet it. When once we find an inner adequacy to meet life no matter what happens, then our fears drop away like dead leaves before the rising sap of adequate life.

Some people find a fear in everything.

> At the heart of everything
> There is a sting, there is a sting,

and that sting is the fear of things, a fear of life itself.

A very nervous and tense type of woman said about a beautiful rug, "This is a beautiful and luxurious rug but moths will get into it." She looked at a beautiful rug and could see only moths in it—no beauty. The rug had been demoted for five years. There are many who cannot see the beauty and blessedness of life; they see only possible moths that eat its beauty—moth-minded!

O God, give me eyes to see—to see Thy beauty and the glory of Thy world. Save me from moth-mindedness. Give me Thy outlook that sees good even in me. Amen.

AFFIRMATION FOR THE DAY: *I shall expect the good and create it by my very expectancy.*

"SLOW SUICIDE BY WORRY"

We must linger longer looking at the effect of fears before we turn to the remedy. Sometimes our anxiety for success becomes disruptive. A young man was successful in all he did. This made him so intent on success that an anxiety tone was produced, which in turn produced stomach ulcers. This kept him from success. It was a vicious circle.

Margaret Stowe rightly says, "You will succeed best when you put the restless anxious side of affairs out of mind and allow the restful side to live in your thoughts." Outer success is a by-product of inner success. When you can live within, you can live without. Then you meet everything in a confident, hopeful mood, there is no strain, hence no drain, and everything you do becomes play. You seem to have more than enough to meet the next thing.

John Dollard puts this matter of fear this way: "Fear has many names and faces. It may be called anxiety, apprehension, or restlessness. Sometimes it is a shuddering reality in the face of a real danger. At times it appears as boredom. Again it is shown by silence, and yet again by a sudden dampening of the spirit. 'Turning away' often reveals fear. Resentment may disguise it; subservience may conceal it. Some people hit upon the art of conquering fear early in life, others never learn."

I know a first-rate man who is always doing second-rate jobs. When confronted with a first-rate job, he pulls back from the responsibility for fear of failure. He takes the job that will not demand too much of him. Fear is cutting down his usefulness. He calls it humility, but it is fear.

Sometimes it is a fear of a disease that isn't there. A mother of three children was convinced she had a cancer. She gave each of the children a toy, bade them good-by, saying that she would never see them again. She committed suicide over a fear of a disease that was not there. She had no cancer. Many do not commit sudden suicide, but a slow suicide, by worry over things that do not exist except in the mind. But if it does exist in the mind, it exists as really, as far as potency is concerned, as if it really existed.

O God, my Father, keep me from inner fears that eat away my soul-substance; give me the inner confidence that is healing. In Jesus' name. Amen.

AFFIRMATION FOR THE DAY: *My confident faith is the antiseptic that kills the germs of fear and anxiety.*

"A CONTINUAL, INDEFINITE, PINING FEAR"

A good many of our fears and anxieties come from seeing someone else sick, especially with heart ailments. We begin to wonder if we haven't the same ailment, and attention concentrated on the organ that is supposed to be affected upsets the functioning of the organ and functional disease is mistaken for structural disease. This is particularly true of the heart.

A businessman said to me: "I'm sixty-six and I find a good many of my friends dropping off with heart disease. My heart is acting up. I'm told by the doctors that there is nothing structurally wrong with my heart." But fear was producing an upset heart. A great many functionally upset hearts come from seeing a friend or loved one with a bad heart. Attention is directed to the heart. Its rhythm is upset by the attention. Fear sets in. Then the heart is more upset. And more fear results.

But fear can be simply a fear of life. Carlyle in *Sartor Resartus* tells of his own fears: "I lived in a continual, indefinite, pining fear; tremulous, pusillanimous, apprehensive of I knew not what; it seemed that all things in the Heavens and the Earth were but boundless jaws of a devouring monster, wherein I, palpitating, waited to be devoured." How he got rid of this chronic state of fear we will see next week.

Some of these fears are unreasonable. There are tree surgeons who lose their nerve up in a tree, and although they are strong and powerful, fear so unnerves them that someone has to go up into the tree to bring them down. They couldn't even hold on to a rope. Fear makes one lose his grip not only on ropes, but on life itself.

Doctors tell us of patients who become skin and bones because of a fear of cancer they haven't got. Some girls lose forty-five pounds through fears of things that are not there. One woman said to me, "I'm afraid to go to a doctor, and I'm afraid not to." No wonder a distinguished physician said, "The commonest and subtlest of all diseases is fear." It is. I asked a doctor: "Is fear Enemy No. 1?" and he replied: "It is Enemy No. 1½." Conquer fear, and you are on the way to life mastery.

O God, my Father, if fear has caught me as a serpent with beady eyes has caught a bird, release me from this nightmare fascination. Make me free. Amen.

AFFIRMATION FOR THE DAY: *I am a man of faith—I think faith, talk faith, am faith.*

"NOTHING IS SOLVED THAT IS EVADED"

Today we conclude looking at fear as a destructive force. A well-known psychologist declares that fear is the most disintegrating enemy of human personality.

Sometimes there is a retreat into illness through fear of being less than perfect. W. Fearon Halliday gives this instance: "A girl on the eve of an important examination developed neuritis in the arm and so withdrew herself effectively from the necessity of undergoing the test. Analysis proved that she feared she would not come out on top. The neuritis had developed as an unconscious protection against the shame (so it seemed to her) of being less than perfect."

Fritz Kunkel says: "Anxiety may be defined as the opposite of creativity. It is the power of creation flowing in the opposite direction: creation being a centrifugal force; anxiety, centripetal. In the state of anxiety the intensity of life increases but its scope decreases. . . . This ebb of creative power is what we feel as anxiety." David Seabury says: "Certainly whoever worries, is nervous, weary, despondent, cynical, censorious, or lonely, is the victim of mental and emotional wounds coming from earlier experience and lying in memory ferment which unnecessarily limits his life and may destroy happiness."

Perhaps the underlying fear is the fear of death. Many go through life with the undertone of a fear of death. Life is spoiled by forebodings about the tomorrow that may hold death within it. Or many just put it out of mind, refusing to think about it. William Randolph Hearst, the publisher, would not let anyone speak of death in his presence. The Japanese dislike the numeral four, for it has the same sound as the word for death. But death is not evaded by evasions. As someone has said, "The refusal to confront death might almost be called 'the twentieth century evasion, for it is the distinctive mark of the modern mind." But nothing is solved that is evaded. It simply comes back as hidden complexes within—an undertone of fear that puts a discord at the center of life. Fears we try to evade come back to pervade.

O Father, my heart grows eager with anticipation as I turn to find Thy way out. For I know Thou hast a way. Put my feet upon it. In Jesus' name. Amen.

AFFIRMATION FOR THE DAY: *There is nothing to fear but fear.*

STEPS OUT OF FEAR

We turn this week to the more pleasant task of seeing how we can be delivered from fears. For we can be delivered from fear, however chronic it may have become. I've seen it in thousands of cases.

In taking our positive steps let us close one door behind us—and let us close it with a bang. It is the door of escape.

First, fix in mind that an attempt to escape from something feared will end not in escape, but in further entanglement. For in running away you only produce a buried complex within yourself that will rise up to plague you. There is no escape in escape. W. Fearon Halliday says: "From a religious point of view, therefore, we arrive at an important life principle, that it is far more dangerous to run away from an enemy than to risk a conflict with it. Indeed we have reason to believe that in a very real sense we cannot run away, and that our troubles arise from thinking we can. . . . If a man has quarrelled with a friend and chooses to avoid him or leave the neighborhood, rather than face the facts of the quarrel, he is unconsciously exchanging one difficulty for another, concealed and far more dangerous."

Walter Alvarez tells of "a fine, public-spirited woman who always seemed sane when I talked to her, but who for years has chosen to live in a psychopathic hospital to avoid the tremendous effort she would otherwise have to make to meet people and to face the problems of a world in turmoil." But did she escape from meeting people? No, the people she compelled herself to meet were nurses and doctors—people, in any case. And did she escape meeting "the problems of a world in turmoil"? She simply transferred the turmoil to her own inner life. Alvarez cites another case of a woman who told such good stories first of gallstones, then of kidney stone, and finally of peptic ulcer that she nearly got operated on. Each time she stayed in the hospital for five or six weeks before she could be induced to go home. Reason: an old husband who bored her nearly to death, so illness and the hospital were her ways of escape. She developed "hospitalitis," a disease as bad as the supposed disease that brings the sufferers there.

Dear Father, I thank Thee that Thou hast hedged me about and I cannot escape from my fears. Give me victory over them. Amen.

AFFIRMATION FOR THE DAY: *I dodge into no roads with dead ends. I'm on the Way!*

"CONFINE YOURSELF TO THE POSSIBLE"

We saw yesterday that the first step out of fear and anxiety is to cease trying to escape. It can't be done.

Second, *give up longing for impossibilities and confine yourself to the possible*. A great many make themselves miserable with worries about goals which they cannot attain. They have laid on themselves the task of setting the whole world right, and when they cannot do it, they are frustrated and worried. Confine yourself to the accomplishable tasks around you and accept the discipline of the possible. There is the *Arabian Nights* tale of a beautiful home where everybody was happy until a chance visitor said, "You ought to have a roc's egg to hang from the gable of your house." Then they all started out on an endless search for this phantom egg. They were never happy again— always pursuing what they could never find. Discipline yourself to tasks that are possible for you and God working together in your situation. He that is faithful in the little shall be made ruler over much.

Third, *look over your worries and fears and pick out the real ones from the imaginary ones*. Isolate the imaginary ones—fears that have been created by your imagining this, that, or the other might happen. You will find that they form about 75 per cent of your fears. You cross bridges which in reality you never have to cross; you meet issues that never arise; you exhaust yourself fighting battles which you never have to fight; you die a hundred deaths—in imagination. You are "barking your shins on stools that ain't there." Someone has defined worry as "thinking with our emotions," and if we would let our minds think a moment, we would see that we are troubling ourselves uselessly with imaginary worries and fears. Samuel Butler wanted someone to invent an assinometer—a gadget by which one could tell just how big an ass he is! Joseph Fort Newton tells of hearing, when a boy, an old Negro say: "If you could jest set on a fence and see yourself pass by, you'd die a-laughin' at the sight." A good laugh at yourself would drive away 75 per cent of your fears.

O God, our Father, give me sense—sense to separate the real from the conjured up. Give me a sense of laughter—at myself. In Jesus' name. Amen.

AFFIRMATION FOR THE DAY: *I have the power to laugh at everything, and thus produce in everything something at which to laugh.*

LOOK FEAR STRAIGHT IN THE FACE

We continue to discuss the steps out of fears. Fourth, *having separated the real fears from the imaginary ones, now look at those real fears—look at them straight in the face.* Suppose the worst should happen, so what? La Rochefoucauld once said, "It is a sort of happiness to know the worst that can befall us." Walter Alvarez says: "Through the years I have gained the impression that people, and especially older people, who are more likely to have cancer, are not as cowardly as we assume them to be. Often they face things beautifully, bravely, philosophically. Many say they have had enough of life; they could enjoy more, but if it is not to be granted them, they are content to go. . . . Many a time I have had persons say that they were relieved to know the worst. Since getting the verdict, they have been able to rest and sleep again." Man can stand almost anything when he knows everything. It is uncertainty that breaks us.

We shall see later that the worst can be transformed into the best, that even death can be made beautiful. Death is one of the least calamities that can happen to the Christian. By surrender of himself the Christian has already died—what can death now do to him? He has already died!

The story is told of a beloved marshal of France who suffered much that he might maintain his Christian Protestant witness: when he was shaving just before a battle his hand trembled violently, and he turned to his own body and said: "Tremblest thou, vile carcass? Thou wouldst tremble more if thou knewest where I am going to take you this day." But though he trembled, he went on. He "trembled bravely."

Luther once wrote to Melanchthon: "I am against those worries which take the heart out of you. Why make God a liar in not believing His wonderful promises when He commands us to be of good cheer and cast all our care upon Him? . . . . What more can the devil do than slay us? . . . . Why then worry since He is at the helm? He who has been our Father will be the Father of our children. . . . As for me, I do not torment myself with such matters." The worst that can happen but throws us into the arms of God. And there our fever is dissolved in the quiet of God. For where God is, there is no fear.

O Gracious God, the worst can but toss me to Thy breast. Then I drown my fears in Thy love. I face life unafraid, for I face it with Thee. Amen.
AFFIRMATION FOR THE DAY: *I am thrown into the arms of God by every event; then let the events come on.*

"NOT GRIM RESISTANCE BUT GRACIOUS RESOURCES"

We are now taking steps to overcome our fears. Fifth, *now that you have separated the real fears from the imaginary ones, not only look at the real fears, but overcome them one by one.*

We saw Carlyle's struggle with fear; we must now look at his deliverance: "All at once, there rose a Thought in me, and I asked myself, What art thou afraid of? Wherefore like a coward, dost thou forever pip and whimper, and go cowering and trembling? Despicable biped! what is the sum total of the worst that lies before thee? Death? Well, Death; and say the pangs of Tophet too, and all that the Devil and Man may, will, or can do against thee! Hast thou not a heart; canst thou not suffer whatso it be; and, as a Child of Freedom, though outcast, trample Tophet itself under thy feet, while it consumes thee? Let it come, then; I will meet it and defy it!' And as I so thought, there rushed like a stream of fire over my whole soul; and I shook base Fear away from me for ever. I was strong, of unknown strength; a spirit, almost a god. Ever from that time, the temper of my misery was changed: not Fear or whining Sorrow was it, but Indignation and grim fire-eyed Defiance. . . . It is from this hour that I incline to date my Spiritual New-Birth; . . . perhaps I directly thereupon began to be a Man."

This is one way to overcome fears: "Indignation and grim fire-eyed Defiance." Obviously this method of grim defiance did help Carlyle out of his fears, but it is not a method to be recommended. It produced a tense, fighting Carlyle, not a very inviting type of character. Since Carlyle's day, we have learned that to fight an evil or a fear is to concentrate your attention upon it. And whatever gets your attention gets you. You must look your fears straight in the face, but not too long. After you have inwardly defied your fear, you must surrender the fear into the hands of God and then look into the face of God with faith and confidence that He will give grace and power to overcome the fear. Your attention is then concentrated on God, not on yourself and your resistance. The end is not grim resistance but gracious Resources.

O God, I turn over to Thee my fears. They are in Thy hands, not mine. And now my attitude turns to faith and confidence and inner serenity. I thank Thee. Amen.

AFFIRMATION FOR THE DAY: *I do not fight my fears—I surrender them and trust God for victory.*

GETTING YOUR IMAGINATION CAPTURED

We saw yesterday that in order to be released from fears we must surrender them to God, not fight them in our own strength.

The New Testament from first to last presents an offer of deliverance from fear. To Joseph: "Fear not" (Matt. 1:20); "Fear not, Mary" (Luke 1:30); "Fear not Zacharias" (Luke 1:13); "Freed from fear" (Luke 1.74, Moffatt); "They were terribly afraid". . . . "Have no fear" (Luke 2:9, 10, Moffatt); "Do not be afraid, I am the first and the last" (Rev. 1:17, R.S.V.). Get your eyes on this offer of deliverance from fear. When your eyes are lifted from your fears to God, then it is as good as done. The fascination of your fears is broken, and with your eyes on God, then faith replaces fear. As long as Peter kept his eyes on Jesus he was able to walk on the water, but when he took his eyes off Jesus, and began to fasten them on himself and his weakness and on the wind and the waves, he began to sink. The capture of the imagination by Jesus guarantees victory; the capture of the imagination by fear guarantees defeat.

William Sadler, the famous psychiatrist, was asked by his wife Lena how long it would take to effect a cure of a young woman suffering from general anxiety and depression. "Oh, about a year," he replied, as he outlined the steps to be followed. His wife said nothing, but not long after, Sadler saw the patient who seemed well and happy. Stumped, he asked the patient what had happened, "Oh," she replied, "Dr. Lena taught me how to pray." Prayer turned her from herself and her anxieties to God and His resources.

The first step in release is to get your eyes on God—that creates faith. "Fear knocked at the door. Faith opened it, and lo! there was no one there." "Faith," says Whitman, "is the antiseptic of the soul." It kills the disease germs of fear and anxiety. But note: "Belief plus trust is faith." It is not belief alone—there must be trust. And trust means entrustment—you must entrust the matter to God and leave it there. Don't take it back again and bear it on your inadequate shoulders. Let God have it and let Him keep having it. "Who daily beareth our burden." Note the "daily"—He can't bear them a week ahead of time; He will meet them day by day with you as they come.

O God, into Thy adequate hands I commend my spirit—my spirit and all its worries and fears. Thou hast them—and me. I thank Thee. Amen.

AFFIRMATION FOR THE DAY: *"Never be anxious, but always make your requests known to God . . . with thanksgiving"* (Phil. 4:6, Moffatt).

TALK FAITH TO YOURSELF

Sixth, *now that you have surrendered your fears to God one by one, or in a lump, begin to do the things you've been afraid of.*

"Do the thing you are afraid of and the death of fear is certain," says Emerson. If you are afraid of the water, go into it. If you are afraid of a certain person, walk up to him or her and begin a friendly conversation. If you are afraid of a situation, walk into it. If you are afraid to stand up and speak, then stand up and speak. "The best remedy for cold feet is to stand on them." Moses was slow of speech, but he got started once and made a speech that covered the whole book of Deuteronomy. When Eddie Rickenbacker was called on to speak at a huge banquet in his honor at the old Waldorf-Astoria, he was terrified. He mumbled a few ungrammatical phrases and sat down. Next day he hired a Metropolitan Opera voice coach to teach him how to talk. He got Damon Runyon to write him a speech, studied grammar, went on a forty-night lecture tour (at $1,000 a night) and conquered his fears. A woman sprained her ankle on a slope. She was afraid of that slope —trembled at the thought of it. I gently led her down the slope and the fear was gone. She could laugh at it.

Seventh, *talk faith to yourself and to others and to God.* Don't talk your fears. If you do, they will grow on your hands. As someone has said, "Snakes crawl, birds fly, rabbits run, but man talks himself forward." Talk yourself forward, not backward. Say the faith-thing, not the fear-thing. William James says: "So to feel brave, act as if you were brave, use all your will to that end, and a courage-fit will very likely replace the fit of fear." He adds: "Worry means always and invariably inhibition of associations and loss of effective power. Of course, the sovereign cure for worry is religious faith." But the "religious faith" contains the trust which means you talk and act faith to God and yourself.

By talking faith to yourself and others you commit yourself to a position of faith, and you thus commit yourself to living to that position—you talk yourself forward. In the same way you can talk yourself backward. Determine that your talk shall be forward-looking speech. And then you will have to catch up with your speech.

O God, I thank Thee that Thou hast delivered me from all my fears. With Thee I am able for anything, anywhere, any time. Amen.

AFFIRMATION FOR THE DAY: *I serve notice on all my fears: I shall do today the thing I fear.*

A SECOND COLLECTION

A chronic worrier analyzing his own situation found that 40 per cent of his worries were about things that were never likely to happen; 30 per cent were about past decisions that could not be changed; 12 per cent concerned others' criticisms of himself that didn't matter anyway; 10 per cent dealt with his health, which he was already doing his best to protect. Only 8 per cent, he decided, were legitimate causes to worry. If we could reduce our worries, as this man did, by 92 per cent we should be getting somewhere. Thus, 8 per cent of real worries —easily handled!

Now that you have worries and fears reduced to a size that can be handled, give the remaining 8 per cent to God. A minister suggested that there should be a second collection—a collection of our fears and worries. Then as the baskets are brought forward, the minister would say, "I hereby declare that you are freed from your fears. Go in peace, and may the peace of God go with you."

A radiant young Christian woman who lived on a farm tells in a letter how she was coming from the Ashram in Texas and was debating whether she should get on the bus with a Negro friend: "I just had to show that woman that my love for her was greater than my fear of the entanglements. The driver got in and looked at me. I remembered what I learned about getting the cows in with the bull in the pasture: always look them in the eye and they'll know you are boss. I looked him in the eye and I was ready for him. I was going to tell him that I had a perfect right to sit there as I had colored blood in my veins, red, just like hers, and that she and I were sisters by a law greater than the great state of Texas. But instead of coming toward me, he just sort of smiled and sat down. I looked at my friend and she gave me the sweetest smile I ever saw and said, 'Honey, praise the Lord for the Ashram where we meet the real thing.' I told her that if I got more of the Real Thing, I'd explode." When she looked her fear straight in the eye she knew she was boss, with the love of God and the laws of the Kingdom sustaining and backing her. With that backing, those who have no natural bravery find that they have a supernatural bravery.

O God, Thou art behind me and in me; then whom shall I fear? Absolutely nothing can now make me afraid. I thank Thee. Amen.

AFFIRMATION FOR THE DAY: *I am free from fear and I shall go out to help others to be free. I shall be a fear-dispeller.*

"CONFIDENT, POISED, AND RADIANT"

Before we leave the subject of fears and anxieties I must tell of those who have found victory over these twin evils.

Here is a minister who came to one of our Ashrams twenty-five pounds underweight, his colon three quarters removed at the Mayo Clinic because of ulceration. He was full of fears. As a boy his older brothers filled him with fears by telling him ghost stories and about finding men with a razor under the bed. His father offered him a nickel if he would go around the house in the dark. When he became a minister, he sometimes got into a panic in the midst of a wedding ceremony and had to be excused. He got into a panic speaking over the radio. His work with his parishioners was a nightmare. Then came the visit to the Ashram and his personal surrender of his fears to God. He has regained the lost pounds and is confident, poised, and radiant. He was examined again at the Mayo Clinic and they were astonished at his recovery.

"See this lunch box under my arm?" said a night watchman in Tacoma. "That means I'm going back to work. I've been sick and couldn't work, but Monday night I came to the meeting, surrendered my worries and fears to God, and I'm well and happy; and I'm going back to work."

The head of a large manufacturing firm had stomach trouble and sinus. He was tense and anxious, especially against labor. A doctor said to him, "What you need is a refreshing well," and handed him a bill for $1,500. Shock treatment! He found that "refreshing well" through personal self-surrender, and his sinus and stomach difficulties disappeared. He was grateful for this new life and began to tell about it. But soon he set up tensions between himself and the new standards. He began to try too hard to be good. His physical difficulties returned. When I talked to him about surrender and receptivity, he took it as a child. "I feel different already. My tensions are gone. For the first time I see it." He surrendered his anxious striving to be good and began to live by receptivity. He was free! His religion was no longer creating tension; it was creating trust. And the trust opened the gates to the resources of God.

O Father, Thou art teaching me not to strive to be good, but to let go and trust—to accept Thy gift. Now I walk to freedom. Amen.

AFFIRMATION FOR THE DAY: *I am free from anxiety, even from the fear of not being good, for Goodness has me.*

"LIVE IN DAY-TIGHT COMPARTMENTS"

We linger one more day to make the last suggestion about how to be free from fear and anxiety. Eighth, *meet each day as it comes—one day at a time.* You can meet each day's cares and sorrows if you meet them one day at a time. But don't let them gang up on you. Meet today to day. Someone has said that "the best thing about the future is that it comes only one day at a time." And that is true. So Jesus was absolutely realistic when He said: "So never be troubled about to morrow; to-morrow will take care of itself. The day's own trouble is enough for the day" (Matt. 6:34, Moffatt). George Macdonald says: "It has been well said that no man ever sank under the burden of the day. It is when tomorrow's burden is added to the burden of today that the weight is more than a man can bear." Note the statement: "No man ever sank under the burden of the day"—and you won't be the exception, not if you meet today's troubles today, and meet tomorrow's troubles when you get to them. Live in "day-tight compartments." Knowing that you can meet anything day by day, then you will know what Robert Louis Stevenson meant when he said: "Quiet minds cannot be perplexed or frightened but go on in fortune or misfortune at their own private pace like the ticking of a clock during a thunder-storm."

And then you will succeed best when anxiety about success or failure is put out of the mind and only the aim to be true to the highest each moment controls us. For I do not have to succeed or fail—I only have to be true to the highest that God has mapped out for me. Wrote Edmund Vance Cooke:

> Oh, a trouble's a ton, or a trouble's an ounce
> Or a trouble is what you make it,
> And it isn't the fact that you're hurt that counts,
> But only how did you take it.

"Anxiety is the expression of the distance between man and God." For He cares—when we let Him. An old woman just made a train and stood in the aisle panting and holding her suitcase. The conductor, noticing, said to her: "You can put it down now, lady. The train will carry it for you." He carries us—and our burdens too!

My God and Father, forgive me that I do myself—and Thee—the wrong in holding burdens which Thou art offering to carry for me. Amen.

AFFIRMATION FOR THE DAY: *I have no burdens, for I have Thee.*

170

"WE TRANSFORM EVERYTHING, EVEN FEAR"

We must sum up our lesson on fear. Fear can transform us up or down. If we surrender to it, then fear will transform us downward, making us into a canceled-out person. Or if the fear is surrendered to God, then it can transform us upward, making us into an augmented person. For every fear overcome is transformed into confidence. Your very fears serve you. Some Africans believe that the strength of a fallen foe enters into the victor. That is true of us in our spiritual battle. The strength of a fear overcome is transmuted into the strength of a faith to overcome. You are taking from your enemy and adding to yourself.

You harness your fears and make them serve faith. The destructive becomes constructive. Then you are no longer afraid of fear, for fear is now your friend, serving you. The surgeon takes his fear of cutting into the wrong places and makes that fear contribute to his skillfulness. The Christian takes the fear of tarnishing or losing this beautiful thing he holds within his heart and transforms that fear into progress. The fear drives him—forward.

Jesus took the fear that shook Him in Gethsemane, laid it into the Father's hands, gained strength to go on to the cross. The fear, overcome and harnessed to His purposes, drove Him forward to a cross and to a complete triumph. Everything serves those who serve God—even fear.

Karl Menninger says: "Conscious rational fear serves a useful function; it warns us from real dangers and has impelled mankind to build up defenses against danger, hunger, disease and other external threats. The irrational fear that cripples and inhibits us is . . . not fear of real danger but rather a fear of ourselves, a fear of our own hatreds or of the hatreds engendered by us in others or projected upon them." But when we have surrendered ourselves and our hates to God, then irrational fear drops away. Only rational fear remains, and that rational fear serves us. We transform everything, even fear. And when fear becomes your servant, then there is nothing left to be afraid of, for you've harnessed your greatest enemy to the chariot of your life purposes.

O God, I thank Thee that I am no longer afraid of fear. It too is my friend to lead me to Thee for added safety and resources. I'm grateful. Amen.

AFFIRMATION FOR THE DAY: *My fears drive me to Him. So fear too is my servant.*

THE RESULTS OF RESENTMENTS

We now turn to look at something which, if not transformed, will transform us and make us into sour, morose, embittered souls: resentments.

A very able minister grasped my hand and said, "Teach me how to overcome my resentments." His large-domed forehead with blood vessels distended showed the tension he was under. Resentments were draining him mentally, spiritually, physically.

For as one professor said to me, "Resentments and anger put the whole physical and mental system on a war basis, instead of on a peace basis." If you live on a war basis all the time, then you are a drained personality. As Walter Alvarez says: "I often tell patients that they cannot afford to carry grudges or maintain hates. Such things can make them ill and can certainly tire them out. I once saw a man kill himself, inch by inch, simply by thinking of nothing but hatred of a relative who had sued him. Within a year or two he was dead."

Is it true that resentments and hate can cause illnesses? A very intelligent young woman said to me: "I had resentments against my father who was in the war. When he was about to come home, I broke out in roselike blotches all over me." Alvarez says: "In cases of giant urticária I keep inquiring about some personal tragedy or great mental strain. For instance, a woman who came to me because of giant wheals finally admitted that the trouble started when she was torn with indecision over the problem of leaving her husband for a man with whom she had become infatuated. A man broke out with giant hives the day after his boss demoted him and cut his salary in half, and another broke out when he saw the position of general manager, which had long been promised him, was going to be given to the boss's son. A nurse I know gets an attack of giant urticaria whenever she loses her temper." So resentments and anger not only leave "splinters in the soul"; they leave splinters in the body as well. And in the mind. You can't think straight if you hold a resentment against a person, for everything you think is pulled off on a tangent—pulled from the straight by that resentment.

God, my Father, teach us how to get these splinters out of our souls—and our bodies. For we are made for love, not hate. Amen.

AFFIRMATION FOR THE DAY: *I am committed to love and will tolerate no resentments, not even marginal ones.*

HATE IS SAND IN THE MACHINERY

We continue to look at the physical effects of hates and resentments. A woman who was a refugee from Latvia came up to me burning with hate against the Russians, for she had been brutally treated by them. She had a case for her hatred, but case or no case, it was disrupting her soul and body. She was consuming herself—with hate. Her eyes were glazed, for back of them was a burned-out soul—burned-out by her own hate.

When we say of another, "He burns me up," that's true. He does. You want to burn him up, and all you succeed in doing is burning yourself up. Again when you say, "I blow up," that's true, you do. You really want to blow up the other fellow, but you succeed only in blowing up yourself.

A farmer with a sadistic sense tied a stick of dynamite to a hawk, lighted a fuse, and then turned it loose, expecting it to blow itself up in midair. Instead, the hawk flew on his barn and the explosion wrecked the barn. Our hates and resentments are always more destructive to us than they are to others whom we hate. Our projected hatreds come back to roost—and how!

Here was the case given by a doctor of a man who previously was very healthy, but in his late fifties became enraged over a lawsuit brought against him by his sister. He could think and talk of nothing else. Immediately his breath became foul and it stayed that way; his appetite left him, his digestion became bad, sleep failed, and his weight dropped off rapidly. Soon his heart and kidneys began to fail, and after some months he was dead. He died from the bodily injuries wrought by painful emotions.

It need not be so absolutely and devastatingly disruptive as in this case. It can just throw the internal machinery out of gear. Here was a rookie ballplayer, Richie Ashburn, who the first year in the big league was a great success, a flash. But the next year he had a bad year. One reason, said the manager, was that he ws not on speaking terms with some of his teammates. This suppressed resentment threw sand in the machinery of co-ordination and slowed down his efficiency. Hate is sand in the machinery of living.

O Father-God, Thou hast fashioned me for love, and love is my native air. All else is poison. Save me from self-brewed poisons. Amen.

AFFIRMATIONS FOR THE DAY: *The oil of love, not the sand of resentments, in the machinery of life today.*

"UNDRAINED WOUNDED EMOTION"

Resentments may cause illness in people who are very healthy otherwise. A woman had gone through hell to rescue her husband from hell —and did. For five years she put up with his drunken fits in which he sometimes would lock her out of her house for a week at a time, sometimes nailing the door shut. She kept her children in college by her own labor, while he let his business go to ruin and bankruptcy. And then he changed, gave up drink, got his business back, and with it, respectability. It was one of the greatest moral victories I have ever seen, won by the Christian patience of this woman. And then after going through all this hell for five years she became resentful that her husband, in spite of all she had gone through for his sake, expected her to go through more sacrifices. The resentment caused a pain in her abdomen, and for six weeks she was in a hospital. When she surrendered that last lingering resentment to God, the pain left her and she became well. But it didn't matter how saintly she had been, the harbored resentment did its devastating work.

A man had a car that wouldn't run properly. He got angry, pulled out a pistol, and began pumping bullets into the engine! That is about as sensible a remedy as getting angry with people! You only blow holes in your own peace and your own health. If you give a person a piece of your mind, you only lose your own peace of mind!

David Seabury says, "Experience shows that the pressure of undrained wounded emotion plays a great part in creating fatigue, nervousness and worry even in youthful days." "Undrained wounded emotion"—nursing a hurt, real or imagined, which becomes a festering sore within. No matter how hard you may try to justify the attitude, nothing can sanctify it. It is a festering sore still. It must be got up and out, drained and cleansed.

A missionary held a lifelong resentment against his mother, and justified it because of the treatment he had received from her. But that did not save him from a mental breakdown through the conflict set up. Apparently resentments are just as deadly in the godly as in the ungodly—more so.

O Christ, help me not to hold stubbornly to my wounded pride. I consent for Thee to lance my inner boils, no matter how much it may hurt. Amen.

AFFIRMATION FOR THE DAY: *My hurts hurt me further when I harbor them. So out with them, forever.*

"I GET PHYSICALLY ILL AROUND HER"

Sometimes our resentments are cloaked under a polite and proper exterior. A Negro schoolteacher said in one of our Ashrams, "I say a polite thing in an impolite way." It was a method of defense. But whether our resentments are clothed in politeness or impoliteness, they are resentments still, and as such are devastating to the personality.

A letter was published in *Time:* "I read the *Daily News* before dinner and I get so darn mad I can't digest my food, and my evening meal is spoiled. I spend my nights composing caustic letters to the editors, which are never sent, and I don't get my sleep." The writer thought she was blowing up the editors, but she was only blowing up the delicate mechanism of her inner life.

Here was a pastor's wife whose mother-in-law was domineering. The mother-in-law never really gave up her son to marriage. She lived with the couple and used to stay in their room till eleven o'clock at night. The young people scarcely had any time to themselves. The mother was always hovering around. The wife cried herself to sleep every night for ten years. She had a sense of guilt because she held the hidden resentments. This combination of resentments and guilt broke her. She had a hemorrhage and a stroke. But when the cause was pointed out and she surrendered that whole thing to God, she was released and happy. Her unjustified and useless self-condemnation dropped away.

Here is a similar case, but this time it was the mother-in-law who got ill. "I was ill for six months because of a sense of separation from my daughter." The daughter fell in love with a nice boy, half Jewish, and she changed from a dutiful daughter to a nonchalant, heavy-smoking type—a pose. But the mother reacted badly. "I feel shut out and angry and resentful, and I have an inferiority complex around her, so much so that I get physically ill around her at times." Her resentments and anger and self-pity were devastating her happiness and her health. And the more she reacted in resentments, the less her daughter could take her into her affections and interests. It was all self-defeating.

O Christ, Thou art trying to save us from the things that destroy us. And now they are all Thine—take them and release us fully. Amen.

AFFIRMATION FOR THE DAY: *My outgoing love will dissolve resentments in me and others.*

UNCONSCIOUS RESENTMENTS

We continue to look at the effects of resentments on the personality. Karl Menninger says: "I can say from clinical experience that in some women the degree of discomfort both in pregnancy and in parturition has been directly proportional to the intensity of their resentment to having to live through this phase of their female role. The excessive vomiting of pregnancy is recognized by many obstetricians as a physiological expression of protest and rejection. I believe this same protest may express itself in excessive pain prior to and during delivery."

It is said that a nursing infant can become poisoned by drinking its mother's milk after she has lost her temper. One child was known to drop dead on its mother's breast after the mother had indulged in a fit of temper.

Sometimes the resentments are unconscious. As one doctor put it, "It is very difficult to get people to see that illness is the price they pay for their unconscious resentments toward the very things they protest they love."

An optometrist said to me, "Anger narrows the field of vision and shuts off the peripheral vision, so it is dangerous to drive when angry, for you can't see things that are not in the direct line of a narrowed vision." I know of a doctor who, when angry, pulls up his car alongside the road and stays there until his anger dies down. So when one says "He made me so mad I couldn't see," that is plain fact. An oculist told me that he simply could not examine the eyes of a person who had just been angry. Everything is out of focus.

Perhaps it is not sudden anger but slow resentments that are even more devastating. Walter Alvarez says: "There are many women around the age of fifty who go to pieces because, with children gone and husband absorbed in business, thy feel unwanted and unloved and unneeded. Similarly, many a man past middle age, who perhaps fails to get a long-awaited promotion and sees a younger man put in over him, loses his drive and joy in life and develops a neurosis."

O Christ, we now see that Thy warnings against hate and bitterness were for our redemption. Save us from ourselves and our hates. Amen.

AFFFIRMATION FOR THE DAY: *"My soul is too glad and too great to be the enemy of any man."*

NO ONE CAN AFFORD A GRUDGE

We continue our study of the effect of hate and resentments on the body—and the soul. There is the case of a woman who lost exactly one hundred pounds in a few months after she discovered that the good-for-nothing husband whom she had long supported was being unfaithful to her. When she decided to forgive the man and go on living with him, she rapidly gained weight again.

John Hunter, a famous English doctor, suffering from a bad heart, said, "I'm at the mercy of any scoundrel who will make me angry." That happened. He got up at a medical meeting to refute something he didn't like, and in a fit of anger fell dead.

A man who knew how dangerous it was for him to get angry was overheard by his secretary saying to a man: "Quick, get the h————out of here, I can't afford to get mad at you." No one can afford to carry around grudges and hates—they are too expensive, expensive to the total person. They are more expensive to the one who holds them than to the other person.

William Sadler says: "There is simply no way to get comfort and delight out of hate—it is truly the archdemon of all the little devils who are subversive of joy and destructive of character."

Here is a daughter who carried under an outer love a hate of her mother: "My poor, dear mother, I love her and she suffered so much. But she had no right to take my life, my beautiful life. I hate her for it." It was the underlying hate that took away her beautiful life.

> The mind is its own place, and in itself
> Can make a heaven of hell, a hell of heaven.

And any heart that holds hate within it holds hell within it. For hate is hell begun.

Someone has said, "Anyone who has ever watched a Mexican woman vomiting bile after a *colera*, or wild debauch of temper, can see how such physiological observations must have influenced the language." That bitter bile is a physical manifestation of the bitterness that has spread through the total person. Hate is self-poisoning.

Father, I know that when I let hate in, I let hell in. Save me from self-created hells. I consent that the poison be removed—now. Amen.

AFFIRMATION FOR THE DAY: *Today I shall live in the climate of heaven, love; not in the climate of hell, hate.*

STEPS OUT OF RESENTMENTS

We have looked enough at the effects of hate and resentment; we must now look at the way out. First, *fix it in your mind as an axiom that all hate, all resentments, are wrong, no matter how apparently justified.* You can make a case to yourself to justify those resentments. "Look what he did to me," and so forth. But justified or unjustified, resentments devastate you. You think you'll hurt the other person, but the resentments hurt you far more than they hurt the other person. Resentments and hate are a wrong to you.

But they are also a wrong to the other person. You think you'll correct the other person by hate, but you cannot do it. "Two hates never made a love affair." "Can Satan cast out Satan?" Can you by acting like the devil get the devil out of people? He sits all the tigher.

I have watched clans of monkeys in India get into war. They go through a definite procedure. The big monkeys begin by making faces at each other at a distance. Then as they get closer they become more and more fierce in their grimacing, baring their teeth, making short rushes at each other, and growling fiercely, each trying to scare the other out and making him turn tail and run. But bared teeth create bared teeth; fierceness produces only counter fierceness. Then they get so close that one of them crosses the line and there is a biting, scratching, tumbling, and the war is on. When I told that story to President Truman, I remarked: "Mr. President, we as nations haven't got much beyond that. We are going through that process with Russia, each trying by bared teeth to scare the other out. But it doesn't work. We are getting very close to that deadline where someone makes an inevitably false move which means war." So among nations and groups and individuals the method of casting out hate by hate is a dead failure. It is a means out of harmony with the ends in view. There is only one way to get rid of hate and that is by love. There is only one way to overcome evil and that is with good. Fix that in your mind.

O God, I know that hate and resentments can so blind us that we cannot see straight, everything is confused. May we see from Thy viewpoint. Amen.

AFFIRMATION FOR THE DAY: *As I cannot get rid of darkness by kicking and beating it, but only by bringing in the light, so today I shall get rid of hate in the only way—by love.*

"I DON'T HOLD ANY GRUDGE"

We are now looking at the steps out of resentments. Second, *if resentments and anger are wrong as far as the effects on you and others are concerned, they are also wrong according to the Christian faith.* You are becoming a Christian. Look to your orders. What does Jesus say? "So if you remember, even when offering your gift at the altar, that your brother has any grievance against you, leave your gift at the very altar and go away; first be reconciled to your brother, then come back and offer your gift" (Matt. 5:23, Moffatt). Stop all religious observance, says Jesus; it is useless if you are not attempting to be reconciled to your brother. For shutting out your brother shuts out your Father—automatically.

This is the case where "your brother has any grievance against you" —you have sinned against him. Now take the other case: "If your brother sins against you, go and reprove him, as between you and him alone. If he listens to you, then you have won your brother over" (Matt. 18:15-16, Moffatt). In either case, whether you have sinned against your brother or your brother has sinned against you, you are under obligations to settle it—to settle it as far as you are concerned. He may not respond. But you have cleared your own soul. The Christian goes halfway, three quarters, the full way—to settle a quarrel. The Christian faith teaches that whatever shuts out your brother automatically shuts out your Father.

Third, *surrender all your resentments to God and consent for Him to take them away.* Don't fight your resentments but surrender them to God. A man was blinded by five assailants who stood before the judge. He said: "I don't feel these boys should go to jail. I don't have any feeling of vengeance. The loss of my sight has hindered me very much, but I expect to overcome the handicap. I don't hold any grudge." He had surrendered it to God.

Here was the case of a woman who was dominated by her mother and raved against her in outbursts. She and her mother lived in separate apartments, couldn't live together. But she surrendered her inferiorities and hates, and became lighted up and free and happy.

O God, give me grace to relinquish this thing within me that makes everything ugly—including myself. I do relinquish it now—now. Amen.

AFFIRMATION FOR THE DAY: *As my resentments will produce resentments in others, so my love will produce love.*

"A HELLCAT TO LIVE WITH"

We continue to look at the steps of inwardly letting go of resentments and letting God handle them. Here is what a woman wrote: "Intellectually I knew I could never be whole until I had completely forgiven those who hurt me, but I couldn't do it except in words! I kept holding back my feelings and saying subconsciously, 'I will someday, and then my troubles will be over—but not yet.' I guess I just enjoyed being sorry for myself. But yesterday, after a night of turmoil and anguish, all of a sudden I let go. It was like a boil bursting! All the pent-up poisons gushed out of me and I was a new person. I am starting a campaign right away to overcome the misunderstandings of years. I know I am finally heading in the right direction. I shall never let my receiving set get full of squeaks and static again."

A Japanese guard cut off the tongue of a captive American soldier, when he gave the wrong answer to a question. His sister, hearing a missionary from Japan, said: "Thank you for telling me about the Japanese. Now I can give more to help them." She was truly Christian —and released and happy.

A missionary's wife resented being sent to a lonely district; resented the coming of a boy, for her husband wanted a boy. As a result of these resentments she had operation after operation. "I've been a hellcat to live with." Then came the prayer and the surrender to God. She wrote the whole thing to her husband, asked forgiveness, and was literally a transformed person.

Here was a highly intelligent woman who was in a very responsible position, but full of resentments and self-pity because her mother, to whom she was deeply attached, was slipping away. She would be left alone in the world. She saw how she was disrupting her life by these resentments, and very quietly and calmly surrendered them to God and passed out of hell into heaven—in a moment! Resentments have no place in a Christian heart. Not even righteous anger, at least for long, for Paul urges that we do not let the sun go down on our wrath —don't keep it overnight lest it corrode the soul.

O Gracious Father, I know Thou art love and that Thy love can transform me, a constricted soul, into a consecrated soul. Amen.

AFFIRMATION FOR THE DAY: *Hate is poison, love is food; today I shall feed on food, not poison.*

FORGIVENESS IS POWER

We continue the steps out of resentments. Fourth, *after surrendering these resentments to God, now actively forgive those against whom you have the resentments*. Not only forgive them, but tell them so. The telling them so will be the catharsis, the cleansing.

A pastor was in charge of a U.S.O. group during World War I. A woman who was jealous of his position and unspeakably nasty to him backed him in a corner and in public struck him on the cheek. He turned the other and said, "That too, please." Said it three times. The woman was dumbfounded. She stood there helpless. The whole community was won to him and revolted against her by this simple act of forgiveness. Forgiveness is power.

A woman wrote a stinging letter to her husband, left it, and drove away, intending to burn the bridges behind her and leave her husband. A friend begged her to go back and tear up that letter. She drove forty miles through rain, got there just before her husband arrived, tore up the letter. They then and there settled matters and have been living happily ever since.

There are many who feel that if they don't stand up and retaliate, they will become everybody's door mat. Everybody's door mat, or everybody's temple of refuge? The camomile plant grows fastest when it is walked on. The soul grows fastest when it has learned to give back love for hate and light for darkness. For you become what you give back.

Lincoln once reprimanded a young army officer for indulging in a violent controversy with an associate. "No man," said Lincoln, "who is resolved to make the most of himself can afford to spare time for personal contention. Still less can he afford to take the consequences, including the vitiation of his temper, and the loss of self-control. Yield larger things to which you show no more than equal rights; and yield lesser ones though clearly your own. Better give your path to a dog than be bitten by him in contesting for the right. Even killing the dog will not cure the bite."

O Christ, Thou who didst pray for enemies on the cross, help me when crucified on some cross of wrong to forgive my enemies too—and to pray for them. Amen.

AFFIRMATION FOR THE DAY: *To indulge in hate or to take offense is too expensive—to me.*

GIVE OUT LOVE, AND ONLY LOVE

Here is the next step to victory over resentment. Fifth, *not only actively forgive, but try to do good to anyone against whom you hold resentments.* A preacher walked fifty miles to beg George Washington to spare the life of a man sentenced to death for neglect of duty. "I am sorry I can't grant the request for your friend's pardon," said Washington. The preacher replied, "He is not my friend; I suppose I do not have a worse enemy living." Washington looked surprised and said, "Surely you are not pleading for your enemy?" "Yes," said the preacher. "Then," said Washington, "I will grant the pardon." The forgiving spirit of the preacher, said J. W. Brougher, so affected the man that he was transformed into a friend.

One of the natives of the South Sea Islands who had been a cannibal went to Communion. As he knelt, he saw that the man kneeling beside him was the man who had slain his father and had drunk his blood, against whom he had sworn that he would kill him the first time he saw him. He went back to his seat. And there he seemed to hear a voice saying, "By this all men will know that you are my disciples, if you have love for one another," and he saw a cross and heard Jesus praying, "Father, forgive them." Then he went back to the altar.

The Delaware Indians were gathered into a Moravian church for a special meeting by some half-intoxicated soldiers, and then the doors were shut and the church burned. The infuriated Indians went on the warpath. This was Christianity! But the daughter of the chief went among them, and by prayer and singing hymns and preaching forgiveness, drew them away from revenge and won them back to Christianity.

Shelley puts it in quivering lines:

> To suffer woes which Hope thinks infinite;
> To forgive wrongs darker than death or night;
>
> . . . .
>
> To love, and bear, to hope till Hope creates
> From its own wreck the thing it contemplates;
> Neither to change, nor falter, nor repent.

So the conclusion we reach is this: Give out love, and only love. For you are born of the qualities you habitually give out.

O God, when I take Thy way, I cannot lose. I win even if I lose. Help me to take Thy way even to seeming defeat. Amen.

AFFIRMATION FOR THE DAY: *To love is the victory, even if it fails.*

"HE WHO TREADS SOFTLY GOES FAR"

We saw last week how we are to overcome resentments and hate. Here are a few remaining observations.

Alan W. Watt says very pertinently: "Our attitude toward evil must be free from hatred. . . . Satan rejoices when he succeeds in in-inspiring us with diabolical feelings towards himself. A continual de-nunciation of evil and its agents merely encourages its growth in the world—a truth sufficiently revealed in the Gospels, but to which we re-main persistently blind."

To get rid of darkness you don't fight it and kick it—you light a candle. The fable of the sun and wind illustrates. They quarreled about which was the stronger and the wind said, "I'll prove I am. See that old man down there with a coat? I bet I can make him take off his coat quicker than you can." So the sun went behind a cloud and the wind blew until it was a tornado, but the harder it blew the tighter the old man wrapped his coat about him. Finally the wind calmed down and gave up. And then the sun came from behind the cloud and smiled kindly on the old man. Presently he mopped his brow and pulled off his coat. The sun then told the wind that gentleness and friendliness were always stronger than fury and force.

The Chinese have a proverb, says Dale Carnegie, "He who treads softly goes far." He does—clear to the inner heart.

In the days when the Japanese government was determined to wipe out Christianity, a test was made. A crucifix was laid on the ground, and when one suspected of being a Christian was brought up, he was told to walk upon the cross. Those who refused were killed; those who did it were freed. One of these crucifixes has been dug up from a ruin, and the face of Christ has been worn down by those stepping on it. Today that face of Christ, walked upon then, is looking with tender compassion on a people who are standing amid the ruin of their civiliza-tion, seeking for guidance. He forgives. So must we if we are to follow Him. The only way to overcome evil is with good, hate by love, the world by a cross. It works. And nothing else will work.

O Father, I know that Thy way of the cross is my way too. Help me to take it and apply it to everybody and everything, everywhere. Amen.

AFFIRMATION FOR THE DAY: *The cross is the magnet of the universe— it draws all things to itself. I use its power as my way of life.*

THE HOLDING OF EXCESSIVE GRIEF

We now turn to something that is akin to resentments—the holding of excessive grief. Grief comes to us all. It is a part of a mortal existence and it is inherent in the nature of ourselves and the world in which we live. Nobody escapes. Even "Jesus wept" at the grave of a loved one. "My son, the world is dark with griefs and graves, so dark that men cry out against the heavens."

Since grief comes to us all, how it affects us determines the results. Some take grief badly and some take it in their stride—and well. Those who take it badly are badly affected by it. Shakespeare asks, "What grief hath set the jaundice on your cheeks?" Many have jaundiced souls, expressing themselves in jaundiced cheeks because they are reacting to grief very badly. Walter C. Alvarez says: "The physician is right when he answers that if the woman would only stop fretting, fussing, overdoing, and getting tired and upset, or if she would only settle some life problems once and for all, her nerves might quiet down and her colon would then have some chance of getting better." And he adds: "Most people with a sore colon are of a tense, sensitive, nervous, or worrisome temperament." If "the colon is the mirror of the mind," then where there is grief in the mind, there will be grief in the colon.

How are we to meet grief and sorrow? First, *make up your mind calmly that grief is bound to come to you.* That attitude will save you from feeling, when grief does come, that you are being singled out for persecution. That creates a persecution illusion, a martyr complex. Say to yourself: "Grief is the lot of every man and I won't be an exception." That shouldn't make you morbid with your arm up ready for the blow to strike. No, settle it once and for all that grief is our common lot and then forget it and go about your tasks. And when grief comes, you won't react into aggrieved, surprised self-pity. The idea that you are being singled out for bad treatment brings a martyr's complex, and this produces unhappiness.

O merciful Father, Thy heart too hast known and dost know grief, for all our griefs are Thine. Help me to share my griefs with Thee, and thus halve them. Amen.

AFFIRMATION FOR THE DAY: *Grief comes to all—sours some, sweetens others. I shall use it to sweeten my spirit.*

"LIVING IN A HALF ACCEPTANCE"

We saw yesterday that the first step out of excessive grief is to accept the fact that grief comes to us all. Second, *don't try to escape grief and sorrow by any illusions or subterfuges.* For the illusions and subterfuges will turn out in the end to be worse than the actual grief. I met a woman who, though blind, kept saying she was not blind—she lived in a make-believe world. I saw another man who, though blind, said: "Anyone who has achieved the perfect happiness I have achieved is no object of pity." He lived realistically, and with solid happiness. Illusions will end in illusions—will let you down.

Today I read: "They rose up, put him out of the town, and brought him to the brow of the hill on which their town was built, in order to hurl him down. But he made his way through them and went off" (Luke 4:29-30, Moffatt). Note: "He made His way through them"— He didn't back off, or dodge, or try to escape; He went straight "through." The Christian word is "through." It never dodges into illusions. It faces everything and transforms everything.

Here is a case of trying to escape into a part illusion: A mother whose entire life had been wrapped up in her only son received the terrible news that he had been killed in World War II. After the first shock of the telegram had worn off, followed by a dull numbness, the mother came to acknowledge the fact that her son had died, since she could not very well do anything else. But she was quite unable to accept the truth of his dying in all its train of consequences and meaning for her continuing life. She could not bring herself to make new friends, or find new interests; she was quite incapable of forming new habits and reordering her plans and hopes. She accepted the fact that her son had died without really believing it and accepting its meaning for herself.

She was living in a half acceptance which turned out to be in its consequences a whole illusion. For it left her unadjusted, ineffective, unhappy. The escape into illusion turned out to be an illusion.

O Christ, I thank Thee that Thou hast shown me the way—the way "through." I surrender to Thee all my impulses to escape. Give me the spirit of reality—the will to go through. Amen.

AFFIRMATION FOR THE DAY: *Only the truth can make me free. I shall think truth, speak truth, trust truth, and be truth.*

SHORTEN THE ADJUSTMENT PERIOD

We are looking at the way out of excessive grief. Karl Menninger says: "Psychiatrists realize from clinical experience what poets have proclaimed in inspired verse, that to retreat into the loneliness of one's own soul is to surrender one's claim upon life." To try to feed on one's loneliness is to try to feed on ashes. "To be is to be in relations," and when we cease relations, we cease to be. We must be rightly related to life, to ongoing life, or cease to live.

That brings us to the next step. Third, *face your grief in the quietness before God and surrender it into His hands.* Really surrender it. Don't put it into His hands and then take it back again into your own. Put it into His hand permanently and finally. Tell Him: "You've got it. I listen now for your answer. I'll obey." And then you'll find the blank wall of your grief now has a little open door through which you can pass to freedom—that little open door is the transforming will of God. He can help you to get through your grief and to make something out of it.

I say "get through your grief." A friend writes: "When my mother died, it took me months and months to get over it, when my brother died, it was only a matter of hours I took to recover and adjust." The time of making the adjustment was shortened. That is victory. The growth in Christian living is measured by the time it takes you to adjust to a calamity or a grief. Some people let their griefs spoil months and years of living. They feel anything else would be disloyal to the absent loved one, so they drape their souls and minds and bodies in grief. They syndicate their sorrows.

Here was a woman highly trained in music in France and the United States. She lost her voice after her mother died, probably by suicide. The grief festered within her. Then she saw she was wrong. She surrendered the grief to God and her voice came back. Now she is free and happy and useful. She walked out of her self-made prison of grief—walked out by surrender and acceptance.

Gracious Lord, I now see that I have selfishly held my griefs. Take them, and you and I will make something out of them together. Now I see the open door. I enter. Amen.

AFFIRMATION FOR THE DAY: *I am shortening my periods of adjustment to grief and sorrow; soon I shall react almost automatically and immediately into victory.*

PRAYER CANCELS LONELINESS

We now come to the next step in getting victory over grief. Fourth, *after surrendering the grief to God, now go out and find someone with a grief or sorrow, and see what you can do for him.*

Meister Eckhart said, "God's every affliction is a lure"—a lure to help you to help others. You are made tender by your sorrow, and that tenderness can make your service tenderly effective.

It was said of Elizabeth Fry that by reading the Bible to the prisoners of England she became one of the best Bible readers of her time. Yet when she was first married, her Bible reading was poor indeed. Janet Whitney in her book, *Elizabeth Fry, Quaker Heroine,* tells us that "on the rare occasions when Joe Fry snatched time to look in at the prison and see what his wife was doing, and beheld her so at home, so queenly and composed, the center of a hundred eyes, yet unembarrassed and concentrated on her task, did he recall those early days of her married life when even to read to himself and brother William and one visitor had covered her with confusion so that she had had to hand the Bible to him 'to finish.'" Her prison reform got her out of the prison of her own self-consciousness and fear. In freeing, she was freed.

Someone has said, "Prayer cancels loneliness." It does, for it brings you into fellowship with God, and in fellowship with Him there can be no loneliness. But prayer just for yourself will not cancel loneliness. It may aggravate it if you are thinking only of yourself. But if you bring the needs and sorrows of others into your prayer hours, then that does cancel loneliness.

I once asked people in a sanitarium to take garments and sew for China relief. I thought there would be a tremendous eagerness to respond, for busy people outside had responded wonderfully. These people had all the time there was on their hands. To my amazement nobody responded. That was one reason why they were there—they were busy thinking about their own griefs and ailments. No time for others. They nursed their griefs and ailments, and they grew!

O God, give me the heart at leisure from itself to soothe and sympathize. And then I shall lighten burdens of my own as I take up the burdens of others. Amen.

AFFIRMATION FOR THE DAY: *Taking the griefs of others inoculates me against the hurts of my own griefs.*

TRANSFORM YOUR GRIEF

We continue the steps out of grief. Fifth, *don't bear your grief; transform it into character and contribution.* Josephine Butler had an only child whom she adored. As she came home in her carriage the girl ran to the balustrade and fell, dying at her mother's feet. An old Quaker to whom she turned for help gave her this message: "God has taken to himself her whom thou didst love; but there are many forlorn young hearts who need that mother love of thine." He told her to go to a certain house, which turned out to be a refuge where forty young lives, rescued from moral peril, were being cared for. Josephine Butler threw herself into that service and became one of the greatest social reformers of the century. She didn't bear her grief; she set it to music.

Someone has said that "one can see farther through a tear than through a telescope." Wrote William Alexander Percy:

> I heard a bird at break of day
> Sing from the autumn trees
> A song so mystical and calm,
> So full of certainties.
> No man, I think, could listen long
> Except upon his knees.
> Yet this was but a simple bird,
> Alone, among the trees.

Robert Spear demonstrated victory over grief when his gifted son was cruelly murdered at Northfield. This is what he says: "During more than forty-three years of incessant struggle, journeying to and fro throughout the world, I have never lost the assurance of Christ's living presence with me. He is not a mere vision, He is no imaginary dream, but a living Presence, who daily inspires me and gives me grace. In Him quite consciously I find strength in time of need." And the "strength in time of need" meant not only comfort but contribution. He gave most when most was taken away.

My Father, I know that Thou knowest what it is to lose a Son. And yet Thou didst use Thy pain and didst make it redemptive. Help me to make my pains into paeans. Amen.

AFFIRMATION FOR THE DAY: *All my sufferings and griefs shall be burnishing powder to polish my soul.*

BE HAPPY AND SPREAD HAPPINESS

We take our last step in transforming griefs. Sixth, *remember that if you have lost a loved one, he is not lost.* The Christian founds his hope in immortality on the nature of God as seen in Christ. If there is the kind of God in the universe that Jesus revealed, then death in any real sense is impossible for those who are in Christ. In ancient Gaul debts were sometimes written to be payable beyond death. In ancient Etruria burial urns were engraved with pictures of the rising sun. If hope was in the pagan's breast, how much more within the Christian's breast? And as Marcus Aurelius put it, "It is good to die if there is a God; and sad to live if there is not."

Among the early Christians this note of triumph in death was described by a Greek named Aristides, who wrote in A.D. 125 to a friend about the new religion called Christianity: "If any righteous man among the Christians passes from this world, they rejoice and offer thanks to God, and they escort his body with songs and thanksgiving as if he were setting out from one place to another nearby."

A mother monkey in India will keep her dead baby, hugging it to her breast long after putrefaction has set in. She has no hope of immortality. Don't be like that mother monkey, refusing to surrender your loved ones to God and to a larger life in heaven. Then your griefs fester and they spoil everything—you included. Give them up gladly, and then go out to live as though you believed in God and eternal life. Lincoln once said, "Most folks are about as happy as they make up their minds to be." Make up your mind to be happy and to spread happiness. It is disloyalty to your loved ones to go around moping and sad and full of self-pity. For at bottom an excess of grief is not a manifestation of love for the absent loved ones; it is a species of self-pity. Say with Fraser of Brea, "This is a harsh-featured messenger, yet he comes from God; what kindness does he bring me?" The harsh-featured messenger brings you the message that your loved one is alive forevermore.

O God, my Father, I repeat the words: "Into Thy hands I commend my loved ones—not into the hands of death, but into Thy hands." They are safe with Thee, and so am I! Amen.

AFFIRMATION FOR THE DAY: *If the greatest human tragedy, death, is only an open door, then what can lesser tragedies do to me? I use them all.*

FIGHTING WITH OURSELVES

We have been looking at the necessity of surrendering fears, resentments, and griefs. At the basis of the hesitation or refusal to surrender these three things is a deeper refusal—the refusal to surrender the self. These others are the symptoms; this is the disease. Back of every failure in regard to fears and resentments and grief is one failure—the failure to surrender the self.

We must then look at egocentricity as the root of all our problems. As long as we make ourselves the center of our universe, none of our problems will come out right, nothing will add up to sense, for we are not the center of the universe—God is. And until we get ourselves off our own hands into the hands of God, we are a problem to ourselve and others.

A lot of people recognize that fact, so they set out to fight themselves. But to fight oneself only aggravates the problem of the self. A robin saw itself in the shiny disc of the hub of a parked car, and began to peck at itself. Then it grew more fierce and flew at itself. This went on for hours, until the beak of the exhausted robin was bleeding. The owner of the car, seeing that the robin would kill itself fighting with itself, had to take the car away. Many of us are like that robin, fighting ourselves and making ourselves all upset and inwardly bloody in the process. And it doesn't get rid of the self. The process is wrong. When a student said in one of our Ashrams, "I've come here to declare a full scale war on myself," it sounded heroic, but it was a wrong method.

Others do not fight themselves, but try to make the self perfect and thus get rid of the problem of the self. A girl, very intelligent and earnest, stood up in one of our meetings and said she wanted to be perfect, to have a perfect personality. Then she confessed in private that everybody accepted her in the beginning, then they fell away for some reason. The reason was that she was not interested in other people; she was interested only in her own perfection. She was engaged to a man who broke it off and hated her. She was not perfect, but perfectly frustrated.

O God, I ask Thee to probe me to my depths, and if I'm trying to be religious for self-centered reasons, bring that up and out. For I want real healing. Help me. Amen.

AFFIRMATION FOR THE DAY: *My self is God-given, and when God controlled, is wonderful and fit to live with. I decide it shall be God controlled.*

"A RESPONSIBILITY HOUND"

We left off yesterday with the girl who was seeking perfection, trying to be a perfected personality. Not only did she lose her friends; she also lost her own self-esteem. She hated herself. Here was a strange outcome: She who wanted to be a perfect person didn't like the perfect person! Her method was all wrong and it left her all wrong. For in trying to be perfect you are the center of your thought and endeavor, and the result is self-centeredness and the consequence is self-disruption. For again, the attempt is to be the center of the universe. She was breaking herself upon the law of life, which says that you must lose your life if you are to find it again.

Another species of self-centeredness is the person who fussily tries to make everything and everyone perfect. Karl Menninger says: "I see several times a month what may well be called the fuss-budget's or the perfectionist's disease. It is the disease that fastens itself upon the woman or man who wants everything just so around the house and office. It tends to grow worse as the patient grows older. Persons of this type wear themselves out and get constantly more irritable and more difficult to live with as through the years they try to force perfection on spouse, servants, or children. . . . One such woman got herself into a serious state of nervousness and exhaustion by visiting in rotation every one of her five daughters in order to clean house and 'put everything to rights.'" Dr. Stokes calls such a person "a responsibility hound." These people are usually good people and conscientious, but they are mistaken. They are on the wrong basis. They are dressing up their service in altruism, but at the back of things is an attempt to impose one's will and superior attitudes on others.

I know of a woman who, though religious and devoted, developed arthritis by her tense anxiety for her family. Down underneath she wanted to dominate, and that tense anxiety, clothed in religion, upset the rhythm of the body and produced very serious disease.

O God, my gracious Father, pull off the cloaks that hide my self from myself and let me stand before Thee as I am, for I want to be different. Amen.

AFFIRMATION FOR THE DAY: *I shall hunt out subtle desires to dominate as one hunts out vermin, and be as ruthless with them.*

THE DESIRE TO BE IMPORTANT

We are looking at the unsurrendered self clothed in various garbs. Many people to get their way and to gain attention retreat into illness.

Dale Carnegie quotes the instance of "a bright, vigorous girl who became an invalid in order to gain a feeling of importance. One day this girl had been obliged to face something, her age perhaps, and the fact that she would never be married. The lonely years were stretching ahead, and there was little left for her to anticipate. She took to her bed; and for ten years her mother traveled to the third floor and back, carrying trays, nursing her. Then one day the old mother, weary with service, lay down and died. For some weeks the invalid languished; then she got up, put on her clothing, and resumed living again."

"The deepest urge," said John Dewey, "is the desire to be important." And if illness makes us important, we take to illness.

Sometimes this desire makes us try to add a cubit to our stature by titles. George Washington wanted to be called "His Mightiness, the President of the United States." Columbus pleaded for the title "Admiral of the Ocean and Viceroy of India." Catherine the Great refused to open letters that were not addressed to "Her Imperial Majesty." Mrs. Lincoln, in the White House, turned on Mrs. Grant like a tigress and shouted, "How dare you be seated in my presence until I invite you!" But the attempt to be great by these extraneous things only makes the one attempting it greatly ridiculous. If you remember yourself, people will forget you, or if they remember you, they do it only to smile. There is a law written into the nature of things and you don't break it; you break yourself upon it—you must lose your life to find it. There are no exceptions.

I stood looking at a tablet put up by a raja of India, with titles stretching through three lines. I said to myself, "You shall call his name Jesus"—just one word. But that one word has become the Word! I cannot remember the raja's name, but how can I ever forget the Man who forgot Himself?

Father, I know that Thou art trying to save me from my self-imposed hurts. Save me from them by saving me from myself. In Jesus' name. Amen.

AFFIRMATION FOR THE DAY: *No attempt to add a cubit to my stature today. I shall be myself—in God.*

IMPORTANCE THROUGH RECOUNTING AILMENTS

We continue to look at the ways in which egocentricity can clothe itself. S. Weir Mitchell gives this letter from a patient: "Under this enforced rest my appetite failed and I began to have nausea. My first vomiting created a sensation in the household, which I think as I recall it, I enjoyed as making me important. Very soon I got to vomiting every day; there was none of the nausea which I had at first, and which I have since been familiar with as a part of seasickness. It gave me no annoyance to cast up my food, and indeed was rather a relief."

A great many gain a supposed sense of importance by recounting their ailments. Samuel Johnson says, "Do not be like the spider, man, and spin conversation incessantly out of thine own bowels." An operation gives an opening to have the conversation center around one's self. A bore is one who talks about his operation when you want to talk about yours!

An old woman in an old folks' home had to be dosed with soda-mint tablets and other digestives after every meal. One day the nurse said to the superintendent, "Have you noticed that Mrs. ——— hasn't taken a digestive for a month?" That was the month when she sat at the table where there was a man! She was so interested in him that she forgot all about her digestion and it was normal. But when she sat at the table where there were only women, her indigestion returned. She began to be absorbed in herself and her problems, and her troubles returned.

Someone has said that if we are to live well, we must have three things: (a) a faith to live by; (b) a self fit to live with; and (c) a work fit to live for—something to which we can give ourselves and thus get ourselves off our own hands. The middle one is the by-product of the first and last. When you have a faith to live by, that breaks the tyranny of self-centeredness; and when you have a work fit to live for, that lifts you out of self-preoccupation; and the two together produce a self fit to live with. A faith and a lifework are lifesavers because they save you from yourself.

O Christ, Thy will is my joy and fulfillment, but my will against Thy will is my sorrow and frustration. Help me to let Thee have me. Amen.

AFFIRMATION FOR THE DAY: *"I shall have no 'organ recital' of my ill-nesses today."*

STEPS OUT OF EGOCENTRICITY

We are looking at the results of egocentricity. We are being driven to the conclusion that to be completely egocentric is to be completely unhappy.

The story goes of a man who got somehow into a state of being where everything he wanted was given to him instantly. He wanted a nice home and it was given to him completely furnished with servants in attendance. He wanted an automobile and it was his. Everything he wanted was given to him at once. But he soon got tired and was bored. He said he wanted to suffer something, to achieve something. Further, he said he would rather go to hell than stay in this place. And the answer came at once, "Where do you think you are?"

To be a completely self-immersed person is to be in hell, no matter where you are. To the degree that you are self-centered, to that degree you are unhappy and frustrated. We are made in the structure of our beings to love something beyond ourselves, and when we do, then we find ourselves coming back to ourselves. If that is true—and all life is a commentary on it—then what are we to do?

First, *decide once and for all that you are not God, that God is God, and that you will surrender your life completely to God.* The basis of your life now is fundamentally changed from yourself to God. You are no longer a self-centered person; you are from this moment a God-centered person. In the ordering of your life you are going to listen to God instead of listening to yourself. That is as complete a change as the shift in astronomy from the Ptolemaic, where the earth was the center of the universe and the heavenly bodies revolved around it, to the Copernican, where the earth revolves around the sun. Your center is God, not yourself. Now your sums will begin to add up, for you are on the right center. As long as you were self-centered, you were tense and anxious and on the defensive, for you knew subconsciously that this was the wrong center. Now you can relax. The universe approves of you, is behind you.

O God, I thank Thee that I am no longer bound by myself. I am loosed from these inner fetters. I am free—in Thee. Now I am at home with myself, for I am at home with Thee. Amen.

AFFIRMATION FOR THE DAY: *Since my center is God, my circumference is everywhere—I am bounded by infinity.*

DON'T FIGHT YOURSELF

We continue our steps out of a self-centered life. Second, *now that you have surrendered to God, give up ways of self-salvation and take salvation as a gift from God.* Alan W. Watt says: "You cannot see what you are looking for because what you are looking for is the one that looks. Every self-conscious attempt to know oneself, to improve oneself, to save oneself, to unite oneself with God, must come to this exasperating and impossible conclusion. . . . Somehow, therefore, man must be persuaded to let go of himself, to stop running around in circles and making himself miserable. . . . This is the same thing as telling him that he is loved and accepted by God, that he must love himself with God's own love, and that he is saved as he is, a sinner, by simple faith in Jesus." If God has you, then your salvation is guaranteed by the simple fact that He has you. For He saves all that He possesses. Accept that fact by simple faith.

This won't be pleasing to your egoism. You will want to do something for which you get credit. "Egoism is like trying to swim without relying on the water, endeavoring to keep afloat by tugging at your own legs; your whole body becomes tense and you sink like a stone." You must learn to let go and accept the gift of God. Don't try—trust!

"But," someone objects, "doesn't the Scripture say: 'Work all the more strenuously at your salvation'?" Yes, it does, but note the rest of the verse: "For it is God who in his goodwill enables you to will this and to achieve it" (Phil. 2:12-13, Moffatt). "God . . . enables you"—that it is the grace at the basis of the working strenuously. He works grace in first.

Don't fight yourself; surrender yourself and accept the gift of deliverance from yourself. You then are relaxed and released. You are no longer afraid of yourself since God has the self. You are not nervously trying to hold it down like a jack-in-the-box. "Delivered from the vicious circle of self-consciousness, the infinite regression of chasing oneself around and around, it is possible for man to move forward."

O God, Thou art breaking the tyranny of self-consciousness and Thou art making me free—free to live with myself and others. I'm grateful. Amen.

AFFIRMATION FOR THE DAY: *Since my horizons are infinity, I'm moving out today to possess more and more of them.*

LOVE YOURSELF—IN GOD

We come now to the next step in our gaining freedom from our selves. Third, *now that you have surrendered yourself to God, you can love yourself in God.* A great many are afflicted with self-hate and to hate yourself is as bad as to hate others. Now "self-loathing must give way to self-acceptance, which is permitting oneself to be loved by God." You accept yourself and love yourself just as you love your neighbor. C. G. Jung, the psychiatrist, puts it this way: "The acceptance of oneself is the essence of the moral problem and the epitome of a whole outlook upon life. That I feed the hungry, that I forgive an insult, that I love my enemy in the name of Christ—all these are undoubtedly great virtues. What I do unto the least of my brethren that I do unto Christ. But what if I should discover that the least amongst them all, the poorest of all the beggars, the most impudent of all the offenders, the very enemy himself—that these are within me, and that I myself stand in need of the alms of my own kindness— that I myself am the enemy who must be loved—what then?"

Now since you are able to live with God, you are able to live with yourself, to be at home with yourself and rather like yourself. For loving Someone beyond yourself, and more than yourself, you are now free to love yourself.

There was a young girl of unusual beauty of character and charming grace. She wore on her neck a locket which no one was ever allowed to open. One day, in a moment of unusual confidence, a friend was allowed to touch its spring and learn its secret. She saw there these words, "Whom having not seen, I love." That love for Christ made it possible for her to love herself in Christ. For she saw herself in Christ not merely as she was, but as she could become in Him. So you can love yourself redemptively. You see in Christ the image of yourself-to-be, and you love that image, and you can love yourself out of everything contrary to that image. The Christian way is the only way I know of which offers a way out of our dilemma—how to love yourself without being self-centered.

O Christ, I see that my self is no longer a problem, but a possibility in Thee. I love myself and rejoice in myself, for I love Thee more and rejoice in Thee more. I'm emancipated. Amen.

AFFIRMATION FOR THE DAY: *I hug myself and pat myself on the back that I had sense enough to surrender myself.*

FROM INFERIORITY TO ADEQUACY

Before we leave our last week's study of deliverance from egocentricity, we must give this illustration of deliverance. A pastor's wife was resentful that her parents, her husband, and others did not give her enough attention. She was resentful that her husband was in Christian work, for it made him neglect her, she thought. The pastor told her he would give up his work for her sake. She was ill, pains here and there. They talked over my sermon on resentments till 2 A.M., and then they prayed and surrendered the wounded ego to God. "Our home is heaven now," he writes. The ego unsurrendered gathered resentments around itself. But the ego surrendered gathered love around itself. The ego produces the kind of world around it suitable to its own attitudes. The attitudes determine the world. The inside produces the outside.

We come now to another transformation—*the transformation from a sense of inferiority to adequacy.* Many feel the need not of being saved from specific sins, but from a sense of inferiority. Many would answer the description of Isaiah: "Listen, ye who are downcast, who feel far from any triumph, I bring my triumph near, right near, my victory is hastening" (Isa. 46:12, Moffatt). Many "are downcast" and "feel far from any triumph"—they are filled with a sense of inferiority.

Karl Stolz gives the fourfold classification of the members of a church. The first group: "They accept with courage the common lot of mankind, expecting no concessions from life." The second: "Those who are somewhat personally dislocated or socially maladjusted, or both, but somehow contrive to accept life's second bests and achieve a measure of satisfaction." The third: "Those who are undone and defeated. . . . They merely exist day by day." The fourth: "Those who have lost out completely, some of them victims of evil habits, some hopeless in chronic invalidism."

If that classification is fair, then all except the first-named need, and need especially, victory over inferiorities and a sense of defeat.

O God, Thy resources and our inferiorities must come together. In Thee we live, in our poverty we perish by slow starvation. Amen.

AFFIRMATION FOR THE DAY: *Shall I be empty in the presence of fullness, inadequate in the presence of Adequacy, uncertain in the presence of Certainty? No!*

LOWER LEVELS OF SOLUTION

Before we look at the remedy for inferiorities we must look at them more closely. The life forces can be converted downward by fears and a sense of inferiorities into various types of diseases as an escape. The soldier who can endure no more combat may be paralyzed in both limbs; a woman who hates the sight of her husband may become blind; a railroad passenger suffering from a minor accident may complain of a backache after a conference with his lawyer. This, in medical terms, is called "conversion hysteria." According to Freud, "An unendurable conflict is converted or transformed into a motor or sensory manifestation which closely simulates a physically caused condition. Yet the patient is entirely unconscious of any deception. The 'conversion' takes place in his subconscious mind for the purpose of a wish fulfillment."

This is conversion downward: the life forces are fastened upon a lower level of solution—an illness, a paralysis, blindness. Christian conversion is a conversion upward: the life forces are fastened upon a higher level of solution—positive instead of negative, on health instead of illness, activity instead of escapism, on outgoing love instead of on self-pity. The probabilities are that if you won't take Christian conversion upward, you will take some form of conversion-downward.

This method of trying to get out of inferiorities by escaping into illnesses is like the remedy, seriously proposed, by a student who when interviewed about how the problem of getting rid of cheating in examinations could be solved, replied, "Do away with the examinations." I once saw in Georgia, where termites are a problem, a sign on a truck: "There Are No Termites in This Load." There was no load! Or like the sign in front of a hotel: "Please Do Not Tip the Doorman." "Good," I said to myself, "this is refreshing." But there was no doorman!

Many try to get rid of inferiorities by dodging out of responsibility into illness so the inferiorities cannot come out!

O God, I see I can't get around my inferiorities—I must go through them—to adequacy. Help me to find release through Thy adequacy. Amen.

AFFIRMATION FOR THE DAY: *All my conversions upward; none downward—all positive; none negative.*

"SHOCK TREATMENT OR A NEW FAITH"

We continue to look at inferiority complexes we build up within ourselves. Here is the case of an able man, but beaten by inward inferiorities and conflicts. His mother was domineering and his father was always comparing him with his very successful brother. He took to unnatural sex expression instead of to the natural expression in the marriage relationship. When he came to the latter, his heart would act up—functional disturbance. He was full of fears and inferiorities. A doctor said to him, "You will have to get shock treatment or a new faith." "Shock treatment or a new faith"—that is the growing alternative. A new faith is a gentle shock treatment that sends the life forces into new channels of constructive life and activity. A new faith gets our eyes off ourselves and puts them on Christ and we find adequacy and power in Him.

> The reason why our way is dark,
> The reason why our eyes are dim,
> Too much we watch our erring feet
> Too little faith have we in Him.

Here was a man who was under his very able father in business. When his father died, he had to take over responsibility for the running of the business and he developed asthma from the tensions and a sense of inferiority when he compared himself with his father. The asthma was functional and gradually dropped away when he faced his tasks, managed the business, and showed to himself and others that he could do it. He could have tried to escape into permanent illness. He fortunately did not try to go around his problems by illness as an excuse, but he went through them—to victory.

A man was such a good worker that he was promoted to a higher job with better pay, a job where he classified potatoes, big and small. After some time he asked to go back to his old job, "I have too many decisions to make each day." A lot of people don't want to take the responsibility of deciding what is big potatoes and what is little potatoes. So they retreat out of responsibility into inferiorities and excuses.

O God, I want to escape into Thee—into Thee and Thy adequacy and power. Save me from any short cuts out that may prove long cuts. Amen.

AFFIRMATION FOR THE DAY: *All my escapes into God; none into things and methods that let me down.*

"PILLARS AND CATERPILLARS"

We continue our meditation on inferiorities and the wrong way to meet them. One woman said, "Whenever I get frustrated, I either go to a movie, or get immersed in work, or I eat and eat." She was far overweight and knew it. All these methods were an attempt at escape. She saw they were all dead ends and turned around and found the way through surrender to God and the appropriation of His adequacy

A man said to a psychiatrist: "I have neither illusions nor delusions Doctor. My problem is that I live in a world of grim reality." He was suffering from the illusion of no illusions! The world of "grim reality" is the place where the battle must be fought and won—or lost. There is no victory in an attempt to escape.

Edward Stracker, University of Pennsylvania psychiatrist, says that there are these marks of emotional maturity: "The ability to stick to a job till it is finished; persistence in face of obstacles; endurance of hardships; decisiveness and determination; the capacity to take orders and co-operate; flexibility in accepting circumstances." All of these add up to being a really functioning Christian—every one a Christian characteristic!

To manufacture alibis, excuses, and reasons for not accomplishing is a sign of immaturity. "I've had an overdose of parents. They made me dependent," said a frustrated man. This was true perhaps, but if he stops with blaming his parents, he won't get anywhere except deeper into the mire. If his human parents let him down, then he has the divine Parent who will lift him up and out if he will co-operate with that divine Parent. There is a way out—for everybody "Success comes in cans, failure in can'ts." Through God you can do anything you ought to do. Drop the vocabulary of "can't" and take the vocabulary of "can"—can, by the grace of God. Somebody has facetiously said that "the members of churches are just two types pillars and caterpillars. The pillars hold up the church, the caterpillars just crawl in and out." Don't go through life just being a caterpillar. But even in a caterpillar there is a butterfly!

O God, I need to see my possibilities in Thee. I have been looking down and I am down. I'm going to look up and I know I will be up. Amen

AFFIRMATION FOR THE DAY: *"Now to him who by the action of his power within us is able to do all, aye far more than we can ever ask or imagine"* (Eph. 3:20, Moffatt).

"THE SICK INTO A POWER"

We look at another cause of inferiority—our own sins. Nothing puts ne down in the dumps so quickly and so lastingly as a consciousness f guilt.

Listen to these penetrating words, "Some, weakened by their sinful vays, were sick and suffering through evildoing; they had a loathing or all food" (Ps. 107:17-18, Moffatt). Again, "Till evildoing wasted hem away" (Ps. 106:43, Moffatt). We have to learn the hard way hat sinful ways do weaken us, do make us sick, do cause suffering, do produce a loathing for all food, and do waste us away. We must make up our minds that we can never get on top of ourselves and the vorld if there is secret, unconfessed sin at the basis of our lives. That produces a central paralysis and inferiority. I once saw in a store vindow a sign: "Wallpaper You Can Live With." But there is somehing more intimate you have to live with—yourself.

Many people settle down into a hopeless acceptance of the supposed act that we are fixed in our present evil condition. But everything is capable of change. Potatoes were once considered poison, and so were omatoes. The juice of peaches was once used in Persia to tip poison irrows. If potatoes, tomatoes, and peaches can be changed from poison o profit, then you can be changed from a poisonous person to a profitble person.

The saying that "all crows are black and will always be black"— even that is not true. For I have seen white crows in Iraq. Besides, the nearest relative to the bird of paradise, the most beautiful bird in the world, is the crow. A crow has been made into the bird of paradise. This passage has a truer ring, "I will make the lame the nucleus of a nation, make the sick into a power" (Mic. 4:7, Moffatt). God is always turning our bad into good, our good into better, and our better into best. "To give them . . . oil of joy for mourning robes, praise for plaintiveness" (Isa. 61:3, Moffatt). "Instead of bronze I will bring gold to you, silver instead of iron" (Isa. 60:17, Moffatt). Bronze is good, gold is better; iron is good, silver is better—all our goods turned into betters.

O Gracious God, I know that Thou art not the God of the dead, but of the living. I do not belong to the dead past but to the living future. I am alive—in Thee. Amen.

AFFIRMATION FOR THE DAY: *I am a bundle of infinite possibilities—in God. Today I shall realize some of those possibilities.*

"MY POWERS HEIGHTENED"

We come now to the steps out of inferiorities. First, *as long as yo feel centered on yourself you feel inferior and alone; now by an act o surrender of yourself and your inferiorities to God, you begin to fee superior in God and not alone.* The secret of victory is surrender Air, when it surrenders to the vocal cords and intelligence, turns from mere air to speech and song. Mere vegetable matter, when it surrenders to and co-operates with the body, is transformed into an organism and a personality. When an isolated individual surrenders to and co operates with a fellowship, he finds himself in a higher life. When the individual and the group surrender to and co-operate with the Kingdom of God, they find themselves transformed.

The four steps which constitute the life climb of the universe ar these: (*a*) Faith in the higher life; (*b*) leading to a surrender to tha higher life; (*c*) leading to a co-operation with that higher life; (*d*) th lower life taking these steps is transformed into the image of th higher life and partakes of that higher life. You are no longer inferio —you are a part of a superior Life.

This is transformation: "For thou hast saved my life from death my feet from stumbling, that I may live, ever mindful of God, in th sunshine of life" (Ps. 56:13, Moffatt). "Life from death"—past; "fee from stumbling"—present; "that I may live, ever mindful of God, in the sunshine of life"—future. Here is something that covers the past the present, and the future—it is a total transformation. Accept it— it is yours for the acceptance.

You are in God and in Him you are not inferior—you are really and intrinsically superior. Say to yourself with Hannah, "My heart thrill to the Eternal, my powers are heightened by my God" (I Sam. 2:1 Moffatt). Your powers are heightened, you are no longer inferior All your natural powers are quickened and heightened by the con tinuous impact of the Supernatural. A continuous creation is taking place by the creative God, your mind is keener, your emotions more sensitive, and your will more decisive.

O God, my Father, all my powers now have a plus to them. They are what they are, plus what Thou art. That adds up to adequacy. Amen.

AFFIRMATION FOR THE DAY: *I think all my thoughts in Thee, feel my feelings in Thee, will my purposes in Thee, live my life in Thee and consequently am plussed by Thee.*

"EVERY NATURAL THING IS INTENSIFIED"

We come to the next step out of inferiorities. Second, *put yourself and your powers at God's disposal each day.* This gives you a sense of mission and direction. It also gives you a sense that all you have is being added to by all that He has.

Listen to this, "Moonlight glows like sunlight, and the sun shines sevenfold strong, on that Day when the Eternal heals his bruised folk, when he binds up their wounds" (Isa. 30:26, Moffatt). Here every natural thing is intensified—moonlight glows like sunlight and the sunshine is sevenfold strong when God's transformation sets in. That happens to your person—your will has an Almighty will working in it; your love has a divine Love intensifying it; your mind is illuminated by a divine Mind; you yourself become a plus.

Note the connection here: "If you are under the sway of the Spirit, you are not under the Law. . . . But the harvest of the Spirit is love, joy, peace, good temper, kindliness, generosity, fidelity, gentleness, self-control—there is no law against those who practise such things" (Gal. 5:1, 22-23, Moffatt). If you are under the sway of the Spirit, then the result is a harvest of the Spirit—you are a fruitful person bringing forth a ninefold crop. The barren becomes the bountiful.

Jesus said one word to the deaf man, "Open!" (Mark 7:54, Moffatt.) Jesus was always saying that one word, "Open!"—to mind, both conscious and unconscious; to opportunity, to love, to joy, to covered guilt, to complexes, to life. He is the great Opener.

When we come under His control, then He brightens all our dullness. "That our God may brighten our eyes" (Ezra 9:8, Moffatt). Dull, lusterless eyes grow bright and dull persons become sparkling. You belong to what a radiant friend of mine—radiant at eighty-two—calls "the heavenly frisky." You have "a New Testament face." Alexis Carrel says, "The human face cannot keep its secret if the owner wears it long enough. Youth is a disguise, concealing character and disposition, but with advancing years the truth comes out. This may be why beauty and dignity are so rarely seen in old faces." The Christian wears both.

Father, I thank Thee that all my inferiorities are lost in Thy amplitudes. I have enough—and to spare. And I shall draw on Thy resources for every demand made on me. Amen.

AFFIRMATION FOR THE DAY: *All my natural intensified by the Supernatural—I am a person with a plus.*

"A VERITABLE BATTLEFIELD"

We saw last week that our inferiorities can be an asset—they drive us to the appropriation of God's resources. If we had felt adequate, we would have gone on feeling adequate for the ordinary, mediocre thing, but feeling inadequate, we are thrown back on God, and then we become ordinary people doing extraordinary things. Those who know say that we are using only about one eighth of our physical resources. If we knew how to call on the other seven eighths, think of what that would mean. And further think of what it would mean to be able to call on infinite resources for our daily living.

Why don't we do it? The reason is that we are divided. We want God, and we want ourselves more than we want God. So we are canceling out ourselves by inner division. *We come now to the study of inner division and how to overcome it and be transformed at the place of motive.*

Jesus said, "A house divided against itself cannot stand," and psychology confirms that. It is a universal law. Jesus said: "Any realm divided against itself comes to ruin, house after house falls down; if Satan is indeed divided against himself, how can his realm stand?" (Luke 11:17-18, Moffatt.) Here He applies this law of ruin through division to "realm," "house," "himself" (Satan); so from the nation down through the family to the individual the law holds good—anywhere division means disruption.

In a Middle Western town taxicabs had two signs on them: on some, "Go to Church Sunday"; on the others, "Drink So-an-So Beer," paid for by the same company. Each canceled out the other. The prophet says, "This guilt of yours shall split you" (Isa. 30:13, Moffatt). That is the pay-off—you become two persons at war with each other. "Below the surface I am a veritable battlefield," said Madame Pastorelli. And there is nothing worse than to live with a civil war within. United within, we can stand anything without; but divided within, the smallest circumstance bowls us over. A girl had a nervous breakdown because of a conflict between her Moody Bible Institute training and her job as a dispenser of beer.

O God, give me that unity within which will enable me to stand anything that happens without. Amen.

AFFIRMATION FOR THE DAY: *I am unanimous for God, a Christian with the consent of all my being.*

"NOT WITH AN UNDIVIDED MIND"

We continue to look at inner division as the root of our personality problems. It was said of Jotham, "So Jotham became powerful because he lived steadily before the Eternal God" (II Chr. 27:6, Moffatt). But of Amaziah it was said, "He did what was right in the eyes of the Eternal, but not with an undivided mind" (II Chr. 25:2, Moffatt). This inner division was his undoing, "Amaziah brought the gods of the men of Seir and set them up to be his gods, bowing in homage before them" (II Chr. 25:14, Moffatt). "No sooner did Amaziah cease to follow the Eternal, than a conspiracy was formed against him" (II Chr. 25:27, Moffatt). Here are the steps: (a) Outwardly correct but inwardly divided; (b) the inner division shows itself in outer disloyalty; (c) this leads to his downfall.

Of Mark Twain it was said, "His mind was a workshop in which two creatures were busy—a creature of hope and a creature of despair." He was on outer humorist covering up an inner sadness.

One writer speaks of "half people"—they are "half people" because the good half is canceled out by the other half. Edward Sandford Martin wrote:

> Within my earthly temple there's a crowd.
> There's one of us that's humble; one that's proud.
> There's one that's brokenhearted for his sins,
> And one who, unrepentant, sits and grins.
> There's one who loves his neighbor as himself,
> And one who cares for naught but fame and pelf.
> From much corroding care would I be free,
> If once I could determine which is me.

David Seabury says there are four dynamic wishes in man: (a) The ego-wish, or the urge to be; (b) the sex-wish, or the impulse for love; (c) the herd-wish, or the longing for society; (d) the life-wish, or the lust for experience. Now if these urges can come under a Central Control and become co-ordinated toward one great end, then life is effective, rhythmical, and happy. But if there is no Central Control—then the result is an inner hell.

O gracious Father, Thou hast made me and Thou alone canst remake me. I'm a candidate to be remade from top to bottom. Amen.

AFFIRMATION FOR THE DAY: *I am one man, not two, and that one man, God's man.*

"A LOT OF PIECES OF PEOPLE"

We continue to look at inward division as the cause of outer in-effectiveness. A very thoughtful man, speaking of a prominent minister, said, "He preaches the gospel, but always as a postscript." The first portion was unmitigated pessimism; the very last portion was the gospel dragged in.

A young man admitted not long ago, "I feel like a lot of pieces of people thrown together." His life wasn't under one central purpose. Seabury says: "Personal achievement is impossible save where the motives of the life are working in harmony. . . . Contentment in life is impossible except when the actual desires are determining its activity; disappointment inevitably follows when self-deception as to the ruling will is confusing the effort. . . . It is always true of the individual who 'doesn't know what he wants to do'—'has no idea what kind of person he could love'—'is not sure of his aim in life.' "

It was said of Oscar Wilde that in the intellectual realm he followed a habit formation, moving ever upward to finer degrees of culture. Emotionally his pattern reactions moved continually downward toward barbaric levels of passional experience. The two inclinations remained long in conflict, but in the climax one inevitably gave way, sweeping the whole man for a time in the downward current.

This inner division may result in very serious consequences even in good people. Frank W. Gunsaulus, the famous preacher, became ill and was left a cripple largely because of indecision about accepting a call to the Broadway Tabernacle in New York. Whether the inner division is in the life of a good man or a bad man, the results are much the same. No one can afford to hold within himself any inner conflict. It should be resolved. The attempt to hold both sides of a dilemma for security results in a central insecurity—an insecurity in the person himself. Throw yourself out decisively on the morally better of the two sides.

O Christ, Thou who didst live with a single eye and a single purpose, give me that inner clarity that comes from a life single-eyed. Amen.

AFFIRMATION FOR THE DAY: *No Dr. Jekyll-Mr. Hyde business for me —I'm all out for God with all I have.*

"LIVING IN TWO OR MORE DIRECTIONS"

We are looking at the life that is inwardly at cross-purposes and at the results of this living in two or more directions.

Many times we wonder what kind of person we are. Patience stands in dismay:

> She began to wonder, and she began to cry,
> Land o' mercy on me, this can't be I?
> But if it be I, as I do hope it be,
> I've a little dog at home, and he'll know me.

We are made for inner integrity, and inner division breaks us down and we sink. Here is a letter: "I lived in deceit and sin for seven years, living with a man to whom I was not married. It held together for seven years and now it has broken down. I became so irritable and so did he. I had a nervous breakdown and he left. Now I'm full of guilt. I'm afraid to go out and look for a job—I'm afraid of everything." Now note: "It held together for seven years and now it has broken down." There is no cement in wrong. It will not hold together. It is bound to break down. "I became so irritable and so did he." There is no happiness—real happiness—in wrong. Irritation sets in. For you are soon fighting with yourself. "When an unclean spirit leaves a man, it roams through dry places in search of ease" (Luke 11:24, Moffatt). "In search of ease"—where there is uncleanness there is uneasiness, inevitably. This unclean spirit sought "ease" in "places." But you can't find "ease" in "places"—it must be found in inner conditions or not at all. This woman mentioned above found release in confession, surrender, and faith in the redeeming Christ—the only way out!

A doctor recommended a sea voyage to a woman in conflict. She would have carried her conflict around the world with her. She surrendered it to Christ and is adjusted and happy, and very contagious as Christian.

O Christ, Thou art the Way—the Way out of my conflicts and divisions. Help me this day to bring up all my conflicts and place them before Thy kindly eye. In Thy name. Amen.

AFFIRMATION FOR THE DAY: *No searching for "ease" today through places or positions, but through the inner assurance that comes to the God-centered.*

207

STEPS OUT OF INNER DIVISION

We come now to the steps out of inner division. First, *make up your mind that to live with inner division and inner conflict is no way to live, and that you are going to cease it.* That making up of the mind is important.

A chameleon, if placed on a red cloth, will turn red, on a blue cloth, will turn blue, and it has been said that when one was placed on a piece of Scottish plaid, he came near splitting himself trying to change to all of these colors! If you try to be too many persons, you will not be a person at all—you'll be a problem. Make up your mind that fitting into everything will end in fitting into nothing.

On the top of a mountain in Virginia a magnificent home was built with thirty rooms. But the two people living there, a man and his wife, could not get along with each other, so each had fifteen rooms and they lived entirely apart. When people looked at that stately building, they didn't see a magnificent mansion but a magnificent misery. It was a home divided against itself, and hence it couldn't stand—couldn't stand as a home, but only a monument of unhappiness and loneliness.

Your life will be like that magnificent misery if there is a central conflict and division. Make up your mind it shall end. Of her husband Mrs. Thomas A. Edison could say: "He could work hard and long then lie on his old couch and go immediately to sleep. . . . Never was there any disunity of mind, never obsessions or impeded flow of energy. He was like a child in God's hands; Nature's man. Perhaps this was one reason God could pour all those wonderful ideas through his mind." Note: "Never was there any disunity of mind"—and because of that his mind literally lights up our civilization. As someone put it: "There may be a score of active motives, but one must dominate, the rest must co-operate—not mutiny." We are made for obedience—it is the first law of life. Then choose what shall dominate. "Seek ye first the kingdom." When the Kingdom is first, then everything falls into its place, co-ordinated and happy and free.

O Father, take these conflicting motives and bring them under one control—Thy control. Then shall my mind be clear and burning—burning with Thee. Amen.

AFFIRMATION FOR THE DAY: *My motives today will not be a crowd but a company with a Commander, and all marching in step in one direction.*

THE INNER DIVISION SUPPRESSED

We come to the next step in the meeting of the problem of inner division. Second, *don't push the conflict down and cover it up as if it were not there.*

There is a quaint vision in Zechariah: "'Raise your eyes and look at this barrel which is emerging. . . . This barrel . . . is their iniquity all over the land.' Then a disc of lead was lifted, and there sat a woman inside the barrel! 'This,' he said, 'is Sin'; and he pushed her down inside the barrel and flung the leaden cover over the opening" (Zech. 5:5-8, Moffatt). Often we try to do just that—we push our conflict down into the subconscious, put the lid on it, and there it works as a hidden complex.

Third, *take the inner conflict and bring it up and surrender it into God's hands.* Now the conflict is not central—God is, for you have surrendered it to Him. Your focus of attention is God—not the conflict. Therefore you are no longer fighting the conflict; you are obeying something beyond the conflict—God.

Fourth, *now that you have surrendered it to God, listen to Him for His solution—and obey.* That obedience may seem costly. "If your hand is a hindrance to you, cut it off, better be maimed and get into Life" (Mark 9:43, Moffatt). For now you are literally getting into Life—into Life, from the death of inner conflict.

Many start out to obey and end with a compromise. Someone has said that our democracy could be called "Democracy Limited." In India we were volunteering to do the sweeper's work, a part of which was the cleaning of the latrines. I asked a Brahman convert when he was going to volunteer, and he replied, "Brother Stanley, I'm converted, but I'm not converted that far." Many of our conversions are "Conversions Limited." If we are going to get full release, we must give full obedience—obedience to health-giving directions.

But many cry out like the demoniac to Jesus, "Do not torture me." He begged Jesus not to torture him, and yet he was torturing himself—"cutting himself with stones." Jesus may give a hard command, but that hardness is a surgeon's knife—to make you well!

My God, all Thy touches loose my chains, all Thy restraints are releases. I am ready to obey, for Thy commands are Life. Amen.

AFFIRMATION FOR THE DAY: *All my discords become concords when they learn to obey Thee, the divine Conductor.*

"THINGS I CAN DO WITHOUT"

We continue our steps out of inner conflict and division. Fifth, *fix in your mind the fact that if you seek first the Kingdom of God, then all these things will be added to you.* If you love God and seek His Kingdom first, then everything you need for living will be added to you. You needn't try to hold mutually incompatible things in order to gain security. That is a losing game. For in the end you get neither of them—they cancel each other out and leave you zero. When you find your good things *in God*, then they are really good things—and good for you. Anything you cannot find in God you can do without—and do without it joyously.

A Texas cowboy went into a department store in New York and a sales girl asked: "Can I do anything for you?" And the Texan slowly replied, "No, I just came in to see how many things I can do without."

There are two ways to be rich—one is in the abundance of your possessions, the other is in the fewness of your wants. When your central "want" is God, then everything you need for abundant living is guaranteed to you. Jesus said two apparently contradictory things: "Yes, I tell you, fear Him" . . . "fear not" (Luke 12:5, 7, Moffatt). But the meaning is this: If you fear God, reverence Him supremely, then you need fear nothing else. Low at His feet, you stand straight before everything else. Loving God supremely, you can love many things marginally. The mixed loyalties have given way to a master loyalty, then all the other loyalties are safe and beautiful. When your eye is single, then your whole body is full of light—when your "eye" —your outlook—is single, then your whole personality is flooded with light. Life is all of a piece; you are not trying to live in all directions at once.

A girl wanted to be a Christian, and yet wanted to run with "the gang." She told a smutty story to a Christian nurse, and the nurse replied, "Why, you're just as bad as the rest of them." This hurt her, for she wanted to be looked on as a Christian. She developed a neurosis as a result of this conflict. Nothing but a real conversion would cure that neurosis—so it's new birth or neurosis.

Gracious Father, I see that when Thou hast me, I have myself. I find myself and everything else in Thee. Thou art my Treasure from which I draw my all. Amen.

AFFIRMATION FOR THE DAY: *I'm on the Way with all I have and all I am, and all I expect to have and be.*

EROS AND AGAPE

We now turn to a side of our nature that produces more heaven and more hell than any one thing—the sex side. Can that be transformed from hell into heaven?

The sex side of us is as natural a part of us as any other function. And used rightly, it can be creative and contributive. Used wrongly, it can play havoc with the personality.

Love manifests itself either as eros or agape. Eros is wanting the other person for one's own purposes. Agape is wanting the other person for the other person's good. Eros thinks of nothing but self. Agape thinks of nothing but the good of the person beloved. Eros would devour, agape would develop the object of the love. Eros blights all it touches, agape makes everything it touches blossom. One is the touch of death, the other is the touch of life.

The Christians of early days had to bring in the word agape to express something absent from that ancient world. Agape was a divine love which sanctified all it touched, including human love, and human love especially. Before divine love or agape came in, there were only two alternatives: unbridled expression or complete suppression. Agape did away with both by making the sex urge the instrument of divine purpose and therefore of human satisfaction.

We as a civilization are now in desperate need of the Christian conception of agape, for eros has taken over the sex situation in large measure. And a vast sexual unhappiness has resulted. A domestic relations court judge says that nine out of ten divorces are caused by sexual troubles. And a large majority of personality troubles come from wrong sex adjustments or lack of them. Eros is working out badly in modern civilization. We are a frustrated generation.

We thought frankness about sex would be the cure-all—it would get rid of repressions. But frankness hasn't dealt with the central difficulty, namely, our relationship to a moral universe. Frankness or no frankness, we are up against it there if sex is merely eros.

Father, I thank Thee that while our answers turn out badly, Thy answers turn out blessedly. They work. And they work our good. Amen.

AFFIRMATION FOR THE DAY: *As a Christian I must be a man of agape instead of a man of eros—I commit myself to agape.*

DOES EROS BRING SELF-EXPRESSION?

We continue to look at the difference between eros and agape. In our civilization we are taking eros and it is turning out badly.

We call eros "self-expression." A worse misnomer could not be chosen. Self-expression is turning out to be self-mutilation. For the most frustrated people are the people who thought they were free in regard to sex. They find they are free, but free to get into trouble with themselves and others and with life itself. It just isn't working—except to work ruin.

"If you repress these libidinous drives, you get into trouble, and if you let them work their will, you are in trouble also. No wonder out of this unhappy condition many a man has said, 'O wretched man, that I am.'"

But psychology, in many cases seeing this dilemma, has attempted to get rid of it by a suppression of consciences. It has substituted repression of impulse with an attempted suppression of conscience. It says that "guilt feeling" is at the basis of many neuroses, and therefore get rid of the sense of guilt by getting rid of conscience. But you cannot get rid of conscience in sex without getting rid of conscience everywhere. If anything is right in sex, then anything is right everywhere, and the whole moral basis of society collapses—and with it society. For Freud says, "Civilization is forged at the cost of instinct satisfactions." I question that statement. It is forged at the cost of instinct satisfaction as eros. But the instincts are not satisfied as eros. They get tangled up and frustrated. But the instincts are satisfied as agape. The whole person is satisfied as agape. I know of a family that dedicated their love as agape, mostly in missionary work. A happier, more adjusted, and useful family could not be found. But one member of the family expressed her love as eros. A more frustrated, unhappy person can scarcely be found. Life has a say and it says, "frustration," or "fruitfulness." We are free to choose, but we are not free to choose the consequences of our choices. They are in hands not our own. The moral universe has the last word, no matter who has the first or the intermediate word.

Father, I know Thou art pushing us by Thy judgments into Life. Help us to obey gladly, lest we disobey sadly. In Jesus' name. Amen.

AFFIRMATION FOR THE DAY: I see the alternatives: life lived as eros= frustration; life lived as agape=fruitfulness. I choose life as agape

CAUSE PERSONALITY PROBLEMS

We said yesterday that we do satisfy our instincts if we work them in God's way. Gerhard Hoffmann, psychiatrist of Western Reserve University, says: "The belief that there are inherent conflicts between man's instinctual needs for pleasure gratification and his moral obligations toward mankind is a myth. Man is essentially a social being and his well-being and happiness as an individual are therefore basically identical with humanity as a whole. Therefore we cannot find true pleasure through any action that disregards the vital interest of his fellow man. Although a certain relative pleasure may be had by many individuals in lust to destroy human values or in taking advantage of other people by deceit or exploitation, a heavy price must unavoidably be paid for such pleasure in terms of loss of inner security."

Not one single sex complex has ever been resolved by sex license. And the psychiatrist who gives the advice of sex license to sex harassed people is bankrupt. And he is passing on his bankruptcy to his patients.

The Soviets have found out that a moral universe exists. They did away with all the restrictions on divorce—one got it for the asking, with or without the consent of the partner, by paying five rubles and signing a paper. It was reduced to its lowest biological level—they thought. Now note: "The October (1917) Socialist revolution wiped out the political, legal, and economic inequality of women, but some people have misunderstood this freedom and have decided that the sex life can be carried on with a disorderly succession of husbands and wives. In a tightly organized socialist society such practices lead to laxity and vulgarization of relationship, unworthy of man, cause personality problems, unhappiness and disruption of the family, making orphans of children." Note: "cause personality problems"—sex laxity caused personality problems. It does inevitably. The moral universe kicks back in frustration. The Communists, who do not believe in any objective moral universe, find themselves up against a Strange Imponderable—the moral universe is the Court of Final Appeal. It has the last word.

O God, I see that I cannot break Thy laws without forfeiting my liberty. I find my way in Thy way, and only in Thy way. Amen.

AFFIRMATION FOR THE DAY: *God's laws are my liberties; my impulses are my impediments.*

ATTEMPTED MORAL JUSTIFICATION FOR THE IMMORAL

We saw yesterday that throwing the reins over the neck of sex results in disaster. Bacchus, the god of wine and revelry, is depicted riding a panther plunging wildly—to inevitable ruin.

But if you can't repress sex, nor express it without moral direction, it is also impossible to try to mingle the loose expression with moral justification. Some try. They try to sin in a moral way. "I committed adultery with this girl only once and then it was on a high and lofty plane," said a man who obviously was suffering from consequences that were anything but high and lofty. He was disrupted. Another man said, "I didn't commit adultery with her until after we had both promised to marry." But both were married to other partners, and the promise of marriage could not justify the unjustifiable. They were both terribly unhappy and frustrated. No, none of these ways will run into anything except a dead end. "It is only when our affection for one another is rooted and grounded in an immortal order that love becomes finally sacred, and life itself sacramental," says W. Fearon Halliday. A man was in Christian service and yet kept up a triangle situation which only hovered around the edge of sex license. He kept away from that, but was ill and sleepless. He confessed it and was released and well again.

Then what is the way out for sex? The way out is agape. And agape means a divine love that sanctifies all lesser loves. You surrender yourself and your sex life to God, begin to love Him centrally, and then that central love makes beautiful and sacred all the lesser loves including sex love. But that central love is in control. The agape controls the eros. This goes beyond sublimation. It is "Christian dedication." All the powers of the eros are at the service of the agape, and then they are no longer eros, but themselves agape. You become creative by turning the creative sex urge into higher channels. This opens the door of hope to those who, having tried sublimation, find it doesn't work. It doesn't work because it doesn't get you beyond yourself—you are trying desperately to sublimate. Agape does get you beyond yourself, therefore is a workable way to live.

My Father, make me pure agape, and then all things will be pure to me. I shall purify all I touch, for Thy agape is divine creation. Amen.

AFFIRMATION FOR THE DAY: *When my urges are dedicated to God, they are dedicated to freedom.*

AGAPE FULFILLS, EROS FRUSTRATES

We come now to the answer of psychology and Christianity in regard to sex-frustration. Psychology, for the most part, teaches sublimation as the way out. "Sublimation," says James Hadfield, "is the process by which instinctive emotions are diverted from their original ends, and redirected to purposes satisfying to the individual and of value to the community." This definition is satisfying except at one place: "the process by which instinctive emotions are diverted from their original ends." I am convinced that the original ends of sex are not merely physical procreation or pleasure, but they include the whole creative side of life. It isn't unnatural to express sex as the creative side of life creating newborn souls, new movements, new hopes, being spiritual parents to groups and individuals. That is just as much a side of sex as the physical is. Therefore it is not an attempt to bend nature to unnatural ends. It fulfills our nature to express love as agape. We are more natural in expressing love as agape than we are expressing love as eros. For to express love as agape would include right physical manifestation of sex within the marriage relationship, but it wouldn't stop there. Therefore agape fulfills, eros frustrates. Sex as an end in itself ends itself. Sex as a means to God's ends becomes a means to man's fulfillment.

When life is controlled by agape, then these words are true:

> Let us not always say,
> "Spite of this flesh to-day
> I strove, made head, gained ground upon the whole!"
> As the bird wing and sings,
> Let us cry, "All good things
> Are ours, nor soul helps flesh more, now, than flesh helps soul!"

This goes beyond sublimation. It is allowing God to use the powers of sex for original purposes—the enrichment of the total person.

Father, I thank Thee that I do not have to struggle to sublimate, but have to surrender to express. In Thy will I am alive in my total being. Amen.

AFFIRMATION FOR THE DAY: *Flesh and soul according well shall beat out vaster music than before.*

STEPS TOWARD TRANSFORMATION OF SEX

We come now to the steps for the transformation of our sex impulses. First, *fix it in your mind as an axiom that sex will work in no way except God's way.* If you try to work it in some other way, it works disillusionment and unhappiness. David schemed to get the wife of Uriah— and succeeded: "She became his wife and bore him a son. Now what David had done displeased the Eternal, and the Eternal sent Nathan to David" (II Sam. 11:27–12:1 Moffatt). He got his private pleasure, plus a displeased God and the prophet's finger, "Thou art the man." Too big a price! There are no exceptions to this, and you will not be the exception.

Second, *surrender your sex life to God to be worked out in His way.* His way is to use sex within the marriage relationship as procreation and as an aid to deeper fellowship. And then both within the marriage relationship and outside, to use the powers of sex as creative activity in creating newborn souls, movements, music, art, poetry, constructive achievement.

Third, *now that you have literally surrendered them to God, do not try to sublimate your sex life, but allow God to use your sex life.* When you try to sublimate your sex life, then you put your attention on it and try hard to sublimate it. But this concentrates the attention on sex, and "whatever gets your attention gets you." It fails. But surrender of sex to God concentrates the attention on God, and then your attention is on the right place.

Sublimation is a striving upward; dedication is a working downward from God. One results in strained activity, the other results in relaxed activity. One tries, the other trusts. One ties you up, the other frees you.

Fourth, *this now takes the fear and strain out of sex, and you look on sex as your ally instead of as your enemy.* Sex is no longer the Trojan horse within, ready to betray you to the enemy. This "horse" has been harnessed to God's purposes and is fulfilling God's will. The whole conception of sex has been transformed from shame and fear to acceptance and appreciation.

O Father, I thank Thee that all that Thou hast created can become re-creative. I thank Thee that I hold within me a friend and a helper to my life purposes. Amen.

AFFIRMATION FOR THE DAY: *I accept all my natural urges frankly and gratefully, and dedicate them all to God's purposes.*

"I WOULD NEVER GET INTO IT"

While we must accept sex as the gift of God and no longer fear it, nevertheless we must not be presumptuous about it. Fifth, *don't allow yourself to get into situations where too great a strain is placed on sex impulses.* Anatole France has a story in which God and the devil are talking of a beautiful young girl. God asks, "How did you dare to tempt so lovely a creature as that?" The devil answers, "She came onto my ground." A man once went to Dwight L. Moody with a tale of moral disaster, and after having narrated the harrowing facts, said, "Now, Mr. Moody, what would you do if you got into such a situation?" Moody replied, "Man, I would never get into it."

R. W. Everrood tells this story: A young man, seeking his fortune, traveled across a desert land and was tired and dusty when he saw a ledge and at its base a cool, shadowy cavern, and within it a beautiful girl spinning at her loom. He asked her if he might have a drink of water and rest on the floor until he was refreshed and could resume his journey. She was willing provided he would permit her to wind around him the gossamer threads she was spinning. He agreed, sure that he could easily brush these threads away as one would do a spider's web. The spinner wound one strand after another around him, and as she wound she sang, and he was soon lulled to slumber. He awoke to find himself in the grip of heavy cords that could not be broken, and he was helpless in the power of one who was no longer a beautiful spinner but had changed to a disgusting and ugly hag.

The best way to get away from some temptations is to run away. John Ruskin says, "No one can ask honestly or happily to be delivered from temptation unless he has honestly and firmly determined to do the best he can to keep out of it." So keep out of the devil's territory.

A speaker propounded the moral dilemma of a surgeon, a married man with a family, an expert in cancer, who was on a mountain-climbing expedition and tied to a worthless character who slipped and fell over the ledge. Would the surgeon cut the rope, or go down with him as mountain climbing codes say he must? The answer was simple— the surgeon should never have let himself get into that moral dilemma.

O God, help me to help myself. Help me not to subject myself to conditions that make a fall almost inevitable. Give me sense. Amen.

AFFIRMATION FOR THE DAY: *I cannot ask God to help me out of situations unless I help myself not to get into them.*

NOT BUILT UP, BUT BUILT INTO

We come now to consider the question of guilt in general. There are some pagan psychiatrists who take the attitude that guilt being dangerous to the personality, undertake to get rid of the guilt by saying that there is no basis for this guilt feeling, that conscience and the moral universe are built-up concepts, must be wiped out, and the person thereby freed from guilt feelings, for there is nothing of which to be guilty.

This is false and creates an illusion of freedom which sooner or later lets one down. For morality is not built up by custom, it is built into the structure of the universe. It is *there*—before and after your action. You do not break those laws; you break yourself on them. Anybody who thinks he can cheat a moral God in a moral universe is a moral imbecile.

You cannot dismiss your actions by waving your hand and saying, "Let bygones be bygones." Both the moral universe and the moral action are there. George Buttrick, commenting on this attempt at dismissal, says: "The memory *cannot* be ignored or repressed. That attempt is like plastering a boil; the poison spreads unseen, to emerge as anxiety neurosis, failure to concentrate, or the 'transfer' in which we try to evade responsibility by criticizing our neighbors. The reader will understand if he asks himself, 'Any names and places from which I shy away in memory?'"

Nor can you get away from sin by joking about it. Oscar Wilde said, "The only way to get rid of a temptation is to yield to it." But you do not get rid of a temptation by yielding to it. It becomes act, and then habit, and then you.

No, we are hedged in—thorn hedges on either side. The only open door is the mercy of God. And these thorn hedges are the creation of God's mercy too. They are God's provision that we should not be comfortable in evil, for the bad is bad for us. He has so arranged the universe that we can be comfortable only in that which is good for us —in His will.

Guilt cannot be banished by subterfuge. "Only God can redeem our wickedness."

O God, I know that I cannot get rid of my sin. Only Thou canst take it away through forgiveness. I bring my guilty heart to Thee. Amen.

AFFIRMATION FOR THE DAY: *I shall not compound, and thus add to my guilt, by saying there is no guilt.*

NOTHING HIDDEN

No one gets away with anything in this universe. "Nothing is hidden that shall not be revealed, or concealed that shall not be made known" (Luke 12:2, Moffatt). It will have to be "revealed" voluntarily and forgiveness sought, or it will be revealed as inner complex, conflict, functional disease, personality disorder. In any case, it is "revealed."

The young doctor in A. J. Cronin's *The Citadel* found it was "revealed." When politics defeated his health measures in a Welsh mining town, he sold his standards for money. So after his wife's tragic death, he found in her handbag snapshots of himself in those crusading days, and letters of gratitude from improverished miners, and other mementoes that she had kept to remind herself of the man he might have been. He knew that his pain was deserved. He shouted at himself in a drunken stupor that could not drug his conscience: "You thought you could get away with it. You thought you were getting away with it. But by God! You weren't."

You do not get away with it, nor can you get away with it by bottling it up within and keeping it to yourself. You cannot keep it to yourself. It "reveals" itself in anxiety in face and manner. Shakespeare puts it thus in *Macbeth*: "Canst thou not minister to a mind diseas'd, pluck from the memory a rooted sorrow, raze out the written troubles of the brain, and with some sweet oblivious antidote cleanse the stuff'd bosom of the perilous stuff which weighs upon the heart?" Again he says: "Out, damned spot! out, I say! . . . Hell is murky. . . . What need we fear who know it, when none can call our power to account? Yet who would have thought the old man to have had so much blood in him? . . . What, will these hands ne'er be clean? . . . Here's the smell of the blood still; all the perfumes of Arabia will not sweeten this little hand." Only Blood can wipe out blood; only Grace can erase guilt. There is no other way.

O God, our Father, we, harassed by sin and its consequences, run into roads with dead ends. Help us to take Thy way. For Thy way is our only open Way. Amen.

AFFIRMATION FOR THE DAY: *Since my suppressed evils will be "revealed" as neurosis and conflict, I decide that my expressed evils shall be "revealed" by confession as newness and concord.*

"NOTHING IS TRUE, EVERYTHING IS ALLOWED"

We continue to look at the ways men take to get out of evil and its consequences. Here is a man who covered his sins by years, hoping they would bury them. He killed a man twenty years before and hid his body in a well. But he came to the police and confessed. "I have only a little left of life. I would like to get this off my chest." The years hadn't covered it—it was on his chest still. Interesting that we react to our sins exactly as Adam and Eve did. The moment they sinned they hid themselves—they wanted to suppress the fact by hiding themselves. We do the same now. We do not hide behind shrubbery, but we do hide behind the shrubbery of various blinds—we put on blasé airs that scarcely hide the unhappiness within; we drink to dull our consciousness of the fact that we are guilty; we use psychological and philosophical terms to cover up plain guilt. But nothing works. Our evils are beyond our power to cure. Nietzsche said blandly: "Nothing is true, everything is allowed." But Nietzsche died mentally deranged. The human brain is not made for that kind of universe and it retreated into insanity.

The Old Testament prophet saw the connection between the fact of guilt and physical illnesses: "Why will you earn fresh strokes, for holding on in your revolt? Your whole head is sick, your whole heart is diseased; from the sole of the foot to the head, no part is sound" (Isa. 1:5-6, Moffatt). The "fresh strokes" were not punishment afflicted directly by God. The revolt itself produced the physical upset. I repeat, "You are not punished *for* your sins; you are punished *by* your sins." You cannot revolt against God without revolting against yourself. If you won't live with God, you cannot live with yourself. That is the pay-off. So the revolt is "revealed"—not always, but often—as disease. Not all diseases are the result of sin, but many are. And as we are becoming more conversant with cause and effect, we are finding that more and more disease is rooted in sin.

O Christ, I know that Thou art a Savior—a Savior from my self-inflicted pain and disease. Help me no longer to keep suppressed within me that which can be only a pain to me. Amen.

AFFIRMATION FOR THE DAY: *There is only one open door in the universe out of evil—the open arms of God. I take that Door.*

"IT HARDENS ALL WITHIN"

We look one more day at the consequences of sin and guilt. The pay-off is in the person. Burns discovered sadly from his own experience what sin does: "It hardens all within, and petrifies the feelings."

I once told the story of a woman who made restitution concerning ducks, and a woman came up and said: "It is easy to make restitution about ducks, but how can I make restitution? I stole another woman's husband. Now we have four children. For a while I was happy, but I've lived with a troubled conscience these years. How can I make restitution to this woman whom I have wronged?" I will not answer that question now, but the point to be noted is that it will not do to tell that woman that no wrong has been done and that her conscience need not be troubled. A wrong was done and her conscience was rightly troubled. And there is a way out. But it is beyond our power to cure.

But the way out is not to deny that anything has happend. Tennyson wrote:

> O purblind race of miserable men,
> How many among us at this very hour
> Do forge a lifelong trouble for ourselves
> By taking true for false, or false for true!

There are many of us who are forging lifelong troubles for ourselves. Arthur John Gossip put it: "Like a creature caught in a trap that struggles and shows its teeth and gnaws at its own limb—anything, everything to get away—he also writhes and twists and tears; but always the trap holds."

Many caught by their past simply give up and accept the bondage. Again Gossip: "I am too old for anything to happen now. The branches are too gnarled to bend. Tug at them, and they do give a little, but they spring back again. My ways are fixed; my character is formed; the channels are long cut in which my life must run on to the end." Is that true? Can a man be born again when he is old? And can we get out of implacable traps? The answer is a resounding "Yes!" There are no insoluble problems with God, no hopeless cases except one—the man who doesn't want to be different.

O God, if Thou art not, then I'm done for. And if Thou art not what Jesus said Thou art, then again I'm done for. But He says Thou art love. It gives me hope. Amen.

AFFIRMATION FOR THE DAY: *My ways snare me; God's ways save me.*

STEPS OUT OF GUILT

We turn now with relief to the answer for the sense of guilt within. First, *remember that a sense of guilt is redemptive*. It is to the soul what pain is to the body. If there were no pain connected with malfunctioning and disease in the body, we would let them work on and in the end they would destroy us. Pain is God's flag of warning that something is wrong and attention must be paid to it. A sense of guilt is God's flag of warning that something is morally wrong and attention must be paid to it, or it will cause moral death. So a sense of guilt is what Matthew Arnold describes:

> He took the suffering human race
> He read each wound, each weakness clear—
> And struck his finger on the place
> And said—Thou ailest here, and here.

So God strikes only to heal. Guilt is God's love at work in us—redemptively at work in us. It pushes you to God for release and freedom. So a sense of guilt is not an enemy; it is a friend. True, if you take it in the wrong way, it can push you into complexes and conflicts. But if it does, it is not the fault of guilt—it is our wrong reaction to guilt.

Second, *don't try to heal yourself*. That can't be done. Seneca in one of his letters says, "I am still toiling with all my might at my old task of seeking to eradicate my faults." But we cannot cure ourselves, for the sense of guilt points us to the One sinned against.

Third, *then we must get forgiveness from God—or we are not healed*. And we can get forgiveness there. "Dear me, Dr. Duncan," people said, as the old Hebrew professor walked along the streets of Edinburgh, his face aglow, cracking his fingers as he walked, "you surely have great news today." "News!" he made answer. "News! Wonderful news—the best of news! The blood of Jesus still cleanses from all sin." That is good news!

Some Hindus asked me to give a contribution to build an idol temple. How could I? They would offer offerings to propitiate their god, and I had looked into the face of the God who offered Himself for us!

O God, I thank Thee that Thy wounds answer my wounds. Thy suffering lifts my suffering. I see the way out—Thy forgiveness. Amen.

AFFIRMATION FOR THE DAY: *Guilt takes me to God for forgiveness; Grace sends me from God with forgiveness.*

"IT IS FOR SINNERS"

We continue to look at the way out of guilt. God forgives you freely and fully and finally. I spoke of Dr. Duncan and the "good news." Arthur John Gossip tells of how the old man would not venture to the table of his Lord, felt he was too unworthy, and was sitting miserably under his pulpit when he saw a girl break down, and pass the cup untasted. Whereat his fears all gone, the old saint cried to her in a loud whisper, "Take it, lassie, take it; it is for sinners," and himself stretched out eager hands to take it for himself. That's it: "Christ Jesus came into the world to save sinners." Anyone can get in under that category!

We are told that in Paris they still show the old state books in which under every town and village there were entered the taxes due from each; and that on the page headed Domrémy, where Joan of Arc lived, there were the usual official figures, but written across them in red ink, "Free for the Maid's sake." So now you can believe that across the pages filled with the debts you owe to God is written, "Free for My Son's sake." God forgives you. Rejoice in it.

A young man in Japan leaned over the back of the bench on which I was seated and whispered, "Are you sure I am forgiven?" I assured him on the authority of the character of God in Christ that he was forgiven. A few minutes later he asked again, "Are you sure I am forgiven?" I assured him that he was. A third time he asked the same question, "Are you sure I am forgiven?" The last time he really accepted my assurance. There is nothing, absolutely nothing that man wants to know as much as to know whether his sins are forgiven. And there is nothing, absolutely nothing that we can say with greater assurance than that God does forgive, and that He forgives graciously and fully and finally. "Scarlet your sins may be, but they can become white as snow" (Isa. 1:18, Moffatt). Your very sins become white, for when you look at them, you no longer see sins, you see grace—the whiteness of grace. That indeed is deliverance.

O God, my Father, is there anything more beautiful in heaven or on earth than Thy forgiving grace? I know of nothing. And I can do no other than gratefully accept. I do. And am I grateful? Amen.

AFFIRMATION FOR THE DAY: *The most absolutely releasing thing in the universe is divine forgiveness—it aligns me with the universe, not against it.*

YOU MUST FORGIVE YOURSELF

We take the next step in accepting forgiveness. Fourth, *now that God forgives you, you must forgive yourself.* A great many get forgiveness from God and then they fail to give it to themselves. They keep lashing themselves for what they have done. They hope to pay God back by their own suffering. This is a false atonement. Don't try to substitute it in place of Christ's atonement. God is paid when we forsake our sins.

Charles T. Holman tells of a church deacon, respected in church and community, who fell ill with high blood pressure, colon infection, and kidney disorders. There had been some wild episodes in the deacon's young manhood, before his conversion, and now, one of the women with whom he had gone astray had returned to town and was trying to see him. He felt threatened with the loss of respect and affection of his friends, and what was worse, shut out from the presence of God.

There was only one way out for him: acknowledge the whole thing, say that it belonged to a past that was forgiven, and then forgive himself. No friends would have looked down on him. They would have honored him for what he *was.* What he had been, had been buried under the love of God.

A woman, now a prominent Christian worker, said to me: "The old drinking days seem to belong to another person. I can look on that person as an entirely different being. I am free." She was. Someone speaks of "the guilt-ridden piety of our day." It is guilt-ridden because people do not boldly accept pardon and do not give it to themselves. We must do both.

I close this week with the statement which has been called the core of the Evangelical Revival: "O let me commend my Savior to you." He saves you from the guilt of sin and from the stinging memory of the guilt. It is buried in the sea of His forgetfulness. And if He forgets it, then we too must forget it. It is a sin against the forgiveness of God to keep bringing up in our memory what God has blotted out of His. It says that God doesn't mean it when He says He blots it out of the book of His remembrance.

O Father, how can I thank Thee enough for this transformation? It is beyond words. I kneel in humble adoration and gratitude. Amen.

AFFIRMATION FOR THE DAY: *As God forgives me, so I forgive myself—in both cases graciously and gladly.*

RESULTS OF WRONG ACTS AND ATTITUDES

These last weeks we have been looking at some of the things that upset the personality, disrupt it, and cause it to deteriorate: fears, resentments, egocentricity, inner divisions, inferiority feelings, wrong sex life, guilts. It is now an axiom that you cannot live with these things—not live, for they cancel out everything called life and substitute mere existence.

Here was a man so full of fears from childhood that he was a wreck. He was afraid of everything. Lost his jobs, and yet he was able. Couldn't live with himself. We prayed together and he surrendered his fears to God. "Now don't talk about your fears any more. They're gone." "Well," he replied, "I don't know what I talked about before I had these fears." He went away released.

I saw a nawab, a petty ruler in India, get in a train and order everyone around with outbursts of temper toward his servants. But I noticed that the last thing he did before going to bed was to order the servant to get his soda-mint tablets. He could order his circumstances—he had money and authority for that—but he couldn't order the processes of digestion. They had the last word, regardless.

George Buttrick tells of a man who, guilty of a secret unworthiness, boarded a train to his country house. His family, eager to meet him, drove two or three stations down the line. They sent the trainman through the coaches calling his name, "Is Mr. So-and-So on this train?" Instantly he feared the police were after him. His sin had so clouded his judgment that he mistook his family for the police.

Here was a man of sixty, married, going with a woman of thirty-five for several years. He was home in the evenings as a faithful husband. But he spent a good deal of the day with the woman. The woman got most of his money. The man threw himself into the river. He could arrange his circumstances, but he couldn't arrange his inner-stances.

The revolt against God on the part of man is turning out badly—badly for man. God is shutting doors one by one until we are shut up to the one alternative that will work—the Way!

O Father, give me an inner life I can live with and live with joyfully. Only Thou canst cleanse my depths of the things I loathe. I give them to Thee. Amen.

AFFIRMATION FOR THE DAY: *The temple of my inner life, cleansed of unclean intruders, is now a sanctuary of tranquillity.*

"LIKE THE RESTLESS SEA"

We continue to gather up the results of wrongs hidden within. Roger Hornsby, manager of the Cardinals, said: "Many a game has been lost by a player holding resentments against a player on the other team, or on his own. You can't play baseball and have resentments." The prophet asks: "Why break the commands of the Eternal? Why defeat yourselves?" (II Chr. 24:20, Moffatt.) Those two things are one and the same thing.

It may not be in deep disruption that the results show themselves, but in just inner dullness and paralysis. A minister said: "You gave me back my sky. I had a resentment against a minister—I left it in the prayer room." Power came back into his life.

In the end "there is nothing covered that shall not be revealed." And that end is often here. A man forged his brother's college degree, put oceans between him and that fact. But while studying to get a post-graduate degree, he confessed to his professors that he had all the conflicts they were talking about in the psychology class. At last the conflict became so intense that he stood up in a student meeting and confessed. He had to, for he was living with something that he couldn't live with.

Here is a vivid picture of the inner life of those in revolt against God and therefore in revolt against themselves, "'Ungodly men are like the restless sea that never can be still, whose waters throw up dirt and mire: no prosperous peace for the ungodly,' says my God" (Isa. 57: 20-21, Moffatt). The disturbed subconscious keeps on throwing up dirt and mire into the conscious, hence there is no prosperous peace.

The figure is changed in this passage, "That no root of bitterness grows up to be a trouble" (Heb. 12:15, Moffatt). Any root of bitterness is bound to be nothing but a trouble. In the beginning it may seem to be a triumph, but it always ends in a trouble. Root it out!

Jesus, the very thought of Thee
With sweetness fills the breast,

and "Resentments, the very thought of thee with bitterness fills my breast." I choose a sweetened breast rather than an embittered one.

Gracious God, I open up the roots of bitterness within me. I consent for Thee to pluck them up root and branch. Make me free. Amen.

AFFIRMATION FOR THE DAY: *My heart cleansed from impossible ways is now living the only possible life—the Christian life.*

"HUMAN NATURE IS INFINITELY PLASTIC"

We have been looking at the things that upset the harmony of the personality. Here is a girl who would not speak to her father for two years. She lost seventeen jobs. The resentments made her inefficient and incapable.

But having no central purpose will make one inefficient and incapable. Gibbon describes the Emperor Gallienus: "He was a master of several curious but useless sciences, a ready orator, an elegant poet, a skillful gardener, an excellent cook, and a most contemptible prince." He was everything, and nothing.

Anything that is against God is against us. Goodness is not only abstractly good—goodness is good for us. Badness is bad for us. Said William James, "Goodness tastes better."

Now what does all this point to? We have been weeks on the disruptions caused by wrong attitudes and actions. Just what does this add up to? To one thing and one thing alone: transformation through conversion. If the need of conversion weren't written in the Bible, it could be read in the needs of our personality. Wipe it out of the Bible, and it is still not written on human nature, but plowed into the necessities of our inner make-up. If we hold our peace, then the stones—the hard, bare facts of life—will cry out, "Ye must be born again."

Fortunately, as David Seabury says, "Human nature is infinitely plastic and potent; capable of correcting itself and rebuilding early devastations." Yes, it can correct itself here and there, but it cannot convert itself, give itself a new birth. Only the God who created us can re-create us. And He can and does wherever the human will consents and co-operates. God is so anxious that, as in the case of St. Simon, it seems like an invasion. "Suddenly," he says, "God came and united Himself to me in a manner quite ineffable; He entered into every part of my being, as fire penetrates iron. I am filled with light and glory. . . . All my members glow with a heavenly light." That is the answer: Transformation through the divine invasion. "God came and united Himself to me." It's incredibly simple.

O Father-God, I thank Thee for this redemptive invasion. I consent to it from the depths. This is the answer. I know it. I accept it. Amen.

AFFIRMATION FOR THE DAY: *"All my members glow with a heavenly light"*—that will be my experience today through receptivity.

POSSESSING YOUR POSSESSIONS

We are now looking at the possibility of being a new man. Here was Gerard Grooterich, a scholar, successful, everything going his way. Watching a game one day, comfortable and at his ease, an old friend of God touched him on the shoulder and said, "Thou shouldst become another man." It was like a bolt from the blue. The summons awoke him and in very truth he became another man.

Perhaps in reading this book the divine Hand touches your shoulder and says, "Thou shouldst become another man." The divine Summons is the divine Offer. He provides everything to become that other man. All you provide is consent and co-operation.

As Robert Frost puts it:

> I bid you to a one-man revolution—
> The only revolution that is coming.

This one-man revolution has the seeds of all the beneficent revolutions that will change the world. Lewis Mumford puts it: "Only in one place can an immediate renewal begin: that is, within the person. . . Today our best plans miscarry because they are in the hands of people who have undergone no inner growth. . . . God must work within us . . . The first step is a personal one: a change in direction of interest within the person. Without that change, no great betterment will take place in the social order. Once that change begins, everything is possible."

That change can begin now. It is yours for the asking—and for the taking. Obadiah says, "The house of Jacob shall possess their possessions." This "possession"—the new birth—is your "possession." It is yours by right of the first birth—your birthright. God created you to re-create you. Walk boldly in and possess your possession. He has said "Yes," now you say, "Yes," and the matter is done—the pact sealed. You are not you—you are another and different you. Can the butterfly believe that he ever came from that worm? No more can you believe that you ever came from that you. You didn't—God has created a new you!

O God, I thank Thee that I can come and possess my possession. I rejoice that I've come to this hour—the hour of the birthday of my soul—my real birthday. Amen.

AFFIRMATION FOR THE DAY: *My earthly birthday and deathday will be forgotten in eternity; my heavenly birthday—never!*

228

THE CONVERSION OF LINCOLN

Many who have loved and admired Lincoln have wondered how he could have the fruits of the Christian life without its roots. He seemed so Christian in his actions and reactions, and yet with no Christian conversion.

But this account of Lincoln's conversion fills the gap. It is taken from the official records at Springfield, Illinois, a part of an address given on September 29, 1897, by the Rev. James F. Jacques, also known as "Colonel Jacques," at the annual reunion of the Seventy-third Regiment of the Illinois Volunteers of which he was a colonel, and transcribed by the Rev. John D. Kruwel, pastor of Kumler Methodist Church, Springfield, Illinois, a personal friend of Colonel Jacques: "I was standing at the Methodist parsonage on Sunday morning when a little boy came up to me and said, 'Mr. Lincoln sent me around to see if you were going to preach today.' I had met Mr. Lincoln but at that time did not think much about him, so I said, 'You go back and tell Mr. Lincoln that if he will come to church, he will see if I am going to preach.' The little fellow stood working his fingers and finally said, 'Mr. Lincoln told me he would give me a quarter if I could find out if you were going to preach.' Then I told him I was. Mr. Lincoln came in after the service had begun and he and Governor French and his wife were given seats inside the altar, for the church was full. I had chosen for my text, 'Ye must be born again,' and I noticed that Mr. Lincoln appeared interested in the sermon. A few days after that Sunday Mr. Lincoln called on me and informed me that he was deeply impressed by my remarks on Sunday, and that he had come to talk with me about the matter. My wife and I talked and prayed with him for hours. Now I have seen many people converted; I have seen hundreds brought to Christ, and if ever a person was converted, Abraham Lincoln was converted that night in my house. . . . He never joined my church, as his wife was a Presbyterian, but I will always believe that since that night Abraham Lincoln lived and died a Christian gentleman." That gives the root from which so much Christian fruit grew in a noble life.

O God, I thank Thee that every hunger of my heart is answered by a deeper hunger of Thy heart—for me. I take one step toward Thee, and Thou dost take two steps toward me. Amen.

AFFIRMATION FOR THE DAY: *As Lincoln's hidden springs were in God, so mine shall be—and today especially.*

A PSYCHOLOGIST'S CONVERSION

The great Lincoln needed conversion—everybody does. Here was a man, able, highly trained, a Ph.D. in psychology, and in charge of child guidance in an important city. But his first words as he sat in the chair were, "I want to be saved." This was so refreshing and straightforward and personal. (In contrast to the story of the man who with two fried eggs on his head and a piece of bacon over his ear, came to a psychiatrist, and when asked by him, "What can I do for you?" replied, "I want to see you, not about myself, but about my brother.")

This educator said that he was tense and inwardly insecure. He was causing a heart condition by his inner conflicts. He had psychoanalyzed himself and saw exactly what was the matter with him. But while he could pick himself to pieces, he couldn't put himself together again. He was long on analysis, but short on synthesis. He had answers, but no Answer. Then the word of prayer, the self-surrender and the accepting of faith, and the miracle happened. Tears of joy filled his eyes as at last, at long last Christ had walked into the chaos of his inner life and made him every whit whole.

Then here was a man who had an inferiority complex because he was short of stature. "This being short is getting me down. I am pulling in upon myself and pulling out of everything. I wouldn't think of asking a girl to marry me because I am so short." I told him of Zacchaeus who made his shortness of stature an asset—he climbed a tree and came face to face with Jesus. He used his infirmity. Then of another friend who laughs about his infirmity and climbs on chairs when he has to be seen. And people love him for it. He uses his infirmity. Then the prayer with the short man, and the surrender of the sense of inferiority, and he went away radiant.

Then here is the little boy who said to his father: "Dad, you hear all this talk about conversion? Well, I've got it." And he had. So from Lincoln to the lad it's all the same. No wonder when I arose from my knees after accepting this incredible Gift that I wanted to put my arms around the world and share it with everybody. I still feel that way!

Father, I thank Thee that I too can be perfectly whole. I am learning to surrender, to accept, and to obey. The light and love stream in. Amen.

AFFIRMATION FOR THE DAY: *God's latchstrings are out, and they hang very low—I enter into my inheritance.*

"YOU MUST BELONG"

On the tombstone of Oliver Goldsmith are these words: "He touched nothing that he did not adorn." That could be said of Jesus in a far deeper sense. To the Samaritan leper at His feet Jesus said, "Get up and go, your faith has made you well" (Luke 17:19, Moffatt). Jesus was always saying to people who were down—and sometimes *out* —"Get up and go." And they do "go"—they go places. And all we have to do is to accept the gift. As George Buttrick says: "The linnet need no longer beat upon the bars: A Hand has opened the cage." And all we have to do is to step out into freedom—a gift!

A monk came to his abbot and said: "I do not know what is wrong with me. I keep all the rules. I fast at all appointed times. I pray according to the prescribed regulations for perfect monks. And yet I am a complete failure. What is the matter with me?" The abbot held up his fingers to the sun until there showed the blood-red light between his fingers and said, "You must become a flame of fire." But in both cases it was short of grace. The monk said, "I must do." The abbot said, "You must be." Grace says, "You must belong."

The new birth can happen to those who are not bad but just ineffective—they lack inner contagion. W. E. Sangster says of John Wesley: "On May 23 he was an extraordinarily equipped man, of deep devotion, of iron will, wide scholarship, and a not inconsiderable experience of life; but he was extraordinarily ineffective too! On May 24 he was an apostle! He left the room at Aldersgate Street, flung his leg across the back of a horse, and rode out to save England." What was it that turned an ineffective believer into a mighty apostle? The "strange warming" of his heart. That strange warming of his heart created what Lecky, the historian, said was "a national epoch in the life of Britain."

A Danish wood carver picked up a piece of driftwood on the shore in Hawaii, and seeing its possibilities, carved out of it an exquisitely beautiful head of Christ. Jesus was and is doing just that: He is taking the moral driftwood—the moral ineffectives—and is carving out of it wonderfully beautiful character. And very effective character too!

O Christ, I thank Thee that Thy saving processes are at work within me. I allow them full rein. I know Thou art savingly at work. Amen.

AFFIRMATION FOR THE DAY: *I have been driftwood; now I'm becoming an image of the Divine.*

TWO WAYS OF DEALING WITH EVIL

There is an exquisite story in the Gospels that got into the canon because they couldn't keep it out. It fits the mind of Christ.

The two methods of dealing with sin are seen in the account of the woman taken in adultery—stones and sympathy. The scribes and Pharisees felt that the way to deal with sin was moral and physical stoning—moral stones of disapproving aloofness and scorn, and physical stones where the case allowed. The evildoers would be corrected by criticism. Jesus took the opposite method—He dealt with evil by sympathy for the evildoer. But "sympathy" in the original sense of sym = "with," and pathy = "suffering," a suffering with the evildoer. As He was hungry in the hunger of the hungry, so He felt sinful in the sinner. He projected Himself into the inner life of the sinner and became so one with him that He was one with his sin. That is what it means when it says that He bore "our sins in his own body on the tree."

This identification with the sin and shame of the sinner comes out in the account here when the religious leaders dragged the woman taken in adultery into the midst of the crowd and said, "Moses has commanded us in the Law to stone such creatures; but what do you say?" (John 8:5, Moffatt.) They felt He would say something different. And He did! His eyes followed the eyes of the woman toward the dust. She was inwardly crumpled with shame and He shared that shame with her. The eyes of the rest were upon the woman in self-righteous disapproval. Jesus suffered with the woman, yet disapproved of her sin.

He began to write His finger in the dust. What was He tracing? I think something like this: "God loves you." So out of the dust came the message of God's redeeming love. If we are in the dust, then in that very dust God writes redemption. He is identified with us at our lowest place of need. If you are in hell, then He is in hell with you —"He descended into hell"—and He's there to get you out. The fact is that He holds the keys to death and hell. He has unlocked both. Walk out of both to freedom. The door is open!

O God, Thou didst stoop to share—to share our lot at the lowest place of our need. Thou hast gone low with us to lift us high with Thee. Am I grateful? See my heart. Amen.

AFFIRMATION FOR THE DAY: *I read Thy writing in the dust of my body, and it all spells "Love."*

"LET THE INNOCENT THROW THE FIRST STONE"

As the leaders "persisted with their question, he raised himself and said to them, 'Let the innocent among you throw the first stone at her'" (John 8:7, Moffatt). And when He looked at *them,* His look must have been different, for His eyes must have looked straight through them, for He felt the burning injustice and hypocrisy of the whole proceeding. Why was the woman alone brought? Where was the man? They had a double standard. And now Jesus made the standards one: "Let the innocent among you throw the first stone." He threw the whole thing back into their own bosoms before their own consciences. They said, "Such creatures"; Jesus said, "You." And having laid the whole matter at the door of their consciences, He rested His case.

And again he stooped down and again he wrote on the ground. This time He must have written another message for the woman, something like this: "God loves you and He has sent me to tell you that you are forgiven. But don't do it again."

And the accusers? "And on hearing what he said, they went away one by one, beginning with the older men till Jesus was left alone with the woman standing before him" (Luke 8:9, Moffatt). They came to pronounce judgment on the woman; they left pronouncing judgment on themselves. For everyone that left, by his very leaving confessed his own guilt. And confessed it to the degree of guilt: "beginning with the older men"—they went first for they had been longest at it.

Was there ever such a judgment scene as this? With such an outcome? The accusers went away guilty but unforgiven, and the guilty went away forgiven.

Then to make the private message written on the ground something public and before all, Jesus said to her: "'Woman, where are they? Has not one condemned you?'" She said, "'No one, sir.'" Jesus said, "'Neither do I; be off and never sin again'" (John 8:10, Moffatt). They expected to condemn Jesus for not condemning her, but ended by condemning themselves and in hearing the woman freed from condemnation—and more, freed from sinning again. Jesus used evil to free from evil.

O Jesus, Thou art a terrible Judge and a tender Redeemer. Thou dost put the judgment seat in our own hearts, and then Thou dost free us with the most tender act of the universe—divine forgiveness. Amen.

AFFIRMATION FOR THE DAY: *God is tender in His terribleness, and terrible in His tenderness—in both cases redemptive.*

WHAT ABOUT THE HOMOSEXUAL?

The last few days we have looked at the story of a heterosexual, the woman taken in adultery. There was forgiveness and release for her. But what about the homosexual? Here we tend to draw the curtain and relapse into silence or into whispers. But why shouldn't this be faced and help given?

I am not convinced that homosexuality is something inherent and therefore cannot be changed—that homosexuals will always be attracted only to their own sex. I am convinced that homosexuality is the normal sex urge perverted. It gets started into grooves of homosexuality for the obvious reason that it is easier to express the sex urge in homosexual relations, for boys are thrown with boys, and girls with girls in intimate relations, and it can be carried on under the cover of legitimacy. Once the sex attention is turned toward one's own sex, it is naturally withdrawn from the other sex—the homosexual is produced. But opportune circumstances and directed attention and choice, rather than nature, produce the homosexual. Therefore the homosexual can be changed with sex urges normalized and redirected, provided there is a real conversion.

Here is a brilliant radio scriptwriter who has gone very high in that field. A telephone call says: "May I see you? I've been a homosexual but I've run smack into God. I want to tell you my story." Obviously sincere, straightforward, and on fire with the love of God, she awes you with the amazing redemption. She was a pagan, with conscience buried so deep that it never squeaked. She lived in homosexuality for seven years, grew increasingly stout through overeating due to a gathering frustration. Then she met by chance or Providence a girl, a childhood friend whom she wanted sexually and yet in whom she saw something else she wanted—the Christ in her. Then began the battle of the urges—the sex-hunger and the Christ-hunger. Which would win? A soul was at stake. The fact is that two souls were at stake. They would go up or down together.

O Christ, I thank Thee that Thy love encompasses all—especially those who have missed the Way. Oh, give them courage to believe that Thou art the Way—the Way out. Amen.

AFFIRMATION FOR THE DAY: *All crookedness can be made straight, all straightness can be made straighter—all can be made over and used.*

THE REDEMPTION OF THE HOMOSEXUAL

We resume the story of the redemption of a homosexual. These two women began to live together, but the one was strong in Christ and would not yield. Then the homosexual came to the place where she tried to compromise—she would take Christ *and* homosexuality, declaring that the latter was not wrong. The other girl saw the crisis hour had come and a choice must be made, so she put on her hat and coat and said, "I'm leaving. You can't have both." And she was leaving—for good. But something called her back and she took the Bible and slowly read: "Their women have exchanged the natural function of sex for what is unnatural, and in the same way the males have abandoned the natural use of women and flamed out in lust for one another, . . . and getting in their own persons the due recompense of their perversity" (Rom. 1:26-27, Moffatt). The struggling woman slowly said, "Well, I guess you're right." And the struggle was over! Her being was flooded with the love of God. Homosexuality dropped away like a dead leaf—irrelevant in the light of this overwhelming divine life that flooded her. She was released and free—and happy. She could scarcely think or talk of anything else.

She poured out this new-found joy over the radio and multitudes feeling the sincerity and simplicity responded. This was *It*. As one put it, "She is terrific." She never quite became an alcoholic, for her drinking was from revolt rather than desire. The drinking dropped away—irrelevant. In her quiet time she had made a mental picture of a pathway of light between her and God, and then one day the pathway seemed clouded with smoke. She took the divine hint and threw away her cigarettes, though she had been smoking four packs a day. No struggle—it was gone. She lost sixty pounds in a year; other appetites began to be normal.

And now the most beautiful thing of all. Those two girls live together in simple, relaxed purity with a very beautiful devotion to each other, but a greater devotion to their Lord. The homosexual urge was redeemed from perversion, and since they now both belonged to Christ supremely, they could belong to each other secondarily.

Christ, Thou art the Answer. When we love Thee supremely, then all our other loves are redeemed. Belonging to Thee, everything belongs to us. Amen.

AFFIRMATION FOR THE DAY: *All my basic drives driving toward God's ends—hence toward their own ends.*

A ROAD WITH A DEAD END

I mentioned incidentally two releases that came to the woman in yesterday's study—the release from smoking and drinking. They are both methods of escape out of reality.

When one is "down," he attempts to escape out of that depressed feeling by a cigarette, which ultimately creates conditions that make him more "down" and demand more cigarettes to save him from the "more down" feeling. It is under the law of decreasing returns. It's a road with a dead end.

And I mean *dead*. Reported the Cancer Research Congress in 1950: "Lung cancer takes 20,000 lives each year in the U.S. and is the fastest growing type of cancer in our country. The number of new lung cancer cases was nearly three times in 1948 what it was in 1939. Out of 900 persons with lung cancer there were only 9 non-smokers. Ninety-five per cent of the men with cancers were moderately heavy smokers—a pack a day. Lung cancer is rarer among women, but it was found that women too had more chance of getting lung cancer when they smoke heavily."

Walter C. Alvarez of the Mayo Clinc says: "It is remarkable how a heavy smoker will sometimes lose his indigestion and will gain in weight and energy and sense of well-being when he gives up his cigarettes, his cigars, and his pipe." And then he adds: "Some of the illnesses and premature ageing of men and women today is doubtless due to their excessive use of tobacco."

Budge Patty, Wimbledon tennis champion of 1950, says: "Just say I won it because I gave up smoking. Seriously, I know it had a lot to do with it. I gave up smoking seven weeks ago. Now I can breathe. And I gained some weight too. If I hadn't done that, I wouldn't have got past the third round."

A lot of people knock themselves out in the third round by cigarette smoking. That is a losing game. And it is a losing game for women to spend money for permanents, make-up, and face lifting, when all the time they are smoking cigarettes which produce a premature aging. And more than that: the life expectancy between the ages of thirty and forty-five is double for nonsmokers over heavy smokers.

O Christ, Thou who didst remain strong and without self-handicaps, save me from weighting my life down with senseless habits. Amen.

AFFIRMATION FOR THE DAY: *I am too big, with goals too great, to be tripped up by little things.*

ALCOHOL A DEPRESSANT

Let me remind you that when people give up smoking, there is usually a blossoming of the personality. A girl, tied in knots and frustrated, threw a whole carton of cigarettes into the lake as a symbol of her change-over. And what a change-over! She went straight to the top of her class in art school. From a problem she became a person. Seeing the change in her, half a dozen or more of the art students have given up smoking. Her father, a doctor, said to her as they drove along, "I'm giving up smoking when I finish this pack." "You coward," she replied. "Why don't you stop now?" He threw the pack out of the window and was on top of the world—both liquor and tobacco under his feet.

Nicotine narrows the arteries, forces the heart to work faster to get the blood through, and that is the "pickup" one gets from smoking. The heart goes at a dingdong pace and wears itself out prematurely. The rise of heart disease as the top killer in our civilization is due in large measure to increased smoking by men and women. Said a heart specialist, "Of all the things that people take into themselves for their supposed pleasure, tobacco is the worst."

Tobacco is a stimulant—a costly one—but a stimulant; liquor is a depressant. Dr. Harold E. Heinwich says: "The chief action of alcohol on the central nervous system, formed by the brain and spinal cord, is that of a depressant. . . . Because of this narcotic effect, alcohol interferes with working efficiency. . . . The feeling of warmth after the drinking of alcohol is illusory." Dr. Haven Emerson, professor of public health administration, figures that from the records of life insurance companies, a man of thirty-five years who is a total abstainer has an expectancy of thirty-two years while a man of the same age who uses alcohol temperately has an expectancy of only twenty-eight years.

A young man who had killed another young man and raped his companion said, "After drinking I got the courage to do it." But drinking did not give him courage, it only deadened the controls—he was free to be murderer and a rapist.

O God, forgive our poor, deluded souls that we dodge into these subterfuges as escapes from reality. Give us sense that we may quit this nonsense. For our nonsense costs heavily. Amen.

AFFIRMATION FOR THE DAY: *Only weak, lame souls turn to the crutches of narcotics. I am no longer weak or lame—I need no crutches.*

"LET ALCOHOL ALONE"

We ended yesterday saying that drinking is a flight from reality, a failure of nerve, an escape mentality. In a hotel there is this sign: "Cocktail Bar—Flight Down." It is a "flight"—a flight from reality, and it is a flight "down." The end is "down"—mentally, morally, and emotionally. Keep it up and you'll not only be "down" but you'll be "down *and* out."

Walter Johnson, the great pitcher, said: "If you expect to stay in the game let alcohol alone. It gets you sooner or later."

William Howard Taft said: "Leave drink alone absolutely. He who drinks is disqualifying himself for advancement." Edison put it: "I have better use for my brain than to poison it with alcohol. To put alcohol in the human brain is like putting sand in the bearing of an engine." Dr. William Mayo: "From the point of view of health there never has been any question but that abstinence from alcoholic liquors proves extremely beneficial." Dr. Richard C. Cabot: "Moderate drinking does at least as much harm as drunkenness. . . . Beer and light wines can poison us and have poisoned us as whisky does. . . . Medically and socially the case against alcohol is just as clear as the case against opium." Dr. Adolph Meyer of John Hopkins says: "Alcohol is a direct and principal cause of several types of mental disease." Dr. Charles W. Mayo says: "You often hear people tell how their wits are quickened for the first half hour after drinking liquor, but they do not tell how, after that, the body does not co-ordinate with the brain."

The liquor dealers, alarmed at the close tie-up between auto accidents and drinking drivers, have put out a sign: "If you drive, don't drink. If you drink, don't drive." If that advice were taken literally, it would wipe out the liquor business.

William E. Gladstone put it: "Intoxicating drinks have produced evils more deadly, because more continuous, than all those caused to mankind by the great historic scourges of war, famine, or pestilence combined." Don't touch it! It's a fool's business, and don't let them fool you into being a fool. It isn't smart to drink—it's weak.

Gracious Father, give me courage and give me sense. Help me to take my feet out of this flypaper. In Jesus' name. Amen.

AFFIRMATION FOR THE DAY: *I am through with all escape mechanisms —I belong to the open road to Reality.*

MORE NEGATIVE THAN POSITIVE

We have been looking at ways of escape through narcotics. Some try to escape through narcotics, others try to escape through negativism. They evade responsibility for positive achievement by being critical and negative. They point out the shortcomings of others and thus hide their own.

This is a deteriorating process. It gets one just exactly nowhere—except backward. For if you take a negative attitude toward others and situations, you become a negative person. The attitude becomes an actuality—in you. That is the pay-off. The critical person begets criticism—of himself. As someone has put it: If you point one finger at another, you point the other three fingers at yourself.

This account illustrates the tendency to blame others when conscious of one's own fault: "But the man who was injuring his neighbour pushed him aside. 'Who made you ruler and umpire over us?' he asked. 'Do you want to kill me, as you killed the Egyptian yesterday?' " (Acts 7:27-28, Moffatt.) It is psychologically a fact that we tend to find the faults in others which we see subconsciously in ourselves.

The man who hid his talent said to his master: "Lord, I knew thee that thou art a hard man, reaping where thou hast not sown, and gathering where thou hast not strawed: and I was afraid, and went and hid thy talent in the earth" (Matt. 25:24-25). He who was conscious of fault began to find fault with his master.

Jeremiah was more negative than positive. He conceived of his commission to be: "To tear up, to break down, to shatter, to pull down, to build up and to plant" (Jer. 1:10, Moffatt). He was negative—four to two—in his attitudes. Hence we call him "the weeping prophet," "the prophet of doom," and we seldom or never turn to him. Agabus in the New Testament prophesied two things—famine, and imprisonment for Paul. Both of them came true. But we don't remember Agabus, or name our children after him. He was negative and his following was negative. The negative person becomes what he gives out.

O God, Thou hast made us for creation. Help me to be creative rather than critical. Help me to see the good and thus create the good. Amen.

AFFIRMATION FOR THE DAY: *"Love is never glad when others go wrong, love is gladdened by goodness"* (I Cor. 13:6, Moffatt).

"SHE SAW EVERYTHING AS EVIL"

We continue to look at critical, negative attitudes as a false way out of our own problems. A woman, obviously full of conflicts and tense and disrupted, poured out a perfect tirade about what was wrong with her father, her brothers, and sisters—everybody was wrong except herself. She was sensitive as a boil about her own faults, wouldn't let you touch them. So my hands were tied. I couldn't do a thing for her, nor could God. We had to leave her in knots—self-tied.

Hornell Hart, after an exhaustive study, sums up his conclusions as follows: "For a large majority of those who lack comradeship the reason is not in the antagonisms of their associates; it is not the misfortune that places them in the midst of unfriendly folks; it is not that they happen to be working under tyrannous, unsympathetic, and emotionally maladjusted chiefs; it is not that there are conspiracies against them. For the great majority of people who lack comradeship the reason is inherent in certain basic qualities in themselves."

"There were extenuating circumstances in all this," said a married man who had robbed and raped numerous women in Dallas. He had built up an inner alibi for all this—others' wrongs. But the alibis dropped away and stark reality remained.

A woman recounted to me a strange experience. She was a highly intelligent, seemingly adjusted social worker. She came a long distance to talk with me about an apparent temporary possession of her by an evil spirit. As long as the evil spirit was upon her she saw everything as evil. Then it passed away suddenly—she felt it go. Whatever we may believe or not believe about evil spirit possession, the thing to be noted is this: *As long as that evil spirit was upon her, she saw everything as evil.* When we are letting in cynical, negative, critical, fault-finding attitudes, then we are letting in an evil spirit which will possess us and make us look on everybody and everything as evil. But when we let in the Holy Spirit, the Spirit of Creation, then we will look on everything and see that it is "good," or can be made "good."

O God, the Spirit, I let Thee in and now I see everything with possibilities in it. Even evil can be turned into good. Amen.

AFFIRMATION FOR THE DAY: *"Always slow to expose, always eager to believe the best"* (I Cor. 13:7, Moffatt).

STEPS OUT OF CRITICAL ATTITUDES

When we get critical of people and surroundings, we end in our own frustration. It is not a way out. A little girl of six felt she wanted to get away from her family, everything was wrong. So when she said she wanted to go away, her mother helped her pack her suitcase and then bade her good-by at the door. Then she kept an eye on her out of the corner of the window. Jane went to the corner, sat on the curb for a long time, apparently in deep thought, then came back and knocked at the door. Her mother opened the door and said, "Why, Jane, I thought you were going to go away and leave home." "Yes," said Jane slowly, "but I didn't know where to go." Her negative, critical, run-away attitudes landed her at zero.

How are we to get out of critical, negative attitudes?

1. *Make up your mind that the way of criticism is a road with a dead end.* Nobody was ever changed by criticism, least of all by a nagging criticism. Nobody is changed except the critic—he is changed into a critical person.

2. *Surrender the way of criticism as a way of life.* Give it up as deliberately as you would discard a torn, spotted coat. For a critical personality is a shabby personality.

3. *Begin to look for good in people and circumstances.* As you see and express the good, a good spirit will take possession of you.

4. *Don't criticize a person until you have projected yourself into his situation and see things from his standpoint.* Here is a red Indian prayer: "O Great Spirit, maker of men, forbid that I should judge any man until I have walked two moons in his moccasins."

5. *Work out a positive technique of relationships based on the positive.* A couple of eighty-nine told of an eighty-year romance and how they were still in love with each other. Asked the secret, they replied: (*a*) A man and his wife should be considerate of each other; (*b*) practice the Golden Rule in everyday life; (*c*) count ten before you begin bawling out your mate—and then give a kiss instead.

O God, who dost judge me only in loving redemption, help me to judge others in the same way. Help me to see the good and create the good in the very seeing. Amen.

AFFIRMATION FOR THE DAY: *"Treat one another with the same spirit as you experience in Christ Jesus"* (Phil. 2:5, Moffatt).

"ANY RECENT NEWS FROM GOD?"

We come to another thing over which we must get victory if we are to be transformed persons—dullness.

The central characteristic of people in this mass production age is just dull sameness. Every town in the country is just the same; see one and you see them all—the same chain stores, the same neon lights, the same lack of spontaneous difference. And where they try to be different, they succeed only in being queer and bizarre. Exceptions, of course. But we are fast becoming a herd-centered civilization and are taking on a protective resemblance to the dull average.

This has passed over into religion. In the New Testament there was a surprise around every corner. Life was popping with novelty and natural spontaneity. People weren't trying to be different—they just were. Creation was at work in them.

A pastor asked his janitor to come to church and the janitor replied, "Have you had any recent news from God?" The Good News had been reduced to musty, stale news. The whole thing was suffering from dry rot.

Studdert-Kennedy says: "After forty, four courses are open to you: (a) You either become a cynic and are damned progressively; (b) or you go mad; (c) or you become like a cow; (d) or you become a saint and are in the process of being saved." Most people unconsciously choose to be the third—a cow. They become what Nietzsche described as "moral cows in their plump comfortableness." Life turns dull and inane. People seek security so ardently that they become secure—in their coffins—before they die. They are dead, but the announcement hasn't been made public.

The religious life of many people is just dull—insufferably dull. But New Testament Christianity was gay, spontaneous, full of laughter; it was joy unspeakable and full of glory. Here is piety set to music —a wedding feast instead of a funeral dirge. When you are cleared up within from conflicts and guilts, you have a hair-trigger laugh— you laugh because of the rhythm of things, you have cosmic approval for your way of life.

O God, my Father, I thank Thee that Thou hast attuned my soul to laughter and gaiety. Give me the laughter that is incorrigibly gay. Amen.

AFFIRMATION FOR THE DAY: *I belong to the gayhearted pilgrims of the Infinite!*

SIN IS DULL

One of the troubles with sin is that it is so dull. The people who go in for it have to invent more and more ways to make life tolerable and interesting. I overheard a man telling another what had happened the night before. "You know what funny things will happen when you get five or six cocktails in you?" And then he recited a story that would make an ordinary decent person sick—literally sick. And they called that "funny." It was "funny" without any fun in it. It was a cackle that laid no egg.

There was nothing left behind except a "hang-over," and a "dark brown taste." I don't have a "hang-over" from being a Christian—not a "hang-over," but a "hallelujah." Not a "dark brown taste," but a taste that leaves an even better taste in the memory of it. Evil tastes sweet but is bitter to digest.

Ezekiel speaks of the river flowing "into the Dead Sea, into the brackish waters which shall turn fresh" (Ezek. 48:8, Moffatt). Sin is a dead sea—its joys are dead joys; its laughter is a hollow death rattle; its smile is like the grin of the Cheshire cat with nothing behind it; its fruit is dead sea fruit. It is the great illusion.

But the River of God flowing into our dead seas turns them fresh. Your whole being is freshened, including your joys. They become joys with a natural spontaneity in them. You learn to laugh—even at hell and high water. You laugh at life—a rhythmical, harmonious laugh, for you're on top of things.

A Christian psychiatrist who had just tasted the joy of being a Christian and surprised at the depths of it said, "It's fun to be a Christian psychiatrist." It's fun to be a Christian at anything you do. It glorifies the commonplace. It throws a halo around what would otherwise be mere dullness.

"It's no fun to be a Christian worker unless it is fun to be a Christian worker." It's no fun doing anything unless it is fun. As Allan Watt says: "Love raises the spirit into one of laughter: a sphere in which the soul says:

> Shall I, a gnat which dances in Thy ray,
> Dare to be reverent?

O God, I thank Thee that Thou hast made me for laughter and for an inner harmony. Give me my birthright. Help me to take it. Amen.

AFFIRMATION FOR THE DAY: *It's fun to be a Christian.*

"THE HOLY SPIRIT IS THE ANSWER"

We continue to look at the dullness so characteristic of many Christians. They are not bad—they are just dull, noncontagious.

And yet this is what God offers to such downcast people: "Listen, ye who are downcast, who feel far from any triumph, I bring my triumph near, right near, my victory is hastening" (Isa. 46:12, Moffatt). Note that this victory is not our victory—it is God's victory, "my victory"; and all we have to do is to take it—a gift! It is near, very near; so near that if you empty your hands you can reach out and take it.

Then again God says: "I am the Eternal your God, training you for your good, leading you by the right way, if only you would listen to my orders, you would have bliss brimming like a river, and welfare ample as the ocean waves" (Isa. 48:17-18, Moffatt). Here is the offer of "bliss brimming," and "welfare ample." Many of us have bliss but not "bliss brimming," and we have welfare, but not "welfare ample." But note this: "Thou hast richly given them gladness, and an ample joy" (Isa. 9:3, Moffatt). An "ample joy"—many of our joys are not "ample," they are not big enough to stand the shocks of life. They crumple under the impact of sorrow or opposition.

This letter in this morning's mail: "In spite of my position as a pastor and a glorious heritage, I do not enjoy the experience about which you preach. I find it difficult to surrender—not that I do not trust God, but I don't trust myself. Too many times have I placed my gift on the altar only to find a few days later that either I had unknowingly kept back part of the price, or that the flesh is too much with me." What is the remedy to this life of death?

The Holy Spirit is the answer. One doesn't have to strive against the flesh or trust oneself. All he has to do is to consent, and the Holy Spirit takes over the inner life. Transformation sets in. And the transformation is not in mere action; it is transformation at the place where it counts most—the depths of the personality. The spring is cleansed and the flow is thereby purified.

O Father, I thank Thee that Thou hast fashioned my spirit to receive Thy Spirit. Now I accept my birthright. I accept Him. Amen.

AFFIRMATION FOR THE DAY: *"For you shall leave with joy, and be led off in blissful bands; the hills shall burst before you into song, and all trees clap their hands"* (Isa. 55:12, Moffatt).

244

"HE KNOWS THE SHEPHERD"

We come now to see what is at the basis of the dullness in Christian lives. It is the absence of the Holy Spirit. The Holy Spirit is the Spirit of Creation, and where He is abiding within, there creation continues.

Up to the coming of the Holy Spirit at Pentecost the disciples were copyists—they were copying Jesus with more or less spotty performance. But when the Holy Spirit moved into them, they were not copyists but creators. They were no longer cold, dead moons lighted by reflected light—they were suns burning with fire and light within them.

They were no longer merely disciples—learners; they were apostles—ones sent. Timid believers had become irresistible apostles. A man with no legal help was assigned two lawyers by the judge, good lawyers. He shook his head and said, "Judge, is there any way I can swap two good lawyers for one good witness?" These disciples were no longer lawyers arguing the case for Jesus, they were witnesses who witnessed to the mighty power of Jesus in their lives to save—and to save now. It was all living and fresh and firsthand and vital. Their spiritual lives were no longer in quotes—they were no longer in quotation marks, but in creation marks.

A great actor read the twenty-third psalm with perfect diction and tones and great applause greeted his performance. A pastor read it stumblingly and at the end there was no applause, but there was not a dry eye in the audience. The actor arose and said, "I know the twenty-third psalm, but he knows the Shepherd."

When the Holy Spirit moves within us in response to surrender and accepting faith, then you know Jesus not by hearsay but by heartsay. You know Him—intimately, vitally, and savingly. An inner dullness gives place to an inner dancing. Everything within you is under the law of creation. You are no longer tense and tired, but relaxed and refreshed. You have learned the secret of drawing upon your inner resources—the Holy Spirit. The Japanese have a saying, "You must be tired." The Christian replies, "No, I'm fresh in God."

O Holy Spirit, I let Thee take possession of my dull inner life and let Thee turn that dullness into creation. I am alive. Amen.

AFFIRMATION FOR THE DAY: *"The harvest of the Spirit is . . . joy"* (Gal. 5:22, Moffatt).

"TO THE TUNE OF 'SUFFERING' "

We now turn from the transformation of dullness to the transformation of suffering and tragedy. Many of us are not dull; we are alive—with pain. Some of that pain is mental and spiritual and some of it is physical—all of it spells pain. The title of Ps. 53 in Moffatt reads: "From the Choirmaster's collection. To the tune of 'Suffering.' " Many of us live our lives to "the tune of 'Suffering' "—that is the dominant note.

What is the Christian answer? It is not merely bearing it, submitting to it as the will of God, as in Islam; nor is it an escaping of it, as in the Old Testament answer. The Christian faith does not promise you exemption from suffering. How could it, when at the heart of that faith is a cross where the purest Heart that ever beat writhed in an agony of unmerited suffering? Then what is the answer? It is found in that very cross where Jesus took the worst thing that could happen to Him, namely, His crucifixion, and made it into the best thing that could happen to the world, namely, its redemption. When you can take the worst and turn it into the best, then you are safe. You can stand anything, because you can *use* everything.

The key is found here: "He withdrew about a stone's throw and knelt in prayer, saying, 'Father, if it please thee, take this cup away from me. But thy will, not mine, be done.' And an angel from heaven appeared to strengthen him" (Luke 22:42-43), Moffatt). Here the answer of God was not to take away the cup, but strength to make that bitter cup into a cup of salvation which He would put to the thirsty lips of humanity. God's answer was strength to use, not exemption from.

I grant that the righteous are exempted from many self-inflicted pains which the unrighteous inflict on themselves. They are not barking their shins upon the system of things. They know their way around better in a world of this kind. But the central answer is here: the angel strengthens Him to use the cup and the cross and make them redemptive. Not around, not over, but through—that is the triumphant Christian way.

O Father, I thank Thee that I need not whine to be released, but can ask for strength to turn my hells into heavens and to make everything sing—even sadness. I thank Thee. Amen.

AFFIRMATION FOR THE DAY: *Not saved from, but saved through the ordinary sorrows of life by using them.*

"POISONED THEIR MINDS, . . . SO"

We are studying the Christian way to live life out when the tune is "Suffering." We found that the answer is to use everything—good, bad and indifferent—and make something out of it. That gives you a practical working philosophy of life. A philosophy of life? No, a practical working *way* of life.

Note how Jesus used this method: "This filled them with fury, and they discussed what they could do to Jesus. It was in these ways that he went to the hillside to pray. He summoned his disciples, choosing twelve" (Luke 6:11-13, Moffatt). Their "fury" furthered Him. It precipitated the decision to choose the twelve with whom He could entrust His message if the "fury" became fact. It was a wise decision, for if He had not chosen the twelve, His movement might have died when He was taken away. Their determination precipitated His decision, and that decision defeated their determination.

Again, take the same thing at work in His apostles who had caught His secret: "The unbelieving Jews . . . poisoned their minds against the brethren. So they remained for a long time, speaking boldly" (Acts 14:2-3, R.S.V.). This is what Halford Luccock calls "crazy logic": "poisoned their minds, . . . so." One would have thought that it would have read: "So they left," but no, "so they remained." And "remained for a long time, speaking boldly." The poison produced persistence and results. The Hindus have the legend of distilling nectar out of poison. Here was nectar from poison. Everything furthers the Christian—everything.

Take another illustration: "Where they opposed and reviled him, . . . he left there and went . . . next door to the synagogue. Crispus, the ruler of the synagogue, believed, . . . and many of the Corinthians" (Acts 18:6-11, R.S.V.). Here Paul was opposed into opportunity. One door was shut and a bigger one was opened. The epistles to the Corinthians came out of that opposition. In I Corinthians 13 the nectar of love is distilled out of this poison of hate. This is victory! When you can produce such a chapter out of opposition and criticism, then you are incorrigibly victorious.

Gracious Father, I thank Thee that by Thy grace I can transform my oppositions into opportunities, my disabilities into doors. Now I can face life with a laugh of triumph. Amen.

AFFIRMATION FOR THE DAY: *"This positive, active way of dealing with suffering gives a new dimension to life."*

247

"A DAWN IN EVERY MIDNIGHT"

We are looking at the Christian way to transform suffering and opposition. We noted yesterday that the apostles stayed at Iconium, but note further: "When an attempt was made . . . to molest them and to stone them, they learned of it and fled to Lystra; . . . there they preached the gospel" (Acts 14:6, 7, R.S.V.). They stayed a long time in spite of opposition and preached the gospel, but in the end they fled—in both cases the end was not staying or fleeing, but preaching the gospel! There was no stubborn adherence to any method—they could stay or flee, but the end was accomplishing their purpose, namely, preaching the gospel. They had fluid minds, but their purposes were not fluid but fixed—preaching the gospel!

Agnes E. Meyer says: "If I were asked to define the principal quality of exceptional women, I should say it is the capacity to accept the triumphs of life without pride and the sufferings of life without despair." The sufferings of life can be met without despair, not because one grits his teeth and says, "I'll bear it," but because he sees an open door in every despair. The Swedish have a saying, "Blessed is he who sees a dawn in every midnight." And there is a dawn in every midnight—pluck it out and rejoice in it before it comes.

A radiant mother and her radiant daughter came up at the close of a service and the mother said: "My daughter was struck with polio and you scared me tonight when you talked of wrong reactions. For I might have reacted wrongly. But both of us reacted in the right way. She is a junior in college and is so happy, and so am I." She rescued out of calamity an opportunity. They were both made by something which could have unmade them. Not what happens to you but what you do with it determines the result. They determined the result by their spirit.

American nasal twang is not beautiful, but I once heard it set to music. An American missionary, brought up on a farm far from the city, brought beautiful music out of humming through her nose and then stroking it with her fingers. A nasal twang turned to tune!

O Christ, Thou art teaching me to turn the ugly into the beautiful, evil into good, and death into life. So now I defy everything, for I can use everything. This is victory, victory. Amen.

AFFIRMATION FOR THE DAY: *"I take every project prisoner to make it obey Christ"* (II Cor. 10:5, Moffatt)—*even the projects of injustice and wrong.*

"A PAIN IN THE MIND"

We continue to look at the way to deal with suffering and frustration. Someone said that "a pain in the mind is the prelude to every discovery." When there is a pain anywhere in life, it is the prelude to a discovery—the discovery of how to use everything. That is the key— the only key to victorious living. A woman came to a doctor in great distress and said, "Doctor, what am I to do with my gray hair?" And the doctor promptly said, "Admire it." That's it! If time puts a white crown on your head, then wear it as a crown, not as a complaint. Glory in everything, and everything will be glorious. A father who had lost his seventeen-year-old daughter the day before, said, "I'm grateful we had her for seventeen years." He picked a gratitude instead of a grouch out of that tragedy. And he was happy—in spite of; and the made those around him happy—in spite of.

In contrast, look at this picture: A woman lost her son in a war. She sorrowed until her throat closed and she couldn't eat, and she lost weight. She is choking herself to death with grief. And she is choking to death the happiness of those around her. She didn't know the secret of living for she didn't know the secret of using. She illustrated the Scripture, "That your souls may not wear out with despondency" (Heb. 12:3). She was wearing out her soul with despondency and it got her just exactly nowhere. She lived by self-pity instead of self-mastery and circumstance-mastery.

Here is what Elsa Maxwell said her father left her as a "legacy"; (a) "Never be afraid of 'they.' (b) Never collect inanimate objects. You don't do it, for they will collect you: own only absolute essentials. (c) Always laugh at yourself first." The power to laugh at yourself is one of the most saving things in the world. When you begin to feel sorry for yourself, walk to the looking glass and burst out laughing. I often do it! That laughter says, "I can rescue a song out of this sorrow." And the song becomes sweeter for the sorrow. So it is a double victory.

O Christ, I thank Thee that I can find my joys in unexpected places— even in my sorrows. Thou hast given me the incorrigibly happy heart. I thank Thee, thank Thee. Amen.

AFFIRMATION FOR THE DAY: *As the plane rises against the wind, so I shall rise against the resistances of the day.*

"BEING CHRISTIAN IS THE TRIUMPH"

We are studying how to rescue good out of evil, a song out of sorrow. Here is the statement of a radiant woman, the target of the jealous barbs of a brilliant "friend": "But all my days are happy, even when she takes me as her target and hits the bull's eye. I seem to heal with as much ease as she pulls the trigger." This is victory. And it is not the victory of a thick-skinned individual who cares for nothing and for nobody, but a person who is highly sensitive and yet knows how to "turn" everything into a "testimony." Her detractor is frustrated; she is fruitful.

Every day you can take hold of life by the handle of fear or the handle of faith. If you take hold of it by the handle of faith, you can find something to rejoice in everything. If nothing in the thing itself, then you can rejoice over the fact that you can rejoice—over everything and nothing. The rejoicing is the victory. Being Christian is the triumph.

In a period of severe criticism, most of it unmerited, one morning I woke up saying to myself: "I hope my critics are as happy as I am. But I doubt it!"

Flannel is made by innumerable needles plucking at the smooth fabric and pulling the cotton out and thus making flannel, so soft and pleasing to the touch. So life's sufferings, like innumerable needles, pluck at the smoothness of your life's fabric and ruffle it. And yet the very ruffling makes life smooth and warm and livable—if you know how to use it! If you fight against life's needling, it may make you raw and sore; if you accept and use it, then it will make you inwardly as snug as flannel.

"Your sorrow will turn into joy," said Jesus. That is the conversion —converting sorrow into joy. Jesus adds: "When a woman is in travail she has sorrow, . . . but when she is delivered of the child, she no longer remembers the anguish, for joy that a child is born" (John 16:20-21, R.S.V.). All sorrow should be not a death pang, but a childbirth. Make every sorrow bring forth something! And when your sorrow brings forth a new soul, it is a soul you can live with.

O God, I thank Thee that in Thee all my sunsets turn to sunrises, all my pangs become birth pangs, all my needlings become flannels. Amen.

AFFIRMATION FOR THE DAY: *"The Prince of this world is coming. . . His coming will only serve"* (John 14:30-31, Moffatt)—*so I too will make even evil serve.*

WILL BEND BUT NOT BREAK

We continue our study of the possibility of transforming sorrow and pain. In a tin plate factory the sheets are put under terrific heat of 2,500° for the purpose of resetting the molecules. After being subjected to this heat, the tin will bend but won't break. Before this process, the sheets would break under bending. The fires of sorrow and trouble will so temper our inner spirit, will so rearrange the elements within us, that we, being harmonized within, can stand pressures. We bend but we don't break. Jesus bent in Gethsemane, at the cross, but He didn't break. A resilience of spirit is created when we know how to take whatever comes and make something out of it.

In the Y.M.C.A. in Erie, Pennsylvania, is a man who at thirty-six has lost his sight completely. He is a masseur in charge of the health department. After losing his sight, he went straight on with his job without self-pity or complaint. When the shock came he bent, but he didn't break.

Susan Peters picked up a 22-caliber rifle and the trigger caught in the branch of a tree. Surgeons removed the slug from her spine and told her she would never walk again. But Susan is radiant and animated; only her body is confined. She became a wheel chair actress and played the part of Elizabeth Barrett Browning. She bent, but she didn't break.

A very effective song leader and evangelist was stricken with a cancer in—of all places!—his throat. His vocal cords and windpipe in the upper portion were taken out completely. He has to breathe through an aperture in his neck. While on the operating table this thought came to him, "To be an old maid is not difficult when you cease to struggle." He surrendered it all to God. He is radiant. He has learned to speak by swallowing air into his stomach and then bringing it back to frame words with his tongue. He is speaking without vocal cords, and expects to be able to preach to an audience again. He learned how to play the violin and to speak at sixty-five! He bent, but he didn't break under the tragedy.

O Christ, I thank Thee that nothing matters except how I take what comes. Give me the spirit that knows how to bend but knows nothing of breaking. Then I shall be afraid of nothing. Amen.

AFFIRMATION FOR THE DAY: *I have the yieldingness and the strength of the bamboo.*

"THE TOP INTO A LYRE"

We spend our last day this week in looking at the possibility of making everything contribute. The lyre pine is a pine tree which has a top arranged like a lyre, with a number of branches forming the top instead of one straight-up top. It is produced, they say, by calamity striking off its original top. Frustrated, it then puts up a whole series of tops stretched on a more or less horizontal bar. Calamity turns the one top into a row of tops and makes the top into a lyre. That is what can happen to us: calamity can turn our prosaic dullness into music—a lone top into a lyre top.

Gayle Pickwell, a professor, was stricken with multiple sclerosis, and the doctors gave him ten years to live. He lived over eighteen years—radiantly. When he could no longer walk, he taught from a wheel chair, and then dictated books and articles when confined to bed. He lost his eyesight, but that didn't stop the march of his spirit. The college yearbook dedicated to him said: "The self-assurance of a strong leader, the insight of a philosopher, the winsomeness of a child—these qualities made of Gayle Pickwell a man never-to-be-forgotten by any who came within his magic circle. He accepted life's every challenge."

This is what happened to a friend: "I was past fifty when I had a heart attack. I am thankful to God for that attack for it cleansed my soul from past sin, took away my tobacco, and pointed me to the way of Christ. I went to Professor Crawford, a man on crutches but whose smile you saw before you saw his crutches, and told him I wanted to go into the ministry. Even at that age he encouraged me. So I'm in the ministry. The shock shocked me out of the old life into the new!"

Oliver Cromwell and John Hampden, utterly weary of the way the king and court and government were ruining the nation, slipped quietly on board ship to go to America. At the last moment a message came from the king that they were not to sail. Angry and frustrated, they came off the ship, their plans ruined. But that was the giving of the Puritan Movement to England!

O Christ, I thank Thee that in Thee everything is opportunity. That in Thee my lone top becomes a lyre and Thy fingers playing upon me make music vaster than before. Amen.

AFFIRMATION FOR THE DAY: *I belong to the incorrigible joy—when I cannot laugh "on account of," I laugh "in spite of"!*

STEPS OUT OF FRUSTRATION

Before we leave the matter of using sorrow and pain and frustration, let me give some steps to take from frustration to freedom.

1. *Fix it in your mind as an axiom that the righteous are not exempt from the ordinary laws that govern accidents, sickness, and death.* A plane full of non-Christian Indian seamen crashed into the Alps; a few days later, fifty-eight Christians fresh from the blessing of the Pope, crashed into the same Alps.

2. *The Christian answer lies along the line of using whatever comes*—justice or injustice, pleasure or pain, compliment or criticism.

3. *Expect strength from God to transform everything that comes into the central purposes for which you live.* Everything is grist to the Christian's mill. "You sold me; . . . God sent me" (Gen. 45:5, Moffatt), said Joseph to his brethren.

4. *Surrender the sorrow or frustration into God's hands—don't keep it bottled up within.* And don't try to deal with it yourself. You and God together can make something out of it.

5. *Now that God has it, look for something good to be rescued out of it.* That will turn your mentality from useless complaint to expectancy, from the negative to the positive.

6. *Thank Him for the good that is emerging, instead of brooding over the loss sustained.* The positive thanksgiving will make your heart receptive to God's power. He can do anything with a thankful heart, but He can do little or nothing for a complaining, self-pitying heart. It is closed to grace.

7. *Speak to others of the good you are finding, instead of the loss you have sustained.* Expression deepens impression. If you syndicate your blessings, they will grow and multiply.

8. *Find someone who has undergone a sorrow or loss too, and help them to your victory.* "Sorrow expands the soul for joy"—the joy of being useful and creative. He has pruned you for fruit bearing. Your tears have washed your eyesight clean. Now look for open doors to creativity.

O Jesus, I know that all my Calvaries can be Easter mornings. I knew that nothing can come that does not contribute. I am free to create everything into something better. Amen.

AFFIRMATION FOR THE DAY: *I have learned the long-sought-for power —the power to distil nectar out of poison.*

"WHAT ARE YOU DOING HERE?"

Many of us are not stricken with sorrow, dramatic sorrow, but with discouragement and inner defeat. We are like Elijah sitting "under a broom-brush, praying for death. 'I have had enough of it,' he cried; 'O Eternal, take away my life now, for I am mortal as my fathers were'" (I Kings 19:4, Moffatt). And God came to him in his discouragement and said, "What are you doing here, Elijah?" God comes to many of us, and seeing us discouraged and beaten, asks us the same question: "What are you doing here? You—a Christian—what are you doing here in defeat and discouragement?"

What had caused this collapse in Elijah? Everything was on the other side of the ledger—why was he in the red? The ravens had fed him; the widow's cruise and the barrel of meal had not failed; a child had died and he prayed him back to life; the fire had fallen upon his sacrifice at Mount Carmel as he prayed. Everything should have produced faith in this mighty man. But the threat of a woman—Jezebel—and he collapsed: "Elijah in terror rose and ran for his life."

Many of us can stand up under the big issues in the big crises, but we stumble and fall into discouragement over the little ones. Some Jezebel threatens us and down we go into the dumps.

There are many of us to whom the words of Eliphaz to Job could apply: "You have yourself set many right, and put strength into feeble souls; your words have kept men on their feet, the weak-kneed you have nerved. But now that your own turn has come, you droop; it touches you close, and you collapse" (Job 4:3-5, Moffatt). Ministers and Christian workers find words like these biting into their souls, for they apply.

Elijah's strong point was courage. In every situation he had shown amazing courage; why did he now sit under a juniper tree and want to die? It was because he was discouraged about himself: "I am not better than my fathers" (K.J.V.) He saw himself in terror running from a woman's threat. He was disgusted with himself. The root of most of our discouragements is discouragement with ourselves.

O Christ, save me from discouragement about myself. When I am sagging inwardly, hold me up there. Give me courage in the inward parts. Amen.

AFFIRMATION FOR THE DAY: *My courage is based on the solid fact that I have cosmic backing for my way of life in Christ.*

GETTING OUT OF THE DUMPS

We come today to see how God got Elijah out of the dumps. And maybe we can follow him out. Elijah felt he was alone: "I am the only one left, and they are after me, to take my life" (I Kings 19:10, Moffatt).

God struck at this sense of being alone in a very dramatic way. As Elijah stood in his cave near the entrance "a strong, fierce wind tore the mountain, crashing the rocks before the Eternal; but the Eternal was not in the wind. After the wind came an earthquake, but the Eternal was not in the earthquake; after the earthquake a fire, but the Eternal was not in the fire; after the fire the breath of a light whisper" (I Kings 19:11-12, Moffatt). And what was God saying through all this? Apparently this: He is not in the big windy, earth-shaking, fiery movements, but in the silent movements of truth—as silent as "the breath of a light whisper," or "a still small voice" (K.J.V.)—provided that voice is God's.

In other words, one man listening to the voice of God whispering in his heart, even if he is all alone, is more than a match for all the outer windy, earth-shaking, fiery movements opposed to him. God is with and behind the one who listens to and obeys the quiet voice of God within. That one man with God is a majority. The future belongs to him. The sum total of reality is behind him. He need be afraid of nothing. He walks the earth with quiet assurance—the assurance of the inner Voice.

In Mark 9, when the evil spirit cast the boy down, "most of them said, 'He is dead.'" If a majority vote had been taken, they would have decided he was dead—"most of them" voted for death. But Jesus, standing alone, voted for life. The boy arose. The truth was with the minority that decided with life.

No man is lonely if he stands alone with truth. He is lonely only if he stands alone, for and by himself. If he stands with truth, then he knows that the universe stands with him. The cure for loneliness is that you stand alone with the still small voice of Truth within.

O Christ, I thank Thee that Thou didst hang alone upon the cross—deserted. And yet that cross has become the center of the gaze of the ages. For there Thou didst have the still small voice within. Amen.

AFFIRMATION FOR THE DAY: *Thy still small voice within me reverberates through all things, and is the final Word.*

"UNBREAKABLY GIVEN TO EACH OTHER"

Our study of the last two days—standing alone with truth—leads us straight into another subject which is a necessary corrective. If we stand alone with truth, we are liable to become anti-social, self-righteous, and queer. The line is a very thin one and we must avoid stepping over it.

We must now pass to the study of the reason for Peter's downfall and collapse when he denied his Lord. Why did he do it? The usual explanation is that he "followed afar off"—the distance he put between himself and Jesus was responsible. But that could hardly account for such a disastrous loyalty collapse. The reason seems deeper. It is found, I believe, in the attitude he showed in the statement, "Supposing they are all disconcerted over you, I will never be disconcerted, never" (Matt. 26:33, Moffatt). It is found in the "they"—"I" attitude of Peter. Inwardly he pulled out of the fellowship and instead of being in a "we" relationship, he was in a "they"—"I" relationship. He was superior and aloof—self-righteous and critical. He broke with the fellowship and that automatically broke the fellowship with Jesus. The denial followed as effect from cause. He broke with the fellowship, and thereby broke with the center of that fellowship—Christ.

For the Christian demand is twofold: "Unreservedly given to God and unbreakably given to each other." A double surrender is inherent —to God and the fellowship. Many are ready to give themselves to God, but they are not ready to give themselves to the fellowship. For look what we are giving ourselves to—streaky, imperfect people! There we hesitate to let our weight down. So we stand off, superior and aloof.

I said to a missionary who was troubled over the appointment she was getting, "You trust God in this matter?" "Yes," she replied, "I can trust God, but I can't trust the bishop and the district superintendent." It is a big demand, isn't it, to trust the fellowship? And yet if we pull apart from that fellowship, we pull apart from Christ. If we deny the fellowship, we will soon, like Peter, deny Christ.

O Christ, give me grace not only to trust Thee but to trust the brotherhood—to trust it in spite of its weaknesses. For in that fellowship Thou art found in spite of its weaknesses. Help me. Amen.

AFFIRMATION FOR THE DAY: *If the fellowship can put up with me, I shall put up with it.*

"THEY"—"I" AND "WE"

We are studying the "they"—"I" and "we" relationship.

You see glimpses of this "we" relationship in the Old Testament. When Ezekiel was sent to speak to the captives by the river, the account says: "I went in bitterness, in the heat of my spirit; but the hand of the Lord was strong upon me" (Ezek. 3:14). He was going to blast them for their sins. It was a "they"—"I" relationship. Then God seemed to say: "Learn what they are going through," so "I sat where they sat, and remained there astonished among them seven days" (Ezek. 3:15). He "sat where they sat"—learned sympathy, changed from "they"—"I" to "we." At the end of seven days God let him speak, for then he spoke from a "we" relationship, and he spoke with power—deep speaking to deep. No one has a right to speak to others until he has earned that right by identification, by a "we" relationship.

The center of the Christian faith is a "we" relationship. Up to the New Testament the relationship of God with man was "I"—"they." God commanded; they obeyed. The relationship was through law. Then came the Incarnation. God literally sat where we sat. He identified Himself with man until at the cross that identification became complete—He became identified with our sins, "became sin for us." There the "I"—"they" merged into the "we"—completely. The relationship was not through law, but through Love.

Since the center of the Christian faith is a "we" relationship between God and man, it follows from its very nature that the relationships we have with each other must be "we" relationships. After Peter repented bitterly for his inner withdrawal, and surrendered to the coming of the Holy Spirit, we note the "we," "us," and "ours" in his language after Pentecost: "We can all bear witness" (Acts 2:32, Moffatt); "Why do you stare at us, as if we had made him walk by any piety or power of ours?" (Acts 3:12, Moffatt); "If we are being cross-examined" (Acts 4:9, Moffatt); "Certainly we cannot give up speaking of what we have seen" (Acts 4:20, Moffatt). He identified himself with the group—passed from a sub-Christian to a Christian relationship, to fellowship.

O Christ, I thank Thee that Thou hast said "We" to the utmost limit. Help me to say it too, with no reservations. Amen.

AFFIRMATION FOR THE DAY: *In my life the breadth of the word "we" determines the depth of the word "I."*

FROM A FEUD TO A FAMILY

We have come to the very center of our problems in the individual and in society and in world relationships. A psychologist says, "The disease of the world is the disease of the individual personality."

Since we are made for social relationships—"to be is to be in relations"—if a child or an adult assumes the "they"—"I" relationship, he turns queer, and if the withdrawal is sufficient, he turns psychopathic. Illusions of difference and grandeur are set up and he lives in a world of make-believe.

The "we" relationship is a fact—an inescapable fact. A boy who pumped the pipe organ by hand behind the scenes said to the organist after the service, "We played well today, didn't we?" And the organist in disdain said, "We? *I* played well." The next Sunday the organist sat down to play, pressed the keys, but nothing happened. The organist sat there nonplussed and helpless when a voice from behind the curtain said, "Is it *we* or *I?*" When the organist said "we" the music went on!

Nothing goes on till we say "we." The family is a feud if each member is saying "they"—"I."

The basic difficulty in industrial relationships is the "they"—"I" attitude of capital and labor. They are not facing the problem of production together. A labor-capital management and a division of the profits and losses would make industry pass from "they"—"I" to "we," and production would go straight up and relationships would turn from competition to co-operation. An official of the First National Bank of Chicago said to me: "Whenever we take over industries to finance them, we try to get them to put in profit sharing as a better business practice. It is enlightened self-interest. It works better. Production goes up and relationships straighten out." An industrialist said to me: "We put in profit sharing this week and you should see the difference in my factory. Everybody is interested in increasing production now." When the "they"—"I" relationship changed to the "we," then a new era began. Industry began to be a fellowship instead of a feud.

O Christ, Thou didst uncover the basic laws of our beings, the laws by which we must live or perish by strife. Help us to obey those laws and live and live fully. In Thy name. Amen.

AFFIRMATION FOR THE DAY: *If I refuse the "we," I shall soon not be able to tolerate the "I."*

THE "WE" IN RACE RELATIONS

We continue to look at the transformation from the "they"—"I" relationship to the "we" relationship.

This is at the basis of our race difficulties—we are trying to live on a "they"—"I" instead of a "we" relationship. We are prepared to be kind to other races, but not to be just. To be kind keeps up the "they" —"I" relationship—you're the brother bountiful and they are the recipients. To be just would put both on the same footing—set up a "we" relationship.

Even in Christian missions this "they"—"I" relationship is sometimes continued. In Africa at a tea party the white missionaries sat on one side and the Africans on the other. I couldn't stand this "they"— "I" business and went over and sat with the Africans. One of them said to me afterwards, "You're a white native, aren't you?" With a lump in my throat I replied, "I'd like to be." In an antireligious museum in Russia I saw the picture of a large mission house in Africa, and the grass huts of the natives around it. It stung. The "they"—"I" relationships are the soil in which communism grows. If we make the word "we" operative in all life, then there will be no toe hold for communism.

Peter had lingering traces of the "they"—"I" relationships even after Pentecost, for he said to the household of Cornelius: "It is illegal for a Jew to join or accost anyone belonging to another nation" (Acts 10:28, Moffatt). See how good I am in coming! There was patronage still in this area of his life—it was "they"—"I," not "we." Our "they" —"I" relationships take peculiar twists. Two women were on the train —one woman from California found she was to have a Japanese woman over her in the upper berth; the other woman from another section of the country found she was to have a Negro woman above her. They both objected to the conductor. The conductor changed the Negro and put her over the California woman and the Japanese over the other, and both were satisfied! The race problem is no longer a problem if we inwardly say "we" instead of "they"—"I." The problem then is not in race, but in our attitudes toward race.

O Christ, Thy way is our way. For if we go against Thy way, we get tangled up with ourselves and others. Amen.

AFFIRMATION FOR THE DAY: *When I meet a person of another race, I shall think "we" until I feel "we."*

"I CHOOSE FEDERAL UNION"

We must continue this week the transformation of our relationships from "they"—"I" to "we."

The churches in their present denominational setup are in a "they" —"I" relationship to one another. We co-operate with one another, but in the framework of "they"—"I" we have never said "we"; we have not come to union.

That union will come either as a union of uniformity or a union of diversity—a merger or a federal union. I choose federal union. A federal union of the churches would mean a union of the churches— an organic union but with a federal structure. The principal of federal union was applied to the colonies and states and produced an organic union—the United States of America, which can act as a single organism, for it is a single organism, but with a federal structure. When the people of the separate colonies said, *"We, the people,"* they passed from a "they"—"I" relationship to a "we" relationship. They became one nation. And a stable one. There is no example in history of a real federal union breaking up. It is the deepest and most lasting form of union, for it satisfies the two urges in human nature—the instinct for union with the whole, and the instinct for local autonomy or self-government. It puts them together in a living blend.

This is the kind of union Jesus prayed for: "May they all be one! As thou, Father, art in me and I in thee, so they may be in us—that the world may believe thou hast sent me" (John 17:21, Moffatt). He prayed that we may have a union like the union He had with the Father—an organic union, but with federal structure, for the Father and Jesus were one, but with distinctive names and personalities. The churches can get together tomorrow on that basis. It is the New Testament basis.

In some drinking fountains three jets of water converge at the place you drink—that is federal union. All three jets have one source, are passed through three channels, but converge at the place of availability. The world would drink of such a fountain!

O God, Thou art calling us to Thy kind of unity. Help us to pass from the "they"—"I" to the "we," Thy kind of "we"—not undifferentiated being, but the "we" of diversity in unity. Amen.

AFFIRMATION FOR THE DAY: *If I belong to Christ and another man belongs to Christ, then we belong to each other automatically.*

FREEDOM FROM WAR

We look at the final place where we are saying "they"—"I" instead of "we" in the international situation. Just what is wrong with us internationally? People don't want war. They hate it. This is true of people on both sides of the iron curtain—they want peace. But the political heads of the nations don't seem to be able to get together. Here is a world hating war, afraid of war, and yet drifting into war. Are we in the hands of a cruel fate, or is there something wrong with us and our attitudes?

Just what is wrong? isn't it found in the attitude of the nations saying "they"—"I" instead of "we"? The fact that we are divided into separate, independent, sovereign nation states makes for the "they"—"I," and yet all the time in reality our relations are "we." "We" have the same problems, the same needs, the same basic longings—"we" are one. And yet we are not acting as one, we are acting as "they"—"I."

The United Nations is an attempt to say "we," but basically each nation is still saying "they"—"I." Each has surrendered no sovereignty to the union. The "veto" is the symbol of a refusal to delegate sovereignty to the union. And the United States insisted on the "veto" like the rest. We are saying "they"—"I," and yet we are able to solve our problems only by saying "we." We are refusing to say "we." We are still adolescent as a race, insisting on our independence when we are not independent and can't be. We are interdependent by the very nature of things, and must be if we are to get out of our problems. We must grow up as a race, become mature. But we can become mature only by saying and meaning one word: "we." But if we said "we," we would come to world government. That is the only effective saying of "we," adequate to the world situation. Everything else is still saying "they"—"I." If we said "we," then we would be free—from war. The education of the human race is education in one word, and only one word—the word "we." When we learn that one word, we shall be mature as a race.

Gracious Father, Thou art trying to teach our trembling lips to say "we." We are hesitant and fearful lest we lose the "I," but we know that only as we lose it shall we find it again. Amen.

AFFIRMATION FOR THE DAY: *"No peace without justice, no justice without law, no law without government."*

EVERY RELATIONSHIP WOULD CLICK TOWARD SOLUTION

We spend another day gathering up the lessons learned in the "they"—"I" relationship. The law of life from the cell to the nation and on to God is that each entity must lose its life to find it again. "Whosoever will save his life shall lose it: and whosoever will lose his life . . . shall find it." That is as deeply engrained in the life of the universe as the law of gravitation. Each cell when it starts out is capable of being the whole organism, but on the way it decides not to be the whole organism, but instead surrenders itself to the organism, takes a differentiated portion, serves the rest, and finds itself in a fellowship. The law of life in the cell is self-surrender. If it breaks that law? It becomes a cancer. A cancer is a group of cells turned selfish—they will not serve the rest, they demand that the rest serve them. They save their lives and they lose them—they eat their way to their own death and to the death of the organism upon which they feed. When the cell loses its life, it is contributive; when it saves its life, it is cancerous.

If we could say "we" in every single human relationship, then all our problems would begin to click toward solution. Now they snarl toward greater snarls. The education of the human race is in trying to get it to say one word—"we." We learn the hard way. If we don't learn to say "we" in time then the words of Kaye Phelps will come true:

> Let not the atom bomb
> Be the final sequel
> In which all men
> Are cremated equal.

So we say "we" willingly or unwillingly—"we" all perish together. Says the Scripture: "Never may there be any root within your soil that bears such bitter poison!" (Deut. 29:18, Moffatt.) The root of our individual and corporate problems—a root that is bearing such bitter poison—is the refusal to say "we." We are trying to say "they"—"I" in a "we" world.

O God, our Father, Thy Son taught us to say, "Our Father, . . . give us," and we are saying, "My Father, . . . give me." And we are in trouble —deep trouble. Save us—we perish. Amen.

AFFIRMATION FOR THE DAY: *God says "we" in the Incarnation; I say "we" today in the extension of that Incarnation.*

EXPERIENCE AND EXPRESSION

We now turn to another application of the "we" relationship. Shall we say "we" in all other relations and not say it in our spiritual relations? Are we still to be "they"—"I" there? Is my spiritual life to be a kind of secret society between God and me? A solitary thing which I share with no one?

Often running through the contribution that each denomination has made to the collective good I have mentioned one that gave us "the warmed heart" and "the world parish"—experience and expression. Around these two phrases the problems of our spiritual life revolve. They are the two focuses of the ellipse of life.

If experience gets low, then expression gets low. If expression gets low, then experience gets low. They are Siamese twins, and if you cut them apart, both die.

The only way to kill a minister is to kill his experience of God. If that dies, then the effect of that central deadness spreads through his work. He is trying to make a stream run without a source, trying to produce an effect without a cause. So Paul said to the young minister, "Take heed to yourself and to your teaching" (I Tim. 4:16, R.S.V.). First "to yourself," then to "your teaching." For the "teaching" is determined by the self behind the teaching. Two people can say the same thing—one falls dead upon the soul, the other falls with kindling, converting power. One speaks out of words, the other out of an experience behind those words. So "yourself" is the first concern. Paul again says to the Ephesian elders, "Take heed to yourselves and to all the flock" (Acts 20:28, R.S.V.). First "to yourselves" and secondarily to "all the flock." The best thing a minister can give to the flock is himself—a self which is warm, living, contagious with God.

But if the experience is one of the problem points of our lives, expression is another problem point. For it is a law of the mind that that which is not expressed dies. The expression deepens the expression. These two things—experience and expression—must be kept intact.

O God, I know if either one of these two things becomes faint within me, I am a spiritual dud. Help me to keep both, and to keep them at their maximum. In Jesus' name. Amen.

AFFIRMATION FOR THE DAY: *Experience—the intake; and expression —the outgo, are going to be the alternate beats of my heart today.*

"LET THE HEARER TOO SAY 'COME'"

In our study of experience and expression we now turn to the expression side of our Christian lives. If that side is not transformed from a bottled-up, noncontagious type of an outflowing, contagious type, then the spiritual life is in a stalemate.

And the transformation is simpler than we suppose. Here was an ordinary layman, owner of a meat market, a spiritual clod until one day a verse awakened him, 'Come', say the Spirit and the Bride: let the hearer too say, 'Come'" (Rev. 22:17, Moffatt). He said to himself: "Why, I've been a hearer all my life and I've never said to anybody, 'Come.' I'm going to begin." He went to his pastor and said to him: "My business is in such a shape that I need only give about four hours a day to it. I'd like to give four hours to Christ and the church. Give me a job." "Well," said the pastor, "here is a list of the people who belong to this great church, but they don't come. See what you can do with them." He called on all of them, talked and prayed and won back a good many. Then he said, "Pastor, I've finished that job, give me another." "Well," said the pastor, "here is a list of the people in this city who ought to be Christians and are not; see what you can do with them." He finished that job, was given a list of the students in the university who had put themselves down as having no religious affiliation, and then when he finished that, he got from the chamber of commerce a list of people who had moved into the city in the last two years. That man who can't make a speech was responsible for five hundred people standing before the altars of that church each year for two years to be received into membership. Before he began this work he had a bad heart. He forgot all about his heart, and his heart settled down to normal. He was a surprise to himself.

A young couple who had been Christians only six months went out together and in one week won twenty-nine people to Christ. They too were a surprise to themselves. They discovered that the only way to do personal work is to just do it. The skill to do it comes from the will to do it. All God's commands are only God's enablings. He guides and He provides.

O God, I would have the channels open—they're clogged; help me to let Thy power through me to others. I'm willing. Thou art able. Amen.

AFFIRMATION FOR THE DAY: *I, who have been a "hearer," am now going to begin to say "Come."*

NOT PROSELYTISM, BUT CONVERSION

In order that we may be able to get guiding principles to help us to win others to the new life, we will look at the Master Worker as He dealt with an individual. Here He lifted up principles which are applicable for us today. In winning the Samaritan woman to the new life He lets us see how it is done. We will take the steps with Him.

1. This story is not one of proselytism, but of conversion—not a mere change of label, but a change of life. The account says: "Now when the Lord learned that the Pharisees had heard of Jesus gaining and baptizing more disciples than John, . . . he left Judaea and went back to Galilee" (John 4:1-3, Moffatt). He would be in no struggle for members—He left at high tide. So this account of the winning of the woman, and through her the village, was not in the setting of proselytism, but of conversion. The Christian convert in the New Testament is never called a proselyte—there were Jewish "proselytes," but no Christian proselytes. It was on a deeper level—the level of conversion, an inner change in life and character, and then, and only then, an outer change. Those of us who would hesitate to enter something on the level of a scramble for numbers are reassured here—this is deeper; it is conversion.

2. Again the account says, "He must needs go through Samaria" (John 4:4, K.J.V.). As He left Judea and went into Galilee, He must needs go through Samaria, for it lay between. He found His evangelistic opportunity in something that was inevitable. He evangelized the inevitable. Find your evangelistic opportunity in the inevitable contacts you have to have day by day. Evangelism isn't something imported into special weeks and special occasions—it must be the breath of the life.

A headmaster of a high school in India told me that he couldn't do evangelistic work since there were too many who came to his office every day. When I asked if the people who came to his office weren't people with problems and sins, and why couldn't he find his evangelistic opportunity there, he saw that he could evangelize the inevitable —and did.

O God, give me the alert heart and the responsive will to find my evangelistic opportunity everywhere in my daily contacts. Help me to make it a natural part of my natural contacts. Amen.

AFFIRMATION FOR THE DAY: *I have the will to evangelize, and now I'm on the lookout for the opportunity.*

FIND THE DOMINANT INTEREST

Yesterday we were studying how Jesus evangelized the inevitable. Here was a young business woman, who although a Christian only six months, found herself in a community that didn't go to church. So she evangelized that inevitable situation. She organized a group on "Abundant Living" in her home. No Christian could come who didn't bring a pagan—that was the admission ticket. They began with games, then went into a study and discussion of "Abundant Living," then more games and refreshments made an evening of it. Soon there were seventy-five present, and then each week they alternated with a high-school group—the young people wanted it! Within a short time twenty-six people had come into the church through that group. She evangelized an inevitable community situation.

3. How did Jesus open the conversation? He began at the Samaritan woman's dominant interest, and led her along the line of that dominant interest. He began at the thing she came for—water—and then went from water to "living water," and then to "a spring of water welling up to eternal life" (John 4:14, R.S.V.).

Find the dominant interest in the person and lead him along the line of that dominant interest. Those who know, say that the ripest evangelistic field in this country is the young married couple setting up a home and children coming. They are interested in the children being Christianized; then lead them through that dominant interest to make a committal themselves.

A friend told me of something I had forgotten, an incident that took place in a Kentucky town when I was a young evangelist before going to India. I stopped at the fence where a town drunk, the ne'er-do-well, was working in his garden, his one interest. I complimented him on his garden and then asked if he had gotten the weeds out of his own heart. It got him. He became a Christian and lived and died honored and respected. I happened upon his dominant interest—a garden—and led him along the line of that interest.

When you show an interest in what people are interested in, they will probably respond and be interested in what you are interested in.

O Christ, give me Thy skill and insight to see what people want, and to lead them from that want to what they ought to want. Amen.

AFFIRMATION FOR THE DAY: *If I show an interest in people's interests, they may show an interest in my interest—Christ.*

RAISE THE HIGHER ISSUE

We must continue this week our study of how Jesus led the Samaritan woman into being a transformed person.

4. When Jesus found the dominant motive and opened the conversation at that point, the woman reacted by putting up a barrier, "How is it that you, a Jew, ask a drink of me, a woman of Samaria?" (John 4:9, R.S.V.) The first reaction was to put up a barrier. That is the usual reaction: we don't let into the inner life any stranger—not easily. There is an instinct of self-protection against intrusion.

Many workers stop right there. They meet this initial rebuff or hesitation and they conclude it is of no use to go farther. Many of the casualties in personal work are right there in front of that barrier. They give up too soon. They should hang around until the second instinct begins to operate. For if the first instinct is to shut people out, the second instinct is to disclose the inner life if there is someone who is sympathetic and understanding. For people have a strong urge within to tell someone of what is troubling them within. They feel the push of these bottled-up difficulties toward expression. They feel that to disclose them might be to dissolve them.

5. How did Jesus get rid of the clash between Jew and Samaritan? He did it by a simple technique which He used all the way through the conversation—He raised a higher issue: "If thou knewest the gift of God, and who it is that saith unto thee, Give me to drink, thou wouldst have asked of him, and he would have given thee living water" (John 4:10, K.J.V.). He raised the higher issue of "the gift of God"—"living water," and when she got her imagination on that "living water," she forgot all about the Jew-Samaritan clash and it simply faded out. Fix that as a principle in a guided conversation: Don't pick up subordinate issues and debate them; you'll get tangled in the little. Raise the higher issue, and the lesser issue will fade out. Drive toward your goals, not theirs.

O God, give me wisdom and insight and help me to lovingly guide toward Thy goals. Make me to be too big to be tangled in little issues when big ones await us. Amen.

AFFIRMATION FOR THE DAY: *"In it [the new nature] there is no room for Greek and Jew, circumcised and uncircumcised, barbarian, Scythian, slave, or free man"* (Col. 3:11, Moffatt).

FINDING THE GOOD IN THE EVIL

We continue our study of the steps into the transformation of a very needy soul.

6. Jesus saw the good in the woman and appealed to it: "If thou knewest the gift of God, . . . thou wouldst have asked" (John 4:10 K.J.V.). In other words, Jesus was saying," If you see the good, you'll want it." Now I suppose everybody else had been saying to that woman, "When you see the bad, you'll want it." And she did. Jesus believes in people when they can't believe in themselves. So they have faith in His faith in them. Paul says, "I live by the faith of the Son of God" (Gal. 2:20, K.J.V.)—one would have thought it was "faith *in* the Son of God," but it is "of." The faith that Jesus had in Paul made him respond with faith in Him. Jesus faiths faith out of the faithless, believes belief out of the beliefless, and loves love out of the loveless. We must have faith in people if we are to influence them. Those who believe in us most influence us most. If we become cynical about people, we become powerless to help people.

"You have expected me into all this," said a very radiant soul who was accomplishing things and going places. But we can keep our faith in people only as we keep our faith in God. For you cannot long believe in man unless you believe in something more than man—something that gives him ultimate meaning and value in spite of his capacity to blunder and sin. If the root—faith in God—withers, the fruit—faith in man—will wither too.

7. The woman was ready for another controversy: "Art thou greater than our father Jacob?" (John 4:12, K.J.V.)—a Jesus-Jacob controversy. Jesus might have said, "Your father Jacob was a scheming liar who stole his brother's birthright." This would have been true, but Jesus would have won His argument and lost the woman. How did Jesus get rid of Jacob? He raised a higher issue, "A well of water springing up into everlasting life" (John 4:14, K.J.V.). She got her eyes on that and Jacob slides out of the picture forgotten.

O God, my Father, help me to help people tangled in little things and controversies to the things that really matter. Help me to be big and lift people to the big. In Jesus' name. Amen.

AFFIRMATION FOR THE DAY: *I will love love out of the loveless, and believe belief out of the beliefless.*

MIXED MOTIVES

Jesus got rid of the Jesus-Jacob controversy by raising a higher issue: a fountain of living water in the heart.

8. Jesus gave His highest teaching to the lowest. This statement "Whosoever drinketh of this water shall thirst again: but whosoever drinketh of the water that I shall give him shall never thirst; but the water that I shall give him shall be in him a well of water springing up into everlasting life" (John 4:13-14, K.J.V.), is one of the most spiritual things He ever uttered, and He uttered it to an outcaste woman. He believed she could take it—and she did!

9. In this statement is something important: "The water that I shall give him shall be in him a well"—the water I shall give from without shall produce a well within. My gift will produce spontaneity. It is difficult to give to people without producing weakness and parasitism. But Jesus gives and the gift becomes a well within. He is the strong Man creating strong men around Him. He is not like a giant oak creating weak saplings around it, because the oak smothers the saplings—His gifts create the spirit of self-reliance and countergiving. That is a miracle of giving.

10. The woman had a new thirst created within her—the thirst for "eternal life." The thirst for physical satisfaction had dominated her life, but now a new thirst began to take hold of her. She therefore said plaintively, "Sir, give me this water, that I thirst not, neither come hither to draw" (John 4:15, K.J.V.). Moffatt translates "sir" as "Ah, sir"—a new craving beginning to well up within, created by contact with Jesus.

But it was still a mixed motive—she wanted this well within the heart and she also wanted to be saved the trouble of coming the mile from the village to draw the water. Her motives were still badly mixed. I think I would have been tempted to dismiss her at that point, telling her that her motives were too mixed. But Jesus takes us as we are, mixed motives and all. He undertook to purify her and her motives.

O God, I'm so grateful that Thou dost not give me up when my motives are mixed. Thou seest that there is a central core of longing for Thee amid the mixture. Cleanse me and my motives. Amen.

AFFIRMATION FOR THE DAY: *I shall not be a man of mixed motives dealing with people with more mixed motives.*

FACING THE MORAL ISSUES

11. In our study of Jesus leading the Samaritan woman to transformation we come now to the moral crux of the process. In every life there is a moral problem which becomes the decision point from which we swing toward darkness or toward light—toward spiritual malformation or spiritual transformation.

If that central moral issue is slurred over or blurred, then the process of transformation is blocked. If faced courageously, then the process and power of redemption is at our disposal. A prominent minister was held up at this point in his seeking to find inner release. Would he act as though the moral lapse had not happened and try to forget it, or would he bring up the whole thing and face it? He faced it, and this Samaritan woman's case gave him the inner push that sent him to peace and victory. You cannot build spirituality on immortality.

How did Jesus get to the moral problem without seeming to invade sanctities? He might have said bluntly, "Woman, you are living a bad, adulterous life," which would have been true; but He would have won his argument and lost the woman. He pointed out her moral need in a very delicate way, "Go, call thy husband, and come hither." When He mentioned the word "husband," a flush must have gone across her face, her eyes dropped, and she looked confused and ashamed. She managed to say limply, "I have no husband." And then Jesus opened the wound to its depths in order to get the whole festering thing up and out: "Thou hast well said, I have no husband: for thou hast had five husbands; and he whom thou now hast is not thy husband: in that saidst thou truly" (John 4:17-18, K.J.V.). He said at the beginning and at the end of his probing, "You are telling the truth"—recognizing the good in her at the very moment of touching the terribly sore depths. Then the woman was face to face with herself and face to face with what she could be if she followed the light dawning upon her darkened depths through this Man. Man had been her weakness— this Man was becoming her strength. She had met a new type of Manhood and she wanted to be like Him.

O Christ, when we stand face to face with ourselves and with Thee, then we stand face to face with destiny. Help us to let Thee decide that destiny. Amen.

AFFIRMATION FOR THE DAY: *I shall see people today not only for what they are, but for what they may be.*

RELIGIOUS BUT ROTTEN

12. When Jesus laid bare the inner moral life of the Samaritan woman, her reaction was the one that many try to take—she attempted to dodge the moral issue by raising a religious issue: "Sir, I perceive that thou art a prophet. Our fathers worshipped in this mountain; and ye say, that in Jerusalem is the place where men ought to worship" (John 4:19-20, K.J.V.). She felt very uncomfortable in discussing her moral life, and so she tried to take Him off the subject by raising a religious issue—"this mountain" or "Jerusalem" as the place to worship. This was a red herring across the trail—it was much more comfortable to discuss an abstract religious question than to face a moral situation.

How did Jesus get rid of the "Jerusalem"—"this mountain" issue? He did it in the same way He got rid of the other issues—He raised a higher issue: "God is a Spirit" (John 4:24, K.J.V.) and if so, then "Jerusalem" as a place to worship is nothing, and "this mountain" is nothing. For in that case, "They that worship him must worship him in spirit and in truth." The statement "in spirit" lifted the whole thing out of designated places, and "in truth" put it right back at the moral issue—"You must worship Him by a life of truth." They were back again where they left off—at her moral condition.

13. The woman replied, "I know that Messiah is coming. . . . When he comes, he will show us all things" (John 4:25, R.S.V.). The woman was apparently a religious woman, wanting to know which is the place to worship, and interested in the coming of the Messiah. Is it possible to be very religious and very rotten? Yes. Many people cannot in unless they sin religiously. They cannot get the consent of themselves unless they sin with a religious frontage.

14. The end of the whole conversation was in this reply of Jesus, "I that speak unto thee am he." The end of the whole conversation was a revelation of who Jesus was. That is the end of our dealing with people—not to win an argument, but to get people to see Jesus as Lord and Savior. If we don't get there, then we don't get anywhere. For all questions are settled at this place.

O God, help me to help people to see past the little issues to the real issue—Thy Son. Help me not to win arguments, but to win people. Amen.

AFFIRMATION FOR THE DAY: *The end of good advertising is not to point to the advertising, but to the thing advertised.*

NOT IN TILL THEY GO OUT

We saw yesterday that the end of the whole conversation was to see who Jesus was, but we must modify that.

15. The end of the conversation is in this verse, "The woman then left her waterpot, and went her way into the city, and saith to the men, Come see a man who told me all things that ever I did" (John 4:28-29, K.J.V.). And when the men heard that, they must have raised their eyebrows and looked at one another as much as to say, "Well, if somebody told that woman everything she ever did, then he told her plenty." And yet when they looked again, they saw that something had happened to her—she was a changed woman, and they soon found themselves following her out of the city to see Jesus. The end of the conversation was to produce an evangelist. The end of evangelism is to produce an evangelist. You haven't got them in until you get them out. For it is a law of the mind that that which is not expressed dies.

16. In the meantime the disciples came back, and when they saw Him in such an exalted state, and that He was in no mood to eat, they urged Him to eat and He replied, "I have meat to eat that ye know not of. . . . My meat is to do the will of him that sent me" (John 4:32, 34, K.J.V.). He who came to found a world order—the Kingdom of God—felt that He was being fed by talking to one lone needy woman. He was great enough to think in world terms and great enough to think in terms of one human soul.

17. He turned to His disciples and said, "You have a saying, have you not, 'Four months yet, then harvest'?" (John 4:35, Moffatt.) It was a saying of procrastination—why be excited: "Four months yet, then harvest." That attitude of procrastination regarding winning people to Christ is still with us—the little pushes out the big, the irrelevant pushes out the relevant. "Four months yet, then harvest—wait till the ingathering at Easter time!" And all the time Jesus is replying, "Lift up your eyes, and look on the fields; for they are white already to harvest" (John 4:35, K.J.V.). Never was this more true than now.

Gracious Father, I know that all our old ways are breaking down. Only Thy way will work. Give me courage to go out and reap. Amen.

AFFIRMATION FOR THE DAY: *No more four-months-attitude for me— go forth to reap.*

272

REASONS AGAINST AND FOR

We come now to the closing moments of the winning of a woman and a whole village through her.

18. The Samaritans came, and when they saw Him, they saw that while He was born a Jew, He had transcended this and belonged to everybody, so they asked Him to stay with them—an unheard of request. But He was different. At the end of the two-day stay the Samaritans said, "We no longer believe on account of what you said; we have heard for ourselves, we know that he is really the Savior of the world" (John 4:42, Moffatt).

Now note the steps she and they went through in their views of who He was: (a) No title: "How is it that thou . . . ?" (b) By contact her respect grew: "Sir, thou hast nothing to draw with"—the title, "Sir." (c) A little further contact and she says: "Sir, I perceive that thou art a prophet"—the title "prophet." (d) A further stay and she said: "Is not this the Christ?"—the title "Christ." (e) Two days with them and they said: "The Savior of the world." Note the steps: Thou, Sir, Prophet, Christ, Savior of the world. No one can stay near Jesus and not have his respect grow until, if he is like me, he will find himself bending his knee and saying, "My Lord, and my God."

19. Now there were a number of reasons why Jesus should not have spoken to the woman: (a) She was a woman. (b) She was a woman, alone. (c) She was a bad woman, alone. (d) She was a Samaritan. (e) She came from Sychar, which literally means "drunken," taken from the character of the inhabitants. "What can you do with a drunken lot?" (f) He was tired: "being wearied with his journey." (g) It was noon, and probably hot. Seven good reasons why He should not have spoken to her. Can you always find good reasons for not speaking to people? Yes! But there were two reasons why He should have spoken—(a) her need and (b) God's will—"the will of Him who sent me." Those two factors persist and were never so valid as today. God wills it—man needs it. That "will" is for everybody—and that need is in everybody. Keep saying that to yourself: "God wills it. Man needs it. I will do it."

O God, Thy will and man's need coincide. Help me to be the instrument of that will and the supplier of that need. Help me to be the hands of Thy redemption. Amen.

AFFIRMATION FOR THE DAY: *God wills it. Man needs it. I will do it.*

"THE ORGAN OF SPIRITUAL TOUCH"

We have been studying how to be spiritually contagious. If we are to have enough and to spare, then we must be sure to provide for replenishing our inner resources. This is done in the Quiet Time.

Those who do not provide for a Quite Time, preferably in the morning, do provide for an unquiet time throughout the day. If you are too busy to have a Quiet Time, you are too busy. The probabilities are that you will have to take time off during, or at the end of, the day for regret, for repentance, for eating humble pie, for realizing a sense of frustration and emptiness, for futility.

A diver who would be too busy to think about getting his pipe line for air in working order before he descends to the depths, would be no more foolish than the man who descends into the stifling atmosphere of today's life without getting his breathing apparatus of prayer connected with the pure air of the Kingdom of God above. If we grow anemic and pale, it is because we have done ourselves this harm—the harm of self-inflicted asphyxiation. The poet says:

> What a frail soul he gave me, and a heart
> Lame, and unlikely for the large events.

But I wonder if more often we haven't given ourselves "a heart lame, and unlikely for the large events." God has offered us infinite resources—for the asking and the taking. And the Quiet Time is where the soul grows receptive, where prayer becomes "the organ of spiritual touch"; where that touch becomes as effective and as healing as the touch of the woman upon the hem of His garment; where Peace flows into our unpeace, where Power floods our impotence, where Love absorbs our resentments, and where Joy heals our griefs, where the cross takes away our sins and buries them in the love of God. The Quiet Time creates an isle of quiet within, and that becomes the atmosphere for the day.

"Arnica is good for bruised flesh, silence is good for a bruised soul." It "Knits up the ravell'd sleave of care." The Quiet Time is quieting and quickening. There the soul becomes at its best.

Gracious Father, give me the sense to keep my balance in an unbalanced world; to keep my peace in an unquiet earth. Amen.

AFFIRMATION FOR THE DAY: *The Quiet Time in me becomes the quiet heart, which becomes the quiet confidence, which becomes quiet power.*

"YOU EAT THE BOOK"

We are looking at the transformation the Quiet Time brings to people whenever it is tried.

In Assam there is a legend among the Khasi people that God gave them a book. When the flood came, the people ate the book so it would not be lost. So the book became a part of them—got into their blood. When Christianity came, the book turned out to be the Book. It's only a legend, but that is fulfilled in every person who keeps the Quiet Time. You eat the Book. It gets into your blood—becomes a part of you. And when the flood of everyday worries or of special griefs and sorrows overflows you, the Book is there intact—within you.

One morning I arose at three o'clock, walked to a mountain peak in The Himalaya to see the sun rise on the most glorious panorama, I suppose, in the world. There as day began to dawn, we saw arise before our enraptured gaze, within a complete semicircle, twenty peaks, each above twenty thousand feet in height, snow-capped with virgin snow. For half an hour the curtain was lifted and we inwardly worshiped. Then the mists began to fill the valleys between, and the view was gone. Gone? Forever laid up in our green and grateful memories. It was ours forever. That is what the Quiet Time does for you. You get up earlier before the mists of worldly happenings close your view of God, and there you take a time exposure to God. It is printed indelibly upon you. After the mists close in, the vision is there within. You live in two worlds at once. You are a two-dimension person, drawing sustenance from a world around you to keep you going physically, and then drawing sustenance from God to keep you going spiritually, mentally, physically—totally.

From the faraway Himalaya to come back to the near at hand: my pen with its cap off was dry at the point and wouldn't write. I put the cap on for a few minutes and it began to run again. When my soul is dry and noncontagious, I shut it up in the Quiet Time and lo, it begins to flow again. To be shut in with God means to be outflowing to men.

O Father God, I thank Thee that my resources are so near at hand. I drop into the shrine of my heart, and there my weakness is absorbed into Thy strength, my all into Thy all. I thank Thee. Amen.

AFFIRMATION FOR THE DAY: *I go to the Quiet Time how weak—I rise how strong! I go how ignorant—I rise how wise!*

THE BUBBLING FROM BENEATH

We continue to meditate upon the Quiet Time. Our ship moved into one of the locks in the Panama Canal. The great sea gates were closed upon us. We, who had sailed the oceans, were blocked, shut in, helpless, our freedom gone. But lo, we felt a lifting, great fountains were opened from beneath, and to our astonishment that great ship was lifted thirty-five feet in just seven minutes. Then the gates opened and we glided out on a higher level, out on the bosom of Lake Gatun.

The Quiet Time does that—it shuts you in with God, the door closes upon you, and you seem so shut-in, so not-doing-anything, so helpless. And then, infinite resources begin to bubble up from within, you are lifted so silently and so powerfully, without noise or strain, onto a higher level. The door opens and you glide out on a higher level of life. You wonder at yourself—and people wonder too—how easily you transcend worries and fears and resentments and live life in general on a higher level. It's the result of being shut in with God.

William R. Inge reminds us: "It is quite natural and inevitable that if we spend sixteen hours daily of our waking life in thinking about the affairs of the world, and five minutes in thinking about God, . . . this world will seem two hundred times more real to us than God."

Pascal once declared that "nearly all the ills of life spring from this simple source, that we are not able to sit still in a room." But what if in that stillness we meet with God—how healing that would be! There all our fears would be hushed in the quiet of God. Isaiah puts it thus, "We have been waiting for thee; be our strong arm, morn after morn, deliver us, all forlorn" (Isa. 33:2, Moffatt). When we, "all forlorn," meet with Him "morn after morn"—then indeed He becomes "our strong arm," our strong Everything. We arise with what Stevenson calls "happy morning faces." We become children of the dawn. As Ruskin says, "We are converted, not to long and gloomy faces, but to round and laughing ones." The Quiet Time is the turntable from one to the other. For in the Quiet Time listening turns to longing, and longing turns to laughter.

O Christ, help me to do what Thou didst do. Give me the strength to take "the pause that refreshes," to drink from a living Fountain, an eternal Spring. Then I shall never thirst. Amen.

AFFIRMATION FOR THE DAY: *The Quiet Time is the turning of the dial till we get God's wave length—then the messages!*

TO MAKE THE QUIET TIME EFFECTIVE

We must look at certain suggestions to make the Quiet Time effective. Wesley gave us a clear-cut measuring rod for testing the reality of our spiritual lives: "(a) Do you pray always? (b) Do you rejoice in God every moment? (c) Do you in everything give thanks—in loss, in pain, in sickness, in weariness, disappointment? (d) Do you desire nothing? (e) Do you fear nothing? (f) Do you feel the love of God continually in your heart? (g) Have you a witness in whatever you speak or do, that it is pleasing to God?" These words search the life relentlessly—the first especially: "Do you pray always?"

If you are to pray always, there must be a specific time for the cultivation of such a spirit of continuous prayer. You cannot pray everywhere unless you pray somewhere. You cannot maintain the spirit of prayer unless you take off specific time or times for prayer. It will fade out. So take these steps:

1. Decide on the amount of time you can give to the Quiet Time, preferably in the morning. The morning is the best—it tunes your instrument for the day.

2. Having fixed the time, stick to it. Pray by the clock, whether or not you feel like it.

3. Take your Bible and read a portion slowly. Let it soak in. If some verse strikes you, let your mind circle around it in meditation. It will render up new meanings to you. Write them in a notebook or on the margin of your Bible.

4. After the reading, let go and relax and say to Him, "Father, have you anything to say to me?" Begin to listen. Become guidable.

5. Then you say to God what you have to say. Prayer is dialogue, not a monologue.

6. Thank Him for the answer. He always answers "Yes" or "No." "No" is an answer as well as "Yes"—sometimes a better answer. The answer sometimes may be in you—you are better for having prayed—you are the answer. In the Quiet Time you become the focal point of transmission for transformation.

Father, help me to come to the Quiet Time with quiet expectancy—expectancy that here my weakness shall become strong, my doubt become faith, my sin become redemption, and I shall be the instrument of Thy peace. Amen.

AFFIRMATION FOR THE DAY: *I fix my habits and then they fix me.*

"A LAMP UNTO OUR FEET"

As we have been meditating on how to get the most out of the Quiet Time we are led to the further question of how we may get the most out of the Bible. For the Bible should be at the very center of our Quiet Time.

I know of a devoted Christian who comes to the Quiet Time without a Bible, just sits in meditation. He thinks he can get to God direct. But does he? He gets to God through the medium of his own conceptions of God. His conceptions are the medium. His conceptions are man's thoughts of God. But the New Testament is God's revelation of Himself. Unless our thoughts are constantly corrected by God's thoughts, our thoughts go off on tangents or mull around on themselves. So my friend is an unstable Christian. He is subject to his own moods. He is bosom-centered instead of Bible-centered, hence moody.

I look into my own heart to see what I am. I look into the Bible to see what I ought to be and can be. As Cardinal Newman said, "I read my Bible to know what people ought to do and any newspaper to know what they are doing." So we have a generation of newspaper-minded people instead of Bible-minded people—one shallow and flighty, the other deep and steady.

Bishop Paul Kern gives these reasons why he reads his Bible: "I read my Bible because (a) within its pages I find power for the ordering of my inner life; (b) it offers a way of escape from those perils which threaten our modern life; (c) in its pages are found the secret by which men walk the pathways of light and hope and freedom; (d) it assures me that man is supremely dear to God; (e) it points the way to world brotherhood; (f) it tells me whither I am bound and why; (g) it offers me sound social philosophy; (h) it teaches me, in the words of Emerson, that the lesson of life is to believe what the years and the centuries say, as against the hours."

Horace Greeley once said, "It is impossible to mentally or socially enslave a Bible-reading people." To start the day without the Bible is like a captain starting on a sea voyage without compass or map.

O God, the entrance of Thy Word giveth light, and the neglecting of Thy Word giveth darkness. Help me to take Thy light as my light; then shall I walk with sure and steady tread. Amen.

AFFIRMATION FOR THE DAY: *When I begin to obey, then the Bible turns from a book to The Book.*

THE INEXHAUSTIBLE BOOK

Some come to the Bible as a book of magic, out of which they pick magic formulas and magic facts. A man told me with evident exultation that he had found the United Nations referred to in Ezekiel.

The Bible is not a magic revelation, but a moral revelation. It uncovers progressively the nature of God as men were able to understand it. Then the final and perfect revelation of the nature of God in Jesus. The Incarnation is the revelation. Everything else is marginal; this is central. Miss this and you miss the focal point of revelation. Where the emphasis is weak on the Incarnation, the sense of revelation is weak, and then people go off into revelations. They "discover Christ within themselves," which turns out to be a Christ of their own creation. The lineaments of Jesus fade out, and a Christ of sentimentalism takes His place. Then the description of philosophers applies:

> They sail away on a sea of mist
> To a land that doesn't exist.

But if the Incarnation is the center, the circumference is everywhere. For if the revelation is fixed, nevertheless it is unfolding. As Pastor Robinson said to the Pilgrims: "Much light will yet break out from the word of God," especially if the "word of God" is the Word of God—"the Word made flesh." The account says "revealing himself to them for forty days" (Acts 1:3, Moffatt)—not merely a physical revealing, but a revealing of His spirit and purpose and meaning. He has been revealing Himself ever since. And the meanings are inexhaustile. He is the Great-I-Am, and the Great-To-Be.

I expect my devotional books to be exhausted of meaning in a couple of years—hence the new ones. But you never exhaust the meanings in Jesus. He is described, "Thanks to the tender mercies of our God, who will cause the Dawn to visit us from on high" (Luke 1:78, Moffatt). He who lives in Jesus is living in a perpetual Dawn. A surprise is around every corner. Life pops with novelty, with the cracking of horizons. "By all the stimulus of Christ" (Phil. 2:1, Moffatt) cries the tingling Paul—tingling with anticipation at the opening vistas and surprises.

O Christ, Thou art there in the Book, Thou are here in my bosom, Thou art yonder beyond my burial. I live because Thou dost live. Amen.

AFFIRMATION FOR THE DAY: *I read other books to get light; I read The Book to get Light and Life.*

STEPS TO GET MOST OUT OF THE BOOK

When Jesus stood up in the synagogue at Nazareth and read the passage from Isaiah the account says: "Then, folding up the book, . . . he proceeded to tell them that 'Today, this scripture is fulfilled in your hearing'" (Luke 4:20-21, Moffatt). Revelation passed at that moment from a law to a Life—from a book to a Person. Now the Person gives meaning to the Book.

In order to get the most out of the Book take these steps: (1) *Come to the Word expectantly.* This Book is alive with meanings. "For the word of God is living and active" (Heb. 4:12, R.S.V.). Expect it to speak and it will. Faith is expectancy—according to your expectancy, be it unto you.

(2) *Come surrendering to the truths here revealed.* "He that is willing to do shall know." In a moral universe the key to knowledge is moral response. The moment we cease to obey, that moment the Revelation ceases to reveal.

(3) *Come expecting to use the truths here revealed.* Not only receive the truths revealed, but make yourself the channel of those truths to others. Nothing will come in that can't get out.

(4) *Come unhurriedly.* If you stalk through a forest, you will probably see and hear little. But sit down and the squirrels will come out, the birds draw near, and everything will speak to you since you are quiet and receptive. Get quiet and receptive and the Word will become alive with meaning.

(5) *Come with a proper emphasis.* Since the Old Testament is not Christianity, but a period of preparation for Christianity—Christianity is Christ—then spend about one fourth of your reading time in the Old Testament and three fourths in the New. Otherwise you'll be an Old Testament Christian, which means that you'll be sub-Christian.

(6) *Come to it even if nothing apparently comes from your coming.* The very fact that you have exposed yourself to the Word is infinitely worth while. For where Love is, silence may be the only language. To be with Him, though unseen and unheard, is the reward.

O God, I thank Thee that "Thy Word is a lamp unto my feet." I shall not walk in darkness if I follow its light. Amen.

AFFIRMATION FOR THE DAY: *The Bible redirects my will, cleanses my emotions, enlightens my mind, and quickens my total being.*

THE TRANSFORMATION OF THE MATERIAL

We come now in our meditations to the transformation of the material. When we face the material, we face this sharp issue: Either we will transform the material into the image of the spiritual, or the material will transform us into its own image.

Some allow the material to get the upper hand. They begin to serve Mammon. Then they begin to look like their god. They become materialized. The light dies out of their eyes. They were born a living soul and become only living flesh. They can repeat the words of Edna St. Vincent Millay:

> I cannot say what loves have come and gone,
> I only know that summer sang in me
> A little while, and in me sings no more.

The winter of materialization sets in. And that is a very frosty winter. Two corpulent people, a man and his wife, who by their querulous attitudes at the table were evidently frustrated and unhappy, sat in the lounge on board ship staring vacantly, doing nothing but staring, when one of them got up and walked to a vase on the mantel, looked in it, came back to his wife and said, "It's empty." My inward comment was, "Yes, it's empty; and so are you." They had nothing, absolutely nothing but money. Actually, money had them.

The story goes of a leopard who was shot and his skin made into a coat and hung in a shopwindow with a price mark of $1,200. The rest of the family of leopards, out walking, stopped at the window and recognized the skin of their father. The comment was, "He was better off when he wasn't worth so much." As least he was alive! Many find an inner deadness as a result of making acquisition their god. They acquired at the cost of inward decay. They acted as if they owned their wealth, and found in dismay that their wealth owned them. "I've learned how to make money, but I've not yet learned how to live," said a very sadly disillusioned multimillionaire who could see no open door but suicide. And entered in. He couldn't live with a materialized soul.

O God, Thou hast made us in Thy image, and we cannot live if we try to live in the image of the material. Save us from trying. Amen.

AFFIRMATION FOR THE DAY: *Since the center of my faith is in the Word become flesh, now my flesh and my material possessions must become word.*

HOW MUCH CAN I KEEP FOR MYSELF?

Now how can we head off this hardening, not of our arteries, but of our inmost souls? How can we keep things from getting us?

We turn to the one note we have to strike again and again—the note of surrender. We turn to it, for it is the turntable on which life turns from materialization to spiritualization. The material must be surrendered to God or we will surrender to the material. When God has the material, then we climb on top of it; but if we have it, then we are under it—it has us.

The real question then for us to ask is this: Who owns my possessions, God or I? Whether we acknowledge it or not, we do not in reality own our possessions. We are only in possession of our possessions for a brief period. A prominent minister was invited by a rich farmer after a service to his house for dinner. He took him to the top of a hill and waved his hand toward the beautiful broad acres stretched before them and said, "You said this morning I don't own anything. If I don't own these acres, who does?" The minister slowly replied, "Ask me that question a hundred years from now."

If in reality we don't own our possessions, then the obvious thing to do is to have sense and say to God: "I'm not owner; I'm only ower. Teach me how to work out that relationship."

He has taught us. The giving of the tithe, one tenth of all we earn, is an acknowledgment of the ownership of God over the nine tenths. Just as we pay rent to acknowledge the ownership of the owner of the house, so we pay a tithe to acknowledge that God is owner and we are only owers, and that nine tenths belong to Him.

When we give the one tenth, we are not really giving—we are only paying an obligation. When we give out of the nine tenths, only then are we giving. A businessman put it wisely: "I've prospered. Now I want to know how much of God's money I can keep for myself." That is the right order: "How much of God's money can I keep for myself?" For everything I needlessly spend for myself is taken from some other person's need. I physically hurt him and morally hurt myself. When I help to meet his need through my surpluses, then I help him physically and myself morally.

O God, Thou hast Thy finger on a nerve center. Help me not to wince. For here the issues of life and death are found. Amen.

AFFIRMATION FOR THE DAY: *Since I belong to God, all I have belongs to God—it's at His disposal.*

"I NEVER CALLED HER MINE"

Holding our possessions at God's disposal does something more than settling a money issue. It settles a life attitude. You are then a man under orders, a man with a sense of mission, a sense of direction and goal.

When you let go of your possessions and let God have them, then life takes on a sense of stewardship. You are handling something in behalf of Another. That does something to the whole of life—puts sacredness into the secular; lifts the sordid into the sacred. Then the Word becomes flesh—and the flesh becomes word. Money becomes a message. When the pastor of the Chicago Temple used to call the collection "an offering of minted personality," he was right. When given to God, it is just as sacred as the words that fall from dedicated lips in the pulpit. Both speak the same message—and equally.

Mammon, then, can become a master or a message. If unsurrendered to God, it is master—and what a master! It drives the driven and lashes the tired. At sixty-five there are twice as many women alive as men. The verdict is "high blood pressure," but it should be "high blood-money pressure." For the money drives men mad or to the mortuary. But if surrendered to God, it can become a beautiful thing.

One of the most beautiful loves ever witnessed was that between George Herbert Palmer and his wife, Alice Freeman Palmer, president of Wellesley College. He said of her, "I never called her mine." Ralph Sockman commented: "He was a trustee of her interests, not a possessor. And as a result, he received a love so rich that it beggared description." When he surrendered her to God, then God gave her back to him—the relationship made sacred and beautiful. That can happen to possessions. When held as a trust, then they bless the trustee and the recipient. Brother Lawrence puts it this way: "Sanctification is not changing your work, but in doing everything which you have done for yourself for the glory of God." Surrender of your possessions to God makes them sanctified and sanctifying. Your Christianity functions in and through the material.

O God, Thou art teaching me how to use Thy entrustments to me. Help me to be a faithful steward of Thy entrustments. Amen.

AFFIRMATION FOR THE DAY: *If I am faithful in material power, God will entrust to me spiritual power.*

MAKING MONEY FOR GOD

Jesus, in sixteen out of the thirty-eight recorded parables, dealt with stewardship. This means that while He taught that "you cannot serve God and Mammon," nevertheless you can serve God with Mammon.

This means that He may call some men to go into business as definitely as He calls some to go into the ministry. There they may use their powers of organization to make money for God.

Someone asked Jane Addams what was the secret of her life, and she replied: "I looked into the faces of ruffian kinds, and then I looked into the face of Christ, and I gave my life to bring them together." I can imagine a businessman saying: "I looked into the faces of the poor of the world, and then I looked into the face of Christ, and I gave my life to business to help meet that need." Or if not the poor, then the other areas of need in the world, at home and abroad. And I can see the businessman go to his tasks with a lightness of step, a sureness of direction, and a sense of mission. He is making money for God. Service of commission should be held for such men and women as they go forth in Christ's name. Then ledgers would be handled with the same sense of sacredness as sacred books in a pulpit.

That fits in with Howard Lowry's definition of the function of religion: "It conceives of all man does as a calling, and of all life as a piece, a unity of richly component parts." "Of all man does as a calling" —that fits in with the New Testament idea of man working out a plan, that plan God's plan.

Sir Christopher Wren, the great architect, asked three men who were building a cathedral what they were doing. One replied, "I'm working till four-thirty." Another, "I'm working for money." The third replied, "I'm helping Sir Christopher Wren build a cathedral." In making the new world every man is important, every man counts. Find God's plan for yourself and work that plan. When you do, you have a sense of cosmic backing. You feel you are a part of a vast design, and you grow big in that vastness. You are a creator under the Creator.

O God, I thank Thee that Thou hast a plan for my life. I am finding that plan by surrender and acceptance of Thy way. In Jesus' name. Amen.

AFFIRMATION FOR THE DAY: *As the little boy gave the five loaves and two fishes to Jesus, so I give my material possessions to Him to bless and break and multiply and give.*

STREAMLINE YOUR LIFE FOR KINGDOM PURPOSES

We are studying the necessity of a sense of stewardship in life. Livingstone had it when he said these immortal words: "I will place no value on anything that I have or possess except in relation to the Kingdom of Christ. If anything I have will advance that Kingdom, it shall be given or kept, as by giving or keeping it I shall best promote the glory of Him to whom I owe all my hopes both for time and eternity." That first sentence should become the life motto of every Christian in the world. Each Christian should repeat it slowly to himself every day, *"I will place no value on anything that I have or possess except in relation to the Kingdom of Christ."* If it furthers that Kingdom, it has value—it can stay. If it is useless to that Kingdom, it is valueless—it must be made useful, or go. Streamline your life for Kingdom purposes.

John Wanamaker, the great Christian merchant-prince, visiting China to see if his gifts were doing anything vital, came across a town where there was a beautiful chapel and near by a man plowing his field with an ox and a young man yoked together. Inquiring what this strange yoking meant, the old man said: "When we were trying to build the chapel, my son and I had no money to give, and then my son said, 'Let us sell one of our two oxen and I will take the yoke of the ox.' We did so, and gave the money to the chapel." Wanamaker adds that he offered up then and there a silent prayer, "Lord, let me be hitched to a plow, so that I may know the joy of such sacrificial giving."

John R. Straton tells of a rich man who went to the sailing of a vessel which contained ten thousand dollars' worth of equipment for a hospital in China, his own gift. He told a friend standing by what the vessel meant to him. And the friend said: "I am glad you made that gift. I too have a gift on that ship—our only daughter is on board, going out to China as a missionary." The wealthy man said: "My dear brother, I feel I have given nothing as I think of what this sacrifice means to you." Both were stewards of the entrustments of God. Both could say: "Such as I have, I give."

Father-God, I hold all that I have at Thy disposal. Thou knowest my needs and the needs of the world—relate them. Amen.

AFFIRMATION FOR THE DAY: *I keep my money in my hands—not in my heart.*

STEWARDSHIP OF TREASURE, TIME, AND TALENT

Stewardship may be of treasure, time, and talent. Everyone has some of each—some have more, some less.

In the Ashram at Sat Tal in The Himalaya is a picture, an original painting of the head of Christ, a gift of the artist, Warner Sallman. When Sallman was in his teens, a friend remarked over his interest in art: "Stay with it. The Christian world needs a great artist." Sallman went into commercial art, but determined at the very least to tithe his ability for Christian ends. Then, says Carl F. H. Henry, in 1924, just in time to make the deadline, he turned out for the cover of old *Covenant Companion* a charcoal sketch of the head of Christ. Ten years later that sketch joined the art immortals, and Sallman today is giving his full time to Christian service in spreading the gospel through art. He put his talent at God's disposal.

Vaughn Shoemaker, chief cartoonist for the *Chicago Daily News*, and former Pulitzer prize winner, whose conversion I mentioned before, dedicates a portion of his time to the production of cartoons that preach the gospel, many of them conceived in prayer, for he confesses that his educational limitations throw him back on God for insights.

"God's Acre" among farmers has produced the sense of working together with God, the produce of that acre going to God. The fact that sunlight, soil, rain, and atmosphere do 93 per cent toward a crop, leaving only 7 per cent dependent upon the work of the farmer, throws vivid light upon the relationship of Owner and ower.

C. B. Keenleyside tells of a college student, smitten with blindness, who accepted his blindness as a gift from God and prayed this prayer: "Father, I thank Thee for the talent of blindness. May I so invest that talent that at the coming of the Lord Jesus He may receive His own with usury." He was William Moon of Brighton, the man who invented the Moon type of raised letters for the blind, which has put the Scriptures within reach of millions of blind people, being utilized in five hundred languages. A dedicated limitation brought unlimited blessing. "The talent of blindness"—if blindness can be a talent, then everything can be a talent. I'm rich in talents!

O God, in Thee nothing is lost, for even our losses become gain. Thou wilt use everything—if we will let Thee. Amen.

AFFIRMATION FOR THE DAY: *Like the man who gave his boat for Jesus to teach from, so I give my talents for His pulpit today.*

STEPS INTO BEING GOD'S STEWARD

Now the steps in becoming a steward of treasure, time, and talent.

1. *Settle it as something fixed: God is Owner, I am ower.* I own nothing—everything I have is a trust. I must give an accounting to God.

2. *As acknowledgment of that Ownership, I will set aside for God one tenth of all I earn.* Then I will give out of the nine tenths as He guides me.

3. *I will keep for myself enough to make me more mentally, physically, and spiritually fit for the purposes of the Kingdom of God.* This belongs to my need, all else belongs to the needs of others. (As a nation we spend 85 per cent of our annual income on ourselves, save 12 per cent, and give 3 per cent; hence much of our wealth has no blessing of God on it. It is touched with death.)

4. *I realize that in giving I am only investing.* Therefore I will follow Wesley's saying, "Make all you can, save all you can, and give all you can," for my giving is investing in eternal values. (On the tombstone in an old graveyard are these words, "What I spent I had; what I saved I lost; what I gave I have.")

5. *Once and for all, I will put at God's disposal my talents and my time.* They belong to Him. Then each day I will ask Him to show new or old ways of using my time and talents for Him. (Some young people discovered that by getting permission of a farmer to glean the cornfields of a three-hundred-acre farm after the mehanical harvester had done its work, they earned $1,200 for a Christian cause.)

6. *I will accept every little task or opportunity as a proving ground of faithfulness, making me ready for bigger tasks.* "He that is faithful in that which is least is faithful also in much." I will not wait for big tasks and responsibilities, doing them or nothing. I will get ready for the bigger by doing the little well.

7. *I will do all my little things in a big way,* bringing to all my tasks a spirit that will make the trivial into the triumphant. I will be a hilarious giver of time, talent, and treasure.

8. *I will make my will under God's guidance,* conscious that I have no right to leave to relatives to waste what God has entrusted me to invest in Kingdom purposes.

O God, my talents are small, but in Thy hands they are multiplied, as everything is when in Thy hands. Amen.

AFFIRMATION FOR THE DAY: *I hold nothing as of any value except in its relationship to the Kingdom of God.*

MAKING THE SECOND-RATE INTO THE FIRST-RATE

We come now to another transformation—the transformation of the commonplace. Often the common tasks make us common. Just as the hands of the dyer are stained by the material in which he works, so our souls are dyed by our tasks. If they are dull and monotonous, we become dull and monotonous too. Our routine becomes rutine, if I may coin a word. We become grooved, insignificant persons, made so by our tasks.

Unless—and this is the point—we make the commonplace a consecrated place by the spirit which we bring to it. We have chosen for our study a man who did just that—Philip. He was really a third-rate man in a second-rate task who did a first-rate job. He was different from the Philip of the Twelve—he didn't belong up there. He was of "the seven"—and among "the seven" he was overshadowed by the outstanding member, Stephen. And then his task was serving tables. He might have folded up under those limitations and might have said, "I'm fenced in." And he was. And yet he wasn't!

He pushed against more barriers and broke more and went farther than any man in the New Testament, not excepting Paul. For Paul simply walked through the breaches that Philip made and extended the implications of what he did. It was Philip who was the pioneer.

Look at the barriers he broke: (*a*) He was a layman and was especially designated to do a meal-serving job which was distinguished from the preaching job of the apostles. ("It is not desirable that we should drop preaching the word of God and attend to meals"—Acts 6:2, Moffatt) and yet he preached so effectively that he was the only one in the New Testament designated as "the evangelist"—"Philip, the evangelist" (Acts 21:8, Moffatt). (*b*) He broke down the walls between the secular and the sacred and made them one. (*c*) He was the first missionary—the first to preach the gospel beyond the walls of Jerusalem, going down to Samaria. (*d*) Not content to go to Samaria, he won an Ethiopian official, who in turn became the founder of the Abyssinian Church in Africa. Philip was a quiet barrier-smasher, a pioneer spirit.

O God, give me the creative heart, the heart that breaks all barriers that life sets up to hem me in. Make me creative. Amen.

AFFIRMATION FOR THE DAY: *I may be a second- or third-rate man, but I'm going to do a first-rate job in life because all I have is linked with Thy power.*

THE RECONCILER

Philip was a man whose actions were seed actions, with the germs of a new world in them.

1. His choice in a crisis and a conflict as one who could be trusted to be just to both Jews and Greeks shows that, along with the other seven, he had transcended race in his personal attitudes. When the complaint was made that the Greek widows were neglected by the Hebrew administrators of food (Acts 6:1-2), the apostles looked around to find men who were big enough in spirit and attitude to bridge this first and dangerous cleft in the solidarity of the Christian brotherhood. He was a man who "stood in the breach" and reconciled both sides in himself.

In every situation from the personal to the international the greatest need in the world today is for men big enough in spirit and attitude to reconcile opposing viewpoints and persons and bring them together in themselves. If we had such men in political life, there would be no war. We have partisans instead of partners, and the result is conflict instead of concord. Someone has defined politics as "the art of seeing trouble everywhere, diagnosing it wrongly, and applying unsuitable remedies." It isn't entirely true, of course, but just enough true to make it sting. The seeing trouble everywhere means the art of seeing enemies everywhere, and in seeing them, making them in the seeing.

Philip with his reconciling spirit is the most needed human in the world today.

2. He reconciled the material and the spiritual, the secular and the sacred. The apostles unwittingly drove a dangerous wedge into life by saying, "It is not desirable that we should drop preaching the word of God and attend to meals" (Acts 6:2, Moffatt). That began a most dangerous and disruptive heresy in Christianity. Christianity would operate within the spiritual, and the material could be managed by lesser and more secular principles. That meaning wasn't intended, but it became the legitimate extension of their attitudes. Jesus fed people as a part of His gospel; they, more holy than their Lord, separated the two and made two worlds—the material and the spiritual.

O Christ, we have torn Thy seamless robe. We have put asunder what Thou hast joined. Help us to find life's unity again. Amen.

AFFIRMATION FOR THE DAY: *The material and the spiritual are brothers, sons of the same Father; I shall bring them into brotherly relations today.*

MENDING THE SEAMLESS ROBE

We saw yesterday that when the apostles made their ministry to operate in the severely spiritual, and another ministry to operate in the severely secular, they put asunder what God had joined. In Jesus the Word became flesh. In the apostles the Word became spirit. A lesser order took over the flesh. There the Christian church laid down a division which has meant that the economic, social, and political are controlled by other than Christian forces, leaving to the Christian forces the spiritual. That doctrine gave rise to communism, which dismisses the spiritual as idealism and organizes life around material forces entirely. It is a revolt against our compartmentalizing life and we are partly responsible.

The Incarnation puts them together. And the Kingdom of God, which is the extension of the Incarnation into all areas of life, makes life all of a piece, organizing the total life around the will of God.

Philip, to whom a secular task was assigned, made the secular and the sacred parts of one whole. For he put evangelism through the tableserving, and made tableserving a part of evangelism. All life spoke one message—the good news.

If reconcilers between groups and races and nations are our greatest need, our second greatest need is reconcilers between the so-called secular and the so-called sacred. We need men and women who see and make no difference, and make all life sacred as Jesus did. He fed, healed, taught, and preached as parts of one whole—the Kingdom of God. Philip, a layman, mended the seamless robe of Christ which the apostles tore asunder. The future lies with him.

For if we do not put these together, then the spiritual is ineffective, not functioning in material terms, therefore not functioning at all, and the material is unredeemed. Both are impoverished.

A bishop asked after an address on the Kingdom, "How do we begin?" And I replied, "I suppose by going out and acting as though it were already here." He took that literally, founded an Ashram, where the Word became flesh, the material and spiritual became one.

O Christ, Thou art calling us to make our Christian calling a life calling —the whole of life expressing one thing, Thy Kingdom. Amen.

AFFIRMATION FOR THE DAY: *Today I shall act as though the Kingdom were already here, and as far as I am concerned, it will be.*

HAVING DOUGH BUT NO LEAVEN

We ended yesterday with the examples of a bishop and a business-man bridging the gap between the secular and the sacred—the bishop incarnating his spirituality and the businessman spiritualizing the otherwise carnal. They met—in the Kingdom!

3. Philip breached another wall of separation—between the Jew and the Samaritan. "The Jews have no dealings with the Samaritans" —that was the forbidding wall. Jesus pointed to its breach, "And you will be my witnesses at Jerusalem, throughout all Judaea and Samaria, and to the end of the earth" (Acts 1:8, Moffatt). But the apostles stopped at the walls and stayed in Jewish territory. Why? This is a revealing sentence, "That day a severe persecution broke out against the church in Jerusalem, and all, except the apostles, were scattered over Judaea and Samaria" (Acts 8:1, Moffatt). "Except the apostles"— why weren't they scattered? Were they braver? Or did the authorities see that the apostles were not the dangerous element—that they would probably fit in and become a Christian sect among Jews? It was these laymen, represented by Stephen and Philip, the dangerous innovators and radicals, who must be suppressed. The apostles played safe—the laymen played Christian! One group stayed behind the walls for safety, the other breached the walls—for salvation!

The leaven of Christianity passed from the hierarchy of apostles to the lay group. The initiative lay with this lay group and with Paul, another layman. The hierarchy could only regularize what these lay-men and Paul produced. When Philip began a revival in Samaria, the apostles came down to regularize it by the laying on of their hands (Acts 8:14-15). The apostles could only approve of Paul's work— they couldn't produce it.

Officialdom is more concerned with its prestige and power. The lay groups, on the whole, are more concerned with the power of the Spirit. So new movements of the Spirit are seldom born out of hier-archies. They have the "dough" but no "leaven." The leaven has passed to the humble, surrendered persons and groups.

Father, I know I am made for the mediocre and the commonplace unless Thou dost remake me and thus remake my tasks into the uncom-monplace. I'm willing. Amen.

AFFIRMATION FOR THE DAY: *Maybe if I am simple, surrendered, and sensitive to the Spirit, I too shall bring forth some deathless move-ment of the Spirit.*

THE REAL APOSTOLIC SUCCESSION

We are studying Philip as the type of the humble, surrendered people through whom the Spirit of God breaks old molds and begins creative movements.

4. Philip was the first of the early disciples to put together the two things Jesus indissolubly put together: Jesus and the Kingdom of God. "But when they believed Philip as he preached good news about the kingdom of God and the name of Jesus Christ" (Acts 8:12, R.S.V.). None of the apostolic hierarchy seems to have grasped this, but Paul did. (See Acts 28:23, 31.) And this was vastly important. In Jesus two important things came together—the Order, the Kingdom of God; and the Person, Jesus Christ. The absolute Person and the absolute Order coincided, making our relationships with Him both personal and social. The whole of life, individual and social, was to come under a single sway, the will of God. This was a completely totalitarian order demanding a total obedience in the total life. But when it is totally obeyed, it brings total freedom.

Had these lines which the laymen Philip and Paul marked out been followed, the Christian centuries would have been different and the world too would have been different today. I am not sure that either Philip or Paul saw clearly the implications of what they were suggesting, but a new world was potential in what they were pointing out.

The hierarchy of the apostles never grasped it at all, and the subsequent hierarchies who drew up the creeds missed it entirely, not even mentioning the Kingdom in the three creeds, except marginally once beyond the borders of this life in heaven.

The insights into the meaning of the gospel come from those who obey that gospel in its full implications. "If any man will do his will, he shall know." When Peter addressed the crowd at Pentecost, although there were before him "people from every nation under heaven," he addressed them: "Men of Judaea and residents in Jerusalem" (Acts 2:14, Moffatt). Peter, his conceptions pot-bound, left out the Samaritans and the Gentiles. Philip took them in. The future lay with Philip and those in the line of his succession.

O God, my Father, Thou art using surrendered, responsive souls. Make me one. For when I see in Thy light, I see. Amen.

AFFIRMATION FOR THE DAY: *The Order and the Person will make my religion intensely social and intensely personal today.*

"GO UP AND JOIN THIS CHARIOT"

We saw yesterday that the line of apostolic Christianity passed from the apostolic hierarchy to Philip and Paul—forerunners of the religion of the Spirit. The apostolic hierarchy had the forms; they had the Spirit. The one led inevitably to the Roman Catholic hierarchy with Peter at the head of it—the religion of authority. The other led to the Evangelical Movement—the religion of the Spirit.

5. There is yet another wall which Philip breached, and through it tens of thousands have marched to world missions. After the amazing revival in Samaria, where whole cities "attended like one man" to what Philip said and did, he felt guided to leave it all and to leave it at high tide and go into a desert. "An angel of the Lord said to Philip, 'Rise and go toward the South [at noon, margin] to the road that goes down from Jerusalem to Gaza.' This is a desert road" (Acts 8:26, R.S.V.).

There time (noon), place (the desert road), and the person (the Ethiopian) converged with Philip at one of the most important moments in history. The Christian missionary enterprise through the centuries was bound up in that moment. This was a seed moment.

The account says: "And the Spirit said to Philip, 'Go up and join this chariot.' So Philip ran to him" (Acts 8:29-30, R.S.V.). There an uninhibited person met an inhibited soul and an uninhibited result followed. That Spirit-guided moment resulted in a far-reaching movement. A person as a person was to be the field of the gospel. Special privileges and class and race and color were all canceled, and man as man was the unit.

Tradition says that this Ethiopian minister-treasurer became the founder of the Abyssinian Church. This was the forerunner of that prophecy that "Ethiopia shall haste to stretch out her hands unto God" (Ps. 68:31, A.S.V.).

Often when God guides us to break with some developed situation and go into a seeming desert, He is really germinating one of those seed situations that may change the face of history. Philip did more in Ethiopia through one man than he did in Samaria.

O Spirit of God, help me to be sensitive at the moment when Thy impulses are within me. And teach me the difference between my impulses and Thine. Amen.

AFFIRMATION FOR THE DAY: *Perhaps the Spirit will say to me today, "Go up and join this chariot"—contact that man—and I shall obey.*

"HE HEIGHTENED EVERYTHING HE TOUCHED"

We come now to gather up the lessons we are to learn through this simple layman, Philip, as he responded to the Spirit.

1. Philip breached the walls between official authority and spiritual authority, between the secular and the sacred, between the Jew and the Samaritan, between the Jew and the Gentile, between white and black.

There is another wall that went down before him—the wall between the areas of responsibility of men and women. The account says, "We entered the house of Philip the evangelist, who was one of the seven, and stayed with him. And he had four unmarried daughters, who prophesied" (Acts 21:8-9, R.S.V.). The attitudes of Philip must have been so universal that all of his daughters felt they need not marry to have the creative instinct within them fulfilled—they could use their creative instincts to produce newborn souls and movements. Here spinsterhood became a vocation and was mightily used in the Kingdom. Spinsterhood is a Christian institution—and can be a very noble one. Some of the greatest work of the world has been done through the spiritual descendants of the daughters of Philip, especially the spinster schoolteachers and missionaries.

2. Philip was the case of a third-rate man, overshadowed by the apostles and by Stephen, doing a bigger work than any of them. He is also the case of a man in a second-rate job—serving tables—doing a first-rate job in human achievement. He was a little man with a great God, and his littleness threw him back on God's greatness.

3. He was the only man in the New Testament called "the evangelist," and yet he wasn't supposed to be an evangelist at all.

4. He belonged to "seven" in Acts 6:3, and turned it into "the Seven." "He belonged to the Seven" (Acts 21:8, Moffatt). He capitalized "the Seven." He transformed a numeral into a name. He heightened everything he touched. He was a man who breached walls, and yet lifted values—destructive and constructive at the same time. Probably he was the most used-of-God man in the New Testament, for Paul walked through the openings in the walls which Philip made. Together they are joint founders of the religion of the Spirit.

O Christ, I thank Thee that Philip was Thy man at Thy hour. Make me Thy man at this hour. Amen.

AFFIRMATION FOR THE DAY: *I may be a little man, but I have a great God, and I expect Him to do great things through my littleness.*

STEPS IN GUIDANCE

Before we leave the very creative story of Philip, we must gather up some lessons from him on guidance.

1. Philip got his guidance through the implications of his own gospel. His gospel was founded on bringing the spiritual and the material together and making them one—"the Word was made flesh." Out of that basic fact he worked out particular guidance regarding his applying it to a so-called secular job. He spiritualized it. Deduction: Our most general guidance will be to work out the implications of our gospel as seen in the person of Jesus.

2. He got his guidance through a set of circumstances not of his choosing: "Now those who were scattered went through the land preaching the gospel. Philip travelled down to a town in Samaria, where he preached Christ to the people" (Acts 8:4-5, Moffatt). He didn't complain about being "scattered" by persecution—he used it. Evil became the instrument of the good. Deduction: Much of our guidance will be to use opportunities which we didn't plan. They may come through evil; we turn them to good.

3. Some of our guidance will come very directly: "An angel of the Lord said to Philip, 'Get up and go'" (Acts 8:26, Moffatt). "The Spirit said to Philip, 'Go up and join'" (Acts 8:29, Moffatt). The first must be interpreted in the light of the second. "An angel," literally "a messenger," turned out to be "the Spirit" speaking within. The whole movement of guidance in the Bible is from the without to the within—from signs and angels to the quiet Voice within. Deduction: Much of our guidance will come from the Spirit's voice within. But not always. Don't confine God to this method, lest you be tempted to produce the Voice from your own subconscious.

4. Some of our guidance will be to let people alone with God. "The Spirit of the Lord caught Philip away, and the eunuch lost sight of him. He went on his way rejoicing" (Acts 8:39, Moffatt). If God guides us to help people, He also guides us not to smother them, but give them spiritual independence. Deduction: Guidance to let people go and grow on their own.

O Spirit of God, Thou art teaching me Thy ways. Help me to be an apt learner in Thy school. In Jesus' name. Amen.

AFFIRMATION FOR THE DAY: *"I will instruct you and teach you what is the road to take; I will give you counsel, O humble soul"* (Ps. 32:8, Moffatt).

CORRECTED BY GROUP GUIDANCE

There is one further lesson we must gather from the guidance of Philip before we go on. At one point the insight and guidance of Philip needed correction by a group. In the enthusiasm of the revival in Samaria, Simon Magus, a sorcerer, was converted and baptized. It was a big fish Philip had caught, and he and the city were impressed—and elated. But it took the impact of the Jerusalem group and their insights to show that Simon Magus, for all his superficial change, was as Peter said, "a bitter poison and a pack of evil" (Acts 8:23, Moffatt). It took corporate guidance to correct the movement of Philip at that point. Individual guidance has to be corrected by group guidance. If individual guidance is uncorrected and unchecked by group guidance, it may go off on a tangent and get tangled up in its own subjective states.

Every religious leader needs a group in which he subjects himself to a group discipline. For many years as an evangelist I had no group discipline. I was telling others what to do, but no one told me what to do. I was the poorer for it. Then I found the discipline of an Ashram group where we pledge each other not to have an inward criticism which we do not bring up. If there is no outward criticism, then we know there is no inward criticism. There is a relaxed fellowship.

But the group life is not for mere correction; it is for contribution as well. If we don't get group correction, we don't get group contribution. In the give and take of a group it is often more "take" than "give." For instance, a convert of a few months said to me in our Ashram in India: "Brother Stanley, I've noticed that whenever you can't really answer a question we put to you, you go off to something interesting and make us forget the point. Is that honest?" That taught me a life lesson, the lesson of saying "I don't know." That lesson has saved me endless tangles and opened many doors to further knowledge. God guides through the group—and guides especially. But the group not only corrects you—it contributes to you as well. The partial idea is filled out by the idea of another. The sparks that fly from the clash of thought upon thought illuminate a subject—and you.

O God, Thou hast made us for corporate living, so help us to accept and rejoice in that possibility and to submit to group guidance. Amen.

AFFIRMATION FOR THE DAY: *"Whoever reverences the Eternal, learns what is the right course to take"* (Ps. 25:12, Moffatt).

THREE STAGES IN GROUP GUIDANCE

Yesterday we noted that individual guidance needs to be checked and, if necessary, corrected by group guidance.

There are three stages in group guidance as seen in Acts 15. (*a*) "Then it seemed good to the apostles and the elders, with the whole church" (Acts 15:22, R.S.V.). "The whole church" is added, but obviously the decision was made by "the apostles and the elders." This is oligarchy. (*b*) "It has seemed good to us in assembly" (Acts 15:23, R.S.V.)—the decision of the total body of believers. This is democracy. (*c*) "For it has seemed good to the Holy Spirit and to us" (Acts 15:28, R.S.V.)—the decision of God and man working together. This is the highest Christian guidance.

These three represent three ascending stages of guidance—the guidance of the people by the few; the guidance of the people by the people in assembly; the guidance of the people by co-ordinating their thinking with God's thinking, but with God first and doing the directing. This last is the highest stage of guidance. For it is not God dictating or merely men deciding—it is a combination of listening to God and of thinking too. Here God is not dictator and man a blank sheet. Nor is it the groping of human wisdom without any sense of being guided. It is a group surrendering their thoughts to God and then thinking too and finding that they and God were thinking the same thoughts. They arose convinced that they had found God's mind.

The Quakers illustrate this method and their conclusions have been dynamic and God-owned. In working out a method for group decision we found in our Indian Ashram this method closely approximated the New Testament pattern: (*a*) the period of silence, of listening to God, (*b*) and then going around the circle, each one is asked what he thinks should be done. It gives a chance for the movement downward from God and the movement upward from man to meet and to merge into "It has seemed good to the Holy Spirit and to us." Decisions reached in this atmosphere and attitude have the backing of Reality. They stand the shock of the years and centuries. When we think God's thoughts, those thoughts stand.

O Spirit of Truth, we think truth and become truth when we think Thy thoughts, will Thy purposes, and feel Thy feelings. Help us this day. Amen.

AFFIRMATION FOR THE DAY: *May all my decisions today seem good to the Holy Spirit and to me.*

"WHY DON'T YOU DRAW ON YOUR FAITH?"

We now turn to look at those who instead of getting guidance from God, tap their way, like a blind man, from event to event, burdened with this business of living. They have never learned to "cast all their care upon Him"—they carry their cares themselves. Jesus described this type thus: "Your hearts . . . weighed down with . . . cares of this life" (Luke 21:34, R.S.V.). Weighed down souls, struggling under the cares of this life.

To all such Jesus says: "Come to me, all ye labouring and burdened; . . . learn from me . . . and you will find your souls refreshed" (Matt. 11:28-29, Moffatt). Jesus offers transformation to the burdened. When one looks at audiences as I do, and scans their faces to find lighted-up souls, he is struck that he finds so few. Most people are simply carrying their own burdens.

Many who are outwardly gay are often hiding by that very gaiety a burdened heart. Mark Twain had little inner humor. He put on his daughter's tomb: "You left behind a desolate father." The outer humor covered the lack of inner harmony. A famous clown, Grimaldi, was convulsing London with laughter. He came to a doctor and the doctor said to him: "There's nothing really wrong with you. You're just depressed. What you need is a good laugh. Go and see and hear Grimaldi." The man replied: "I'm that unhappy man."

No one has any right to be unhappy—no matter in what conditions he is. To be unhappy makes you the center of a contagion of unhappiness. I said to a doctor concerning a sour, morose-looking nurse, "Can't you give her an injection of sunshine?" She needed it.

The biography of many people could be summed up in three words: womb, gloom, tomb. Between womb and tomb they live in gloom. And it is no place for a Christian to live. A man who had everything except happiness and health told me what a simple Christian who knew his Bible said to him: "You Christian people should be ashamed of yourselves, running away to sanitariums. Why don't you draw on your faith?" Yes, why not? A psychiatrist said to a prominent minister, "You have a faith, haven't you?" And when the minister replied, "Yes," he said, "Then why don't you use it?" Yes, why not?

O God, Thou hast everything for me, including joy—and joy especially. Help me to take it, for it is my birthright. In Jesus' name. Amen.

AFFIRMATION FOR THE DAY: *My life history shall not be womb, gloom, tomb; but birth, bloom, blessedness.*

"SYNDICATING PAINS AND TROUBLES"

We are thinking upon the right and duty to be happy. We have no business syndicating our sorrows and miseries. A doctor said he went to the Mayo Clinic and saw the streets of Rochester and the clinics crowded with people, so he said to a resident doctor: "What's the matter? Is there a special festival on here today—all these crowds?" "No," said the doctor, "this is what is happening. We're living too close together. A man gets a slight pain around his heart and it frightens him, so he tells a friend on the street about it. The friend listens, begins to pay attention to his heart, and he also gets a pain. Then he tells somebody about his pain. And thus it goes. And these crowds are largely the result of that process of syndicating pains and troubles. We get the wreckage."

And it need not be. We can spread the opposite. I mentioned a young wife who scatters sunshine so abundantly that someone said to her, "You look as though you've swallowed an electric-light bulb." Someone addressed a letter to her and began, "My dear Electric-Light Bulb." Many of us could be like that if we made up our minds not to entertain gloomy thoughts, and not to utter any, and soon we'd have none. One woman said of herself: "I used to screw the electric-light bulb in in the morning Quiet Time, and then unscrew it during the day. Now I keep it screwed in all day." And she was alight all day. It was as simple as that!

But getting rid of gloom is a twofold process—the first is to make up our minds that it is a wrong to God, to ourselves, and to others to spread gloom; the second is that we will pay the price of sunshine.

Take the first. Nietzsche once said, "The redeemed must look more redeemed if they are going to get us to believe in redemption." A dramatic student saw the face of a redeemed Christian psychiatrist as she talked, and remarked to a friend, "I'd be a Christian if I could have eyes that sparkle like that." Not a high motive! But it shows that people want to get out of the dull drabness of things. And one of the things—only one—that Christ brings is deliverance from dullness and drabness.

O Christ, Thou dost give me a sense of adventure, and life with Thee is full of novelty and sparkle. I thank Thee. I thank Thee. Amen.

AFFIRMATION FOR THE DAY: *As I live in the creative Christ, so I shall live in continuous creation, therefore in constant surprise and adventure.*

"TURNED ONLY HALFWAY ON"

We are looking at the necessity of being transformed from gloom to gladness. It is a sin against God to be gloomy. It says to the world that God is a gloomy God and produces gloomy followers. A complete reversal of the facts! For there is more joy to the square inch in being a Christian than there is to the square mile outside.

A young man stood up in a meeting and with radiant face said, "My brand has been ————," naming a brand of cigarettes. "Now my brand is Christ. I'm going to spread Him." And you can't spread Christ with gloom. A Japanese, not too good in English, wrote to a friend, quoting a passage of Scripture, "The Lord bless you and pickle you." Some of us look more "pickled" than "preserved"!

There are two great reasons for not being happy, radiant Christians. One is a halfwayness about the whole business of being Christian. We are only tentatively Christian. A sign on a radiator in a hotel room said: "Please turn the radiators all the way on or all the way off. If they are turned only partially on, they will leak and be noisy." A lot of Christians have lives that are squeaky and noisy and they can't hold happiness and joy for long—they leak. Why? Turned only halfway on! Many Christians have just enough religion to set up a conflict, but not enough to set up a concord. A half-Christianity is a problem instead of a power.

The second reason for gloomy Christianity is not realizing our resources. I saw a Brahmany bull in India eating out of a garbage can when right nearby was a field of green grass. Many of us eat out of garbage cans of current pessimisms and fears instead of eating in the green fields of God's grace and power. We should realize our Resources and possess our Possessions.

Whenever we have been troubled in conscience about our spiritual impotence, we have added a new wheel to our machinery—a new commission or a new committee, a new plan or program, and in the end we have added one more wheel with little or no power to run either the old or the new. We are busy turning old and new wheels with hand power instead of lighting central fires. We do not realize our Resources.

O Christ, give me the grace to take Thy joy, that Thy joy may be in me and my joy may be full. In Thy name. Amen.

AFFIRMATION FOR THE DAY: *I shall not have just enough religion to make me miserable, but enough to make me merry—with God.*

STEPS OUT OF GLOOM

1. *Fix it that it is your birthright to be happy.* God wills your happiness. He couldn't be God and will anything else.

2. *But if you seek happiness, it will elude you.* Seek God's will for your life, and happiness will come as a by-product.

3. *See God's redemptive will in everything.* The thing that strikes you may not be God's will, but God will rescue out of that thing *something good for you.* Everything that happens can be redemptive if you take it in the right way. A friend, being slowly paralyzed by a wasting disease, said to me: "I can't walk now, but I'm going to walk all over God's heaven. God saves me from gloom. I'm happy."

4. *Forgive everybody for everything in which he has wronged you.* Hold no grudges. Grudges become glooms. A Japanese boy in an oratorical contest announced his subject: "The Sacredness of Work," and people inwardly smiled—and then they didn't! His parents and his home were burned to ashes in the atomic bomb at Nagasaki. The three children knelt in the ashes of the home and prayed to know what to do. The eldest boy of sixteen years said, "I know what we can do; we can work." So they set to work, gathering bits of tin and boards, and soon they had a hut to live in. They could have nursed their grudge and been gloomy; instead, they forgave, forgot, and went to work—and were radiant.

5. *Laugh your unhappinesses away.* I felt a stiffness in my knees while on a train coming out of New York, looked up and saw a building with a sign on it "Hospital for Joint Diseases." I said to my joints, "Now stop complaining or that's where you'll land." My joints and I laughed and they immediately felt better. Raymond Calkins told me he took his "aching joints to a circus and showed them the suppleness of the actors and shamed the stiffness out of them!" His laughter helped.

6. *Go out and every day do something to lift somebody else's burden and gloom.* The most absolutely happy people in the world are the people who are deliberately taking on themselves the burdens of others. As they think about the troubles of others, their own troubles lessen and vanish. They're not solved, they're dissolved.

O Christ of the glad mind and heart, I go out with Thee today to gladden every mind and heart I touch. Help me to be a gloom-lifter. Amen.

AFFIRMATION FOR THE DAY: *I will to be happy, I will to make others happy—I shall swish love and happiness around me today.*

FROM ANXIETY TO RECEPTIVITY

Before we leave the subject of being transformed from a morose to a merry person, I must give instances of how people have been able to get out the blocks to blessedness.

A man threw his bankbook on the counter of the bank and said, "She can pay the rest." The president overheard him and asked to see him. He found the man and his wife were about to separate. He asked the man to go home, get down on his knees with his wife, and say the Lord's Prayer together. The man laughed: "My wife? She'd probably swear in the name of God instead of praying." But he promised. Later the wife came into the bank and the president asked to see her. He asked the same thing of her. She laughed: "My husband? He'd probably start swearing instead of praying." But she promised, and was then told what her husband had promised. Six months later she told the bank president what had happened: "We got on our knees, said the Lord's Prayer together, arose, and kissed each other. And we had a wonderful six months together. And then he died. But those six months were heaven." Get out the blocks and happiness will flood you.

A man told me that when he sat down in the big chair "the boys" gave him on retirement, he had bad pains in the back of his neck. But when he went out and began to be interested in paroled people, his head was perfectly normal. It was attention pains. Get interested in others, and your own troubles will vanish.

K. V. Rajan, a convert from the family of a raja, became a Christian and then began to feel sorry for himself as he felt the world was unjust to him. As the train whistle blew I called to him: "Don't expect justice in a world of this kind, not even from your mother. But when it comes to you, be sure to give it to others." This lifted his whole burden of self-pity. And then a further stage came, when after hours of prayer, a saintly Indian Christian said to him: "Why do you worry God this way? Give Him a rest. Accept what He has offered to you." "There," he said, "I turned from anxiety to receptivity." Accept the gift of Joy—it's yours.

O God, I thank Thee that I see my privilege of joy and I'm taking it. No longer shall I live in gloom. And I shall give gladness to everybody I meet. Amen.

AFFIRMATION FOR THE DAY: *Since my stream of joy has its source in the eternal Fountain, it will never run dry.*

"LET'S HAVE A GOOD LAUGH"

One more day must we pause upon the subject of the lifting of inner gloom. Joseph Sizoo tells how he got out of a rut of gloom and unhappiness: "Years ago, in a day of uncertainty and disillusionment, when my whole life seemed to be overwhelmed by forces beyond my control, one morning quite casually I opened the New Testament and my eyes fell upon this sentence: 'He that sent me is with me: the Father hath not left me alone.' My life has not been the same since that hour. It is the Golden Text of my life." That verse struck at the very center of his uncertainty and consequent unhappiness—he was no longer *alone*.

May I drop a verse into your mind and soul: "Whoever is walking in the dark without a ray of light, let him have confidence in the Eternal, and lean upon his God" (Isa. 50:10, Moffatt). When we have "confidence" and "lean upon," we are leaning upon Reality—ultimate Reality, the only Reality. In a bus going over a temporary bridge over a swollen river, as the bridge creaked and rocked, one girl said to another, "Aren't you scared?" "No," replied the girl, "for my father built the bridge." Your Father built this universe, and when you let go and trust Him, you are simply trusting a wisdom which has provided for stresses and strains in life, and He has also provided grace sufficient for all of this.

This story deserves the climactic place as a gloom-chaser: A missionary went back to her lonely station in the interior of Japan after the World War II, when food was very scarce. Two last precious bits of bacon were looked on as a luxury, so she invited a little Japanese girl of six, who dearly loved bacon, to share the feast. As the bacon was being fried they were called out, and when they came back, the precious bits were burned black. The little girl fought back the tears, and them smiled and said: "Let's have a good laugh." And they did! Then they ate the charred bits with more laughter. They made a game of it! When life hits you hard with a big calamity or a small one, then throw back your head and say, "Let's have a good laugh."

O Christ, Thou hast my gloom; bury it, with my consent, at the foot of the cross. I belong to "the sunshine of life." I thank Thee. Amen.

AFFIRMATION FOR THE DAY: *I belong to the incorrigibly gay because I am backed by Reality. I can wait amid my circumstances till Reality asserts itself.*

ON TRANSFORMING DEATH

We must now look a little longer at the central cause of our gloom —death. For unless we conquer the fear of death—the central fear— we are subject to an unrelieved gloom. The concern regarding death throws a shadow across all our hopes and achievements—across us— unless we see light there.

But suppose there is no light there? If the worst came to the worst and there is no future life, is all lost? No, if I come to the end of this life and look out and see nothing but a vast blank, a vast oblivion, I shall look the universe in the face and say: "Well, I thought better of you. I thought this thing that I have in Christ had the feel of the eternal upon it, but now I see it didn't. Well, I don't repent that I was a Christian. It was a better way to live. I've had a brief heaven, though denied an eternal one. I shout my victory in the face of oblivion." That's not rhetoric. I mean that.

Arthur John Gossip in a vivid passage depicts Jesus leaving the world, and after being gone some time, He returns weeping bitterly: "Oh," He says, "it's all a mistake. I misled you. I told you there was a heavenly Father back of things, but I've explored all the universe and there is no heavenly Father. It's all blank. I'm sorry, I'm sorry I misled you." What would we say if we heard that announcement fall upon our incredulous ears? Well, after the first shock was over, I'd turn to Jesus and say: "With You, I'm sorry too. But I've still got You. Your way of life has worked. I'm glad I followed it. It's been wonderful to live in company with You. I do not repent or regret, I am full of gratitude. If there is nothing after death, it does fill me with awe and gratitude that I had such a wonderful Companion on my way to oblivion."

Will such a thing happen? If so, then everything we know about the universe would be reversed. The conservation of values would be obliterated. The highest value is character, and if that value is obliterated by death, the universe adds up to nonsense.

O God, I know that oblivion is unbelievably impossible. Thou art not the God of the dead, but of the living. I live in Thee now, I shall live in Thee forever. I thank Thee. Amen.

AFFIRMATION FOR THE DAY: *If the final enemy, Death, has been vanquished, what can little enemies along the way do to me now?*

"THEY BELIEVED IN HIS BELIEFS"

We must look again today at that central cause of gloom—death. My central faith in eternal life is found in Jesus. The best Man who ever lived went down through death and came back, and the first thing He said was, "Fear not"—there is nothing here to fear. He who was so right in everything else, the ages being witness, is He wrong here? He who never let us down in one single area of life, will He let us down in this central area? It is impossible.

The Christian faith is the only faith that lights up that dark area of life—death. And it lights it up not with word, but with a Word made flesh. Jesus went through it, and the word of resurrection became flesh in Him. Anyone who lives in Him is as deathless as He is deathless. As was said of Emerson, "He did not argue; he let in the light," so it can be said of Jesus: He did not argue immortality; He showed Himself alive. It was said of Tennyson, "He laid his mind upon theirs and they believed in his beliefs." Well, Jesus lays His mind upon ours, and I believe in His beliefs, and He believed in and demonstrated immortality.

The monks of a certain order sit in a circle and the name of each one is called and each answers "Present." Then the names of the dead members are called, and someone answers "Present" for each one. Then the name of "Jesus Christ" is called, and they all reply "Present." Those two things are connected. Jesus said, "Because I live, ye shall live also." His living guarantees our living. A woman was teaching a class of Japanese children in Hawaii about the death of Jesus. A little fellow couldn't stand it. He jumped into the aisle and said, "Ah, no fair, Him one swell guy." The teacher left the story at the death of Jesus. One girl who knew the story, talking to the others afterward said: "Don't feel too bad. He didn't stay dead."

Well, if He didn't stay dead, I too shall not stay dead! William James gave this reply to the query "Do you believe in a personal immortality?" "Never keenly; but more strongly as I grow older. Why? Because I am just getting fit to live." I too am just getting fit to live!

O Christ, I look at Thee and my soul dances with an inexpressible joy that will dance its way through death—and beyond. In Thee I'm free—from death. I know it. Amen.

AFFIRMATION FOR THE DAY: *I shall need eternity to grow up in—I'm already bursting the seams of my earthly environment.*

"A THOUSANDTH PART OF WHAT IS IN ME"

We continue to look at the necessity for eternal life. Victor Hugo said: "Winter is on my head, but eternal spring is in my heart. The nearer I approach the end, the plainer I hear around me the immortal symphonies of the world to come. For half a century I have been writing my thoughts in prose and verse; but I feel I have not said a thousandth part of what is in me. When I have gone down to the grave I shall have ended my day's work; but another day will begin the next morning. Life closes with the twilight, but opens with the dawn."

That is the man of faith. Now listen to the man who was a skeptic. Robert Ingersoll said at his brother's grave: "Life is a narrow vale between the cold and barren peaks of two eternities. We strive in vain to look beyond the heights. We cry aloud, and the only answer is the echo of our wailing cry. From the voiceless lips of the unreplying dead there comes no word. But in the night of death, Hope sees a star and listening Love can hear the rustle of a wing." That is beautiful in the last lines—beautiful but pathetic, for the Christian not only sees a star and hears the rustle of a wing—he sees a Figure come out of the night of death saying, "I am the resurrection and the life: he that . . . believeth in me shall never die." That is solid reality. And we can say with Sir William Osler: "Some of you will wander through all phases to come at last, I trust, to the opinion of Cicero, who had 'rather be mistaken with Plato than with those who deny altogether a life after death,' and this is my own *confessio fidei*."

I had rather be wrong with Jesus than right with anyone else! He affirmed and illustrated life after death. I sink or swim with Him! On the Damascus road Paul cried out, "Who art thou, Lord?" And the voice replied, "I am Jesus." He was alive! And that fact transformed Paul from a tangled-up unhappy persecutor to a free, incorrigibly happy proclaimer of the good news. Can a lie produce that—a lie produce life? A falsehood produce fruitfulness? A make-believe produce solid reality? I laugh a long incredulous and victorious laugh. And life catches the music of that laughter and laughs too.

O God, my Father, I thank Thee that one glimpse of Thy Son and we know that eternal life is now. For there is life for a look—both now and forever. Amen.

AFFIRMATION FOR THE DAY: *I look at Jesus, and then I laugh at both life and death.*

"IT'S A DEAD CERTAINTY!"

We now look at those who, having faced the fact of death, believe in immortality. Bishop William F. McDowell, a prince of a man, lost his beloved wife, and while preaching saw on the front bench a friend, a colonel, who had also lost his wife. He stepped to the front of the platform and said: "Colonel, you and I are Christians. We have suffered loss, but we can go down through God's acre, put our feet on the mound of our loved ones, and sing the 'Hallelujah Chorus.'" That is the Christian attitude.

Here is Helen Keller's longing for the larger freedom of immortality: "Here and now our misfortune is irreparable. Our service to others is limited. Our thirst for larger activity is unsatisfied. The greatest workers for the race are at times shaken with a mighty cry of the soul, a longing more fully to body forth the energy, the fire, the richness of fancy and of human impulse which overburden them. What wonder, then, that we with our more limited senses and more humble powers should with passionate desire crave wider range and scope of usefulness!" The bird was beating its wings against its bars and longing for the perfect freedom of eternal life.

D. A. MacLerman tells of the last words of the beloved teacher, W. Cosley Bell, who when he knew he was going, sent this message to his students: "Tell the boys that I've grown surer of God every year of my life, and I've never been so sure as I am right now. Why it's all so! It's a fact—it's a dead certainty. I'm so glad I haven't the least shadow of shrinking or uncertainty. I've been teaching and preaching these things all my life, and I'm so interested to find that all we've been believing and hoping is so. I've always thought so, and now that I'm right up against it, I know. I can see now that death is just the smallest thing—just an incident—that it means nothing."

As Alfred W. Levan says, "Without immortality, nothing is intelligible; with it, everything is." In other words, if there isn't immortality, then we'd have to make it in order to house and environ this thing we have in Christ. For it is eternal life now!

O Christ, Thou hast "brought life and immortality to light." For in Thee death seems so utterly impossible, and life, eternal life, so utterly possible—nay, necessary. Amen.

AFFIRMATION FOR THE DAY: *I shall live today as one of the immortals!*

307

"AN IMMENSE AND REVERENT CURIOSITY"

On our last day's meditation on immortality let us emphasize that Jesus didn't use the word. He spoke of "eternal life," and that meant life not merely in eternal duration, but in a quality so rich, so inexhaustible, so abundant now that it simply could not be confined to this life. Eternal life is a quality of life as different from the ordinary life as the ordinary life is different from the animal. That quality of life bursts the bonds of death as a seed rends a rock.

When Charles Kingsley was approaching death he said: "God forgive me if I am wrong, but I look toward it with an immense and reverent curiosity." And Carlyle says: "Eternity, which cannot be far off now, is my one strong city. I look into it fixedly now and then. All terrors about it seem superfluous." The happiest woman I've ever seen was a dying woman. She lay there and clapped her hands at the approach of death. She said to me: "They tell me this is death. It's life. 'O Death, throw open the door.'" And then she laughingly said: "They tell me to be tickled to death is an hyperbole, but I'm being literally tickled to death." Streams of people came to look on her angel face. People were converted by her bedside, including her son. I knelt beside the bed to pray, but I couldn't. There was nothing to pray for. She had everything, including Death, within her grasp. But while I couldn't pray for her, she could pray for me. She put her hands upon my head as I knelt there and prayed that I might preach this gospel of joy, joy, joy. I've been ordained by a bishop and I'm grateful for that ordination, but the mightiest ordination I've ever had was not by a bishop, but by this dying woman! She ordained me out of death to preach life, eternal life.

No wonder the early Christians shut up within dark underground prisons wrote on the walls of the prison the words: "Vita, Vita, Vita"— "Life, Life, Life." Prison walls could not stifle or quench this life, nor can death extinguish it. By its very nature it is bound to go beyond the borders of this life. Can the shell confine the growing seed? Can death stop the Christian? Stop him? It only frees him—forever.

O Christ, Thy empty tomb makes all our fears lies and all our hopes truths. Thy empty tomb is the birthplace of eternal certainty. I thank Thee, thank Thee. Amen.

AFFIRMATION FOR THE DAY: *I shall write on all my confining walls today, "Vita, Vita, Vita."*

GOOD ADVICE AND GOOD NEWS

If what I have been saying about transformation—a transformation that extends from redemption from past sins, from present inner conflicts and fears and egocentricity, and redemption that stretches through all the ages and aeons to come—then this is good news.

For we are destined to awaken in His likeness. "We shall be like him; for we shall see him as he is." I, who have soiled my soul and have spoiled my life, have a destiny which includes being like the most wonderful Character our planet has ever seen. That, I repeat, is good news!

There are just two great views about religion—all systems fall into two categories: those that give good advice and those that bring good news. There are really no other divisions. But note, that in the good news there is good advice—the best advice—but it is a corollary of the acceptance the good news. It is contained within the good news, but it is not the good news. The good news is not mere good views, but when you accept the good news, all the good views are there ready to be unfolded. You have a right orientation to life as a whole. You have the key. Life now begins to add up to sense. All you have to do is to follow out the implications of what you have.

But if you begin at good advice, you soon get threadbare and peter out. Because it begins with man's advice, then another man's better advice may supersede it. But you never exhaust the good news. It has past, present, and eternal meanings wrapped up in it. It is an eternal unfolding of what has been infolded. Then life is full of adventure and surprise.

The presidents of the synagogue at Pisidian Antioch said to Paul and Barnabas: "Brothers, if you have any word of counsel for the people, say it" (Acts 13:15, Moffatt). He expected them to give a "word of counsel"—expected them to add to the billions of words of advice offered to a sin-burdened and morally helpless people. He expected good views, and Paul broke into this discouraged and beaten group with good news! It was the fresh air of another world into the fetid atmosphere of a legal and self salvation.

O God, how can I thank Thee enough that Thou art putting grace at my disposal? I don't have to tug and pull at my own bootstraps; I have to accept Thy gift of grace. I thank Thee. Amen.

AFFIRMATION FOR THE DAY: *Not asserting self-salvation, but accepting God's salvation.*

"IT'S ALL WIPED OUT"

Instead of "any word of counsel," there poured forth from the soul and lips of Paul, not words of counsel—human advice about living—but the astonishing news of God assuming human form to redeem us —"a saviour in Jesus" (Acts 13:23, Moffatt). A radio speaker announces each day a Bible study and with it the statement: "The Bible —the greatest book on self-help." The greatest book on self-help? On the contrary, the Bible unfolds the astonishing drama of divine help, culminating in this sentence, "But God proves his love for us by this, that Christ died for us when we were still sinners" (Rom. 5:8, Moffatt). That isn't an exhortation to self-help—it's an invitation to throw yourself on divine help, no matter what you are, or what you've been. This is not a demand—it's an offer!

No wonder Paul continues and says, "So we now preach to you the glad news" (Acts 13:32, Moffatt). This wasn't a human shout of encouragement to a tired and beaten struggler in the sea—it was a life-line! The only self-help in it was that we let God help us! Then the nature of the offer was unfolded: "Remission of sins is proclaimed to you through him" (Acts 13:38, Moffatt). You don't have to balance your sins with a corresponding good and thus lay up a balance to your account—a hopeless procedure. You accept a gift—remission! He wipes them out. The red Indians, when someone had confessed his sin, made piles of different colored sand and then wiped out the piles as a sign that the sin was wiped out. That happens in Christ! It's all wiped out.

No wonder the account says, "The people begged to have all this repeated to them on the following sabbath" (Acts 13:42, Moffatt). And no wonder, "And on the next sabbath nearly all the town gathered to hear the word of the Lord" (Acts 13:44, Moffatt). And further, "The word of the Lord went far and wide over the whole country" (Acts 13:49, Moffatt). People will go to a fire, and if one gets started in the minister's heart, they will flock to see the great sight. These men had a fresh word from God and it wasn't good advice—it was good news!

Father, how can I thank Thee enough that I am not merely reaching up in aspiration; Thou art reaching down in redemption. My uplifted hand is clasped by Thine. I thank Thee, I thank Thee. Amen.

AFFIRMATION FOR THE DAY: *Today I am living at the junction point of my upreach and God's downreach.*

"TO DO PENANCE FOR PAST SINS"

One day I stood on a cliff and there below me was an enclosed peninsula where the famous leper colony of Molokai, one of the Hawaiian Islands, lay. It was there that Father Damien, the Belgian priest, after being with the leper colony for three years, discovered that he too was a leper and announced the fact by saying to his congregation, "We lepers." It was no longer the "they"—"I" relationship, it was "we."

The man who took over the work of Father Damien was Brother Joseph, a lay brother who served the lepers for forty-four years. Of him the writer of the preface to his memoirs says: "Thus Brother Joseph Dutton came to Molokai to do penance for past sins by spending the remainder of his life as God's servant among unfortunate lepers." There is something very touchingly beautiful about that statement, and yet how utterly foreign to the New Testament. For here was a piety trying to do penance for past sins, trying to atone for past sins by serving lepers. That is not the atmosphere of the service, say, of Paul. He did not have a guilt-ridden piety which he was trying to work off by serving others.

He accepted the gift of grace—something that God had worked out from His side through a cross of self-giving. When he accepted the gift of grace and forgiveness, he went out not to do penance for past sins, but to share with others the amazing gift of God's grace. The transformation was not wrought by penance, by a long-drawn-out sorrow for, but by repentance, a sorrow for and a once-and-for-all turning from, and that made not a guilt-ridden piety, but one grace-inspired and abounding in a spontaneous, ever-active gratitude and joy.

This is the New Testament view, "By grace are ye saved through faith; and that not of yourselves: it is the gift of God." When that gift is accepted, you do not spend the balance of your days wearing hair shirts for past sins. God forgives you, you forgive yourself, and the balance of your days you spend in showing your gratitude by sharing with others what you have found. Penance brings consciousness of sin; repentance and faith bring consciousness of freedom from sin.

O Christ, I thank Thee that I am not healed by the stripes I inflict on myself, but I am healed by Thy stripes. Help me to take it gladly and live it joyously. Amen.

AFFIRMATION FOR THE DAY: *I look today not at my shed blood, but at His!*

FRUSTRATING THE GRACE OF GOD

We continue to look at transformation through grace. This presupposes surrender and receptivity. These two attitudes keep the channels open and allow grace to operate. It is our part of the co-operation.

But we can block the working of redemptive grace within us. Paul could say, "I do not frustrate the grace of God" (Gal. 2:21). That meant that Paul was the freest man in history. Nothing bound him—circumstances, chains, opposition—for he was free at the center.

On the other hand, it was said of the Pharisees and jurists that they "frustrated God's purpose for themselves" (Luke 7:30, Moffatt). They discovered what we all discover sooner or later, that to frustrate God's purpose is to frustrate your own person. Since God's purpose and our own inherent destiny coincide, to revolt against God is to revolt against ourselves. To fulfill the purpose of God is to fulfill ourselves. When I am most His, I am most my own. Bound to Him, I walk the earth free. Low at His feet, I stand straight before everything.

When the leaders of the Jewish nation frustrated God's purposes for themselves, they found themselves behind "a Wailing Wall," weeping over a departed glory. That's where everyone ends up when he frustrates the grace of God for himself—a Wailing Wall. And there are no exceptions.

God had a purpose for Ananias and Sapphira, but they frustrated that purpose by keeping back a part of the price. They gave, but didn't give up. That divided loyalty proved their undoing. They probably died of apoplexy from the inner conflict. On the other hand, Barnabas took all he had and put it at God's disposal and walked into an open door. He leaves behind one of the most beautiful memories of any man in history. He did not frustrate the purpose of God for himself. No "Wailing Wall" in his life.

The rich young ruler could have gone down in history as an apostle. He made the great refusal and "went away sorrowful." Matthew, on the other hand, offered his all and "made a great feast." One ended in sorrow and the other in song. You fulfill or frustrate the purpose of God and fulfill or frustrate yourself. There is no alternative.

O God, I see that Thy purpose is good and is good for me. Thou art willing my highest. Help me to accept it and joyously work it out. Amen.

AFFIRMATION FOR THE DAY: *No blocking of the great by the little today.*

GOD'S PURPOSES AND GOD'S ENABLINGS

The purpose of God and the grace of God are two sides of one medal —if you take the purpose, you have the grace. If you refuse the purpose, you annul the grace.

This was vividly brought home to me as I took a journey, a journey which I had taken twenty-two years before. When I resigned from the bishopric through an inner compulsion of the Spirit, I walked off the platform straight to the railway in Kansas City to go to St. Joseph. It was all a leap in the dark. But I felt it was God's purpose. Twenty-two years later I took the same railway journey from Kansas City to St. Joseph. And during the whole journey I could think of nothing but grace. The intervening years had been filled with grace. People thought I was making a sacrifice. Sacrifice? There was none—none whatever. All I could say to myself was "Grace and glory."

God's purposes are always God's enablings. When "He guides, He provides." And He provides the little things. I sat in a plane and made notes on how the angel who delivered Peter from the prison said to him, "Put on your sandals," and "Put on your coat" (Acts 12:8, Moffatt). The angel thought about minute details of need—sandals and coat. I bowed my head and asked, "Father, have you anything to say to me through this?" "Yes," He replied, "I'm looking after the details of your need." I walked out of the plane at San Francisco to change to another plane for Honolulu, and as I walked out, there was my shaving kit which I had left in the washroom and someone had picked it up and put it in the passageway. I picked it up, thanked the Father for looking after the details of need—a shaving kit, comparable to sandals and a coat.

God's purposes and God's grace are always equal. Anything He purposes for you He gives you grace to do. John speaks of "grace upon grace." Dwight Moody tells of a rich man who wanted to help a poor man, so he sent five pounds through another: "This is thine. Use it wisely. There is more to follow." Again and yet again another five pounds came and with it the note: "More to follow." So every time you receive grace there is always a note attached: "More to follow"—"grace upon grace."

O Father God, Thou dost overwhelm me with Thy grace. Thou art showering me with it. I'm grateful, grateful. Amen.

AFFIRMATION FOR THE DAY: *I shall be a living illustration of "grace upon grace."*

ON SNUFFING OUT THE LIGHT

Once I watched two young people dressed in long robes go forward and light the candles by the altar. Then toward the close I saw them go forward again, this time with snuffers, and they snuffed out the candles. Some of us are candle bearers—lighting up ourselves and others. Others are snuffer bearers, going around snuffing out lights.

Today we meditate on snuffers. The first we look at is inner division. A divided heart is a heart with its light snuffed out. A man in Eire lives on the boundary line of Eire and Ulster. He sleeps with his feet in Ulster and his head in Eire. Many of us live in two kingdoms at once—or try to. A divided loyalty means a snuffed-out light. This from a letter: "A young man, teacher of fifteen-year-old boys in a Sunday school, complained of feeling physically upset over a Saturday night drinking bout. A friend asked, 'Isn't there a word in the Bible for that?' 'I suppose you mean the word 'hypocrisy'? 'That's it.' 'Oh, I can give the finest talk on temperance to those boys you ever heard.' " But with all the assumed gaiety and banter the light had been snuffed out. Grace had been frustrated in his life. He wanted two worlds at once and got neither, but something different—a world of headaches.

You can snuff out the light within you by thinking and talking pessimism. Two letters came to me, both from the same situation—one was filled with pessimism about everything, the other filled with hope and appreciation. One outlook produced a melancholy character, the other a radiant hopeful character. The latter had a candle lighting everything, the other had a snuffer putting out every light.

Here is a letter from one who changed an inner attitude from pessimism to faith: "I was brought back to Christ through reading *Abundant Living*. At that time I was bound up with fears as my baby was ill with croup. After reading the page on 'Worry Is Atheism,' I realized that Christ was near me at all times and there is nothing to fear. From that time I have been living with faith instead of fear." The fear attitude untied her knots and spread health to herself and child.

O God, help me to be one who thinks, talks, and becomes light. Give me a candle this day that I may light every situation I touch. In Jesus' name. Amen.

AFFIRMATION FOR THE DAY: *I light life, I do not snuff it.*

"FINDS THE FOUNTAIN"

There are those who just settle down after forty and the light goes out. The churches of Japan are filled with young people or old people —the middle-aged group has dropped out. I asked an audience of church people how many were above forty. Only twenty-six out of five hundred were above forty. The pull of secularism sucks the young people into the vortex of the world—slowly damned. At forty the idealisms of youth begin to fade, and the soul may turn into an ash—or into a flame!

That leads to the last way we snuff out our lights: by just sheer neglect of the means of cultivation. Thomas was absent from that first gathering behind closed doors after the Resurrection. Doubts set in. The writer says, "Let us consider how to stir up one another to love and good deeds, not ceasing to meet together, as is the habit of some" (Heb. 10:24-25, Moffatt). Note the connection: When you cease to meet together, then you are no longer subject to the mutual stirring up to love and good deeds.

Others stay within the church but neglect a personal Quiet Time. That snuffs out the light. When you have a Quiet Time, you can stand anything that happens during the day. "He who has heard the Word of God," said Ignatius, "can bear his silences." For you know He is there. You have met Him in the morning. The one who keeps the Quiet Time fulfills the lines of Tennyson:

> She spies the summer thro' the winter bud,
> She tastes the fruit before the blossom falls,
> She hears the lark within the songless egg,
> She finds the fountain where they wail'd, "Mirage!"

There is the principle of osmosis: two cells are separated by a membrane. Fluid will pass from the more dense body to the less dense body. So it is with your soul and society. If society is more dense than your soul, its life will flow into you. But if you are more dense than the world, then your life will flow into it. Without the Quiet Time, you become inwardly thin and the world flows into you. With the Quiet Time, you go on the spiritual offensive and flow into the world.

O Father, save me from putting my light under a bushel or in the cellar. Help me to burn with steady, pure light. Amen.

AFFIRMATION FOR THE DAY: *I shall flow into the world today—it shall not flow into me.*

"MYSELF IS MY GREATEST PROBLEM"

We come this week to look at those who were blind and now see, who were all messed up and now are transformed. In our Ashram (place of spiritual retreat) we have "The Morning of the Open Heart," when we face on the first day, "Why have I come? What do I want? What do I really need?" No one is urged to speak, but they speak very willingly, eager to get festering things up and out. In the ten years and more experience of this period I've never known any off-color situation to arise. It has all been natural and normal and healthy —a real catharsis. We give these statements of the first day and then follow the statements of the last day—before and after.

(1) I want to be straightened out regarding war. I am too critical. I want something that will keep me from being upset all the time. (2) I want to be perfect, but I want to be perfect for my own sake— to be a perfect person for selfish reasons. (3) I have two great fears— cars, and I'm always in them; and audiences, and I've got to stand before them all the time. (4) I want to be converted—convert me! (5) I am so lonely. I hate people in the ———— Home. (6) I've blown my top and my people say, "Poor fellow, he had cold coffee." I have a tension within, probably a pride as I see others succeed better than I. (7) I have come here to wage a full-scale war on myself. (8) My self is my greatest problem. I need to throw away my self and come to Christ. (9) I need to overcome the frustration of too many interests. I need to put first things first. (10) I want to know why I was born, why I am here. (11) My child said to me, "Mother, what good does it do you to read all those books? You're still sick." I am. (12) I am here because I'm afraid of religion and yet can't get away from it. I was brought up in a home where there was a strict self-righteousness. (13) I'm little and vile and jealous and full of resentments. I've been afraid of this hour of sharing. (14) I need the blocks taken out of my life. If they were gone, I'd be well.

O God, my Father, Thou seest the depths. Help me to bring them up to Thy kindly, healing eye. For I want to be whole—perfectly whole. Amen.

AFFIRMATION FOR THE DAY: *"The wisdom from above is . . . unambiguous, straightforward"* (Jas. 3:17, Moffatt).

"MY LIFE IS ON A LOW PLATEAU"

We continue to look at those who, in "The Morning of the Open Heart," talk about themselves frankly. (15) I'm a pretender to the throne. The song "Bewitched, Bothered, and Bewildered" fits me. (16) I'm a selfish, vindictive man. I want to bury him. (17) I've got butterflies in my stomach. I've got to get rid of them. I'm afraid. (18) I'm a Christian, but I'm a marginal Christian. I'm still a disappointment to myself. I have nervous exhaustion. (19) I'm fed up with my fellow ministers. We are in a cutthroat competition over members. (20) I am a battleground between two selves—one a retiring self, the other a domineering self.

(21) I can't escape. The Hound of Heaven is on my trail. I have a superiority complex which is really an inferiority complex. (22) It bothers me when I am not well thought of. I'm self-conscious. (23) I'm a pastor and I'm bogged down with details. I'm always trying to wangle people into liking me. (24) I have not only cold feet, I have weak knees as well. I'm scatterbrained too. Combination of cold feet, weak knees, and scatterbrains—God needs to make me over entirely. (25) I know what it means to be on the Way. And I know what it means to be off the Way. I'm off the Way now and I want to get back. (26) I'm tired of being tired. I know my tiredness comes from incomplete union with God.

(27) My life is on a low plateau. I'm drunk with the wine of the world. (28) I need a complete surrender, but I don't want it. I'm afraid of my family—what will they think? Will they laugh at me? They're very accomplished people. (29) I have high blood pressure. Nothing organically wrong, but I'm under a tension all the time. (30) I need somebody to knock my ears down. I'm alone. I can't get on without resources. (31) My old problem still remains—preoccupation with myself. (32) My belief is intellectual. It has no fire in it. (33) I am an urgent case of soul sickness. I am a relative of the demoniac in the Gadarenes. I'm full of fears, self-preoccupied. I'm a counterfeit, I can give advice, but I don't live it.

O Christ, like evening time in Galilee, the sick around Thee lie. Give us healing, full healing of all our self-inflicted hurts. Amen.

AFFIRMATION FOR THE DAY: *My straightforward honesty shall throw open the gates to God's grace.*

"LIFE IS AWFULLY SIMPLE OR SIMPLY AWFUL"

We continue for one more day looking at ourselves through looking at others. (34) I am a half-full vessel trying to run over. (35) I have a lot of knots that need to be untied. (36) I have fled to this Ashram —I didn't come—I fled. I have come to get security. (37) I have been bitter over retiring. I want to be a creative person. (38) I have a sense of superiority. I look down on Negro and white. I need to get down from my pedestals. (39) I hear of a "hilarious giver," but I want to be a "hilarious forgiver." (40) My barriers are self-pity, boredom, fear, swearing, self-centeredness. (41) I seem to be going around in circles. I am in a conflict. If I go back to China, I'll have to go to an Indoctrination camp. I feel I'll be a coward if I don't go back.

(42) I feel resentments against a former pastor's wife who lives in our community. (43) My resentments stay too long. The period of their stay is shortening, but I don't want them to stay at all. (44) I do not forgive myself. I need to. I forgive others but not myself. I'm a coward. I've been running away. I've not had the guts—I've been backwatering. (45) The thing I need I resist. I need a spontaneous honesty and a spontaneous gaiety. (46) I need to get out of myself. I rush hobnailed over the feelings of others. I need empathy. (47) I have had a bad temper for eight years, though my husband doesn't know it. I feel like blowing the roof off sometimes. (48) I want to be what my friends think I am. (49) I know all the answers but I don't live the answers. (50) I've studied psychology and anthropology and my Christianity has faded out. I need to become Christian again.

(51) I have had the shock of being retired. I get out of patience with the saints who are blind to the needs of the world. (52) I need to be less complicated for I am a musician. Life is simply awful or awfully simple. (53) I need reconversion. I deal with ideas but they are not alive. I need release and reserve.

Father-God, we've been looking into the depths of each other's hearts. Now let us look into the depths of Thy heart—to see Thy resources. In Jesus' name. Amen.

AFFIRMATION FOR THE DAY: *All my fading colors retouched by the hand of the living God.*

318

"I'VE LOST MY IMPORTANCE—IN GOD"

We have been looking intimately into the depths of need as revealed by honest souls. We now turn to what these same people said on the last day—"The Morning of the Overflowing Heart."

(1) I feel I have been converted all over again. I've had Jesus so deeply planted in me that I'll never call God a principle of being again. I spent three hours in the prayer room. (2) I held a grief in my heart —my son was killed in the war. Also a great fear. Both grief and fear are gone. (3) I held resentments and called it righteous indignation. I gave it up. I found myself running and bounding up the stairs. I've been made over again. (4) I surrendered my emotions. All my life I've surrendered my will, but I had never surrendered my emotions. Hence I've had a nervous breakdown. But now I've surrendered my emotions and I'm free. (5) I've learned to cease to look at my problems. I've looked at God and had no problems. (6) Had a chart made which showed I had forty allergies, paid $70 for it. I've been full of fears. I've gotten rid of those fears and I believe the allergies will take care of themselves.

(7) I came here and when I heard what we had to do, I felt like dying, now I feel like flying. (8) I came here a very important person, competent and smug. But I've lost my importance—in God. (9) I came here resentful, feeling that the church had no special passion. I've had my resentments taken away and my faith in the church restored. I'm free. (10) I accepted the Kingdom of God ten years ago. But I've been stepping in and out of the Kingdom. Now I'm in. (11) I've had a bunch of allergies, but I've gotten rid of of bottled-up sins and my allergies have dropped away, even asthma. (12) I came here to run away from my family. But I've been running away from myself. I go home with changed attitudes. (13) I came here race-conscious, denomination-conscious, also self-conscious. I've gotten rid of all three. (14) I've been lonely because I've not been in right relations with Christ. I've straightened out that and I'm no longer lonely.

O Christ, while on others Thou art calling, do not pass me by. Thou art healing others, heal me. I know Thy healing is near, so near I have but to take it. Amen.

AFFIRMATION FOR THE DAY: *My receiving set in tune and in operating order today.*

"I WAS EXHAUSTED"

We continue the glorious notes of victory from glad and free hearts. (15) I tried too hard to prove that I was not too old, so I became peevish and fretful and tense. I sinned against the Holy Spirit. I've let go my tensions. (16) Halfway through I got rid of my tensions and the rest was fun. (17) I came here striving for perfection, but the more people came to know me, the more they drew away from me, for they saw I was essentially selfish. Now I'm seeking my perfection in God; I've lost myself by surrender to God and now I've begun to live. I'm free. (18) I've been herd-guided instead of Spirit-guided, so my river became a trickle. Now I've become Spirit-guided and the rivers are beginning to flow.

(19) I've been the victim of half-truth. I've not taken the gift. I thought I was under a demand, now I see it is an offer. It's a whole new vista. (20) I can't breathe when there is someone around me antagonistic. I gave a woman a dessert I didn't like. She gave me one she didn't like. Now we're friends. (21) I was exhausted. My subconscious worked all night and my conscious all day. But I surrendered both to God and I'm released. I'm rested. (22) I lost my grip on reality. I was sermonizing instead of preaching. The cutting edge of my message was gone. There was an interfiltration of egoism, fear, working under tension, most of all, a strong reaction to a wrong situation, was full of resentments. I came to this Ashram with a heavy depression. I've found again what I lost.

(23) I've got back to God. I came up here to fish, but I've never gone once. Besides, people have fished for me and I got caught. (24) A submerged pride was within. It came out as false humility. It's gone. I'm myself. (25) I came here for techniques and information. I go away with the Holy Spirit. (26) I've had a fear of individuals as individuals. I was bold in the pulpit, but outside I was afraid. It's gone. (27) I got rid of my tiny circle of self, and now I'm released to all the world. (28) I've had my spiritual batteries recharged.

O God, as I listen to these victories I begin to feel the possibility of my sharing them. I accept them too—by faith I do. Amen.

AFFIRMATION FOR THE DAY: *Today I rely not on information and technique alone, but on the Holy Spirit primarily.*

"GOD JUST LAUGHED AND LAUGHED"

We listen again to what released souls are saying about their release. (29) I wrote out all my faults. The first one was "Disposition," the last one "Ego." I burned them all in the kitchen stove. (30) I came here with a lot of chips on my shoulders. I also came here with a lot of ice in my heart. I'm a Lutheran and I felt superior. I came with all the answers, but with no smile on my face. My ice has all melted. I'm different. (31) I'm the champion worrier. I'm not happy unless I have something to worry about. But here I've forgotten to worry. It's all gone. (32) I came to the Ashram for the Hound of Heaven was on my trail. God was here and I was over there and we couldn't get together. My resentments have created an atmosphere into which I have to go back. But I'm not afraid now.

(33) I came here mentally, spiritually, and physically tired, and I go away refreshed. (34) I was full of tensions but didn't want to admit it. I got the answer: God just laughed and laughed and I got to laughing too, and I've been laughing ever since. (35) I had a lot of resentments toward those whom I love most. I tried to correct my family by criticism. Now I go back to go at it differently—I'm going back to love. My resentments are all gone. (36) I'm exhibit "A" in knots. I couldn't even smile except it turned into a snarl. I didn't know how to smile. It seems incredible that they could all go in so short a time. But they're all gone—just like that.

(37) I gave a forlorn testimony the other day, but since then I've had a face lifting. The issue has been: How to accept the grace of God. My little five-year-old girl said, "I don't know Jesus, but my Daddy knows Him personally." It was misplaced. But now there is nothing between—I do know Him personally. (38) I came here with a long list of allergies—things I couldn't eat. I've eaten them all and nothing happened. I found it was not enough to hold no resentments —I must have positive outgoing love. (39) The doctor said I shouldn't come as I have a bad heart, but I go away with a rested heart.

O Father God, I thank Thee that Thou hast the answers to all my needs —all of them. I am taking Thy answers—now. Amen.

AFFIRMATION FOR THE DAY: *Too full of love for resentments; too full of joy for gloom; too full of peace for disquietude.*

"I WAS BORN TO LOVE"

We come to our last day of looking at those who found victory and release at the Ashrams. It is a wonderful story of profoundly transformed lives. (40) I was benighted ten days ago; now I am rich. (41) This has been an amazing week of self-revelation. I would have said I didn't have any resentments, but they were there and have been the source of my criticism of others. I came into the Christian faith out of atheism on the basis of a long evening of meditation. But this week I realized that I still had Him on trial. I had never actually surrendered my life to God. Now I have. (42) I had let self creep in and let myself crawl into a shell. I have been released. (43) I have been aware of God above, around, and at my side. Since I came to the Ashram it has been Jesus Christ within.

(44) This week has restored unto me the joy of my salvation. I like pie with meringue, but the trouble is that the meringue so often rubs off. In a chiffon pie the meringue is all through the pie and it can't rub off. This experience is like the meringue in a chiffon pie—it will never rub off. (45) I said I hoped I could get rid of my resentments and suspicions and I found I resented and suspected everyone except the one who ought to have been resented and suspected—myself. I've surrendered that. (46) I needed my call revalidated as a minister. I've gotten on the beam again. (47) Whereas I was dawn, now I'm noonday. My new name is Grace. I've been afraid of receiving in prayer. Now I'm no longer afraid to receive. (48) I've never seen so many wonderful people together. Now I'm going out to love everybody. I wondered why I was born. Now I see why I was born—I was born to love. (49) I was all tied up and nervous when I came, and now I'm all light and free. (50) I've been like a hen trying to gather a brood of rebellious chickens, but now I'm going back to preach and live grace. (51) I lacked confidence in myself, for I lacked confidence in God. I've found confidence in God, so I've gained confidence in myself. (52) You gave me back my sky. I had a resentment against a minister. I left it in the prayer room.

O Loving Father, I am on Thy hands—no longer on my own. I'm taking Thy grace and resources. I am learning to take. I thank Thee. Amen.

AFFIRMATION FOR THE DAY: *I pass from the rank of the transformed to rank of the transforming.*

THE TRANSFORMATION OF THE BODY

We have been listening in to a marvelous recital of transformation of mind and spirit, and incidentally, of the body. We now pause for this week on the matter of transformation of the body.

God wills health. We often create our own sickness. T. E. Murphy says: "In the last twenty years physicians have come to a realization that worry, fear, anger, and hatred are poisons that can cripple and destroy the body as well as the mind; grudges can bring arthritis, rage can bring about the need for surgery. A man's thoughts are the theater of his soul." Christian attitudes toward life would clear up a great many physical illnesses. When Jesus said to the man sick of the palsy, "Man, thy sins are forgiven thee," He saw that there was a connection between the sense of guilt and the paralysis of the body. He lifted the guilt first and then the body was released from its bondage. God wills health. For salvation is wholeness—wholeness to the total person, including the body.

Every emotion that upsets the body is an unchristian emotion. Every emotion that sets up the body is a Christian emotion. An eminent doctor, Charles T. Bingham, says: "Worry, fear, and anger are the greatest disease causers. If we had perfect faith, we wouldn't worry. Faith is the great healer." William James said, "The molecules of his brain have registered his sin against him." But every cell of the body registers our sins or our goodnesses. There is not a single cell of the body removed from the effects, for good or ill, of our emotional states.

Walter C. Alvarez says: "I have had a woman make the air of the consulting room foul with her breath when she was terribly anxious as to what the verdict of her examination would be." A doctor told a girl who was ill to go home and read a chapter of the Bible each day for a month. She did, and when she came back, she was well. The reading of the Bible centered her mind on God instead of on her self and she got well. A man who had to take soda-mint tablets before every meal came to our Ashram and surrendered himself to God and ate everything—even wieners!

O God, I see I owe it to Thee and to myself to make every emotion contribute to health. Help me to give up all disease-producing emotions. Amen.

AFFIRMATION FOR THE DAY: *All my emotions today will produce health, not disease.*

"THE RESENTMENT BECAME AN OBSESSION"

We continue to look at the effect of emotions upon the body. T. E. Murphy tells of a businessman, vice-president of a firm, who was deeply disappointed that an outsider was appointed as president and he was passed over. The resentment became an obsession. One day he was shocked to find two office boys talking about him, how he was going to pieces. In despair he asked a wise friend what to do. "Love the man you resent. Help him," was the answer. Next day he tried it; forced himself to make a suggestion. The new president thanked him and said, "I'm scared of this new job. You know more about it than I do. Please help me." Life changed then and there for both.

A medical authority says: "Of all skin diseases, 30 per cent are produced by blood vessels in the skin reacting in this way to anger, disgust, and fear. The tissues become thickened with serum, become reddish, finally the serum is actually pushed up through the surface of the skin where it becomes scaly, crusty, and itchy, and the result is neurodermatitis."

Here was the case of a man who, every time he had a date with a dentist, started to overbreathe. By the time he was in the dental chair he was a tetany and would fall out of the chair. He overbreathed through fear.

A man hadn't worked for a year. Three months before he got ill his wife died, a month later his son was killed. Then he went around thinking to himself. "Why did this happen to me?" Through self-pity he became ill.

Hans Selye of Toronto University tells of an experiment with rats in a cage with dogs looking at them through a glass panel. The rats became tired. Blood from the tired rats was put into the veins of a normal rat and immediately it became tired. He took blood from a person who was having a nervous breakdown and put it into a normal rat and that rat became tired.

An Indian young man wrote me: "I intended to tell you about my tour but I am not feeling well. I had a very disturbing letter from my brother." The disturbing letter produced disturbed health.

Father, I see that I must be healthy in mind and soul if I am to be healthy in body. I want to be every whit whole. And Thou who hast made the whole hast willed health for the whole. I'm grateful. Amen.

AFFIRMATION FOR THE DAY: *I am not tired—I'm fresh in God!*

"THE SPIRIT IN TROUBLE"

We continue to look at the effect of emotional unhealth upon the health of the body. The Japanese have a very significant character for disease. It means "the spirit in trouble." For a long time medical science thought disease was "the body in trouble." So much physical disease, so much physical remedy. As a result of this, operations were performed for physical difficulties not there. Then they began to come to psychosomatic medicine—a medicine that recognizes that some diseases root in the soma, the body, and some in the psyche, the mind or soul. Opinions differ as to the proportion, but it is now conceded that it is fifty-fifty or more on the side of the psyche. Doctors at the Mayo Clinic say they can deal with only 25 per cent of the patients that come to them with the instruments of science. The 75 per cent cannot be touched by the instruments of science—they need to change their attitudes of mind and soul before they will get well.

Dr. Hamilton Robinson of Ohio State College of Dentistry says that mental upsets may produce mouth diseases, even tooth decay. So mental and spiritual upsets can reach in their effects clear to the marrow of the bones and to the center of the teeth.

I sat in a barber's chair and as a man was leaving he called out to the barber, "Well, be good." And the barber thoughtfully replied, "I'll have to." For if he wasn't good, the results would register themselves in every cell of his body. So humanity that wouldn't listen to goodness and right living as preached by the Bible now has to listen to it as preached by the unfolding facts of life. Both Bible and blood are now saying the same thing: Be Christian.

One woman estimated that she saved each year $500 in medicines since she surrendered herself and her wrong emotional attitudes to God. So she gives that amount each year to God. The economic waste of living in unchristian ways is appalling. If for no other reason than economics, we should be Christian. But that is the least of the reasons. The whole of the reasons adds up to a life reason—life demands it.

O Christ, everything in heaven and on earth, within me and without me, is pushing me to Thy feet. I come pushed and impelled. Amen.

AFFIRMATION FOR THE DAY: *If disease is often "my spirit in trouble," today my health shall be "my spirit in adjustment."*

STEPS INTO HEALTH

The effects of emotions on health are seen in this striking case. Here was a man, treasurer of a company, drawing a salary of $15,000 a year. At a party he took one too many drinks, coming home he had an accident and had his license taken away. He was let out in a reduction of staff, got another job, but not so good. His wife at a party took too many drinks, left in anger at another woman's paying attention to her husband. On the way home she ran into a parked car. Her license was taken away too. Both were humiliated. He became ill and in thirty-six hours was dead. An autopsy couldn't find a thing the matter. His will to live had snapped, and with no faith to sustain him, he died of mental suicide.

We have seen enough of the effects of wrong emotion on the body. We must now turn to see the effect of right emotions on the body and the steps we are to take into health.

1. *Since God wills health, then when you will it, you are in line with the purposes of God.* You are working with the grain of the universe, not against it. You are natural when you are healthy, for your body is made for health, not disease.

2. *So relax and let the healing processes inherent in you and inherent in God work within you.* Tension ties them up and relaxed receptivity lets them operate.

3. *Let the climate of your life be cheerful faith instead of fearful anxiety.* In Japan, where this is written, a great many people go around their daily tasks with influenza masks over their mouths and noses to keep out the influenza germs. Wearing them all day long, they probably accumulate germs in these pads. At any rate, the constant thought of germs suggested by the pads creates an inner condition of anxiety susceptible to germs. Your very breathing an atmosphere of faith sterilizes most if not all of these germs. Ninety per cent of disease germs falling on a healthy skin die within ten minutes—killed by health. The best germicide is a happy, outgoing, trustful type of mind. God's health pours through it.

O God, I thank Thee that Thy will and my inner structure and my attitudes converge on health. I am the meeting ground for victorious health. I'm grateful. Amen.

AFFIRMATION FOR THE DAY: *My affirmative, hopeful attitude toward life will be my best germicide today.*

"I SHALL WEAVE THOSE WRINKLES INTO SMILES"

We left off yesterday at the place of the climate of life being health. When I was about to sail on a ship from New York in winter time, the ship was covered with snow and ice. I wondered why they didn't attempt to get rid of it before sailing. I saw the answer in a few days, for we were soon in the Gulf Stream and all that snow and ice which could have been chipped away only laboriously now simply melted away by the change of climate. It was all done so easily. Don't try to chip away your clinging diseases by tense anxiety—live in the warm Gulf Stream of faith and confidence and many of the diseases will simply melt away.

4. *Don't let old age invade your mind when the calendar says it's time to do so.* Assert your eternal youthfulness in God. You are literally youthful in Him. So let the Holy Ghost put back your shoulders. I wrote in my notebook: "I'm going to beat my body into shape—from within! When Time's blows dent it, I shall beat out those dents by my ardent spirit's answering blows. When age presses on me and wrinkles my exterior, I shall press out those wrinkles by my expanding spirit. Or if I can't, then I shall weave those wrinkles into smiles. And I shall make my outer into the image of this gay, youthful Within!"

5. *Learn the power of laughter.* There is a village in Suffolk, England, a population of 694, with 125 "laughing Methuselahs," 32 of them over 80, who qualify for old age pensions. The reason, Chester James says, is that "we laugh and joke more than most." Almost nothing tones up the body as good healthy laughter which comes from the depths—not surface cackles induced by drink and entertainment, but laughter that laughs at the rhythm of life.

6. *Hold in the back of your thinking the backlog thought that when you will health, God is willing it too; so is your body, since it is made in its inner structure for health; all three converge on one thing —your health.* So in willing health you are working with God, not against Him. You are in line with Creation's meaning.

O God, my Father, I thank Thee that Thou art conspiring with me to give me the best body I can have. Help me to work with Thee. Amen.

AFFIRMATION FOR THE DAY: *God, the universe and my body are conspiring to make me healthy—I enter the conspiracy.*

HEALTH THROUGH THE INDWELLING SPIRIT

Here are the concluding suggestions for health:

7. *The Spirit of God quickens you into health if you will allow Him:* "He . . . will also make your mortal bodies live by his indwelling Spirit in your lives" (Rom. 8:11, Moffatt). Now note the indwelling Spirit makes the body live indirectly, that is, He does it by being "in your lives," not merely in your bodies. The indirect effects of the Holy Spirit in the life are greater possibly than the direct effects on the body. A climate of life is produced where health is a by-product. When the Holy Spirit saves us from fears, anxieties, resentments, egocentricity, and guilts, then the result is inward harmony and rhythm and consequent physical health. One psychologist estimates that half of our diseases would drop off tomorrow if we lived in a truly Christian way.

8. *But sometimes the Holy Spirit touches our bodies not indirectly, but directly and vitally.* Take this case of a prominent theological professor who, between the ages of fifteen and twenty-two, had Pott's disease of the lumbar region of the spine and was unable to work. There was a structural lesion involving two vertebrae. He wore a plaster cast from hips to armpits, then a mechanical brace. But he grew worse. At the age of twenty-two, since he belonged to the Church of the Brethren, he called for an anointing service. During the service he knew in his body that a change had taken place. Gradually the sores in his spine were healed and no trace of active tuberculosis was discernible through a long and active life. This healing took place over fifty years ago and he is still active and teaching today.

Then here was the case of a banker who was expected to die of an incurable heart condition. The doctors stood waiting for the end when a group praying felt he would be healed—and he was. He was soon back at his office and lived a very useful and radiant life. When he did die, the doctors, anxious to see if they had made a wrong diagnosis, held an autopsy and found that they were right, but an actual healing had taken place.

O Spirit of Health and Healing, touch all my weaknesses into strength, all my diseases into health and all my feeblenesses into fruitfulness. Amen.

AFFIRMATION FOR THE DAY: *I work co-operatively with the health-giving Spirit within me today.*

"THE PULL IS GONE"

We continue to meditate upon the possibility of God touching directly our bodies into health. A very cultured woman, wife of the dean of a great university, had effected neck muscles which turned her head to one side and compelled her to wear a cast. An operation was contemplated. We went into the prayer chapel and prayed, and there she received assurance that she was healed. She hadn't been able to sit and look at a speaker for long without great pain, the neck twisting to one side. Now she sat for hours without pain or pressure, the pull was gone. She was radiant and told of it freely at the Ashram and when she got home. Friends, trying to rationalize it, suggested that she had gained rest at the Ashram and that was responsible. Her reply was that this took place on the second day before she had any time for rest!

But it was more than a physical touch—the whole person was made new. She writes: "I've found too that when a person enters God's Kingdom, there's another change that comes over him. He has an assurance he didn't have before, not that he feels he is any better than anyone else, but he feels that no one else has anything better than he has—unless he has more of it. It just gives an assurance that is different."

And then she adds: "I'm glad you gave us the thought of using the things to which our minds might wander during prayer time—use them as starting points for prayer. It's fun to use those wandering thoughts. I found myself during prayer time listening to the refrigerator: 'God, freeze all unkind thoughts that would keep my mind and heart from being lifted up.' And I found myself thinking about a telephone cord one of my teen-agers had broken: 'God, telephone into my soul the things Thou wouldst have me do for Thee today.' O. K.? That's lots better than feeling guilty about mind wandering." She gave to missions the cost of the operation that didn't take place, and then playfully said, "Now, I won't be able to talk about my operation!" But she can and does talk about the Saviour from an operation—and from very much more!

O Christ, Thou art the Saviour from everything that keeps me from being the kind of person I ought to be. Thou art the perfect Transformer. I thank Thee. Amen.

AFFIRMATION FOR THE DAY: *I bombard every cell of my body with life-giving rays of Thy Spirit.*

THE TRANSFORMATION OF HUMAN RELATIONSHIPS

We now come in our study of transformation to the transformation of human relationships. The history of human relationships might be summed up as five stages: (*a*) Owner and slave; (*b*) master and servant; (*c*) employer and employee; (*d*) comrades and deviators; (*e*) brothers.

The first stage was owner and slave. This was an almost universal relationship in humanity. And it was considered inherent. Aristotle could say, "Some men are born naturally rulers and others are born naturally slaves, as a dog is naturally a dog and a cat is naturally a cat." It was not only inherent but God-approved. "When Israel became a power, they forced the Canaanites to slave for them" (Josh. 17:13, Moffatt). And in the passage which Jesus quoted in the synagogue at Nazareth, beginning with "The Spirit of the Lord is upon me . . . to preach good news to the poor," there is this verse, "The foreigner shall serve you as a herdsman, the alien shall work your fields and vineyards" (Isa. 61:5, Moffatt). Jesus left that out.

In the New Testament slavery is not fought directly but by an indirect method. Someone has said that there is no method of reform so powerful as this: Alongside of a corrupt practice there is laid an incompatible principle. That incompatible principle will silently work against that corrupt practice and will overthrow it. Alongside the practice of slavery there was laid the incompatible principle of human brotherhood, that a man was no longer a man, but "a man for whom Christ died." That incompatible principle killed slavery. Christians began to free their slaves on certain festivals, and when there were no more slaves to be freed, they would loose a white dove as a symbol.

Paul wrote to Philemon, the owner of Onesimus, a slave, and said, "No longer a mere slave but something more than a slave—a beloved brother" (Philem. 16, Moffatt). In every man there was seen "something more," and that "something more" was the leaven that permeated society and killed slavery. Master and slave knelt together at the same communion rail and received the same Communion and thus slavery died—asphyxiated.

O Christ, I thank Thee that Thou hast put such an infinite worth in each one of us that we can never, never again be satisfied with chains. Thou art liberty. Amen.

AFFIRMATION FOR THE DAY: *I shall look at every man today with the eyes of Christ.*

DISSATISFACTION WITH UNEQUAL RELATIONSHIPS

We continue our meditation on the transformation of human relationships. While slavery, as the complete ownership of one man by another was abolished as such, yet it was not dead and came back in milder guises. Slavery, put out at the door, came back by the window as master and servant. The servant was not the property of the master, but was compelled by economic necessity to work for a master if he was to survive. It was voluntary servitude through economic necessity. The master's conscience was a bit easier with this relationship since the servant voluntarily attached himself to him for wages. But he failed to see that the system which he had set up compelled the servant to seek that relationship in order to survive. The servant was a slave still —the slave of economic necessity.

The master-and-servant relationship left both master and servant unhappy—down underneath. No one has a right to make of another man a means to his ends. The servant was a means to the ends of the master's wealth, just as a plow or an ox was. He was an instrument and not an individual—a means and not an end in himself. Jesus said, "Neither be ye called masters: for one is your Master, even Christ" and "All ye are brethren" (Matt. 23:10, 8).

Here again was the incompatible principle laid alongside of a wrong relationship—the principle of "all ye are brethren" laid alongside of the practice of master and servant. They are incompatible, and the brotherhood principle is silently fighting the master-and-servant relationship.

The barons of Britain could say to the king: "We who are as good as you are, say to you who are no better than we are, that we will make you our lord and king, provided you promise to protect our liberties and our rights. If not, then not." This was a step forward—the servants were choosing their own masters. But the brotherhood extended to barons as barons—a class. The common people were still *common* people. James I decreed that no one less than a baron could eat pie! There is a statute still upon the statute books of Massachusetts forbidding the common people to wear the clothes of gentry.

O Christ, Thou art pressing upon our inequalities with Thy mind— and that pressure disturbs us into revolution. We thank Thee. Amen.

AFFIRMATION FOR THE DAY: *Today I shall think about man, not as man thinks, but as God thinks.*

"MAN SHALL NOT LIVE BY BREAD ALONE"

We continue to look at the pressure of the mind of Christ upon our relationships causing ferment and change.

The relationship of master and servant, being untenable in a society where the Christian principle of "all ye are brethren" is at work, we softened the relationship by making it into employer and employee. The words "master" and "servant" were done away with and the words "employer" and "employee" substituted as expressing a contract relationship. The employee may be as good as the employer theoretically, but a contract relationship is entered into. Actually, it was the old relationship of master and servant back again in a softened form, for the employer owned the means of production and could hire and fire. The employee was a servant still—a servant not now of a master, but of a system. He was a cog in an industrial machine, the purpose of which was to earn dividends for the owners and in the process supply him with wages sufficient to keep him working.

Unions were organized, their primary purpose being to keep up wages. Through collective bargaining and the power of the strike they have succeeded in making wages in the United States the highest in human history. The workman who has a job within the system is better off than the employee has ever been.

But is he contented? No, for man does not live by bread alone. He is not just a hungry animal who is contented when well fed. He is a person—a person for whom Christ died, and he feels brotherhood stirring within him. He is not content to have his "brotherhood" extend only to his fellow employees. He is excluded from management and from the profits of the system. He feels he is a servant still, though a very well-off servant. The business is not his—he is a servant of it. In that is the area of his inner discontent. And mere higher wages and greater privileges will not cure that discontent.

A baron said to me in Holland: "Look at the number of people to whom I give employment on my estate. They should be grateful." They were—in a way. But only "in a way"—they were servants still. Servants of hereditary barons or money barons are servants still—as such, discontented.

O Christ, Thou art disturbing our relationships to set them on a right basis—Thy basis, a brotherhood basis. Help us to respond. Amen.

AFFIRMATION FOR THE DAY: *The moral universe guarantees the instability of an unjust situation.*

JOSEPH SERVED HIS MASTERS WELL!

Before we leave the employer-and-employee relationship, we must look at a vivid account of how Joseph, representing management for Pharaoh, the owner, got the wealth of the people into the hands of his employer.

Joseph got the Pharaoh "to annex" a fifth part of the grain of the country during the prosperous years. Then during the famine years the people paid for the grain (really their own annexed grain) till their money gave out. Then Joseph got the people to bring their cattle and livestock. Then the people said: "We have nothing left for my lord except our persons and our lands. . . . Buy us and our land for food. . . . The land became the property of the Pharaoh, and as for the people, they were reduced to thraldom from one end of Egypt to the other." Then taking advantage of the people's hunger, "Joseph drew up a regulation for Egypt to this day, that a fifth should fall to the Pharaoh" (Gen. 47:18-19, 21, 26, Moffatt). Thus shrewd management got the land for his employer. Joseph got the applause of his employer and found a sense of importance. Joseph lost touch with the people in his drive for profits for his employer. He, a man of the people, let the people down.

Often today when men come up from the ranks of the people into the ranks of the managers, they lose touch with the people and become harder than their employers.

But the people are there still seething in their often unuttered discontent. They are servants still, even if they are called employees. And no man can be content to be a servant. He has a divine destiny and therefore "a divine discontent." He feels that he has not come into his heritage as yet. For his heritage is more than good wages. He must be a part, and an important part, in the direction of the system of which he is a part. If "good government is no substitute for self-government" in governmental affairs, it is also true in economic affairs. Man wants to help manage that which he serves. Only then will he serve well and with his whole heart. He wants to be a person.

O Lord and Master of us all, forgive us that we try to make our brothers means to our ends. Save us from exploiting others for our ends. Amen.

AFFIRMATION FOR THE DAY: *I shall strive in the love and power of Christ to bring everybody and everything into a brotherhood relationship.*

COMRADES, LTD.

Into this relationship of employer and employee there steps a very compelling person and says, "You are to be no longer employer and employee. You are comrades." That is the voice of the Communist.

And this voice is very catching to the discontented masses. They are at last to be "comrades" in the industrial and social and political process. It sounds emancipating. A new dignity is offered to the common people—they are comrades.

There is no doubt that in some ways there is emancipation. The common man and woman do have a larger share in the direction of the industrial machine. When the young people carried loads of dirt out of the subway in Moscow and chanted, "We're making a new world," they doubtless felt they were in a new era of freedom to create. And within the system they were.

But only within the system. The word "comrade" expresses the relationship. The word comes from the Spanish *camarada*—a chamber fellow—one who is in the same room with you. You are a comrade to one who is in the same room with you. But you are not a comrade to anyone occupying another room in the house of humanity. Wear my label and you get my love, otherwise you get my hate. The word "comrade" is too small a word to fit a world need. For the house of humanity has more than one room. The iron curtain is an attempt to make it one room by shutting out the rest of humanity.

Besides, the freedom from employer and employee is only seeming. For now everyone becomes an employee of the state. The state employs everybody—a state capitalism. The peasants of China were told that they would get the land from the large landowners. They did. But they got it—to work it for the government. No deeds were given them. The land belongs to the state and the peasants to their dismay found they have a new employer, the state. And the state brooks no criticism. "Stalin is my conscience," was written on the walls of a prison in Assam. But Stalin is the state. The individual has no conscience apart from the state. Siberia is the answer to the protest of the individual conscience.

O God, the half answers don't answer. They let us down. We are looking for Thy Answer, for Thy Answer alone will answer. In Jesus' name. Amen.

AFFIRMATION FOR THE DAY: *Today I shall stand not for "Comrades, Ltd.," but for "Brothers, Unlimited."*

THE WORLD'S STRUGGLE WITH A WORD

The human race is struggling with words—words which express relationships. We have seen the struggle with the words owner, slave, master, servant, employer, employee, comrade, deviator. At each stage there is an attempt to get to an ultimate basis of relationship. The Communists think they have it in the word "comrade," but the comradeship extends to those of the same room, Communists. They are ruthless to non-Communists. Their comradeship is a comradeship of belief and practice. They are ruthless to those who deviate from their line. And that "line" comes from the Kremlin.

Now humanity is trying to come to an ultimate word, a Christian word—brother. We are trying to say that one word and don't know how. But until we say it, we are doomed to clash and strife in every department of life. Jesus said, "All ye are brethren, . . . one is your Father" (Matt. 23:8-9). And He said this not merely to His disciples but "to the crowds and to his disciples." He did not say, "You ought to be brethren"; He said, "ye are"—inescapably so. Now of course there is a deeper sense in which only those who are reborn into the family of God are fundamentally brothers. But we are brothers by the fact of a common origin in God, of common needs, and of a human solidarity. We are one.

Jesus therefore proposed that life be organized on a brother basis. Is that revolutionary? Yes, very. And rightly so. For the slight upset of getting to a brother basis would be nothing compared to the vast human confusion and upset now operative in human affairs as we try to live on a nonbrother basis. We are trying to work life in a way that life won't work. For we are made for the brother basis of living and in no other way. From the lowest cell of the body to the vast organism called humanity there is one law of life, and only one—co-operation. Where there is non-co-operation and hostility there is one result, and only one result—death. Our individual, economic, social, political, and international relationships must come to a brother basis or we perish.

O God, our Father, we are trying to live against Thy cosmic plan and we are hurting ourselves with self-inflicted hurts. Forgive us. And help us to take Thy way. Amen.

AFFIRMATION FOR THE DAY: *I shall say and mean the word "brother," even if I am the only one who says it.*

"A FAMILY INSTEAD OF A FEUD"

We are studying the ultimate word in relationships—"brother." Jesus described that relationship as "Thou shalt love thy neighbor as thyself," and then He defined the neighbor as a man of another race in need. The Jews had that same commandment and took the teeth out of it by defining the "neighbor" as a Jew. They didn't reject it—they reduced it.

We do the same. Near an atomic energy plant is a large placard entitled: "How We Protect Our Neighbors," with the description of how the chickens, cattle, plants, and the people living around the plant were protected from radioactivity. But as I looked at this description I kept saying to myself, "Protect our neighbors?" Who is my neighbor? Here you are making atomic bombs to drop on people somewhere—innocent or guilty—and all the time talking of protecting our neighbors. Yes, who is my neighbor? This is the same position as "comrade"—a comrade to those of my room—the United States! This is sub-Christian. The brother basis extends to a person as a person.

Applied to our relationships, what would the word and attitude of "brother" mean? (*a*) It would mean a society in which there is equality of opportunity to everyone, regardless of race and class and religion and sex. (*b*) It would mean in economics a labor-capital management and a division of the profits and losses. This would mean what Kagawa calls "brotherhood economics." (*c*) It would mean world government under which there would be equal security to all nations to carry out their way of life within their own boundary lines.

That would let down tensions in three great realms: (*a*) personal and social relationships, (*b*) economic relationships, and (*c*) international relationships.

The struggle in the world is the struggle with a word—that word "brother." We are dissatisfied with owner and slave, master and servant, employer and employee, comrade and deviator, and are reaching for a long-lost word—a word Jesus taught us, the word "brother." When we take that word and act on it, the world will be a family instead of a feud.

O Father, we cannot escape brotherhood for it is inherent. Help us to come to what we are—a world of brothers. Amen.

AFFIRMATION FOR THE DAY: *We can save the employer-employee basis by shifting it to a brotherhood basis.*

WORLD TRANSFORMATION

We come now in our study of transformation to the question of world transformation. There are many who are convinced that the Christian way is the way of transformation, but question whether it can transform the world except incidentally through transformed individuals. Its influence is indirect—it has no head-on proposal or plan for world transformation. Secular forces must control the collective life of mankind.

Well, the control of secular forces has led us to the collective mess we are in—two world wars in one generation and now we tremble on the brink of a third. Does Christianity let us down in the area where direction and control is most needed—the collective?

Not the Christianity of Christ. For Christ presented something that is a head-on and all-inclusive proposal for the control of the individual and collective life. That proposal was the Kingdom of God. The Kingdom of God on earth is the most astonishing and radical proposal ever presented to humanity. It is nothing less than that the whole of life shall be organized around one center—the will of God. If that total demand on the total life is totally obeyed, then there would be total freedom. When you totally obey the other totalitarianisms, you find total bondage.

The Kingdom of God is the answer which men are dimly reaching for through the half answers of fascism, nazism, and communism—something to bring the total life into coherence and direction and goal. Men are finding that their freedom based on their own individual wills is the freedom to tie themselves into knots; the freedom to become problems to themselves and others. They want something to command them, something that they can obey, and yet they want their freedom too. Only the Kingdom of God puts those two things together.

But the Christian church pushed the Kingdom of God back into the inner spirit as individual experience, and then pushed it beyond the borders of this life in heaven as collective experience and left the economic, social, and political unredeemed. Into that vacuum rushed the modern totalitarianisms and took over where we abdicated.

O Christ, forgive us this wrong that we have made Thy answer into an answer too small for world need. Help us to rediscover Thy way for our total life. Amen.

AFFIRMATION FOR THE DAY: *The Kingdom is God's answer—may it be my answer.*

337

THAT IMPONDERABLE SOMETHING

The Kingdom of God is God's total answer to man's total need. The totalitarianisms took over where we abdicated, saying to us, "We will leave you the inner mystical personal experience of the Kingdom of God now, and the collective experience hereafter in heaven, we will take over the rest and control it." And yet they can't—simply can't. They are always running up against something imponderable—something that always breaks them. What is it?

It is nothing less than the Kingdom of God which is written into the nature of things. Jesus said that the Kingdom of God would come in three ways: First, by gradualism, the mustard seed that becomes a great tree, the leaven that leavens the whole. Second, by apocalypticism, or the sudden coming of the Kingdom by the return of Christ to set it up. Third, by the realization that the Kingdom *is*: "The Kingdom of God is within you"—it is written into your being as the laws of your being. "The Kingdom of God is in the midst of you" (R.S.V.)—the Kingdom is "in the midst of you" as the laws of your relationships to each other and to the material universe, it is "in the midst of you."

That Kingdom has been "prepared for you from the foundation of the world"—it is built into the structure of the world as the laws of its being. If we live according to the Kingdom, we live ("the Kingdom of God" and "Life" are used synonymously, Mark 9:45, 47, Moffatt), if we live against it, we perish.

Suppose nazism or fascism or communism could claim that the laws they promulgate by decree are the laws of the beings over whom they rule—that these laws are simply the way men are made to live—what an advantage they would have! But the Kingdom of God is not something imposed on humanity—its laws are not imposed, but exposed from the nature of things. Here is a Kingdom whose decrees are the very decrees of our necessities; are the complement of us. When we find them, we find ourselves; when we break them, we break ourselves. What an advantage that is! A Kingdom which has its seat in our nerves, our blood, our tissues, our organs, our relationships—how ultimate and inescapable it is!

O God, I thank Thee that Order and subject are made for each other and that when we obey that Order we obey the order of our necessities. Amen.

AFFIRMATION FOR THE DAY: *"The Kingdom of God is within you"*—the laws of my being are the laws of the Kingdom.

DESTROYED BY NO MORTAL BLADE

We ended yesterday on the thought that the Kingdom of God is not a set of laws imposed, but the law of life exposed. It is against this strange imponderable that the kingdoms break themselves.

Isaiah saw this strange imponderable as the final arbiter of human destiny, "Then falls Assyria, by no hero's sword, destroyed, but by no mortal blade, Assyrians fly before the Sword" (Isa. 31:8, Moffatt). He saw that Assyria would fall by "no hero's sword," but by "the Sword." Men and nations are cut down by a moral universe when they fall afoul of it—cut down by the Sword! Evil has the seeds of its own destruction within it, for evil is an attempt to live against the nature of things, against Reality. Evil is not only bad; it is stupid, for it is an attempt to live life in a way life is not made to work. "Sin is plainly a vandalism against life, a rebel flag of pride lifted against the creation." So all sin and sinners, individual and collective, perish—they perish by "the Sword."

When someone spoke about the "liquidations" that take place under communism, and their ruthless suppressions, my remark was: "I'm not so much afraid of their badness as of their goodness, for the more ruthless and oppressive they become, the quicker they go. It is the good things in the system that keep it going." When they use the sword to suppress all "deviations," they "shall perish with the sword." It is quite possible to capitalize the s in the statement of Jesus and make it read, "They that take the sword shall perish with the Sword," and thus emphasize the statement of Isaiah. For it would fit in with that statement of Jesus referring to Himself: "Everyone who falls on that stone will be shattered, and whoever it falls upon will be crushed" (Luke 20:18, Moffatt). We see that shattering and that crushing taking place before our very eyes—individuals who go against Him go to pieces; nations that refuse to build on this Stone stumble over it to their doom. Today the judgment seat of Christ is set up and all men stand before it and hear the inexorable verdict of the final Word.

O Christ, Thou art the terrible meek. We tremble at Thy word, for it is the final judgment of life. Help us to build on that word now. Amen.

AFFIRMATION FOR THE DAY: *Everything and everybody is being brought now before the judgment seat of Christ.*

"HEWN . . . BY NO HUMAN HANDS"

The Kingdom of God as embodied in Christ has the final say in human affairs. Daniel puts it vividly in his vision of the huge image with its "head of fine gold, its breasts and arms of silver, its belly and thighs of bronze, its legs of iron, its feet partly iron and partly clay." Then he "saw a stone being hewn out by no human hands" strike "the image on its feet, part iron and part clay, breaking them to bits; and then the iron, the clay, the bronze, the silver, and the gold, were all broken to bits, and whirled away by the wind . . . till they could not be found. The stone that struck the image became a great mountain, filling all the earth" (Dan. 2:32-35, Moffatt). Then he interprets the vision: the mixture of the iron and the clay represents a kingdom of strength and weakness: "but they shall not hold together, any more than iron blends with clay; and in the days of these kings the God of heaven shall set up a kingdom never to be swept away, with a sovereignty that shall never pass to others; it shall break all these kingdoms to bits and make an end of them, but it shall stand for ever, as you saw how the stone was hewn from the mountain by no human hands and how it broke to bits the iron, the bronze, the clay, the silver, and the gold" (Dan. 2:43-45, Moffatt).

Is the stone hewn out by no human hands—not set up by man and thus incapable of being overthrown by man—the Kingdom of God which shall break in pieces all the kingdoms whose brilliant civilizations have heads of gold and feet of clay? Yes! The systems set up by man kick against the rock of the Kingdom with their feet of iron and clay and go to pieces in the kicking. The dust heaps of the centuries are filled with ruined kingdoms—ruined because they went against the strange Imponderable.

And let not the proud civilizations of today point to the strength of those civilizations—the iron in them. It is the clay that ruins them, even if that clay is mixed with iron. If we treat men as means instead of ends—that's clay. If we refuse to divide the profits of industry with labor—that's clay. If we clash instead of co-operate—that's clay. If we depend on military might instead of moral right—that's clay. And God's stone is rolling!

O God, we know that we are clay when we do not obey. And we get hurt. Help us. Amen.

AFFIRMATION FOR THE DAY: *Whenever I depart from Christ I'm clay —and I know it!*

"THE DETHRONED POWERS WHO RULE"

We are studying the Kingdom which, like a rock hewn out by no human hands, smites all our images with feet of clay, destroys them, and then fills the earth.

The reply is a sigh, "Yes, but the man-made images are still in the earth and they are still the centers of ruling power." They are, but they are doomed. Paul gives an accurate description in these words, "The dethroned Powers who rule this world" (I Cor. 2:6), Moffatt). They were still ruling but they were dethroned—the sentence of doom, of dethronement, had been passed on them. There are a lot of people and systems still ruling today, but they are dethroned. They do not fit in with God's order, the Kingdom, and so they silently decay or suddenly collapse.

The racialisms of the world, which take as their premise the superiority of one race over another, rule on, but they are dethroned. The equal worth of every man before God silently presses on them and they will topple. An economic system which can hire and fire at will, and will not share its profits with labor, still rules on, but it is dethroned. It must change into a system of capital-labor management and a sharing of profits and losses; then it can be saved. A labor union organizer, after I had spoken on labor-capital management and profit sharing, said, "Does Stanley Jones want to put the unions out of business?" Co-operation between capital and labor would ruin his union, which is based on conflict. That kind of unionism may still rule, but it is dethroned. It doesn't fit into the Kingdom, for its central drive is "Thou shalt love thyself," while the Kingdom drive is "Thou shalt love thy neighbor as thyself."

A system of armed balances of power still rules, but it is dethroned. It is repudiated inwardly by the common people. In their hearts they want collective security for all through world government. Give the peoples of the earth a chance to vote and they will vote overwhelmingly for world government. Systems of power politics still rule, but they are dethroned from the affections and confidence of men. We hope they will go without pulling civilization down with them like blind Samson.

O God, we know that Thy judgments are in the earth and all that is shakable will be removed. Help us to build on Thy rock. Amen.

AFFIRMATION FOR THE DAY: *Everything is inwardly dethroned except that which fits into Christ.*

"A KINGDOM THAT CANNOT BE SHAKEN"

We ended yesterday with the dethroned powers which rule this world. They are on the way out, every one of them. They are shakable.

There is a passage which tells of an unshakable Kingdom. In Moscow one morning at my Quiet Time it arose out of the Scriptures and "spoke to my condition": "Wherefore, receiving a kingdom that cannot be shaken let us have thankfulness" (Heb. 12:28, A.S.V.). We are in the midst of world-shaking movements, and the things that are "shaken" are being removed. (V. 27) Amid the crashing of systems built up through the centuries, did anything remain unshaken and unshakable? Yes. The Kingdom of God was not only unshaken, it was unshakable—"a kingdom that cannot be shaken"—literally "cannot," for it is the very foundation of the universe.

Communism has iron in it; it is strong and makes an appeal to some who want a better order for the common man, but amid that iron is clay—a lot of clay. Communists have no God, no stable moral universe, are ready to use any means to get to the ends of communism, believe that all the great changes of history are made by force and force alone, and are ruthless toward all who differ. This clay will be struck by the Stone cut out by no human hand and it will cause the image to crash. Today? Tomorrow? Maybe not. But the third day? Yes! The truth of God's Kingdom will rise and will have the last word. Am I thankful that we have a Kingdom that cannot be shaken? To my finger tips!

The next day in Moscow I went again to the Quiet Time and another verse arose and again spoke to my condition, "Jesus Christ is the same yesterday and today and forever" (Heb. 13:8, R.S.V.). Here is an unchanging Person—"the same yesterday and today and forever." Change everywhere, but not in Him. He forces change on everything by His moral authority—Himself unchanged! I came out of Russia with two things in my heart: An unshakable Kingdom and an unchanging Person. They were two then. Now they have coalesced and have become one—an unchanging Person embodying an unshakable Kingdom, the absolute Person and the absolute Order. That is the answer!

O God, I am thankful that I can receive this Kingdom and live in it and let it live in me. That is my ultimate security—and the world's. I am thankful. Amen.

AFFIRMATION FOR THE DAY: *If I am identified with the Kingdom, I am identified with ultimate security.*

"THE KINGDOM WILL COME"

The final transformation is given in this vivid language: "Then I saw the new heaven and the new earth, for the first heaven and the first earth had passed away. . . . And I saw the holy City, the new Jerusalem, descending from God out of heaven, all ready like a bride arrayed for her husband. And I heard a loud voice out of the throne, crying, 'Lo, God's dwelling-place is with men.' . . . Then he who was seated on the throne said, 'Lo, I make all things new.' . . . Then he said, 'All is over! I am the alpha and the omega, the beginning and the end'" (Rev. 21:1-3, 5-6, Moffatt).

Here the goal of history is seen as the coming of the holy city, the new Jerusalem, to earth—a city, a corporate entity is to replace the present world order. This is pictorial language for what Jesus called the coming of the Kingdom, "Thy kingdom come, thy will be done, on earth as it is in heaven." He would not give us an impossible prayer to pray—a prayer that has no fulfillment. The Kingdom will come! The Kingdom is coming—coming now as destruction to all who will not fit into it. And after all the ways have been tried and have broken themselves upon the Way, then the Kingdom will be manifested as reality—the only Reality.

This "holy City" is depicted as "a bride arrayed for her husband." Heaven and earth are to be married. They are made for each other. The period of estrangement between earth and heaven is over and they are wedded forevermore. There will be the marriage of the individual and the collective, the personal and the social, the material and the spiritual—all things are made new in a higher synthesis.

The first Incarnation was the divine Word become flesh—God incarnate in a Person. The second Incarnation will be the divine Order become incarnate in a new earth. Then the two Incarnations will complete the coming together of the Person and the Order in actual realization on earth. This is the omega—the final Word. So the Christ of the beginning, the alpha, becomes the Christ of the final word, the omega. This is the final consummation, the final transformation.

O God, I know that the whole creation groans and travails with pain awaiting the manifestation of the sons of God, awaiting the coming of the Kingdom. May Thy Kingdom come. Amen.

AFFIRMATION FOR THE DAY: *Today, as far as I am concerned, the Kingdom is here!*

343

CONTINUOUS TRANSFORMATION

We now turn this week to look at continuous transformation. Our main stress has been upon the crisis in transformation, and I believe this emphasis has been sound, for "the soul gets on by a series of crises." The crisis precipitates decision, the decision precipitates acceptance of grace, and acceptance of grace precipitates transformation.

But while transformation comes through crisis, it also comes through process—a continuing transformation. This passage gives that continuing process better perhaps than any in Scripture: "But we all mirror the glory of the Lord with face unveiled, and so we are being transformed into the same likeness as himself, passing from one glory to another—for this comes of the Lord the Spirit" (II Cor. 3:18, Moffatt). The phrase "we are being transformed" depicts that continuous process of transformation—a process, I believe, that has no end. It will continue for eternity.

Here then is the figure the apostle uses: We stand with unveiled face continuously gazing at the face of Christ as the center of our attention and love, and we are gradually and continuously changed into the likeness of Christ, thus proceeding from one degree of glory to another, the Spirit within us being the silent Artist who makes us into His image. It is a breath-taking conception and so simple! And yet how profound!

First of all, it is sound in that it gets you to look beyond yourself to Another. It frees you from self-preoccupation and gets you to look at Someone outside yourself. All the cults that get you to look within to discover Christ within you end in self-preoccupation with your own states of mind and emotion. As someone has said, "If Smith worships the divinity within Smith, he will probably end in worshiping Smith." In any case, he is tangled up with Smith. This verse gets our gaze fastened at the right place—the face of Christ. That fulfills the law of losing your life and finding it again. The attention is important, for "whatever gets your attention gets you." Christ gets attention, so He gets you. And what a getting!

O Christ, I thank Thee that Thou art drawing me from the poisonous center of myself to the healing center of Thy face. Now I know that my gaze is on the Center. I thank Thee. Amen.

AFFIRMATION FOR THE DAY: *My oscillating gaze has found its center and has come to its rest—Christ.*

"WE KEEP MOVING"

We saw yesterday that the first thing of importance is to get your attention and gaze fixed at the right place. If you look within at yourself, you'll be discouraged; if you look around at others, you'll be distracted; if you look at Christ, you'll pass into His likeness.

You become like that which you gaze at habitually. If you gaze at nothing, are continuously shifting your attention to the latest attraction, if nothing has your attention and love, then you look like nothing. Your face looks like what you are looking at—nothing. No character signs on the face—just a blur called a face. "Do you keep stationery here?" asked a prospective customer of a store. "No," she replied, "we keep moving." The modern person keeps moving not only his body, but his attention and interest, and the result is a blurred face.

But there are those who see a Face and give themselves forever to the gazing on that Face. On the desk in front of me as I sit writing in Okayama, Japan, is the face of a lovely old Japanese woman of eighty years. When I first saw her, I inwardly exclaimed, "What a lovely face." Fifty-two years ago she graduated at Mt. Holyoke College, went back to Japan, started a girls' school. Never married—married herself to the needs of the girls of Japan. "I have a large family," she laughingly said, "six thousand graduates are all my children." The war came and Okayama was burned out in one dreadful night, with it the school she had built through the years by faith and toil and prayer. At seventy-five she might have said: "I'm too old to begin again. We'll call it a day and quit." Not she. She rebuilt the school and now has eleven hundred girls in it, and every day at eighty she is in active charge. Fifty-two years of looking at the face of Christ, and then at the faces of her girls, has made her beautiful—at eighty!

It was said of a blacksmith in New England that he had lived in thought so much with Emerson that he looked more like Emerson than Emerson himself! He became what he looked at habitually. The psalmist says, "They looked unto him, and were lightened" (Ps. 34:5, K.J.V.). Look at Light and you'll be light.

O Christ, Thou hast my heart; soon Thou shalt have my face too—it shall look as though it belonged to Thee. I thank Thee. Amen.

AFFIRMATION FOR THE DAY: *"My heart is fixed,"* therefore my gaze is fixed.

"THERE GOES PHILLIPS BROOKS"

We saw yesterday that we become like that at which we habitually gaze. The youth in the story of The Great Stone Face became like this noble image of the great stone face. We have all seen husbands and wives, deeply in love with each other, who have looked into the limpid depths of each other's souls so long that they have become like each other in face.

Someone asked a Harvard professor how he would define a Christian. He got up, walked to the window, and looking out said: "It's hard to define a Christian. But there goes Phillips Brooks." There was a walking definition of a Christian. Someone asked Brooks the secret of his life and he replied in substance: "Perhaps, if there is any secret, it could be found in the fact that I find myself as the years come and go with an increasing love for Christ. He holds my heart." In front of Trinity Church, Boston, where Brooks preached, is a very telling statue of Christ standing behind Brooks with His hand on his shoulder. There is one flaw: Christ is smaller than Brooks and the impression left is of a small Christ putting His hand of approval on a very big man. It was the opposite: a great Christ making a small man into greatness.

Not long ago I saw a radiant blind man studying at a university. He was a lieutenant in the Japanese navy, and when the peace was signed, he was delegated to go to the deck of his destroyer and there announce the signing of the peace. The war was over. Just then an American submarine, not knowing of the end of the war, sank the destroyer. The lieutenant was left blind. He was in such despair that he stole out on what he thought was a dark night to throw himself beneath a train. A Korean seeing him, called to him of the danger. He pulled back, felt there might be some kindly purpose in the universe. A pastor invited him to his church and there quoted the verse "Ask, and ye shall receive." He began to ask and he did receive. The burden of his despair was lifted. When he looked from his chaos to Christ, he was lightened. He became radiant—marched out of his inner dungeon to Light.

O Christ, Thou art Light and Thou art making me light. I feel Thy radiance stealing into every darkened corner of my being. I'm light—in Thee. Amen.

AFFIRMATION FOR THE DAY: *As the moon turned toward the light becomes light, so I am turned toward the Light and I am light.*

Luke 9:28-29   **Week 50—WEDNESDAY**

"I JUST WANT TO LOOK AT YOU"

We may add a sentence or two to complete the picture of a blind man full of despair turning into Light. He heard the statement of Andrew Carnegie that "the first step into success is the willingness to accept responsibility," and he turned from the temptation of self-pity and asked what responsibility he could assume as a blind man in a world of this kind. He decided he would be a minister and help turn people from darkness to Light. He is now in the university, his young wife reading the books to him, is radiant and tingling with anticipation of sharing the world's work. Had he continued to look at his inner darkness, he would have been made in the image of despair, but he began to fix his gaze on the face of Jesus, and hope sprang up.

For looking at Jesus creates faith within, "Looking unto Jesus the author and finisher of our faith" (Heb. 12:2). He is the author, the inspirer of our faith, and having inspired the faith, He finishes it, brings it to its consummation—no halfway business.

The Quiet Time is a period of just gazing at the face of Christ. "Prayer is a time exposure to God." If no prayers are made or answered, nevertheless it is worth while for you become like that at which you gaze. You are made one degree more Christlike by your Christ-gaze. A little fellow came into his father's study and the father asked him what he wanted, and the boy replied: "I don't want anything. I just want to look at you." So the boy sat and gazed into his loved father's face and in the process became more like him. We often say "Prayer changes things"—it does, but more important: Prayer changes the pray-er into the image of the Face he gazes on.

> That one Face, far from vanish, rather grows,
> . . . .
> Become my universe that feels and knows.

The Quiet Time brings the quiet heart. For you know that the One into whose face you gaze will have the last word in human affairs. The beholding produces a holding—a holding of the depths by quiet faith. You leave with something left within you—faith.

O Christ, as I behold Thee I am pulled out of what I am to what Thou art. I am made into the pattern of Thy mind and spirit. Amen.

AFFIRMATION FOR THE DAY: *I am no longer a comet, racing to my ruin. I've been caught by Christ, and now I revolve serenely around Him—forever.*

347

"WITH FACE UNVEILED"

We come now in our studying of being transformed into the same likenes as Jesus by beholding, to the central condition of that transformation. The central condition is the "face unveiled." We have to lift the veils if we are to be transformed.

The moment we do anything wrong we instinctively drop a veil to let no one know. It is the tribute we pay to goodness. Hypocrisy is also a tribute we pay to goodness. The man who is a hypocrite is really a better man than the one who is openly and brazenly evil. For at least he shows by hiding evil that he really prefers to be good.

But the dropping of the veil is no solution. For the veil that shuts others out shuts us in—with ourselves. And to be shut in with a self you cannot respect and love is to carry a living hell within. Besides, we know that the One that matters knows—God. We know that there our veil is of no avail. He sees. I went past the naval base of Kure, Japan, where formerly a high board fence was along the railway track so no one could look from the car windows and see the base. But the board fence was to no avail, for the base was open to the sky and bombers laid it waste.

The veils we put over our faces do shut people out, but we are vulnerable from above. He sees and we see, and they are the two that matter.

So we must lift our veils and become completely honest with God, ourselves, and people. "Don't lie to God" is Jeremy Taylor's first curt rule for spiritual life.

It may hurt our egoistic pride to lift the veils, but it must be done. The Japanese, when they are compelled to live by selling ancestral heirlooms and necessary articles around the home, as they have had to do in these postwar days, say they are then living by an "onionskin economy"—they peel off one layer after another and do it with tears. You too may have to peel off the veils with tears from a hurt pride, but the veils must go. For when they go, He comes! His glory takes the place of shut-in gloom.

O Christ, help me to lift my veils and let Thee see my all, for seeing all, Thou dost forgive all. Then give me courage to do it now. In Thy name. Amen.

AFFIRMATION FOR THE DAY: *With complete honesty and frankness I face Thee and life today.*

"I'M GOING TO DO SOMETHING ABOUT IT"

One of the veils which we must take down, if we are to be transformed into the same image, is the veil that was lying on the heart when Moses was read—the veil of legalism, that you can find salvation and release by what you do.

As long as you take that attitude you are on the basis of your self—*you* are doing it. You call in Christ to help you in what you do. You use Christ. The unveiled face means that you surrender yourself, transfer the center from yourself to Christ. Christ uses you. You are the recipient of grace. And grace touches the springs of love within you. You love in return. Now you can say with the little boy who said to his father, "Daddy, I love you and I'm going to do something about it." So you can say, "Jesus, I love You and I'm going to do something about it." The doing springs out of the loving and the loving springs out of surrender. For you don't love a person until you inwardly surrender to that person. You don't love Christ until you completely surrender to Him.

Along with the lifting of the veil of legalism is the lifting of the veil of impure thinking. For as long as you were on the basis of doing you were always free to say, "Well, I don't do the impure deed," even if the mind indulges the impure thought. Now the impure thought must go as well as the impure deed. For to think the impure thought would be disloyalty to the love relationship between you and Christ. "I'm filled with rotten thinking," said an earnest and devoted follower of Christ who did everything for Christ except to surrender to Him. To live behind the veil of impure thinking is to live in a hell of disloyalty where self-respect is replaced by self-contempt. But when gazing at Him with unveiled face, the white thought of Jesus sterilizes an incipient impure thought as an X ray sterilizes a cancer germ. We are made pure within by simple gazing.

When Jesus was crucified, the veil of the temple was rent in twain, symbol of the fact that the heart of the universe was laid bare as redemptive Love. Since God has unveiled Himself in Jesus, so we in response unveil our faces, drop our masks, gaze in wonder, and in the gazing are made like Him.

O Christ, in simplicity of heart I gaze on Thee with unveiled face and feel redemption steal into every pore of my being. Amen.

AFFIRMATION FOR THE DAY: *Complete honesty in thought, attitude, and word.*

"FROM GLORY TO GLORY"

We come now to note the most astonishing fact about transformation—we are being transformed into the likeness of Christ: "We are being transformed into the same likeness as himself, passing from one glory to another" (II Cor. 3:18, Moffatt). This passage gives the same breath-taking truth: "We are children of God now, beloved; what we are to be is not apparent yet, but we do know that when he appears we are to be like him" (I John 3:2, Moffatt).

We who are born of the dust are being gradually transformed into the most beautiful image that this planet has ever seen—the image of Christ. What a destiny! The emperor of Japan renounces his divinity —that he is not a son of the sun-goddess; I, a commoner, announce that I am a son of God—and that I am being made into the image of the Son of God. What a royal dignity beats within my veins!

And the road to this is the glory road: "passing from one glory to another." This transformation is "from"—and that is wonderful; but it is also "to"—and that is more wonderful. It is "from glory to glory." The Christian transformation is negative—from sin and its consequences; but it is far more positive—from one degree of glory to another. The state of being produced by this transformation can be described only by the word "glory"—it is glorified human living. The drabness, the dullness, the inanity of living is replaced by living that has a halo around it. I have looked down from a plane and have seen the plane's shadow on the white clouds below traveling in an encircling halo. That is Christian living. The commonplace tasks become uncommonplace. The ordinary relationships are touched into sacred beauty. Your very words have a new meaning, for they are a glorified vocabulary. Not cant nor sanctimoniousness, but a heightening of words and meanings until they have the glory touch upon them. "Grace" and "glory" are often connected in the New Testament—take the "grace" and you get the "glory." And this forever, going from one state of glory to another—forever. What a redemption! Glory, glory, glory!

O Christ, to think that I shall be made into Thy likeness from one state of glory to another—I, who am the least, shall be made into that. I bow my heart in gratitude. Amen.

AFFIRMATION FOR THE DAY: *"As you believe in our Lord Jesus Christ, who is the Glory, pay no servile regard to people"* (Jas. 2:1, Moffatt).

THE MEANS TO TRANSFORMATION

We study this week the means used in transformation. The means are important. You cannot use wrong means to get to right ends. For the means pre-exist in and determine the ends. If you use force in the means, you'll have to keep force in the ends. Whatever is won by force must be held by force. That is the rock upon which Marxian communism will go to pieces ultimately. Lenin said, "All great changes of history are made by force." And then he could have added, "And those changes will be overthrown by force." If you want love in the ends, you must use love in the means.

That is the unique thing about the Christian transformation. In the person of Christ it never succumbed to the temptation of using force in the means. That was the temptation in the wilderness: "Take my method, use force, worship me, and all these kingdoms I will give unto you," was the tempter's suggestion. Christ refused. If the Kingdom had come by those means, it wouldn't have been the Kingdom. It would have been transformed into the image of the means.

So God, being love, uses love in the means to bring in the transformation, individual and collective. That rules out the method of war. For war is a means out of harmony with the ends it proposes. When it gets to those ends, the ends are spoiled by the very means. War therefore is the vast illusion—the illusion that you can get to right ends by wrong means. It simply can't be done. Twice in one generation we thought we were making a new world—through a world war. We succeeded not in making a new world, but in making a new war. Like produced like. We cling to the illusion that though this has been true of war in the past, it will not be true of the next one. But each time we are let down. The only good that can possibly come out of war is something good rescued out of it in spite of war. And all these goods could have been had by other means. All human attempts at getting into a new world by wrong means have ended in dead ends. Only God's method will get us there. And that method is love. That method works to the degree it is tried. History has rendered one verdict, and that verdict is that only that which is founded on love lasts—everything else perishes.

O Christ, we try our impossible ways. They break down, and then we try them again in another form. Forgive us. Amen.

AFFIRMATION FOR THE DAY: *I use right means to get to my ends today.*

LOVE IS HEALING

If the Revolutionary War and the Civil War seem to be exceptions to what we said yesterday, they are only apparent exceptions. It was the Constitution, which was love embodied in a document, that brought and held the people together. There they saw "liberty and justice for all" enshrined. Around that documented love the country was made one.

At the close of the Civil War it was in the person of Lincoln that the North and South were made one. When the South was about to surrender, Lincoln went to Richmond, refused a triumphal entry, walked with head bowed to the house of Jefferson Davis. He entered Davis' office, and after an hour an officer looked in and saw the giant frame of Lincoln with his head bowed on his arms, shaking with sobs. Lincoln, "a child of the men who bore the gray, a leader of the men who wore the blue" was weeping for the 600,000 boys of the North and South who would never return. In such a love as his, Lincoln united the shattered nation again. A grateful nation loves him for his love, and because of that love he grows taller as the years go by.

I write this in Japan, where I see the miracle of two nations, embittered by a cruel war, forgetting their bitterness and learning to love. In Hiroshima, where the first atomic bomb fell, two women live together—one an American woman who lost her husband in Okinawa, the other a Japanese woman who lost her doctor-husband and three children by the atomic bomb. The sight of these two women with their arms around each other and telling me of their real affection for each other is indelibly planted upon my memory.

When I saw a long row of American dolls in Japan, I asked what it meant, and was told that the story back of them was this: A GI gave a little Japanese girl a chocolate bar in the early days of the occupation when candy was a rarity, and the little girl in response ran to her home and brought the most precious thing she had and gave it to the GI—her doll. Moved, the GI took the doll to the United States, told its story, and got the American children to send their dolls to Japan. Love, embodied in a doll, helped transform enemies into friends.

O Christ, Thy love is the most healing thing on our planet. Help me to embody it today for everybody, everywhere. In Thy name. Amen.

AFFIRMATION FOR THE DAY: *A missionary was called "The Person of the Healing Hands." I shall be that—today.*

"HE LOVED THEM TO THE END"

Out of Korea, just a hundred miles away, comes this amazing story of a pastor's love. His two sons were brought before a People's Court in Korea to be tried by the Communists because they were Christians. The oldest son, studying for the ministry, stood before the court and preached the gospel to them with great boldness. They decided he should be shot. The younger son begged that his elder brother be spared that he might go back and support the family—that he be taken instead. The elder brother refused this offer saying, "No, they want me." When he was blindfolded, he prayed a prayer, "Father, forgive them. Into Thy hands I commend my spirit." He was shot.

The younger brother jumped up before the court and said: "I believe exactly as my brother did. Why don't you shoot me?" And he preached the gospel to them. "You're as bad as your brother. We'll shoot you." And when they tied him up, he prayed the same prayer, "Father, forgive them. Into Thy hands I commend my spirit." He too was shot. When the pastor, the father, heard this he walked the forty-five miles, went before the court and asked that the student who was the ringleader in the shooting of his two sons, be not prosecuted but be entrusted to him as his adopted son. This was done. The parents of this boy, moved by this love, asked that the pastor's daughter be permitted to come and live with their daughter and teach her the Way. It was done. The adopted son, moved by this attitude, became a Christian and began to study for the ministry. Hundreds were converted by this new Way.

During the war, when the Communists overran the country, the pastor was put into prison. There he continued to preach the gospel and to sing hymns. While he was singing one day in his cell, a guard shot him sideways through the lips to stop the singing. The pastor, not able to eat, gave his meager rations to the other prisoners saying, "You take this and get strong and be ready to serve your country." They finally shot the pastor in order to quiet his spirit. Quiet his spirit? That spirit will march down through the ages inspiring men and women by his deathless love. It is power.

O Christ, I bow my head in gratitude for Thy faithful servant. May I too catch some of his ardent spirit. Amen.

AFFIRMATION FOR THE DAY: *If my love fails, yet my love itself is the victory.*

"LOVE NEVER FAILS"

We have been studying the power of love to transform people and situations. Before Pearl Harbor, Admiral Kichisaburo Nomura, the Japanese ambassador at Washington, took my hand and said: "Thank you for what you are trying to do. You are doing the work of heaven. It is heaven's work to reconcile us." Later, in Tokyo after the war, I paid a public tribute before a large audience to Admiral Nomura for his sincere efforts at peace. The crowd roared its applause. Before I went in to see the Japanese emperor, Mr. Terasaki, one of the members of the embassy staff at Washington, now an advisor to the emperor, took a letter from his pocket and said: "Do you see that letter? It kept my soul alive during the war. To think you would believe in us when everybody thought we were playing a double game." It was a letter I had written on December 10, 1941, three days after Pearl Harbor, thanking them for what they tried to do before Pearl Harbor to head off the war, and assuring them of my prayers during the trying days ahead. My confidence was not misplaced, as events have shown. The fact that they have never been tried by a war guilt tribunal shows the military believed they were of the peace party. General Douglas Mac-Arthur agreed with me when I raised the question in an interview. When the newspapers printed a statement that these three envoys at Washington were going to be tried by the war guilt tribunal then going on, General MacArthur sent a special messenger to Karuizawa, four hours' journey by train, to assure them there was no truth in the newspaper report. That was a very thoughtful thing to do.

In the new International Christian University being put up in Japan to cement these two nations, I am being privileged to provide the pulpit and lectern in the chapel. There is a book of remembrance being kept in the chapel, and my inscription is this: "To my three Japanese friends, the envoys at Washington, who before the war strove valiantly for peace." Since the close of the war I have had the privilege of seeing one of them, Saburo Kurusu, led to Christ. Love heals—the only healing.

O Christ, I thank Thee that love never fails. All else may fail, but love never does. Let Thy love work through me this day. Amen.

AFFIRMATION FOR THE DAY: *Love creates the atmosphere in which the impossible becomes possible.*

"AND DO IT ALL OVER AGAIN?"

We are looking at the power of love to transform. Charles A. Wells, writer, cartoonist, and world traveler, tells how he was once caught between contending armies in China and sought refuge in a cellar. Another refugee, an English missionary doctor, had built a hospital, a church, and a school through thirty years and had seen it all destroyed in as many minutes. He said to Wells, "Do you think, Sir, that God would ask a man to come back and do it all over again?" Five years later Wells visited the same place and found to his surprise a new hospital, a new church, and a new school. "He did come back," said Wells to himself. When he inquired at the church about the doctor, a Chinese Christian took him to a newly made grave with this simple inscription over it: "Here lies one who has found that the winds of war and the flames of hate cannot tear from the hearts of men the seed that love has planted there."

I sat at breakfast with a dentist who had spent five years in prison before the war for preaching against war and the myth of the sun-goddess, from whom the Japanese emperor was supposed to be descended. In jail he was so hungry that he ate the paste used to glue the match boxes on which he worked. When the atom bomb fell on Hiroshima, he was in jail there, and when the jail was shattered and the prisoners free to go he refused to run away—he was a Christian. Freed at the end of the war, he sold oranges from door to door to gain a living. Now he has re-established his dental business, works fifteen hours a day, runs three Sunday schools, one on Saturday! He has conquered his tuberculosis, is radiant, and has lived to see his nation renounce war in its constitution, and his emperor renounce the myth of the sun-gooddess. His was a courageous love that had to bend but did not break. His love won through.

Two years ago I heard the "Hallelujah Chorus" sung by the girls of a Japanese school—sung in the concrete basement of a burned-out school. Yesterday I heard the same schoolgirls sing the "Hallelujah Chorus," this time in the same basement, but with a rebuilt school. Love sings in a basement if it has to, but love builds a new world.

O Christ, Thy love conquers all—has conquered me. Help me to conquer all through my love for everybody today. Amen.

AFFIRMATION FOR THE DAY: *My love shall sing its "Hallelujah Chorus" either in a burned-out basement or in an unbombed cathedral—everywhere I raise my song!*

THE WORD OF LOVE MADE FLESH

The transforming power of love is not only the most effective way of transforming men and situations, but it is beneficial to the person who is doing the transforming. It is psychologically sound.

All the problems of psychology revolve around the problem of self-preoccupation. Love, by taking you out of yourself, is therefore the best therapeutic that could be devised by divine wisdom. Paul says: "If I am in distress, it is in the interests of your comfort and salvation; if I am comforted, it is in the interests of your comfort" (II Cor. 1:6, Moffatt). Here was a "distress" "in the interests of," and a "comfort" "in the interests of"—both of them, distress and comfort, lifting him outside himself. Distress might have left him in self-centered misery—a miserable man; comfort might have left him in self-centered satisfaction—a smug clod; but now whatever happened to him left him with the right center—something outside himself.

Here is the blessing and the blight of some modern movements centered around broadcasting love to everybody. Meetings in which love is mentally broadcast to everybody are popular.

This is psychologically helpful up to a certain point, in that you are thinking in terms of others. But it can leave a subtle blight, in that this may take the place of loving people in concrete situations and providing help in concrete situations. It may and does produce a sentimental type of spirituality that loves everybody in general and nobody in particular. The word of love broadcast remains a word, not the Word become flesh. Jesus did not sit on a hillside broadcasting love to everybody. That would have been the Word become word. He loved people with concrete acts of healing, of feeding, of teaching, and of dying for men. That was the Word become flesh.

Broadcasting love to everybody doesn't produce movements, except movements for further emotion. Creative movements come out of creative thinking, and creative praying resulting in concrete acts in concrete situations for concrete people. Loving in the air may leave you up in the air without roots.

O Christ, sitting on the hillside Thou didst broadcast Thy love to Jerusalem, but then Thou didst go into it and die for it. Thy word of love became flesh in the deed of the cross. Make all my words flesh. Amen.

AFFIRMATION FOR THE DAY: *My love shall take feet and walk today.*

"THEY ARE IN THE BASEMENT"

The Christian way of love seems foolish. In a psychiatry class a very radiant Christian told the class how he had been able to transform a woman through prayer and self-surrender. The reaction of the class was voiced by one of them: "What a fool you were. You could have made $3,000 out of her." He probably could have done so by prolonging the number of interviews endlessly and stringing the patient along and using her as a means to his monetary ends. But what would have happened to the psychiatrist in the meantime? Exactly what does happen to psychiatrists who do that. They become queer. They often become like their patients—neurotic. Why? Because you cannot break the law of love any more than you can break the law of gravitation and not get hurt. If psychiatrists are self-centered in their interests to help others, then they suffer from the neuroses of the self-centered. Therefore Christian love in the psychiatrist, and as the motive of his work, is the only thing that can save the method and the patient—and the psychiatrist!

A little girl looked at the picture of Christ knocking at the door. "Why don't they let Him in?" she asked, and then added, "It must be that they are in the basement and can't hear Him." Pagan psychiatry has been too much in the basement of using the disrupted for financial ends to hear the knocking of Christ at the door of the method. Moreover, it has dwelt too much in the basement of the subconscious to hear the knocking of the Superconscious. An invasion of divine love from the Superconscious would cleanse and clear and co-ordinate the subconscious.

In the twinkling of an eye,
The blood of Christ can sanctify.

So the Christian method of transformation is turning out to be what Paul said it was: "Christ Jesus, whom God has made our 'Wisdom,' . . . and redemption" (I Cor. 1:30, Moffatt). It is Wisdom because it turns out as redemption—the total person is transformed, redeemed. So the Christian Way is not only wisdom, but Wisdom.

O Christ, I thank Thee that in Thee all our foolishness becomes Wisdom and out of Thee all our wisdom becomes foolish. Help me to be wise—in Thee. Amen.

AFFIRMATION FOR THE DAY: *Love is more knowing than knowledge, and wiser than wisdom.*

WILL IT FADE?

We come to our last week's study and here we must raise the ultimate question about being a transformed person: How secure are the transformations? Do they let us down ultimately?

For we are in an age of disillusionment. William R. Inge calls this "the century of disappointment." For things that men put their weight down heavily upon are cracking beneath them. These disappointments in pursuing life's ends range from the disillusioned astonishment of greyhounds on a Florida track when the mechanical rabbit they were pursuing blew up in front of them, to the awful inner letdown of a nation, in which I find myself just now, who banked their earthly and heavenly all on the idea that their emperor was a divine being, they were therefore a divine people with a divine destiny. That whole conception went down in blood and ruin, and the emperor announced that it was all a mistake—he is not divine. The ensuing inner chaos within their souls has been devastating. Recently I went past the famous shrine at Kotohira, dedicated to the patron saint of navigation —he protected shipping especially. Then this saint must have gone on a moral holiday, for the shipping of Japan has been swept from the seven seas and her proud navy sunk. And yet men of evident intelligence got off our train, formed a procession with a banner in front, to make offerings at the shrine of the saint who let them down. Men still pathetically lift banners to forlorn, dead hopes.

And yet men still build up vast illusions to gain the temporary allegiance of temporary multitudes. Someone asked me what I thought of "the assumption of the Virgin Mary." I replied, "It is rightly named—it is an 'assumption.'" This prayer of Peter Marshall is a good one: "Lord, give us courage to stand for something, lest we fall for everything." Men are falling for everything, for nothing they have is certain. They add one more illusion in hope it will not be an illusion.

Is this transformation a transformation from one illusion to another? Or is it a transformation from illusions to ultimate Reality?

O Christ, in this age of letdown help us to feel the solid rock of Thy Way beneath our feet. Let us see that if Thou art not ultimate Reality there is none. In Thy name. Amen.

AFFIRMATION FOR THE DAY: *The God whose universe is timed to exact regularity is not going to be slipshod with me.*

"BADLY PLACED FOR WINTERING IN"

Many religious cults are fair-weather cults. It was said of the harbor named Fair Havens, on the island of Crete, that it was "badly placed for wintering in" (Acts 27:8, 12, Moffatt). A good many are taking shelter in harbors named "Fair Havens," but they are "badly placed for wintering in"—they give no protection when the winter winds of sorrow, of sickness, of death blow. Is what has been expounded in this book just another "Fair Haven," "badly placed for wintering in"?

You cannot give the beautiful camellia plant to a sick person in Japan, for the flower, instead of falling petal by petal falls as a whole flower—suddenly. We are afraid of beautiful camellia flowers of faith and allegiance which suddenly fall as a whole—centrally weak.

But there is one place of complete security in the universe: "Thus there is no doom now for those who are in Christ Jesus" (Rom. 8:1, Moffatt). "There is no doom"—what a sweeping judgment of immunity! You have been lifted out of the law of decay and have been brought into the place of complete security for everything that is in Christ Jesus. If your all is there, then your all is secure from any doom of decay or of being made irrelevant or by-passed. It is secure in substance and meaning. Beyond that which is found in Christ, the human race will never progress.

There is no doom in your inherent being. You will hold together whatever happens. "In him all things cohere"—they hold together. You are not canceling yourself out with a way of life incompatible with the universe. Your personality will hold together and develop for eternity.

You are immortal and your relationships held in Him are immortal too. As William Cowper wrote: "There is not room enough for friendship to unfold itself in full bloom in such a life as this. Therefore I am, and will be, yours forever. William Cowper."

The saddest sight on our planet is a graveyard without a cross in it, and I see them every day in Japan. But the gladdest sight on our planet is a graveyard with a cross—and hence a resurrection! "There is no doom" to our relationships!

O Christ, Thou art my surety and my security. Thou dost guarantee against the decay and shock of death. It's all there—forevermore. I thank Thee. Amen.

AFFIRMATION FOR THE DAY: *In the creative God there is no decay—I'm in the creative God.*

"SECURE AGAINST OUR FAILURES"

We continue to look at the fact that to the Christian there is no doom. We are secure against our failures. For our very failures in Him lay the foundation for the ultimate success.

Look at Lincoln. When he was a young man he ran for the legislature in Illinois and was badly swamped. He entered business, failed, and spent seventeen years paying the debts of a worthless partner. He fell in love with a beautiful woman to whom he became engaged, and then she died. He tried to win an election to the United States Senate and was badly defeated in 1858. In spite of defeats he eventually achieved the highest success attainable in life, and undying fame till the end of time. Why? He was essentially honest, so that his very failures furthered him. He made those disappointments prepare him for the great appointment—the freeing of the slaves and the holding together of the Union. "There is no doom" to a man like that.

Paul could say: "My opponent says, 'Paul's letters are weighty and telling, but his personality is weak and his delivery is beneath contempt'" (II Cor. 10:10, Moffatt). But suppose it had been the other way around: that his personality and delivery were weighty and telling, but his letters were weak and his way of writing beneath contempt. That would have left the world, which has fed on his letters, impoverished. But Paul took the weakness of his personality and his lack of oratorical ability and made them contribute to his power to write letters that have changed the world. He made his failure in personality and speech into contribution instead of collapse. "There is no doom" for the man who can make his weaknesses and mistakes work for higher ends.

It is said that fire opals are opals into which dust has found its way, and the opal turns the dust into fire, and through it becomes a fire opal. When you can turn your dust into delight—then "there is no doom."

O Christ, everything I have is safe in Thee—even my failures. Thou dost turn failures into fruitfulness. So I am afraid of nothing, for I can use everything. Amen.

AFFIRMATION FOR THE DAY: *I am in God's cupped hands; periodically He opens His hand and smiles at me.*

"FOR ALL TIME THROUGH HIS GRACE"

Many of us are not afraid of our failures in marginal things, but we are afraid of losing the transformations which have become ours. They are precious but precarious. Will they stay and become an abiding part of us?

If this book proposed transformation by fighting this sin here, that fear there, and that weakness yonder, then it would all be very precarious. You would be sitting on a lid. But when we propose release by grace, then we are striking at the roots. The grace of God takes over the sources of life, and so every act and attitude is a strengthening of life at the center. We become habituated to goodness. So the future should make us more secure, not less. For the accumulations of habit are in the direction of security upon security.

The two methods of transformation and their results are seen in this vivid account from a member of our Ashrams: "Six years ago I suddenly awakened one night with a great difficulty in breathing, followed by rigors. The next day my friends said that I looked as though I had passed through a long siege of illness. My doctor suggested an overdose of thyroid, but I now know it was resentment toward my husband who had suddenly enlisted in the Seabees. . . . Four years ago I experienced many symptoms of pregnancy. One night I knew for sure I was on the verge of miscarriage. The doctor's examination assured me I was not pregnant and the symptoms disappeared. Now I know that the symptoms appeared because of a fear of pregnancy. . . . Last year I suddenly developed cutting, gnawing pains in my stomach. Two or three hours after meals and in the middle of the night I would suffer intense pain. A complete X-ray examination revealed nothing. The fear of ulcers immediately vanished. As I look back over it all, I can see that the doctors allayed one fear after the other, but new fears constantly arose. Not until I looked to the Great Physician did freedom from fear come into my soul. Thank God I am free once again and for all time through His grace." Grace delivered from individual fears by wiping out the cause of all fears—an unsurrendered self.

O Christ, all fears of fear are gone. In Thee, who art the same yesterday, today, and forever, I'm secure—eternally secure. I thank Thee, thank Thee. Amen.

AFFIRMATION FOR THE DAY: *I am as secure as Security, as safe as Safety.*

"OUR VERY SINS MAKE US SING"

No fears need creep into today from past sins and blunders. For Grace covers them all. We do not see them, we see "Grace" written across them. And seen through Grace they produce not a paralysis but a paean. Our reaction is gratitude, not gloom. Our very sins make us sing—sing at the redemption from them. The last words of the saintly Bishop William F. Oldham were "A sinner saved by grace."

Emerson says: "Finish every day and be done with it. You have done what you could. Some blunders and absurdities no doubt crept in; forget them as soon as you can. Tomorrow is a new day; begin it well and serenely and with too high a spirit to be cumbered with your old nonsense. This day is all that is good and fair. It is too dear with its hopes and invitations to waste a moment on the yesterdays." This is good, but not good enough. You cannot "forget them as soon as you can," unless you are sure God forgets them, that across them is written "Grace." If so, you can forget them and rejoice, even if you remember them. For you are reminded of Grace, not of them. If the past can't hurt you, then the present and the future are secure, for they too are under Grace. It covers my future falls as well as my past. "There is no doom" from any direction to those who are in Christ Jesus.

The Old Testament ends with these words: "lest I come to strike the land down with a curse" (Mal. 3:6, Moffatt). It ends with "a curse." The New Testament ends: "The grace of the Lord Jesus Christ" (Rev. 22:21, Moffatt). One ends with a "curse," the other with "grace." So Grace doesn't simply look back at past deeds, it looks forward to the future to hold that future steady. We *are* under Grace, we *will be* under Grace. Revelation points to "grace" in the future as well as to the past.

Someone writing of experiences in a Russian prison camp told of a nun who would continually say "Now I have suffered almost as much as Jesus Christ. Now I will certainly be redeemed soon." But we are redeemed, not by our sufferings, but by His. Our security is based, not on what we have done, but on what He has done. That's different. And more secure!

O Christ, Thou hast the keys of Death and Hell, and Thou hast also the keys of Life and Heaven, locking the one and opening the other.

AFFIRMATION FOR THE DAY: *Grace sends me tripping down the years, and into my tasks each day.*

THE CHRISTIAN WAY IS THE WAY

We look today at the ultimate basis of our security—the fact that the Christian way is the Way. A missionary in Japan who was in the process of restoring his burned-out school plant—a complete wreck from bombing—asked me which of my books I would choose from the ones I wrote, and I replied: "Evidently from the sales my readers would not agree, but I would choose *The Way*. For if the thesis of that book is true, then it's all over but the shouting." He replied: "I hoped you'd say that, for I agree. If the Christian way is the Way, then that's devastating. It sweeps aside everything but one thing—the Way." In that faith he could build, be bombed and build again, knowing that if he and his projects were on the Way, then the future is secure. "There is no doom."

Robert Louis Stevenson put it in these words:

To go on forever and fail and go on again,
And be mauled to the earth and arise,
And contend for the shade of a word and a thing not seen with the eyes,
With the half of a broken hope for a pillow at night
That somehow the right is the right
And the smooth shall bloom from the rough.

That sentence, "That somehow the right is the right," sums it up. If the right is the right, then it will turn out right. This from the German: "The absolute victory of the absolute good is written into the fiber of the universe." And the absolute good is revealed in Jesus Christ. He is the guarantee of the absolute victory of the absolute good.

I agree with these penetrating words of Tolstoi: "The human soul is Christian in its nature. Christianity is accepted by man as a reminiscence of something forgotten. . . . This faith, far from being artificial, exceptional—inculcated by education—is in human nature; we connot do without it any more than birds that have lost their wings can fly."

If sin and evil are an alien revolt against the nature of things, then they are doomed. You cannot live against life and live. The Christian way is not a way, or the best of ways—it is the Way.

O Christ, how can I thank Thee enough that Thou hast allayed all my fears by presenting Thyself as the Way. I walk that Way, and all life agrees that this is the Way. Amen.

AFFIRMATION FOR THE DAY: *All good ways converge into the Way, or they cease to be good.*

ALL LIFE IS BASED ON TRANSFORMATION

Today, our last day together, we sum up the meaning and message of this book: All life is based on transformation.

We take air into our lungs and transform the blood from impure to pure and send it on its healing, life-sustaining way; we take in food and transform it into blood and tissue and cell; we transform mere sense impressions upon the retina into sight; we take wild sounds and tame them to time and tune and make them into music; we take two people, tie them together with bonds of love and make them into a family; we take the self-centered soul and get him to surrender all this to Christ and he is transformed, not only into a living soul, but into a life-giving spirit.

In Christ's name and power we take hold, as the Japanese do, of an ugly root, and transform the ugliness of life into beauty. We transform the commonplace and the trivial round into dancing duties—done in His name. We take hold of humanity, tearing itself by wars, like the man in the Gadarenes, and transform it into the Kingdom of God. We touch everything and we transform everything. And all this because God transformed Himself into man—became like us, that we might become like Him.

If anybody can be transformed into anything, then I shall lay large plans. The ground plan shall be God's will, nothing more, nothing less, nothing else. For His will is my freedom. And the superstructure shall be after the pattern of the lines loved and chosen by the girls and the missionary of a school in atom-bombed Nagasaki, as they rebuilt:

Give me wide walls to build my house of Life.

. . . .

The North shall be of Love, against the winds of fate;
The South shall be of Tolerance, that I may outreach hate;
The East of Faith, that rises, clear and new each day;
The West of Hope, that even dies a glorious way.
The threshold 'neath my feet shall be Humility;
The roof—the very sky itself—Infinity.
Give me wide walls to build my house of Life.

O Christ, I thank Thee for the pilgrimage into transformation. I have been privileged to begin—with Thee. Now on into transformation forever and forever and forever—with Thee. Amen.

AFFIRMATION FOR THE DAY: *I see no end to this transformation—an open vista forever!*